THE
VIKING
BLITZKRIEG

THE
VIKING
BLITZKRIEG
AD 789–1098

MARTYN WHITTOCK AND HANNAH WHITTOCK

The
History
Press

In memory of Jeffrey Martin Whittock (1927–2013),
much-loved and respected father and papa.

First published 2013

The History Press
The Mill, Brimscombe Port
Stroud, Gloucestershire, GL5 2QG
www.thehistorypress.co.uk

British Library Cataloguing in Publication Data.
A catalogue record for this book is available from the British Library.

ISBN 978 0 7524 6799 3

Typesetting and origination by The History Press
Printed in Great Britain

CONTENTS

Acknowledgements

A number of people provided valuable advice which assisted in the preparation of this book; without them, of course, carrying any responsibility for the interpretations offered by the book. We are particularly indebted to our agent Robert Dudley who, as always, offered guidance and support, as did Simon Hamlet and Mark Beynon at The History Press. In addition, Bradford-on-Avon library, and the Wiltshire and the Somerset Library services, provided access to resources through the inter-library loans service. For their help and for this service we are very grateful. Through Hannah's undergraduate BA studies and then MPhil studies in the department of Anglo-Saxon, Norse and Celtic (ASNC) at Cambridge University (2008–12), the invaluable input of many brilliant academics has shaped our understanding of this exciting and complex period of history, and its challenging sources of evidence. The resulting familiarity with Old English, Old Norse and Insular Latin has greatly assisted in critical reflection on the written sources.

As always, the support and interest provided by close family and friends cannot be measured but is much appreciated. And they have been patient as meal-time conversations have given way to discussions of the achievements of Alfred and Athelstan, the impact of Eric Bloodaxe and the agendas of the compilers of the *Anglo-Saxon Chronicle*.

INTRODUCTION

This book explores the impact of the Viking Wars on England between the first recorded attack in AD 789 and the last major Scandinavian interventions in the late eleventh century, with a few stray events occurring even later than this. It is the argument of this study that these events constituted some of the most formative influences on the making of England. Time and again, major features of Late Anglo-Saxon England – and the Early Middle Ages generally – can be traced directly, or indirectly, to the 'blitzkrieg' of attacks, resistance, conquest and settlement that characterised these wars. The effects of these events range from the creation of one unified English state to the compilation of Domesday Book; from the establishment of a unified national taxation system to the Norman Conquest – and many more.

In order to investigate this claim, we have aimed to provide readers with an overview of the key events of these wars, including insights from the latest archaeological finds and from close analysis of the written sources. Where controversies exist, and there are many, we have identified the issues and suggested the solution that seems best to fit the available evidence. This involves a process of detective work using a wide variety of fascinating clues. And, wherever possible, we have striven to put the people into the history by exploring individual experiences and outlooks.

It is worth drawing readers' attention to the fact that we have used the term 'Viking' as a group-name to describe the Scandinavian adventurers who descended on England in this period. This is because the term is so familiar in the popular consciousness that it serves as a useful label, even if its use has been reduced in some academic circles. That it remains a very useful shorthand label is seen in the use of the term in recent academic papers and books.[1] Where 'Vikings' were clearly from a particular area of Scandinavia – Danes, Norwegians and, occasionally, Swedes – we have indicated this, but have retained the group-name as a useful and convenient way to describe those involved in these extraordinary events. However, it should be borne in mind that the term 'Viking', when it was originally used, was employed to describe the warrior adventurers, rather than the humbler farmer-settlers, craftspeople and merchants who followed in their wake, and that many other terms were used in the original sources.

The issue of language

The sources explored in this investigation are largely written in Old English, Old Norse and Latin. In order to engage with these we have used accessible modern translations and the system of references will allow readers to understand these references in context, should they wish to take their studies further. Whenever we have referred to an event or phenomena in the original language, this has been made more accessible by using only a short phrase, accompanied by its translation, so that its meaning is obvious. Occasionally we have then continued to use a phrase in the original language because it has become embedded in modern scholarship. An example would be our references to the *micel hæðen here* (the great heathen army) which devastated England in the 860s and 870s. These examples, however, are few in number, and all other descriptions/phrases are in modern English. Where words in the original language reveal more than their modern English translations would suggest, we have drawn attention to the original word/phrase and explained why it is important and what it reveals. For example, the Anglo-Scandinavian word *lið* (seaborne military) was used in the *Anglo-Saxon Chronicle* to describe both the forces of the Anglo-Saxon Harold Godwinson's sons and those of Svein Estrithson of Denmark after 1066. It seems that it was hard to tell who was the 'Viking' and who was the Anglo-Saxon at this point in time, and the reason for this is explored. In another example, the modern word 'army' does not always represent one single word used in the original source. As a consequence, in the *Anglo-Saxon*

Chronicle the Viking forces are usually described as a '*here*', whereas Anglo-Saxon forces are usually described using the terms '*fyrd*', or occasionally '*folc*'. In translation into modern English, this difference can get submerged under the general term 'army', but the difference was important and revealing; and we explore its importance to our understanding of the events described.

We have used the title of medieval written sources in their original language although, on the first occasion of use, we have also given their titles in translation in order to explain the meaning. An example would be the *Encomium Emmae Reginae* (*In Praise of Queen Emma*) which, after the first use, is thereafter simply referred to as the *Encomium Emmae* or the *Encomium*. This is because it has become customary to use its original title, rather than the title in translation. Another example is the *Vita Ædwardi Regis* (*Life of King Edward*). In a similar way, where Old Norse sources are usually now referred to by their Old Norse name, we have continued to do so. Examples would be: *Heimskringla* (*Circle of the World*), the great history of Norwegian Viking kings; *Eiríksmál* (*Erik's Story*), the anonymous elegy for King Eric Bloodaxe; *Orkneyinga Saga* (*Saga of the Orcadians*), the history of the Earls of Orkney; *Knútsdrápa* (*The drápa* – a long series of poetic stanzas – *of Cnut*). This is common usage and the convoluted direct translation of the last example explains why the original Old Norse name is usually used. It also means that, should readers come across these sources in other studies, they will recognise them from these frequently used titles. Other sources, though, are commonly referred to just in their translated form and we have continued that in this study. Examples would be Simeon of Durham's *History of the Church of Durham* and the anonymous *History of St Cuthbert*.

The Old English and Old Norse languages used letters that are no longer found in modern English. The most commonly used ones were: Æ or lower case æ (ash), Ð or lower case ð (eth) and Þ or lower case þ (thorn). The last two are approximated to the 'th' sound in modern English. The one we have employed when referring to personal names is Æ or æ because it was so commonly used and does not have a direct parallel in modern English. For this reason, we refer to Æthelred and Æthelflæd, not Ethelred and Ethelfled. However, where a name has become more familiar in a modernised form, we have used the modern appearance; so we refer to Alfred not Ælfred, and Athelstan not Æthelstan. We have only used Ð or ð and Þ or þ on the very few occasions when a word or phrase quoted in the original language uses them. An example would be *micel hæðen here* (the great heathen army).

The nature of the evidence and the dating of events

The most frequently used source of written information is the *Anglo-Saxon Chronicle*, which was first compiled in Old English, in Wessex, in the 880s. In this study, after its first use in each chapter, it is usually just referred to as the *Chronicle*. Once one allows for its largely West Saxon agenda – except when it clearly incorporates other materials with their own specific agendas – it provides a crucial insight into events, even though seen from a particular angle, with attendant assumptions and values. The most authoritative and easily accessible modern translation of the *Anglo-Saxon Chronicle* is that by D. Whitelock[2] and is found in her invaluable collection of documents, which also includes many other sources quoted in this study. Since, in this collection of documents, her translation of the *Chronicle* only extends to 1042, it is necessary with regard to later annals to use the translation of D. Whitelock, D.C. Douglas and S.I. Tucker, which gives the full run of annals to 1154.[3] Another accessible translation of the *Chronicle* is that by G.N. Garmonsway,[4] although the way in which he lays out the different manuscripts of the *Chronicle* may appear a little confusing to the uninitiated reader. It is fair to say that the different manuscripts of the *Chronicle* can almost be studied as different documents in their own right, rather than as aspects of one document, since the motivations and methods used in each continuation from the 'common stock' reveals much about the context in which each subsequent manuscript was copied, continued and adapted.[5] This is why, at critical points, we refer to distinct manuscripts of the *Chronicle* as part of our disentangling of its motivations, sources and agendas.

Within the *Chronicle* there are often dislocations in dating, which mean that the dates given for events can vary in different secondary sources which refer to the same entries. In this exploration we have followed the – corrected – dates given in bold in Whitelock. The dating of events to particular years in the *Chronicle* is made more complex by the fact that there was no consistent contemporary practice of deciding when a given year actually started. Some ninth-century annals were clearly working from a start-date at Christmas, others from a year-start on 24 September. A reversion to Christmas can be seen in the tenth-century annals, although some events were still dated using the 24 September system, particularly with regard to the dating of the deaths of a number of kings. In the eleventh century, another method was also sometimes used, which dated the start of the year from the Annunciation, on 25 March. Following the 'corrected' dates in

Whitelock provides consistency in the various dates used in this examination of the Viking Wars.

The *Chronicle* is not our only English version of events. The contemporary ninth-century *Life of King Alfred* by the Welsh bishop, Asser, gives us a pro-Alfred view of events from the circle of the West Saxon court. The anonymous *History of St Cuthbert*, compiled at Chester-le-Street in the mid-tenth century, contains some authentic information amongst its legendary accounts and was later used by Simeon of Durham when writing his *History of the Church of Durham*. Other valuable insights can be gleaned from later chroniclers who clearly preserved earlier traditions and material in their accounts. These range from the late-tenth-century *Æthelweard's Chronicle*, to post-Conquest sources such as the twelfth-century *Annals of St Neots*, the *Chronicon ex Chronicis* (*Chronicle of other Chronicles*) of John of Worcester (and once attributed to Florence of Worcester), Henry of Huntingdon's *Historia Anglorum (History of the English)*, Simeon of Durham's *History of the Church of Durham*, and William of Malmesbury's *Gesta Regum Anglorum* (*Deeds of the Kings of the English*). Unlike the *Anglo-Saxon Chronicle*, these other sources were written in Latin. Although most were compiled much later than the events they described, these writers often had access to sources of information now lost to us. In particular, we are especially indebted to William of Malmesbury for much of our knowledge regarding King Athelstan. Without the work of this twelfth-century monastic historian we would know very little about this major player in the tenth-century phase of the Viking Wars. However, despite writing two centuries after Athelstan, William clearly had access to much earlier evidence, including traditions preserved at Malmesbury (Athelstan's burial place). Even a thirteenth-century writer, such as Roger of Wendover, in his *Flores Historiarum* (*Flowers of the Histories*), can reveal a northern take on earlier events through his use of materials which themselves preserved much earlier traditions.

Other writers had a specific motivation, such as the author of the *Encomium Emmae Reginae* (*In Praise of Queen Emma*) in the 1040s, or the earlier celebration of the life of Eric Bloodaxe, the *Eiríksmál* (*Erik's story*), or the eleventh-century poetry on the subject of the deeds of Cnut the Great, the *Knútsdrápa*. These, though clearly written to promote the fame of a particular person, still give us an insight into general events, even if these were viewed from a peculiar slant and reveal a distinct agenda.

Written sources from the Viking side are generally more problematic. Many of our most engaging Old Norse accounts are very late indeed and date from thirteenth-century Iceland.[6] Whilst these were clearly based on ancient traditions, they also wove the legendary into the historic narrative and were part of a revival of interest in the 'Viking past'. As such, they need to be used with great caution when attempting to reconstruct the actual events of the Viking Wars. Nevertheless, at the very least, they reveal how these earlier events were later remembered, interpreted and celebrated. Amongst these accounts are Snorri Sturluson's *Heimskringla* (*Circle of the world*), *Jómsvíkinga saga* (*Saga of the* – legendary – *Jómsvíkings*), *Orkneyinga Saga* (*Saga of the Orcadians*) and *Egil's Saga* (*Egils Saga Skalla-Grímsson*). The stories they contain about kings as famous as Eric Bloodaxe of York and Harald Hardrada of Norway are as dramatic as they are problematic, though some may preserve the authentic 'voice' of the eleventh century. One such is *Liðsmannaflokkr* (the *flokkr* – poem without a refrain – *of the men of the fleet*), a poem that purports to date from Cnut's reign and perhaps was composed by members of his household troop, although any attribution is uncertain. Here we may actually hear something of the victory song of Cnut's army which conquered England in 1016.

Other literary and linguistic insights can be gleaned from the study of royal charters, the titles and symbols on coins, and from place names. This last body of evidence is as complicated as it is abundant, but reveals a great deal about the dramatic changes which occurred in eastern and northern England in the ninth and tenth centuries.

Archaeology is continually adding to our picture of life and developments. Urban archaeology is revealing the origins of towns fortified under Alfred the Great and Edward the Elder. Continued excavations in York have added to the amazing insights provided by the earlier Coppergate excavations; an engaging and thought-provoking way to experience this York-based evidence is provided by the Jorvik Viking Centre, York.[7] The archaeology of rural sites and of scarce Viking-period pagan burials raises questions about how great was the change that was actually brought about by Scandinavian settlers to Christian Anglo-Saxon England. On the other hand, the huge increase in small finds (cheap copper-alloy brooches) due to the growth of metal detecting has caused us to re-evaluate the scale of the Viking settlement of Lincolnshire, which now looks to have been substantial. Recent finds are giving us a much more detailed view of the wealth and complexity of the societies being forged by the Viking newcomers in the tenth century. These include the Cumwhitton burials (discovered in 2004), with their links to Viking Ireland; the 'Huxley Hoard' of silver arm rings (also discovered in 2004), which show a thriving economy using fixed weights of silver in transactions; and the 'Vale of York Hoard' or 'Harrogate Hoard' (discovered in 2007), the most important Viking find for 150 years, which contained artefacts linking the hoard to Afghanistan, the Carolingian Empire (in modern France and western Germany), Ireland, the Middle East, Russia and Scandinavia. A further two significant hoards were discovered in 2011: a coin in the 'Silverdale Hoard' revealed the name of an otherwise unknown Viking king in northern England; while the 'Furness Hoard' bears mute testimony to the revival of Viking power in the kingdom of York in the middle of the tenth century, before it was eclipsed by the death of Eric Bloodaxe in 954. As a consequence of these new discoveries, we are gaining a more detailed and nuanced understanding of the impact of the 'Viking Blitzkrieg' on England.

It is the combining and evaluating of such varied forms of evidence that makes the study of the Viking Wars so intriguing, informative and rewarding. Together, the evidence indicates that these events had a huge impact on England and that this impact still affects the culture, place names and outlook of twenty-first-century England. And, in a modern time of cultural change and the re-evaluation of notions of national identity, this period of history has a great deal to teach us about the way in which a multi-cultural society – in a period of massive change – could still forge a coherent and recognisable identity and a sense of national unity around negotiated shared values.

1

THE GATHERING CLOUDS

The Viking Wars are more than just a feature of the second half of that period of time we call 'Anglo-Saxon England' for they radically altered England. Indeed, it can be argued that, unintentionally, they helped to create a united 'England' from a patchwork of Anglo-Saxon kingdoms which characterised the ninth century. In the severity of their impact these wars fell like an early medieval blitzkrieg on the kingdoms of western Europe. Furthermore, the Viking Wars gave rise to some of the great myths of English national history: Alfred and the burnt cakes; Eric Bloodaxe, king of York; Æthelred 'the Unready'; the Massacre of St Brice's Day and the skins of Danes nailed to church doors; and Cnut and the waves on the seashore. Each of these myths reveals the ways that these traumatic events have been interpreted. As if this was not enough, the great national account, the *Anglo-Saxon Chronicle*, was created in the 880s as a direct consequence of the Viking invasions. It was written following what might be termed the West Saxons' 'Finest Hour', when they had survived the ninth-century Viking assault and were creating an epic story of the rise of their people to the position of the sole surviving Anglo-Saxon kingdom. The Viking Wars made 'England' and did so as much in people's heads as in their institutions and archaeology.

For twenty-first-century readers these wars strike familiar chords: there are debates about the 'clash of civilizations'; we see the stresses and strains inherent in the formation of a multi-cultural society; national identities are questioned, forged and challenged; religion, economics and power-politics intersect, interact and, at times, explode; immigrants and native inhabitants both clash and cooperate; and propaganda is created and re-created in a battle for hearts and minds.

A whole range of myths, stereotypes and assumptions cloud our view of these events. However, the latest archaeological finds and new explorations of the written records are challenging many of these views, giving us a clearer picture of the events and impact of the Viking Wars.

The Viking Wars lasted from the late eighth until the late eleventh centuries. In this series of wars there were a number of discernible phases: from *c.* 790 until 866, raids escalated in their frequency and ferocity; from 866 until 896, these raids gave way to a conquest and settlement which involved the overthrow of every Anglo-Saxon kingdom except Wessex; in the first half of the tenth century that surviving kingdom launched a counter-offensive against the newly established Viking elites in England; in the mid-tenth century, invasions of Dublin Norse and other ambitious Viking leaders once more challenged Anglo-Saxon rule; from *c.* 980 until 1016, a wave of attacks comparable with the first phase of Viking activity eventually led to the Viking conquest of England; from 1016 until 1042 England was inextricable drawn into the rule and complications of an Anglo-Danish empire; following the Norman Conquest of 1066, Scandinavian rulers once again fished in the troubled waters of English politics and added their own unique contribution to the cocktail of rebellions and bloody reprisals that marked the two decades following the Battle of Hastings; in the 1090s the last – failed – Viking interventions brought this astonishing period of history to a close.

But who were these Vikings? And where did they come from? Even more importantly, why did they explode on to the scene in the late eighth century? In short, what caused 'the First Blitzkrieg'?

A '9/11 moment'?

Every educated Anglo-Saxon – whether monk, nun or noble – would probably have later been able to recall where they were when they first heard the news that the monastery of Lindisfarne (Northumberland) had been sacked, in 793. Situated at the end of a causeway, off the coast of the northern Anglo-Saxon kingdom of Northumbria, Lindisfarne was a spiritual, cultural and intellectual powerhouse. Not for nothing is it still known as Holy Island. In 635 the Irish-born monk, Aidan, had been invited by

King Oswald of Northumbria to set up a base for preaching and teaching the Christian message in the north. Arriving from the equally famous monastery of Iona, the place Aidan eventually chose as his base was this tidal island close to the royal fortress, which was situated on the nearby Rock of Bamburgh. This placed it close to a centre of political power, where the great decisions of the north were being made; while still being sited far enough into the sea to make it an island at high tide and so a place of solitude and reflection. It would soon become famous for its saintly monk, Cuthbert, who became abbot of the monastery, a bishop and the patron saint of Northumbria. It was also at this monastery that the literary and artistic treasure of the Lindisfarne Gospels was created in the early eighth century. Anyone who has seen its beautifully illuminated pages, glowing in the subdued twenty-first-century lighting of London's British Library, cannot fail but be impressed by both its stunning beauty and by the skill and religious devotion it embodies. As a book to glorify God and spread the Christian message, it sums up all that Lindisfarne was established to achieve.

Then, in 793, the place was trashed. It is often risky to draw parallels between events occurring in different periods of history. Values, ideas and outlooks do not always travel as easily as we sometimes make them do. But 793 was surely an Anglo-Saxon '9/11 moment'. It struck at national security and cultural values in an iconic place and in a brutal and bloody manner. If anything represented a 'clash of civilizations' then surely it was the sack of Lindisfarne.

For those Anglo-Saxons who heard of it, the destruction of Lindisfarne was an offence against God, learning and the sense that the Anglo-Saxon kingdoms were safe from external threats. That the ancestors of the shocked and appalled listeners to the breaking news of 793 had done much the same things to Romano-British citizens in the fifth century was an irony lost on most who heard it. At that previous time the Anglo-Saxon raiders had themselves been pagans, like those pirates who now devastated Lindisfarne. However, Anglo-Saxon England had moved on since then and devastation at the hands of pagans was totally unexpected. Similarly, the fact that Anglo-Saxon warbands in the eighth century were not above sacking monasteries loyal to rival neighbouring kingdoms within England did not diminish the shock of this attack from the sea by 'outsiders'.

Far away, in Aachen (modern-day Germany), at the court of the Frankish ruler Charlemagne, the Northumbrian churchman, scholar and educationalist, Alcuin, provides us with the only significant contemporary account of the attack (since the equally famous account in the *Anglo-Saxon Chronicle* was not penned until the 880s). Head-hunted by the ruler of the superpower of his day, in order to revolutionise educational standards in the Frankish royal court, Alcuin eloquently recorded his shock at the events that had unfolded off the Northumbrian coast in a letter he wrote, in 793, to Æthelred, king of Northumbria:

> It is nearly 350 years that we and our fathers have inhabited this most lovely land, and never before has such a terror appeared in Britain as we have now suffered from a pagan race, nor was it thought that such an inroad from the sea could be made. Behold, the church of St Cuthbert spattered with the blood of the priests of God, despoiled of all its ornaments; a place more venerable than all in Britain is given as a prey to pagan peoples.[1]

Contemporary Christians saw in this event the fulfilment of the Old Testament prophecy of Jeremiah chapter 1, verse 14: 'The LORD said to me, "From the north disaster will be poured out on all who live in the land" '.[2] This may have inspired Alcuin's reminder – in the same letter – of a bloody rain which had fallen from a clear sky on the north side of the church at York. To Alcuin this suggested that 'from the north there will come upon our nation retribution of blood'.[3] Alcuin went on to attempt to explain why such a disaster had occurred. He identified sins as varied as hair fashion which imitated that of the northern pagans, luxurious clothing and the impoverishment of the common people as a result of the wealth enjoyed by their leaders. Curiously, a fragment of an early eleventh-century letter, written following another phase of Viking incursions, also complains about Anglo-Saxons who 'dress in Danish fashion with bared necks and blinded eyes'.[4] This seems to be another reference to unacceptable Viking-inspired hairstyles.

In a second letter, also written in 793, but this time to Higbald, bishop of Lindisfarne, Alcuin wrestled with the same dilemma of explaining why 'St Cuthbert, with so great a number of saints, defends not his own?'[5] Again, Alcuin concluded that 'it has not happened by chance, but is a sign that it was well merited by someone'.[6] He strongly advised the bishop to consider what sins in himself and in his community might have caused this judgement to fall, and to see they were remedied swiftly. Otherwise there was a real danger that what had occurred was the start of more tribulation to follow. In the meantime, Alcuin promised to try to use his influence with the

Frankish ruler, Charlemagne, to see if anything could be done to secure the release of the monks enslaved by the Vikings.

Alcuin's letters are not our only record of the disaster which hit Lindisfarne. A later source – a manuscript of the *Anglo-Saxon Chronicle* (*manuscript E*) which included northern events to augment its southern focus – took up the theme dramatically:

> In this year dire portents appeared over Northumbria and sorely frightened the people. They consisted of immense whirlwinds and flashes of lightning, and fiery dragons were seen flying in the air. A great famine immediately followed those signs, and a little after that in the same year, on 8 June, the rav-ages of heathen men miserably destroyed God's church in Lindisfarne, with plunder and slaughter.[7]

The Viking Wars had started with a vengeance. The opening strike of what can only be described as 'the First Blitzkrieg' had fallen on Anglo-Saxon England. Some other manuscripts of the *Chronicle* date the attack as occur-ring in January, but *manuscript E* was well informed about northern events and a summer attack is more credible than one in the depth of winter.

Not surprisingly, many histories of the Vikings in England start with this raid on Lindisfarne. They use this to illustrate the utter devastation caused by these first Viking attacks. This is not surprising, but it does not actually take account of some crucial evidence. A closer examination of the traditional account is more revealing and challenges some of these commonly held assumptions.

On closer examination

The evidence regarding the first Viking attack is less straightforward than it first appears. The Viking Wars are full of historical surprises which test the critical skills of the historian. For a start, Alcuin's second outraged letter was written to the bishop and community of monks on Lindisfarne, so monas-tic life had clearly survived the assault of 793. A later, mid-tenth-century source (the *History of St Cuthbert*) indicates that it was not until 830–45 that the relics of St Cuthbert were translated from Lindisfarne to Norham-on-Tweed. This seems to have been accompanied by a dismantling of much of the church building on Lindisfarne itself. However, this occurred two generations after the raid of 793 and, whilst it may have been prompted by escalating Viking activity in the ninth century, may equally have been due to the monastic community gaining estates inland.[8] By 875 the community had returned to Lindisfarne as, in this year, it relocated yet again. This is a point often overlooked in modern accounts of the raid of 793.

Similarly, the famous gravestone from Lindisfarne, which is often interpreted as showing seven weapon-waving Viking marauders advancing from left-to-right across the stone slab, probably dates from the ninth century.[9] Obviously, a Christian religious community continued to bury its dead there until the site finally became too dangerous a generation or two later. And the menacing warriors could just as easily represent warfare in general, in a scene from events leading up to the Day of Judgement, for there is nothing specifically Viking about them. This is particularly important as most references to this gravestone assume beyond doubt that it commemorates the famous Viking attack. This may be an assumption too far. Recently, analysis of Viking raids in Ireland, for example, show that, of the 113 attacks on monasteries between 795 and 820, only twenty-six were carried out by Vikings. The rest were either carried out by Irish kings on Irish monasteries or were even the work of monks from rival religious communities.[10] We should not expect anything different for Anglo-Saxon England. As early as the late seventh century, Aldhelm, abbot of Malmesbury (Wiltshire), had been forced to negotiate a special arrangement with the kings of Mercia and Wessex to prevent them targeting his monastery, since it was sited in a border zone between the two rival Christian Anglo-Saxon kingdoms.[11] In 684 Ecgfrith of Northumbria launched an attack on Ireland which was accompanied by the destruction of Irish churches. There was, therefore, nothing specifically Viking about the tendency to loot vulnerable religious communities which were situated in enemy kingdoms. This is a point often ignored when assessing the impact of the early Viking raids.

A more fundamental problem lies in the fact that the attack on Lindisfarne was not actually the first recorded Viking raid on England. Although written in a later source of evidence, the first appearance of the Vikings dates not from 793 and not from the North Sea coast, but from 789 and from Dorset. It is not surprising, though, that this earlier event was eclipsed by the later attack on Lindisfarne. It seems that only one man died in the first attack and, rather more fundamentally, no one had written a national treasure like the Lindisfarne Gospels on the beach at Portland. But it was to Portland, in Dorset, that the dubious honour goes of being the first English victim of the Viking Wars. The account of that earlier event, however, is rather short of the 'shock and awe' that we associate with the raids from Scandinavia, although it is very revealing if one reads between the lines.

The record is found in the *Anglo-Saxon Chronicle*, which was compiled in Old English, in Wessex, from a range of earlier material about a century after the event in Dorset (probably in the 880s). The simplest and oldest surviving version of the attack is found in *manuscript A*, also called the *Parker Chronicle*, which is now found in the Parker Library at Corpus Christi College, at the University of Cambridge. Written in Winchester in the late ninth or very early tenth century, this manuscript of the *Chronicle* does not even mention the more famous attack on Lindisfarne. The annal in question (wrongly dated in the original to 787) reads:

> ... and in his days [this refers to Brihtric, king of Wessex] there came for the first time three ships of Northmen and then the *reeve* [the king's local representative] rode to them and wished to force them to the king's residence, for he did not know what they were; and they slew him. Those were the first ships of Danish men which came to the land of the English. [12]

This is all rather vague and leaves us guessing exactly where this occurred, although at least we know the origin of the raiders: Denmark. Rather more information is provided by a later manuscript of the *Chronicle. Manuscript E*, the *Laud* or *Peterborough Chronicle*, was written in East Anglia, beginning in 1121 and continuing until 1154, probably to replace an earlier version destroyed in a fire in 1116. The version used in making the replacement copy seems to have taken some additional information from a northern source and identifies the raiders as 'from Hörthaland' (in Norway), although it then, confusingly, continues with the same information that the raiders were Danes. Clearly, there was some confusion in the geography here.

In these rather garbled accounts we have the evidence of the first Vikings in England. Other, later, records join up a few more of the dots to give us a more rounded picture. In *Æthelweard's Chronicle*, written in Latin for a wealthy West Country aristocrat sometime in the late tenth century, we are told that the murdered royal official was named Beaduheard and that he had come down to the coast from the nearby town of Dorchester (Dorset). This town was a *villa regalis*, a royal estate centre. *Æthelweard's Chronicle* adds that the *reeve* thought that the new arrivals were traders. To this the Latin *Annals of St Neots* – confusingly compiled at Bury St Edmunds (Suffolk) in the early twelfth century – adds that the violence erupted at Portland.

So, the picture finally emerges. A ship docked at Portland, in Dorset. Its crew were from Norway, but since every Viking later got lumped together under the catch-all title of 'Danes', this ethnic label became attached to the record, despite more accurate intelligence that later became available from a northern source. The local royal official rode down from nearby Dorchester to establish their tax status. This involved them accompanying him back to his base at Dorchester in order to check out their credentials. He clearly thought they were merchants and this was standard practice for anyone seeking to enter an Anglo-Saxon kingdom in the eighth century. The later, ninth-century laws of King Alfred specifically state that, with regard to traders: 'they are to bring before the king's *reeve* in a public meeting the men whom they take up into the country with them, and it is to be established how many of them there are to be'.[13] This allowed the local royal agent time to check how many people were entering his local area and on what business. It upheld the security of the kingdom by keeping track of travellers and was all very tidy and tax efficient. But on this occasion things turned nasty – they killed him.

What the killing on Portland beach reveals about the Vikings

What is interesting about the violence at Portland is, in fact, what did not happen. There is no record of mass slaughter; no account of pillaging; no burning or looting; and, as far as we can tell, only one man died (although *Æthelweard's Chronicle* says a few men were killed alongside the *reeve*). There was presumably an altercation over procedure, accompanied by resentment at the unwanted orders being issued by a royal administrator, then a quick resort to violence and away. Clearly, Viking 'raids' were not always what we might imagine. Trade and opportunism, rather than massacre, was often on the agenda. This is rather closer to the image of traders and settlers that we find in many modern histories of the Vikings, and that we can see embodied in the animatronics who speak in Old Norse at the Jorvik Viking Centre in York. Furthermore, Alcuin's letters to King Æthelred and Bishop Higbald suggest that there were existing social and economic connections between the suffering communities and Scandinavia. If there were not, then how were the Northumbrians aware of the Viking hairstyles of which Alcuin disapproved and how else might it be possible for the Franks to negotiate the return of the enslaved monks? These little pieces of evidence are easily missed when reading his letters, but they are certainly there and they are significant. Clearly, the Vikings had not appeared from nowhere; they must already have been familiar coastal traders by the late eighth century.

Nevertheless, this aspect of Viking realities should not erase the more brutal image. There is plenty of evidence in support of that too and we will explore it later. But the account probably gives us a realistic insight into these first tentative incursions. Young Scandinavian men in these situations might drift from trade to violence depending on the circumstances. These were violent opportunists, not men setting out to level kingdoms. That would come, but the escalation to that phase would have its own reasons and its own dynamics. At first, things were less clear-cut, and, even later, the image of the Viking trader and the Viking raider could blur, depending on the make-up of the group involved and the strength of the opposition.

On the other hand, a royal official died. The quick resort to violence and the refusal to accept local authority would also be a characteristic of the Vikings. So, we should not go too far in a rehabilitation of those groups about to descend on England. As an historian commented, on a violently named tenth-century Viking king of York: 'He wasn't called Eric Bloodaxe because he was good with the children.'[14]

What is a Viking?

'Danes', 'Northmen', 'heathen', 'pagans' and 'Vikings' were all terms used to describe the Scandinavian raiders and eventual settlers by those experiencing their attacks. In Anglo-Saxon sources, the labels 'Danes', 'Northmen' and 'pagans' or 'heathens' were the terms most often used. As we have seen, with regard to the incident at Portland, this did not always convey much geographical accuracy. When we read 'Danes' in the accounts of raids we cannot be certain that those involved actually originated in Denmark. Despite this, other evidence does suggest that, for most Anglo-Saxons, it was in fact Danish Vikings that they faced most of the time.

What is more surprising is that we hardly ever come across the term 'Viking' being used in any accounts from outside of Scandinavia. This was true for almost all those who encountered Scandinavian raiders. The Franks called them '*Nordmanni*' (northmen) and an area eventually ceded to them in the tenth century would become Normandy as a result. Slavs knew them from their perceived ruddy complexions as the '*Rus*' (red) and a similar word, 'Rhos', was used by the Byzantines, in modern Greece and Turkey, who employed them as mercenaries and met Scandinavian traders who had ventured down the rivers leading into the Black Sea and from there had travelled into the eastern Mediterranean. This word would eventually survive in the national name of Russia, since a Viking state centred on Kiev was at the core of the early Russian nation. Amongst the Byzantines they were also known as 'Varangians' (those who swear loyalty) and the Varangian Guard served the Eastern Roman Emperor in Constantinople. In Ireland they were the 'Lochlannach' (northmen); with the Norwegians differentiated as 'Finn-gaill' (white foreigners) and the Danes were the 'Dubh-gaill' (black foreigners). Islamic sources knew them as 'al-madjus' (heathens). No one called them Vikings.

So where does the word 'Viking' come from? There is no certain answer, but there are a number of possible derivations. The Old Icelandic word 'vík' (bay or creek) may have developed into a term used to describe seamen hiding in, or sailing from, these coastal inlets. Since an area of southern Norway was called Vik, it may alternatively be that this became attached to those sailing from this area and, eventually, gained a wider application. We have seen that the first raiders along the English coast were apparently Norwegians. On the other hand, the Old Icelandic verb for 'moving, turning aside' is 'víkja' and may have come to describe seafarers far from home. Old Norse Scandinavian written sources (and these came very late to Scandinavia) describe a pirate raider as a 'víkingr' and a raiding expedition as a 'víking'. It has recently been memorably stated that 'the word "Viking" is something you *did* rather than what you *were*.' [15] And for many this would have been a part-time occupation. [16] In these Old Norse sources the negative connotations of pirates were probably not in the thoughts of the writers, and a more adventurous sense of freebooters was probably what they had in mind. In its Old English form 'wicing' or 'wicingas' does not appear as a label for Scandinavian pirates until the tenth century and, surprisingly, it is only used five times in the annals of the *Anglo-Saxon Chronicle*. However, it does appear in some east-coast place names where it may have been derived from a personal name. As a result, we have Wickenby (Lincolnshire) meaning 'Viking's by' (village), Wiganthorpe (Yorkshire) meaning 'Viking's thorp' (dependent farm) and Wigston (Leicestershire) meaning 'Viking's tun' (village). [17]

After sparing use in Old English, the word had no Middle English form and it did not become the standard term for Scandinavian invaders in

Britain until the nineteenth century. In fact, it is not known in its modern spelling 'Viking' (as opposed to the Old Norse *vikingr*) before 1840. Since then the term has really taken off and has become applied not only to those involved in raiding expeditions but to Scandinavians generally during the 'Viking Age'. As a result, it is the term used in this book. But it comes with the warning that few Anglo-Saxons living through the 'Viking Wars' would have recognised it and most Scandinavian merchants and settlers would not have thought that it applied to them.

The origins, destinations and motives of the early Viking raiders

Most of those involved in attacking and settling in England – and Britain generally – came from what we now know as Denmark and Norway. Norwegians (often simply described as the Norse) targeted Shetland, Orkney, northern Scotland, the Western Isles and Ireland. They would eventually establish a Viking kingdom based on Dublin and from there would 'fish' in the troubled waters of northern English politics. The Danes raided the coasts of eastern and southern England, and the coast of France, and were those who would have the greatest impact on Anglo-Saxon consciousness; hence the tendency to describe all raiders as 'Danes'. Swedish adventurers tended to sail eastward into the Baltic and down the river systems of what would become Russia. Only from the late tenth and early eleventh century do we learn of Swedish Vikings joining the fleets sailing for England. The homelands of these Vikings were not developed nations, but this was changing as the Viking Wars started and is significant, as we shall shortly see.

Denmark dominated trade routes from the North Sea to the Baltic and so had the potential to develop into a formidable threat to its southern neighbours. It also controlled regions in southern Sweden. Denmark became increasingly centralised by the eighth century and was strong enough to threaten the coast of the Frankish empire by the ninth century. It then fragmented in the late ninth and early tenth centuries between dynasties competing for control of the kingdom, before being reunited again.

Norway on the other hand was, prior to the late ninth century, divided and dominated by Denmark. The richest area was Vestfold, with its trading centre of Kaupang. In the late ninth century it became increasingly united under a ruler named Harald Finehair, but was still dominated by Denmark.

Regarding Sweden, Denmark ruled much of the south, while the rest of the country lacked political cohesion. In the ninth century, petty kings are mentioned in the written sources which were compiled outside Sweden. There appear to have been two main political units: the Svear (with a centre at Uppsala) and the Götar (centred on the plains of Östergötland and Västergötland, near Lake Vättern).[18]

It was a combination of changes occurring within Scandinavia, coinciding with events outside of the region, which appear to have triggered the start of raids and later settlement. In the eighth century increased population in Norway may have sparked competition for resources. Even more important may have been the growing power of Norwegian chieftains, who extended their authority and control of land at the expense of lesser nobles. Frustrated at home, these warriors looked elsewhere for a means of gaining wealth and prestige. This may have been why it was Norwegians who appeared off Portland in 789. Increased political unity in the ninth century may have provided another spur to unsuccessful competitors to leave Norway and seek opportunities elsewhere. Within Denmark there were internal and external triggers. Externally the southern Danish frontier was threatened by the expansion of the Christian Frankish empire. This seems to have prompted moves towards greater Danish political unity as a defence against Frankish attack. This led to internal push factors by driving some dissidents abroad who had lost out in this process and, on top of this, the Danish elites who triumphed in this power struggle appear to have decided to finance their new political power from raiding expeditions abroad. In addition, the emerging Danish rulers rewarded their supporters with grants of land, creating an elite land-hunger as there was not enough land to go round. The answer to this land-hunger lay in conquests abroad.

A recent analysis of factors has concluded that the roots of the Viking Age expansion are long: mercenary participation in Roman wars encouraged the development of military hierarchies as these warriors returned home; an almost constant state of war within Scandinavia encouraged the development of centralised government and naval transportation; increasingly centralised power in southern Scandinavia brought stability and encouraged international trade by the seventh century; the Danish elites in this area then turned to external trading and raiding in order to generate further wealth and this was assisted by the development of ocean-going ships.[19]

This Danish expansion may have had another feature which gave it a particularly striking character. The Frankish empire was expansionist in both its political and its religious policy, and the threat of a Christian superpower on the border appears to have prompted aggressive defensive reactions from the still-pagan communities in Denmark. We are used to explaining the attacks on western European monasteries as being motivated by the desire to seize portable wealth from undefended communities. However, the first century of raids may have had an extra ideological motive; it was an attack on the very ideology of the Franks and their Christian neighbours. This remains a very controversial modern theory, but may suggest that the many accounts of looted monasteries may not simply be due to monks doing the record-keeping. There may, in fact, have really been a religious conflict going on: a 'clash of civilizations' may really have occurred with treasure houses of Christian sacred art and literature looted or burnt. However, the situation was complex and at least one modern study has suggested that the dearth of surviving documentary sources from East Anglia, for example, is due less to Viking destruction than to poor curation of records in a diocese which underwent significant organisational changes in the period up to 1095.[20]

One other ingredient was also added to this volatile and violent cocktail of factors. Danish attacks on Francia and England coincided with disruptions in the flow of silver from the Middle Eastern Islamic Caliphate to Scandinavia. This escalated further when the Caliphate lost control of the silver mines in what is now Tajikistan. The drying up of supplies of Arab silver had far-reaching consequences as Scandinavian economies faltered due to the decline in trade. And the lack of silver struck at the heart of the gift-giving which reinforced the relationships between nobles and their followers, since it was more difficult for silver-poor Scandinavian elites to purchase luxury goods from western Europe. Raiding offered an alternative method of obtaining these valuables and slaves.[21] Consequently, storm clouds from the north were gathering over the communities of Anglo-Saxon England and its neighbours, and in the late eighth century the storm began to break.

2

STORM FROM THE NORTH,
789–866

Between the years 789 and 866, Viking attacks on England escalated. In 794, only one year after the famous attack on the monastery at Lindisfarne, *manuscript D* of the *Anglo-Saxon Chronicle* records another raid against the North Sea coast of the kingdom of Northumbria. This time the 'heathens ravaged in Northumbria and plundered Ecgfrith's monastery at *Donemuthan*'.[1] The location of this unfortunate community of monks is not entirely clear. The name means 'mouth of the River Don' and has not survived as a modern place name and, to add to the complexity, there appears to have been another northern monastery with a similar name – *Donaemuthe* – which is recorded in a letter written by the pope to a king of Northumbria in 757. Its location is also uncertain, although the details of the earlier letter suggests it was a different place to the monastery recorded as the subject of the raid of 794. However, in the early twelfth-century account of the Church in northern England (the *History of the Church of Durham*), written by Simeon of Durham, a tradition is recorded which locates the plundered community as being the monastery of Jarrow (Tyne and Wear).[2] The case for Jarrow is strengthened by the reference to the plundered monastery in the *Chronicle* as being 'Ecgfrith's monastery', since King Ecgfrith of Northumbria had granted land to the Church for the foundation of a monastery at Jarrow in 681. In which case, yet another famous northern monastery – the community where Bede, the famous Northumbrian historian had died in 735 – was being targeted.

This time, though, the attackers did not have things entirely their own way. Despite the description of ravaging and plundering, one of the Viking leaders was killed, storms destroyed some of the Viking ships and many of their crews were drowned. Those who survived to reach the shore were immediately killed by the Northumbrians.

Extreme violence, in an age of extreme violence

Shocking as the attacks on Portland, Lindisfarne (see Chapter 1) and Jarrow were, there was nothing as yet to suggest that a new era of seaborne devastation was starting. Only hindsight would suggest that, and the decade of the 790s was more noteworthy for home-grown atrocities. In 798, *manuscript C* of the *Chronicle* records that 'Cenwulf, king of the Mercians, ravaged the people of Kent' and also of Romney Marsh. The king of Kent, named Præn, was brought 'in fetters into Mercia'[3] and, according to *manuscript F* of the *Chronicle*, 'had his eyes put out and his hands cut off'.[4] The brutality of this event reminds us of the context in which the Viking attacks occurred. State-sanctioned acts of extreme violence against rivals, inter-kingdom raiding and general destruction were features of Anglo-Saxon England long before the Viking Wars occurred, and therefore the destruction of the raids needs to be seen against this background. Had there been no Viking assault, the people of England could still have found themselves enslaved and their resources destroyed, or looted, as a result of the military adventures of neighbouring Anglo-Saxon kingdoms. This is not to claim that these were everyday events, but their occurrence is confirmed by a range of Anglo-Saxon sources and they clearly were not rare experiences. When, in 815, Egbert of Wessex 'ravaged in Cornwall, from east to west'[5] it would have been the crops and houses of ordinary farmers that were destroyed and, no doubt, people would have been killed and others raped by the West Saxon army. These victims, though, were British citizens of the still-independent Cornish ('West Welsh') kingdom of the far south-west, so no doubt were particularly vulnerable to being simply dismissed as collateral damage in a strike at the economic viability of the Cornish elites. However, the same strategies were also deployed against other Anglo-Saxon kingdoms for warfare was hardwired into Anglo-Saxon society. As one recent study of the exercise of power in Anglo-Saxon England has noted: 'Even before the Viking attacks of the ninth century, conflict between English kings and their foreign neighbours was common, if not yet on the scale of the 860s and 870s.'[6]

There is, though, an interesting link between the West Saxon attack on Cornwall in 815 and the escalating Viking raids since when, in 838, a Viking fleet landed in Cornwall the 'West Welsh' joined them in a coordinated attack on Egbert of Wessex. Clearly, one person's 'ravaging heathens' could become another person's 'useful ally' in retaliation against the aggressive West Saxons. And, of course, the Cornish were Christians, though of the Brittonic Church which elsewhere had been absorbed and disparaged by the dominant Anglo-Saxon Church. Clearly, the heathen nature of the Vikings was no barrier to the Cornish in establishing an alliance and, similarly, the Vikings were amenable to a tactical working relationship with the Christian Cornish in order to benefit from a combined assault on the far wealthier West Saxon kingdom. This complexity is important to note, as it is the first recorded example of many, and no doubt many more went unrecorded in the surviving documentary sources. The Viking Blitzkrieg would throw up a range of surprising alliances.

Escalating attacks from the 830s onwards

What is undeniable is that, after a comparative lull, the pace of attacks escalated from the 830s onwards. The lull is explainable since Irish sources tell us that Ireland experienced heavy raiding in the first thirty years of the ninth century, followed by settlement in the 840s; the raiders – seemingly Danes at this time – were clearly preoccupied on the other side of the Irish Sea. However, this was not to last. In 835 'heathen men ravaged Sheppey' (Kent).[7] In 836 a large fleet of thirty-five Viking ships landed on the Somerset coast and fought the West Saxon king, Egbert, at Carhampton – the battle ended in a Viking victory. Carhampton was again the scene of a battle in 843, this time between King Æthelwulf of Wessex and Viking raiders and, again, the invaders were victorious. That neither Egbert nor Æthelwulf were killed suggests that they were forced to withdraw, rather than that they were comprehensively defeated; nevertheless, these reversals show the extent of the threat Wessex was now facing. The repeated attacks on Carhampton were probably due to its importance as a royal estate centre where abundant resources were available to plunder.[8] In which case the raiders were showing an awareness of local opportunities, suggesting a sophisticated level of intelligence gathering.

The *Chronicle* simply records these Scandinavians as raiders but, at this point, they may have been active in the Bristol Channel as both raiders and traders, depending on the opportunities available, and this will have assisted in the collection of intelligence information that could be used in aggression, as well as in peaceful trading negotiations. That they based themselves in the Bristol Channel in order to facilitate raiding and trading into Wales and the West Country, is evidenced from the Norse names for the islands of Steepholm and Flatholm. Whilst Steepholm simply means 'steep island', the name of Flatholm is more revealing. It is the '*flota-holm*' (fleet island) and clearly took its name from its role as a Viking naval base. The island of Lundy, off the coast of Devon, also carries a Norse name, in this case 'puffin island'.[9] Exactly when these islands gained these Norse names is unknown, but they suggest a significant Viking presence in the Bristol Channel and they most probably date from the ninth century. Taking into account varied pieces of evidence, including these island names, an Irish-Norse trade weight found at Ilchester (Somerset) and the later, eleventh-century record of a thriving slave-trade from Bristol to Ireland, has led one recent study to suggest that, in the ninth century, the Scandinavian visitors to the Bristol Channel may have combined trading with raiding.[10] There are echoes of the first arrival at Portland but, by the 830s, the balance was swinging far more in the direction of pirate raids.

The size of the force that the West Saxons confronted at Carhampton is a matter of some debate. *Manuscript C* of the *Chronicle* claims the force landed in thirty-five ships in 836, whereas *manuscripts D, E* and *F* downgrade this to twenty-five. The fact that the same sized force of thirty-five ships appears in all manuscripts of the *Chronicle* regarding the 843 battle suggests there is a confusion in our sources between the two battles. It has even been suggested that the record of the later battle is a duplicate of the earlier one.[11] Extrapolating from numbers of ships to size of army is extremely hazardous, however; a figure of thirty to forty men per ship is reasonable[12] and this would suggest a Viking force at each of the Carhampton battles of somewhere is the region of 1,000 warriors,[13] perhaps as many as 2,000.[14] The compiler of this larger figure, though, thinks that a figure in the region of 1,000–1,100 is more likely. The larger figure assumes the presence of bigger warships, but we simply cannot tell the size of the ships being deployed and, even if some were of the largest kind, this does not mean that all were of this type. And such very large warships, carrying at least sixty men, for which there is some evidence,[15] are always likely to have been few and far between[16] due to the immense cost of their construction and the fact that only kings and the most successful Viking *jarls* (nobles) could have afforded them. Perhaps the most significant fact in any assessment of the size of the Viking forces at the two battles of Carhampton is that they were large enough to inflict defeat on the West Saxon armies, but not large enough to make these defeats crushing ones.

Even more alarming is the distinct possibility that these defeats allowed the Vikings ample opportunity to plunder at will. There is no other raid reported in English sources for 843, so the contemporary Frankish report of a major Viking attack on England this year may very well refer to the same event. If so, the *Chronicle* account is very economical with the truth. The Frankish *Annals of St Bertin* records: 'After a battle lasting three days, the Northmen emerged the winners: plundering, looting, slaughtering everywhere, they wielded power over the land at will'.[17]

If the consequences were worse than the *Chronicle* would admit to, but not as bad as the Frankish source suggests, we are still left with a serious crisis affecting western Wessex in the early 840s. We have already considered the Viking force which landed in Cornwall in 838 and in 840 the major trading port of Southampton (Hampshire) was attacked. Here the *ealdorman* (the king's regional representative), Wulfheard, inflicted a defeat on the raiders. Wulfheard died that same year, but the later tenth-century chronicler, Æthelweard, adds to his version of this record 'in peace', as if to emphasise the success of this fighting royal official. However, not all royal representatives were so successful. That same year *Ealdorman* Æthelhelm of Dorset was killed fighting a Viking army at Portland; Æthelweard adds, 'and his companions with him'.[18] In 841 another *ealdorman* was killed on Romney Marsh. Wessex was not alone, however, as that same year many Anglo-Saxons were killed in Lindsey (Lincolnshire), in East Anglia and again in Kent. The lack of detail about the first two of these disasters is almost certainly due to the West Saxon focus of the *Chronicle*.

The fate of London

Whatever trading aspects there had been to earlier Viking arrivals, the scene was now set for devastation. In 842, according to the *Chronicle*, three major trading centres were raided. These were London and Rochester (Kent) in

England and Quentovic on the Continent. The first was the foremost trading centre in England, the last was the principal early medieval port for northern France and was the most important of the Frankish seaports. The fact that the *Chronicle* records 'great slaughter'[19] at these two places clearly indicates the severity of the attacks on these rich trading centres. This was a real blow to the trade of Anglo-Saxon England as London had been a major trading centre since the late seventh century. In 731, Bede had described it as 'a trading centre for many nations who visit it by land and sea.'[20] At that point it was the main city of the kingdom of the East Saxons (Essex) but, during the course of the eighth century, it was brought under the control of the Mercian kingdom. Even before Bede wrote, the city was already coming under Mercian domination. The earliest reference to '*portum Lundoniae*' (the port of London) is from a charter of *c.* 672–74 that was issued by Frithuwold, sub-king of Wulfhere of Mercia. Domination of London gave landlocked Mercia access to the sea. A few years later we have the first record of its name in the form '*Lundenwuuic*' (*Lundenwic*). The city that Bede described was situated to the west of the Roman city and sprawled along what is now the Strand, with modern evidence for its expansion being found by archaeologists in the vicinity of Covent Garden and Trafalgar Square. Its name – *Lundenwic* – indicated its trading nature and differentiated it from the older Roman city. It was ideally situated for communication with the Continent and archaeological finds from the Strand area include: quernstones from the Rhineland, whetstones from Norway and pottery from northern France, Normandy, the Seine valley and from Rhenish production centres.[21] Its exports included Anglo-Saxon slaves taken in warfare between the many rival kingdoms and sold on through Frisian middle-men based in *Lundenwic*. Again this reminds us that enslaving and the slave trade was endemic in Anglo-Saxon England, although it is recounted with particular horror when later carried out by Viking intruders.

By the mid-ninth century, settlement at this trading centre had ceased. At the same time occupation, as evidenced by archaeology, expanded within the walls of the old Roman city. What would eventually be called *Lundenburh* (London-fort) was to replace the undefended settlement to its west. The old settlement of *Lundenwic* was later remembered as the *ealdwic* (old trading settlement), a name which survives today in the modern Aldwych. It is not difficult to explain the failure of the foremost trading centre of Anglo-Saxon England. *Lundenwic* was attacked again in 851, making two major assaults in just under a decade. At the same time as *Lundenwic* was abandoned, other settlements in its hinterland also declined. Archaeological excavation suggests that the same period saw the end of occupation at Barking, Battersea and Bermondsey. All would have been vulnerable to incursions up the River Thames by Viking fleets. However, the Vikings may not have been the only factor behind the demise of *Lundenwic*. Archaeological evidence indicates that the settlement suffered a series of disastrous fires in the late eighth century which had nothing to do with Scandinavian attacks. Rising river levels may also have seriously disrupted the settlement. In addition, civil wars in the Frankish empire, after 829, undermined economic growth across the English Channel and damaged trade with England. Nevertheless, the same analysis of factors which reminds us of these many reasons for the failure of *Lundenwic* concludes that Viking activity, more than any other, should be seen as instrumental in the decline of the settlement.[22] Fundamentally, it seems it was the Vikings who were to blame.

Prelude to disaster

From the mid-840s to mid-850s, the *Anglo-Saxon Chronicle* records suggest that a number of raids met with defeats at the hands of Anglo-Saxon forces. In 845 the men of Somerset and Dorset, fighting under their respective *ealdormen*, and in the company of Ealhstan, bishop of Sherborne (Dorset), defeated a Viking force at the mouth of the River Parrett (Somerset). The *Chronicle* insists that this was a major victory and, given its frankness in admitting later defeats, there is every reason to think that this is an accurate record. What is interesting is that this again draws our attention to the Bristol Channel area and reminds us that, in addition to those Viking fleets operating down the eastern coast of England, a significant number were now active in the Bristol Channel and Irish Sea region. Given the Irish records for Viking activity in the 830s, there is every likelihood that the Vikings who were attacking the Somerset coast and northern Devon did so from bases in Ireland, probably augmented by ones on islands such as Flatholm, which were located closer to their targets. This is reinforced by an attack on Devon in 851. The location of this battle is uncertain since *Wicganbeorg* (Wicga's hill) has not survived as a modern place name, although the personal name Wicga occurs in a number of minor-names in Devon, so it could have been anywhere in the county. This may have been another example of Bristol Channel Vikings in action, but the matter must remain open to debate.

What is clear is that there was a growing intensity to the attacks. That same year, in 851, King Æthelwulf of Wessex defeated a Viking army, at the unidentified place *Aclea*, in such stunning fashion that the chronicler – looking back from the 880s – wrote 'and there inflicted the greatest slaughter on a heathen army that we have ever heard of until this present day'.[23] In the same campaigning season, King Athelstan – eldest of the five sons of Æthelwulf of Wessex, and who ruled as sub-king of Kent – intercepted a Viking force at sea, off Sandwich (Kent), and captured nine of the Viking ships. This was clearly an unusual event and the first time that anything of this nature is described in the *Chronicle*. It suggests that, either patrols were operating off the English coast designed to intercept incoming Viking fleets, or that coastal land-based patrols alerted a waiting Anglo-Saxon fleet to Vikings who were seeking a landing place. Either way, it speaks of a significant level of preparedness and of investment in defence.

At the same time as these victories were occurring, other, more ominous events pointed to disasters soon to follow. While the West Saxons were enjoying some measure of success, the Mercians were defeated in their defence of London; the city was stormed, along with Canterbury, and King Brihtwulf of Mercia and his army put to flight. It was this same Viking army that Æthelwulf of Wessex defeated at *Aclea*. It is highly likely that Mercia was facing more threats than those recorded in the Wessex-orientated *Chronicle* since, two years later, King Burgred of Mercia requested the assistance of Æthelwulf of Wessex to subdue the Welsh on his western border. Since the Mercians and West Saxons were old rivals, this suggests both that Mercia was a much weaker player on the English stage than it had been at the beginning of the ninth century, and also that the crisis precipitated by the Vikings was causing one-time rivals to bury their differences in the face of common enemies. The reality of this is based on more than just the account in the *Chronicle* since, within a generation, Mercia and Wessex were cooperating on coinage reform and some kind of monetary union (see Chapters 5 and 6).

The assault on Canterbury and London was on a scale not seen before. It seems that this attacking army came in 350 ships into the mouth of the Thames. This raises the question of the size of these Viking fleets, something which has divided historians for some time. Clearly, if this figure is anywhere near correct we are looking at a force on a very different scale compared to the thirty-five ships that brought an army to the vicinity of Carhampton in 836 and 843. But can we believe such a figure? The baseline for criticism was provided, in 1962, by Peter Sawyer, who argued that, since the 851 *Chronicle* entry is not a contemporary record, the number was probably exaggerated and meant no more than that it was a 'large fleet'.[24] This is an understandable point of view since the round numbers usually used to describe such massive naval deployments sound less than convincing. On the other hand, this does not mean that the numbers are meaningless. The fleets may not have been exactly as large as stated, but the accounts may give something of the order of magnitude. Later accounts were contemporary with the events they described and similar numbers still occur. More significantly, Anglo-Saxon, Irish and Frankish sources, when they do offer contemporary accounts, do so very consistently and these range from a handful of ships to fleets that were 200+ in size.[25] There is no possibility that these various sources were in collusion and so we are left with independent sources of evidence providing corroborative evidence for very large fleets. Furthermore, we have an Islamic account from Spain which records a fleet of 100 Viking ships causing destruction on the coast of *Al-Andalus* in 844.[26] It seems that we have to entertain the possibility that, as the numbers of attacks escalated, so did their size. If there were just thirty men (or less) per ship in 851, we are still left with a Viking army numbering many thousands.

In the winter of 851–52 an even more significant event occurred in south-eastern England, for until then the raids had been seasonal: spring had seen the start of operations and autumn had closed them down. Given the fact that Viking fleets were operating from bases outside of England, this is hardly surprising as winter storms made seaborne operations far too risky. What happened that winter was a water-shed in the history of Viking attacks. Whether its significance was noted at the time we cannot say but, looking back from the 880s, it was correctly identified as a seminal event. *Manuscript C* of the *Chronicle* records the fateful change in tactics: 'And for the first time, heathen men stayed through the winter on Thanet.'[27] This was highly significant for three reasons: firstly, it meant that the next campaigning season would start at the very first opportunity; secondly, the over-wintering Viking army required provisioning – for those unfortunate enough to live anywhere near this winter camp there would be no respite from theft and murder over the winter months; and thirdly, it raised the real possibility that the Viking armies might be here to stay, raiding might be transitioning into land seizure and that Anglo-Saxon society was now facing conquest rather than the smash-and-grab raids of the past. And there was a particular irony in the location of this first over-wintering: Thanet was, according to tradition, the place where the mythical founders of Anglo-Saxon England, Hengist and Horsa, had first landed and been granted land. The Anglo-Saxon kingdoms now faced the same possibility of defeat and conquest that they had visited on the Romano-British communities of the fifth century.

There is every likelihood that this event really did occur at Thanet. In the mid-ninth century it was still an island, separated from mainland Kent by the, now silted up, Wantsum Channel. As such, it offered a secure base with access to the open sea and was ideally placed for further incursions into south-eastern England. However, the later chronicler may have been drawn to this place because it resonated so strongly with Anglo-Saxon history. *Manuscript C* of the *Chronicle* identifies the location of the camp as being on Thanet, as does the late tenth-century *Æthelweard's Chronicle*. Conversely, *manuscript A* omits the location altogether and the biography of Alfred, written by the Welsh Bishop Asser in 893, locates the event on Sheppey, off the coast of north Kent and further into the mouth of the Thames. Asser wrote his account in the same decade that the first version of the *Chronicle* was compiled and seems to have had access to an early manuscript of it. In addition, he wrote at Alfred's court, possibly in the same context as the compilation of the first version of the *Chronicle*, and he had access to official documents and other royal and ecclesiastical sources. Consequently, the divergence is puzzling and may suggest that, by the 890s, the traditions concerning this event of forty years earlier were divided. Whatever the location of the first over-wintering, both places were soon again in the news. In 853 two *ealdormen* were killed in a fierce battle at Thanet. Since this time Asser concurs with the *Chronicle* by giving the island's British name – *Ruim* – the location seems secure. In 855 the Viking fleet over-wintered on Sheppey (based there for the first time according to the *Chronicle*).

The decade of the 860s opened with slightly more promising events from an Anglo-Saxon perspective. After an initial disaster, when a large Viking force looted Winchester (Hampshire), the *ealdormen* of Hampshire and Berkshire rallied their forces and intercepted the invaders as they returned to their ships anchored in the Solent and defeated them. According to Asser, the defeated Vikings had been 'returning to the ships with immense booty.'[28] However, the success was not to last. In 865 a Viking army once again returned to Thanet and demonstrated a deviousness that was to be characteristic of Scandinavian raiders, if the chroniclers are to be believed. Having been paid off by the people of Kent, they broke the agreement, took the money and ravaged eastern Kent anyway. Clearly, an agreement with a submissive enemy was no agreement at all. It is the first record of the paying of what would later be called *Danegeld* in the late tenth and early eleventh century. And, as Kipling would remind his readers in his famous poem of 1911:

> ... if once you have paid him the Dane-geld
> You never get rid of the Dane.

Therefore, this is a significant time to consider the price that Anglo-Saxon England would have to pay as the Viking Blitzkrieg intensified.

What was the impact of the Vikings raids on England in the first half of the ninth century?

What was the damage caused by these Vikings raids? The traditional view, bolstered by contemporary and near-contemporary accounts, is that of slaughter, enslavement and of social and economic devastation. We also have King Alfred's own verdict on the effects of the Viking attacks. In a remarkable document, written between 890 and 895, Alfred wrote his own preface to a translation of the *Pastoral Care* that he had overseen (see Chapters 6 and 7). In it he recounted the devastation caused by the Viking Wars and that he, 'remembered how, before everything was ravaged and burnt, the churches throughout all England stood filled with treasures and books...' These were, he reflected, 'temporal punishments' because the Anglo-Saxon peoples had lost their love for the study of the Christian scriptures. This was clearly a major theme in Alfred's account of events because a surviving letter to him from Fulk, archbishop of Reims, written between 883 and 886, quotes a letter from Alfred which had described how the Anglo-Saxon Church had 'fallen in ruins in many respects' and that this was in large part due to 'the frequent invasion and attack of pagans'.[29] This is the fire-and-the-sword image of the Vikings that continues to dominate the popular imagination, and it is not without justification. A magnificent Gospel book (the *Stockholm Codex Aureus*), produced in Kent and now in the Royal Library in Stockholm, Sweden, contains a mid-ninth-century inscription recording how the book was ransomed from Vikings (from 'a heathen army') for gold by *Ealdorman* Alfred (the *ealdorman* of Surrey or Kent) and his wife, Werburh.

It was returned to Christian use by being presented to the high altar at Christ Church, Canterbury (Kent).[30] Many other treasures would have been lost forever.

This view of the impact of Viking attacks has not gone unchallenged by historians. We have already seen how Peter Sawyer's 1962 publication of *The Age of the Vikings* challenged the numbers of ships that made up Viking fleets and with this the scale of violence that might be expected from such sizeable numbers of invaders.[31] Sawyer argued that contemporary expectations of what constituted an army (see Chapter 3) should be considered when we assess what chroniclers thought was a large army in the Viking Wars. Since, according to the Law Code of Ine of Wessex (688–726), any force larger than thirty-five constituted a *here* (an army), an invading 'army' might be no larger in number than four modern football teams. This dramatically down-scales our expectations of the likely devastation such a force might inflict on an enemy society. For Sawyer, Viking warfare was simply an extension of 'normal Dark Age activity'[32] and this view has remained influential. A number of historians have argued that Viking violence was exaggerated because they were seen as different due to their non-Christian culture. To the late tenth-century chronicler Æthelweard they were 'a most vile people', 'that filthy race', 'disgusting squaddies' and 'a filthy pestilence'. Æthelweard wrote probably sometime between 978 and 988, before the renewal of Viking attacks in the second great invasion phase of the Viking Wars and after some fifty years of relative peace. And yet his vehemence was undiminished, revealing how memories of the ninth-century assaults could still stir up loathing towards the Viking enemy.[33] Such feelings did not make for objective commentary, though. This is a point made strongly by Sarah Foot, who has argued that for Christian churchmen the key element in describing the violence of the Vikings was that it was 'heathen violence',[34] rather than its scale as such. A further twist was provided by the seaborne nature of the attacks. Contemporary Anglo-Saxon society was geared to taking revenge, or compensation, against those who had killed members of their communities. This was fairly straightforward with regard to the land-based Anglo-Saxon armies which conducted warfare in England, but seaborne invaders upset the whole system. How could revenge or compensation be pursued against those whose bases could not be located? It was this sense that Vikings 'played outside the rules', in addition to their pagan identity, which added to the horror and anxiety that their attacks caused.[35]

Given these factors, it is highly likely that the extent of the destruction may have been exaggerated by churchmen who were motivated by a greater degree of sensitivity to pagan violence than to acts committed by Christian rulers and who, additionally, emphasised the scale of destruction as a method of persuading their fellow countrymen and women to repent of their moral failings. Added to this, we might well argue that King Alfred had a strong incentive to magnify the scale of the disaster in order to more convincingly show the importance of his own achievements and to encourage Anglo-Saxons living outside Wessex to welcome the West Saxons as liberators, rather than as rivals. A recent analysis of the reduced finds of Anglo-Saxon coins minted from *c.* 830 onwards cautions against the tendency to seek one cause of this monetary decline (i.e., the Vikings), since a number of factors appear to lie behind it.[36]

These revisions of the traditional picture, though, may be going too far in downplaying the damage and horror of the mid-ninth century. We will return to this in greater depth later (Chapter 8), but suffice it to say at this point that it is not only the evidence from Anglo-Saxon commentators which suggests such catastrophic impacts caused by the first phase of the Viking Wars. D.M. Hadley has pointed out that charters of this period often note that the land was granted for 'as long as the Christian faith should last in Britain', which suggests some thought its continuation was in doubt, whilst many bishoprics vanished at this time including Hexham, Leicester and *Dommac*. Church land holdings also reduced, with the Church at Domesday (1086) owning 20–33 per cent of the land in the country as a whole, but consistently less than 10 per cent in the north and eastern Midlands – the areas most affected by the attacks as they spiralled out of control in the 860s and 870s. In support of Alfred's lament, there are very few surviving pre-Viking charters, suggesting a great loss of Church libraries and records, and therefore a consequent decline in the standards of literacy.[37] Between 844 and 864, when a Kentish noblewomen promised regular provisions from her estate at Bradbourne (Kent) to the monks at St Augustine's Abbey, Canterbury (Kent); she declared that the monks could have the entire estate if the promised supplies were unforthcoming for three successive years due to the '*hæðen here*' (heathen army). That such a clause was necessary is 'eloquent testimony to the local destructive power of the raiders'.[38] In addition, the sense of facing an enemy who did not follow the established conventions of warfare further increased the stress and anxiety of those on the receiving end of Viking attacks.

What is beyond question is that, in 866, the Viking Wars entered a new phase. In 851, raiding had been extended by over-wintering and, in 866, extended raiding turned to outright conquest. A series of devastating campaigns would destroy every Anglo-Saxon kingdom in England, except Wessex, in the space of just eleven years and would cause the ruler of that remaining kingdom to run for his life into the marshes of Somerset. If anything deserves description as an early medieval blitzkrieg it is the devastating Viking strategies that led to such stunning victories during this period.

Seventy-three years earlier, in 793, Alcuin had written to the king of Northumbria warning him that the Vikings were a punishment sent by God as a consequence of the sins of the Anglo-Saxon people, and that, in the past, 'for sins of this kind kings lost kingdoms and peoples their country…'[39]

In 866, Alcuin's warning was about to unfold. In that year the *Chronicle* records the landing in East Anglia of the '*micel hæðen here*' (the great heathen army) and, as a consequence, Anglo-Saxon England would never be the same again.

3

THE 'FIRST BLITZKRIEG': WHY WERE THE VIKINGS SO SUCCESSFUL?

Given the devastation caused by Viking armies in England and their eventual conquest of every Anglo-Saxon kingdom except Wessex, it is reasonable to ask why they were so successful. Anglo-Saxon England by the late eighth century contained well-organised and militarily powerful kingdoms. Kings, such as Offa of Mercia (king from 757 until his death in 796) or Egbert of Wessex (king from 802 until his death in 839), were formidable war leaders whose power was built on the well-structured nature of Anglo-Saxon kingship and were allowed to call on and deploy the military resources of their respective kingdoms. While not every Anglo-Saxon king and kingdom *c.*800 was comparable with Mercia and Wessex, it is clear that Anglo-Saxon kings were formidable opponents. So, why were their kingdoms unable to inflict bloody defeats on the Scandinavians who invaded them and why did they fall in quick succession within a decade after 866? Looking back from a twenty-first-century perspective, the Viking successes certainly resemble an early medieval blitzkrieg: skilfully planned and executed, and devastating in their impact. Even the raids that occurred between 789 and 866 – whilst falling short of conquest – appear to reveal raiders who were able to attack without warning, loot, fund their adventures, and impose their agenda on the various kingdoms of Anglo-Saxon England. How was this possible and why was the Viking Blitzkrieg so successful?

In order to answer this crucial question, we need to explore how Anglo-Saxon government functioned, especially with regard to its organisation for war.[1] We then need to reflect on how this system operated within the context of Viking strategies and why responses to the Vikings appear to have been so ineffective when, for centuries, Anglo-Saxons had been highly proficient in warfare. As part of this we will also need to explore the evidence for Viking ship-building technology, since this enabled them to strike with devastating effect. New understanding of Viking tactics and strategies, alongside a better grasp of how Anglo-Saxon kingdoms functioned, is helping us to understand why the Anglo-Saxon kingdoms found resistance so difficult. This exploration will focus on the reasons for Viking successes in the first great phase of attacks from 789–896. The reason for the Viking successes in the second phase of attacks, from *c.* 980–1016, are explored in a later chapter, since the circumstances of the late tenth and early eleventh century were very different from those of the first phase of Viking attacks.

What constituted an 'army' in the late eighth and ninth centuries?

As explored in Chapter 2, the size and make-up of eighth- and ninth-century armies continues to divide historians and archaeologists, as does the Old English terminology used to describe them. The seventh-century law code of Ine of Wessex stated that an armed group up to seven in number were classified as 'thieves'; a group numbering between seven and thirty-five was a 'band of marauders' (*bloþ*); and anything larger was a 'raid' (*here*). This has led some historians to suggest that this last word does not apply to an army as such; the term used for a formal army being *fyrd* or *fierd*.[2] If this is the case, then this reference in Ine's law code cannot be used to infer the size of any army, since *here* does not refer to an army. However, this may be taking too strict a line on how the term was used. There is, in fact, plenty of evidence to indicate that the word was used to imply an 'invading army', 'host', 'army' or 'devastation'. This is surely why it is found compounded in literature to form *herefolc* (army), *heregeatu* (war equipment), *herehuð* (plunder) and *heretoga* (military leader).[3] Place names also indicate its use to convey the meaning 'army' or 'military'. In this sense the word *here* appears in the place names Hereford (Herefordshire), Harlow (Essex) and Harwich (Essex). The compound *herepæþ* is found in a number of locations and means 'army road, road large enough to march soldiers upon'.[4] This is found in two Harpfords, one in Devon and the other in Somerset. These and other examples suggest that *herepæþ* came to mean something like 'main road'. It is true that in the *Anglo-Saxon Chronicle* the term *here* is almost always used to describe Vikings, whereas alternative Old English words were used to describe Anglo-Saxon armies, and this certainly suggests that, to the chronicler, *here* did indeed mean something like 'raiding army'. But the term in its wider usage was clearly more flexible than this and its use in literature and in place names reveals that it did also have the meaning 'army' in a conventional sense and was not inevitably bound up with concepts of criminal gangs. As a result, it is not inappropriate to use the evidence of the law code of Ine to get some idea of the possible size of armies.

The role of warfare in Anglo-Saxon England

Having established that armies could be small, when measured against twenty-first-century expectations, it is now necessary to consider how they were constituted. What role did warfare play in the functioning of the Anglo-Saxon kingdoms? Who was eligible to fight? How were armies assembled and deployed in the field? What were the discernible military tactics and how successful were they in operation? It makes sense to begin this analysis with the defenders – the kingdoms of Anglo-Saxon England – since we have a range of evidence to help us gain a picture of the military disposition of the defending side.

Warfare was a key feature in the formation of the Anglo-Saxon kingdoms and their expansion, and was crucial to the careers of the most successful Anglo-Saxon kings. Writing *c.* 731, Bede referred to seven kings exercising *imperium* (overlordship) up until that date. These were Ælle (South Saxons), Ceawlin (West Saxons), Æthelbert (Kent), Rædwald (East Anglia), Edwin (Northumbria), Oswald (Northumbria) and Oswiu (Northumbria). Bede did not include the Mercians, Wulfhere (658–74) and Æthelbald (716–57) but elsewhere he did admit that they too exercised *imperium*. The *Chronicle* entry for 829 adds Egbert of Wessex (ruled 802–39) to Bede's list. *Manuscript A* of the *Chronicle* calls them by the title, '*Bretwalda*' (ruler of Britain), but better manuscript evidence suggests this should be '*Brytenwalda*' (wide ruler).

With the notable exception of Æthelbert of Kent (died *c.* 616), all Anglo-Saxon kings who exercised *imperium* over other kingdoms were proficient warlords. Æthelbert is the exception as it seems that his pre-eminence was based on a favourable relationship with his Frankish neighbours across the Straits of Dover, since the Franks were the superpower of the age. In such a society, stronger kingdoms absorbed smaller ones, and this was sometimes accompanied by the extermination of rival royal lines. Wessex destroyed the seventh-century dynasty of Arwald of the Isle of Wight; within the same century, Northumbria saw the kingdoms of Bernicia and Deira battle for dominance; in the eighth century, Offa of Mercia overawed his neighbours, subjugating Kent and Sussex, defeating Wessex and executing the king of East Anglia in 794. Absorption by larger kingdoms saw the royal titles of smaller kingdoms reduced by their new over-rulers until all vestiges of independence disappeared. The *Hwicce* of the south-west Midlands were absorbed into Mercia and the recorded titles of its rulers show the downwardly mobile process at work: '*reges*' (kings), '*reguli*' (princes), '*subreguli*' (petty-princes/vassal rulers) and then '*duces*' (dukes). This entire process was driven by military activities as, ultimately, it was violence which overawed lesser rulers. The amazing arts and crafts represented in the Staffordshire Hoard (discovered in 2009) should not obscure the fact that this was war-booty. It was undoubtedly worn by skilled practitioners of violence and taken from them by those whose skills in this department were even more effective. We may surmise, too, that the previous owners were not alive to see their treasures paraded by the victors.

In short, warfare and violence was an integral part of Anglo-Saxon royal power-politics. It was not, of course, the only feature, but it was a crucial one. Kingdoms rose and fell according to their proficiency on the battle-field, alongside their skills in diplomacy and negotiation. It was probably the ready availability of tribute and slaves (seized from the Welsh) that explains why Mercia and Wessex rose to such prominence and why kingdoms further east – such as Kent and East Anglia – which lacked ready access to such exploitable 'resources', declined after their early dominance. None of the kings mentioned so far were trying to create a united English kingdom, but they were using violence to enhance their own prestige, increase their access to wealth and status and overawe their rivals. This was an heroic age, in which military force was celebrated in reality as well as in poetry. For example, in Britain, north of Mercia, in the period 608–878, about 30 per cent of kings died in battle, a further 6 per cent were murdered by relations or rivals, and a further 12 per cent were assassinated by their own warband. This illustrates the dynamics of warfare within politics to a striking degree.

Organisation of war in Anglo-Saxon England

Given the importance of warfare, it is hardly surprising that the kingdoms of Anglo-Saxon England were proficient in its organisation and deployment. We know more about this system from Wessex than from the other Anglo-Saxon kingdoms and more about the later period than the earlier. Nevertheless, a cautious analysis of later clues, when allied with evidence from the ninth century, can suggest something of how this system functioned. By the time of the first Viking raids, Anglo-Saxon kings fought in the company of their personal bodyguards and household retainers, but also relied on a regional framework which called on the freemen of each shire for military service when the need arose.

The former had developed out of the ancient warband, made up of the hearth-companions of the king. These were the '*king's thegns*' who attended the king personally. Dependent on the king for the grants of land which would establish them as local lords and enable them to marry and form their own households, the youngest and unmarried members of this group made up the king's personal household troops. These warriors were a force to be reckoned with and were capable of decisive and independent action. The *Chronicle* entry for 871 records small groups of *king's thegns* operating against Viking foragers in Wessex. It would have been such a group that made up the 'small force' which accompanied King Alfred when he retreated into the Somerset marshes in 878.[5] However, the professional expertise of this group of warriors has to be set against their relatively small numbers.

The need for larger groups of armed men was met by the *fyrd*, led by the king's local representatives, the *ealdormen*. As early as the late seventh century, the law code of Ine of Wessex required all freemen, aged 15 to 60, to provide military service if called on. Sources dating from later Anglo-Saxon England frequently refer to the three-fold obligation imposed on land owners of military service, fortress work and bridge repair. The first record of this three-fold obligation dates from late eighth-century Mercia and it seems to already have been a well-established expectation by that date. The kinds of battles fought in the ninth century were only possible because Anglo-Saxon kings could call on more than their personal household warriors and the three-fold obligation provided the means by which this could be done. At times we see this system in operation in contemporary sources, although the chronicler takes for granted that his readers would understand the arrangements. So, in 802, the *Chronicle* records how the

Mercian *Ealdorman* Æthelmund crossed the border of Wessex at Kempsford (Gloucestershire) and was defeated by the West Saxon '*Ealdorman* Weohstan with the people of Wiltshire'.[6] In a similar way, the *Chronicle* records battles fought against Viking raiders in 840 by *Ealdorman* Wulfheard of Hampshire and '*Ealdorman* Æthelhelm with the people of Dorset'.[7] In 860 the 'great naval force' which sacked Winchester was put to flight, not by the king of Wessex but by '*Ealdorman* Osric with the men of Hampshire and *Ealdorman* Æthelwulf with the men of Berkshire'.[8] In each of these cases the *ealdormen* in question acted independently by raising and deploying their shire levies against invaders. There are many such examples. At other times we read of *ealdormen* commanding component parts of the royal army under the direct command of the king in the field. In this way we hear of the deaths of two *ealdormen* – Duda and Osmod – killed in battle against a Viking army at Carhampton (Somerset), in 836, while fighting in the company of King Egbert of Wessex. Again, there are many examples illustrating this leadership of units of the *fyrd* under royal command.

Fighting in the *fyrd* were freemen of differing rank, whose role varied depending on that rank. The *ealdormen* would themselves have had their own household troops and *thegns*. Below these were the ranks of ordinary freemen, the *ceorliscmen*. These *ceorls* were the free farmers who formed the bulk of the rural population; they existed in a range of classes depending on the extent of their land ownership and freedom from labour services owed to superior lords. In time a *ceorl* might – according to the early eleventh-century legal tract *Geþynctho* – come to own five *hides* of land and be regarded as a *thegn*; in effect, a local lord of the manor (although there is some debate amongst historians over whether every landholder of five *hides* was automatically considered a *thegn*). A *hide* was a notional unit of taxable land; sometimes regarded as *c.*120 acres, it was considered to be sufficient for the maintenance of a household of moderate means. While the lack of military training, experience and equipment of many of these men will have meant they were best deployed as support troops, guards and in military construction projects, there were attempts made to raise the capability of the *fyrd*; although how early in the Anglo-Saxon period this occurred remains a matter of debate. This involved drawing one man from every five *hides* of land. This would have raised a much smaller number of men than by a general call-up of the armed free population, but it allowed for a greater concentration of resources on the training and equipping of that man. Modern historians have coined the term '*select fyrd*',[9] as opposed to the '*great*' or '*general*' fyrd of all freemen, to describe this more specialist military force. At the time, though, the shire forces were simply called the '*fyrd*' and differentiating terms are modern inventions. There has been a great deal of debate over whether such a differentiation really existed within the *fyrd*,[10] but recent research suggests that it did indeed have a basis in fact.[11]

Given the link between the ownership of five *hides* and *thegnhood*, many of these *select fyrd* warriors would have formed the local minor aristocracy, the squirearchy, of the Anglo-Saxon countryside. In other areas a group of lesser landowners might have clubbed together to equip and send one of their number. By the late eleventh century, the monetary value of this commitment was expressed as twenty shillings, which would support the warrior for about a sixty day call-up period. We know this because the Domesday Book entry for Berkshire (1086) describes a system of five-*hide*-warriors with their twenty shilling wages for two months' service.[12] However, a unique charter of 801 from Middlesex, which stipulates five armed warriors from an estate of thirty *hides*, suggests that something like this had probably operated from at least the late eighth century.[13]

The problem is that we do not know at what point Ine's general levy of freemen turned into this more professional and experienced force. Given the successes that the *fyrd* could achieve against Viking raiders by the ninth century, it is hard to believe that it was made up solely of masses of free peasant farmers. In which case, something like the so-called *select fyrd* must have developed by that point in time. If this is correct, this created an experienced, well-equipped and mounted force which was a long way removed from a peasant militia and could be rapidly deployed across the shire and beyond its borders. Something like the feudal levy of post-Conquest knights was being created. And it should be remembered that the word 'knight' is actually derived from the Old English *cniht*: youth, attendant and, hence, military servant.

The main equipment of such troops consisted of spear and shield, with wealthier members carrying a sword. Poetry talks of the spear shafts being formed out of ash wood. It is noticeable that, in the later poem *The Battle of Maldon* (fought in 991), *Ealdorman* Byrhtnoth is described as having fought extensively with his spear before turning to his sword. The elites would have also had a helmet and a mail-shirt. The fact that the *Beowulf* poem refers to men swimming while wearing mail suggests that it was of fairly light construction, with corresponding limitations to the protection it afforded. The rarity of the helmet is illustrated by the fact that only four have been found from the entire Anglo-Saxon period (*c.* 450–1066): at Sutton Hoo

(Suffolk), Benty Grange (Derbyshire), Wollaston (Northamptonshire) and Coppergate, York. Until the eleventh century – and the spread of kite-shaped shields – most shields would have been round and formed from a tough but flexible wood such as linden. Single-edged knives would have been carried by men of all ranks, while lower class members of the *great fyrd* may also have used clubs and slings. Battle tactics are harder to discern but Asser, writing in 893, describes how at Edington (Wiltshire), in 878, the West Saxon army fought 'fiercely with a compact shield-wall against the entire Viking army.'[14] Clearly, fighting in relatively close order had occurred in this battle at least. The Old English word *bordweall*, or 'shield-wall', occurs in a number of varied Old English sources to compare with the Latin account by Asser, including *Beowulf*, *The Battle of Brunanburh* and *The Battle of Maldon*. The phrase suggests that interlocking shields played a part in creating a position of mutual defence for all warriors in the front line. How long this formation survived the shock of contact with the enemy in battle is harder to assess and the striking metaphor may have been more of a poetic device that an accurate description of how shields were actually deployed in battle, since a solid 'wall' may have restricted freedom of action.[15]

Exactly how the call-up was achieved is unclear, but study of later Anglo-Saxon local government structures suggests that it was probably through the system of *hundreds* that made up the shire. This sub-division of the shire was made up of twenty five-*hide* units which would probably have supported twenty well-armed warriors of the *select fyrd*. Given the regular transactions of business at *hundred* courts, this would have provided a focal point for calling up and assembling warriors, and these warriors may well have fought together as a unit within the overall shire force, under the *ealdorman*. Hints of this may lie behind the rendezvous points of Alfred's army as they gathered before the battle at Edington in 878. They almost certainly met at well-known muster-points and at least one – Iley, near Warminster, Wiltshire – was later recorded as a *hundred* meeting point. As a result, we can reconstruct a system whereby a royal summons to the *ealdorman* of the shire (or a local alarm caused by appearance of Viking raiders) led to the order being transmitted to the *hundreds* and resulted in previously selected and equipped warriors gathering at pre-determined muster-points until the whole shire *fyrd* was assembled. It was this system that had served Anglo-Saxon kings well in the past and which was used to respond to Viking attacks from the late eighth century. The question is: why did this tried and trusted system eventually fail in virtually every kingdom?

Viking weapons, tactics and capabilities

In terms of weapons technology, the Viking forces were comparable with their Anglo-Saxon opponents. The main difference appears to have been that the spear was a lower status weapon and that swords and axes played a greater role. This did not necessarily confer any tactical advantage, though, since spearmen enjoyed a greater reach and the quality of swords was very variable. In the thirteenth-century Icelandic *Eyrbyggja Saga* a warrior, named Steinthor, found his sword blade was of such inferior quality that it would not cut through armour and he was forced to straighten it with his foot.[16] Whilst this is a work of later literature and not an historic source, its literary effect would have been diminished if such an event was unlikely to occur. Consequently, in the ninth and tenth centuries there was a large export trade of pattern-welded sword blades from the Rhineland into Scandinavia, which is ironic given the targeting of Viking attacks on Frankish coastal areas. It is a reminder of the complex relationship between Viking forces and their victims. Many carried the Frankish (or Scandinavian-Frankish hybrid) name *UFLBERHT* inlaid in the fuller of the blade. It is probable that these were manufactured on the Middle Rhine, with Solingen identified as a likely centre. Others may have been exported from the vicinity of Passau on the Upper Danube. Swords bearing the *UFLBERHT* brand date from *c.*850 to the late eleventh century, so the name clearly became associated with a workshop that had a long production life. A rival manufacturing outfit, operating in the tenth century, carried the name *INGELRI*.[17] An *UFLBERHT* sword has been recovered from the Thames where it was dredged from Battersea Bridge in 1897. Becoming heavier from the eighth century, Viking sword design improved again in the tenth century, becoming lighter, tougher and more flexible, and could be used for both thrusting and cutting.

The weapon most closely associated with Vikings was the two-handed axe. In the earlier period of Viking attacks, experts describe the type of axe as the 'bearded axe' or *skeggox*. During the two centuries after the first recorded eighth-century raids, this developed into the so-called 'broad axe' until it became the dominant form of Viking axe by the eleventh century. By this later period a swung axe could fell horse and rider in one sweep, as is revealed on the *Bayeaux Tapestry*, and the *huscarls* (bodyguards) of the kings of England after Cnut (ruled 1016–35) were closely associated with this particular Scandinavian weapon. In terms of battle tactics, Viking armies resembled the Anglo-Saxons they faced. The shield-wall provided protection against enemy assault and, when driven forward, could cause enemy forces to break. It was then that individual combat would replace a more organised approach and the numbers, strength and experience of individual combatants would decide the outcome. There is nothing to suggest that Vikings were particularly innovative in these tactics and the annals of the *Chronicle* describe battles against an enemy that was no different in terms of weapons or behaviour.[18]

Like Anglo-Saxon warriors, Vikings tended to carry round shields and wealthier warriors owned mail-shirts and helmets, though both are rare in the archaeological record. Horned and winged helmets, though, are the stuff of Victorian paintings and Hollywood and have never been found. Demanding horses as tribute, or simply stealing them, provided mobility and increased the element of surprise, though Asser described an event in 885 when a Viking army shipped horses across the English Channel from Francia. Similarly, the *Chronicle's* account of a major Viking incursion in 892 records how they crossed from Boulogne 'in one journey, horses and all'.[19]

The most significant strategic weapon in the Viking arsenal was the warship. We know little about the warships of the eighth and ninth centuries, since it is only from the tenth century onwards that we get an insight into the varied ships available. By this time distinctions were being drawn between merchant ships (described by terms such as *knörr* and *kaupskip*) and warships (described variously as *snekkja*, *drekar* and *langskip*). While the term '*langskip*' almost certainly describe the specialist 'longships' employed in the second great phase of Viking attacks, *c.* 980–1016, the earlier seaborne movements may have made use of a far wider range of vessels. The great majority of the later longships carried twenty to twenty-five rowing benches according to the eleventh-century Norwegian law collection called the *Gulathing's Law*; although some late tenth- and eleventh-century ships may have been far larger (such as King Olaf Tryggvason's thirty-four bench *Long Serpent* and Harald Hardrada's thirty-five bench *Great Dragon*, both from Norway). Some of those used earlier, in the ninth century, might have been described as merchant ships by later generations of Viking seamen. This would certainly explain the use of ships to transport horses and this would not have happened in the specialised longships being built in the late tenth and eleventh centuries. However, we do have some idea of earlier ships from two ninth-century ship burials containing remarkably well preserved Norwegian ships at Gokstad (discovered in 1880) and Oseberg (discovered in 1903). Gokstad may give us a good idea of the ships which carried raiding parties to England in the ninth century, since its sixteen rowing benches accords almost exactly with the *Chronicle's* statement, in 896, that King Alfred's design of ships, at thirty benches, was twice the size of those of his Viking adversaries. The rowing benches on the Gokstad ship are actually notional since none were found and the oarsmen presumably sat on their sea-chests. The ship itself is 23.24m (76.2ft) long and 5.20m (17.1ft) wide, and clinker built (with overlapping planks) made mostly of oak, felled *c.*890 according to dendrochronology. Its sail could, it is estimated, have propelled the ship at a speed of over 12 knots, or 14 mph (22 km/h), and it would have carried a crew of about forty men. The Gokstad ship would have been far more seaworthy than the less sturdily built Oseberg ship. However, the carved spiral prow of the Oseberg ship, with its carved serpent's head, may indicate that the famous dragon's head prows so common in popular depictions of Viking vessels were indeed seen in English waters. Certainly, the thirteenth-century *King Harald's Saga* describes the later *Great Dragon* as having a prow decorated with a dragon's head and a stern decorated with a dragon's tail; however, this saga, as with most of this genre, was not a contemporary account. In the case of *King Harald's Saga*, it forms part of the *Heimskringla*, a complete history of Norway from prehistoric times to 1177, written by the Icelandic historian, Snorri Sturluson, whose writing output is justly famous.[20] Nevertheless, it may give us some idea of how the most prestigious warships were decorated.

Why were the Vikings so successful?

Unlike the members of the Anglo-Saxon *fyrd*, the crew of a Viking longship were, in effect, professional warriors. In this they had a great deal in common with the *king's thegns* and hearth troops of the Anglo-Saxon kings. The great advantage that they enjoyed, though, was their relatively large numbers. Whilst it is likely that some of the descriptions of Viking armies were inflated by chroniclers, there is every likelihood that some were very large indeed. This was because they were made up of separate groups of adventurers which coalesced in loose alliances and could, in the right combination, overwhelm defensive forces thrown against them. Being opportunistic raiders – at least in the period up to 866 – they would also dissolve and scatter when opposition was too great. This made it hard to know exactly what constituted the enemy force, since its size and form was prone to fluctuation.

There are hints of this in the *Chronicle's* accounts. Taking the annal for 871 as an example, we hear of part of an invading Viking army striking into Berkshire under two Viking earls (a rank similar to that of the Anglo-Saxon *ealdorman*); eight days later, at Ashdown, it was 'the whole [Viking] army' that was on the move and under the command of two kings and at least five earls; later a 'great summer army arrived'; then, at Wilton (Wiltshire), Alfred later again fought 'the whole army'; and in total that year the Viking invaders suffered the losses of nine earls and one king. Reading between the lines, the evidence suggests that a large number of Viking groups took part in that year's conflict, sometimes in unison and at other times apart. The mention of 'kings' and 'earls' gives the impression of a unified hierarchical command but, in fact, the opposite was probably true and, while we cannot now unravel the relationship between these 'kings' and 'earls', it is likely that what actually occurred involved a range of independent groups under leaders of varying rank. Deploying against such a fast-changing combination must have presented a logistical and organisational nightmare.

The seaborne nature of the attackers added to the difficulties faced by Anglo-Saxon defenders, and the element of surprise lay with the Vikings. Moving swiftly along the coast they could strike and be gone before the *fyrd* could be raised, or could penetrate far inland along England's river systems. As a consequence, these raiders posed a profound set of problems to the Anglo-Saxon authorities charged with their apprehension and defeat. In this we see one of the key ingredients which made the Vikings so hard to defeat and which often wrong-footed their Anglo-Saxon opponents. In this the development of ocean-going warships was the most significant innovation, since in other areas – such as weapon technology, battle tactics and motivation – there was little to differentiate Viking warriors from their Anglo-Saxon counterparts. However, the presence of superior naval technology gave Viking raiders the advantage of surprise, since these forces could appear off the coast without warning and could penetrate rivers of a depth of as little as 1m (3ft).[21] Given the length of the British coastline the potential number of landing sites was enormous. The Ordnance Survey gives the coastline of Great Britain as 11,073 miles (17,820km). Clearly, removing modern Scotland and Wales reduces this length considerably – the modern English coastline is in the region of 5,581 miles (8,982km)[22] – but this still left a massive coastline to be defended in the ninth century. Furthermore, nowhere in Britain is more than 70 miles (113km) from the sea. This left the land highly vulnerable to coastal raids and this vulnerability increased massively when riverine penetration was factored into the equation. Many of these river systems – such as the Humber, Trent, Severn and Thames – provided major entry points into England. Moreover, even much small rivers gave ready access from the sea and placed inland communities at risk. We hear therefore of Viking ships based far from the coast; for example, in 896, on the higher reaches of the River Lea, some 20 miles (32km) north of London.

The combination of seaborne attack, transportation of horses (or seizure of horses), produced an attacking force which was fast, flexible and versatile. This was the main difference between the earliest Viking raiders and the larger groups which devastated England in the 860s and 870s. The later seizing of horses gave them speed and reach that became difficult to resist without either a 'rapid-reaction force' to counter them, or protected bases from which defenders could operate and in which the civilian population could shelter. What is interesting is that when these began to appear, as an Anglo-Saxon response from the 880s onwards, the first phase of the Viking Blitzkrieg faltered in England. As a consequence, a large number of Vikings then shifted their operations to the Continent and there deployed the tactics which had earlier been so effective in England.[23] As a result, these raiders were soon penetrating northern Francia, making use of the rivers Scheldt and Somme and seizing horses in order to devastate the wider regions beyond the river valleys.

These then were the essential features of the Viking Blitzkrieg: seaborne attack and the element of surprise; absence of defensive systems geared to countering such assaults; large numbers of seasoned warriors, even if some operated seasonally in the first phase of the attacks; the shifting nature of Viking armies which made their movements difficult to predict or contain; and tactical flexibility which, by the 860s, was developing a mounted capability based on horses seized from the local population. Added to this was the natural advantage of an aggressive attacker whose own communities and non-combatants were safely out of harm's way and secure from retaliation. The significance of this latter factor becomes clearer when we see how Viking communities themselves became vulnerable once the initial phase of raiding turned to settlement. Once this occurred, a key feature of their aggressive character became undermined by the need to defend their own non-combatants and resources. A subtle shift occurred in the 890s as we first hear both of Viking armies having to defend their families from Anglo-Saxon aggression and of the capture of Viking non-combatants.

Once this began, the initial strength of the Viking assault began to be compromised by defensive requirements. Now the playing field was being levelled and, when combined with Anglo-Saxon defensive innovations, the first period of the Viking Blitzkrieg began to give way to land-based military campaigns more familiar from earlier periods of Anglo-Saxon history. And, in such circumstances, Anglo-Saxon victories began to increase dramatically as the ninth-century defensive actions of King Alfred gave way to an aggressive forward policy associated with Edward the Elder and then Athelstan in the tenth century.

4

THE SHADOW OF
THE 'BLOOD-EAGLE'

The arrival of a Viking force in 866, described in the *Anglo-Saxon Chronicle* as the '*micel hæðen here*' (the great heathen army), marked a step-change in the Viking assault on the kingdoms of Anglo-Saxon England. What had been a series of escalating raids now turned into outright conquest and settlement. The rise in coin hoards dating from the 870s reveals the attempts of Anglo-Saxons to preserve their wealth in the face of this unprecedented Viking threat.[1] These new raids were conducted by – as in the majority of raids experienced so far – Danish Vikings. The Viking Blitzkrieg had entered a new and devastating phase, and if anything deserved the description of an 'Early Medieval Lightning War' it was what followed over the next few campaigning seasons, because the assaults that started in 866 brought the kingdoms of Anglo-Saxon England to their knees. What no ambitious Anglo-Saxon ruler had ever achieved in the previous four centuries was accomplished in just over a decade: the destruction of every independent competitor kingdom, except one. Where rival kings and royal houses had survived the imperial ambitions of rulers such as Edwin (of Northumbria), or Penda (of Mercia), in the seventh century, and the actions of rulers such as Æthelbald and Offa (of Mercia) in the eighth century, or Egbert (of Wessex) in the ninth century, what occurred after 866 was the elimination of every independent kingdom with the sole exception of Wessex. By the time this process had been completed, the political landscape had been transformed.

Before this, the ambitions of powerful kings had tended towards *imperium* over other competitor kingdoms. As long as these weaker kingdoms accepted this *imperium*, paid tribute, provided military support when demanded and kept their policies in line with that of their overlord, there was every hope that they and their dynasty would survive. There were, of course, exceptions to this rule. The Northumbrians had forged one kingdom out of the previously independent peoples of Bernicia and Deira; the Mercians had absorbed minor kingdoms, such as the *Hwicce* in the south-west Midlands, had subjugated Kent and, in the 790s, had beheaded a king of East Anglia; Wessex had annexed Sussex, Surrey, Kent and Essex in the 820s, during the reign of Alfred the Great's grandfather, Egbert. But the total removal of the major rival kingdoms and dynasties on a permanent basis had proved beyond the capabilities of these earlier warrior-kings. Even a king as powerful as the eighth-century Offa of Mercia had failed to do this, assuming that he even considered it a desirable political necessity, which is far from certain. Consequently, by the mid-ninth century, East Anglia, Mercia, Northumbria and Wessex all maintained their own independent royal houses and administrations under kings who, by one route or another, claimed descent from heroic and semi-mythical founders who had forged kingdoms out of the wreckage of post-Roman Britain. The arrival of the *micel hæðen here* put an end to this *status quo*. As such, the achievements of this invading force were quite remarkable for – even if to start with they seemed content to work through subservient native rulers or compliant client-kings that they placed on the throne – the final end product was the removal of all these native rulers when circumstances so demanded. In 866 this all lay ahead, but clearly something had changed.

We do not know exactly what caused this change but there are circumstantial clues which may point towards an answer. Viking attacks by groups of Danish raiders on northern Francia had prompted a reorganisation of the Frankish defences and, as a result, it was becoming more difficult to campaign there. The Frankish king, Charles the Bald, had overseen the construction of a number of fortified bridges; the first was built at Pont-de-l'Arche, on the River Seine, in 862, to protect the royal place at Pîtres. Similar fortified bridges were also erected on the rivers Loire and Oise. These were a major obstacle to Viking raiders who used the river systems to penetrate deep into target territory. In 865, a final raid up the River Seine, with Paris as its target, was followed by a shifting of attention across the English Channel.[2] This relocation was also prompted by a treaty signed with Charles the Bald, which had paid off the Vikings with 4,000lb (1,814kg) of silver and large quantities of wine as long as they left western Francia. At the same time, Frankish work on the defended bridge on the Seine accelerated; clearly Charles was making preparation for the possible failure of his peace deal. This time he was successful, though one kingdom's success was another kingdom's crisis. It seems that the Viking leaders had decided that they had temporarily exhausted their Frankish option and that England offered an easier target. One group of Danish Vikings landed in Kent, in 865, and proceeded to break a treaty they had made there and plunder eastern Kent. As Asser bitterly commented: 'they knew they could get more money from stolen booty than from peace'.[3] The next year another, larger, force landed on the coast of East Anglia. The late tenth-century *Æthelweard's Chronicle* claimed they came 'from the north' and Asser thought they had originated 'from the Danube'.[4] The latter is clearly wrong and the former unlikely, given the evidence of Vikings moving out of Francia that same year.

There is a temptation to see this as a planned pincer movement, but this probably assumes far too high a level of planning and coordination. What we should envisage is the arrival of a number of raiding armies which enjoyed a loose connection, coalesced, broke up and reformed as circumstances changed. The simultaneous arrival of different groups, therefore, does not necessarily imply anything beyond the most rudimentary planning and coordination. However, despite these reservations, it is clear that – to start with at least – the force which landed in East Anglia possessed a size and a degree of unified command that caused it to have a devastating effect on its opponents. One recent assessment of their progress over the next five years has drawn attention to their 'keen awareness of the strategic military situation within England, coupled with a firm grasp of the political position within each of the Anglo-Saxon kingdoms.' Such was only possible through a combination of 'shock tactics and acute intelligence gathering'.[5] Clearly, this capability makes it clear that such a force was very different to the mindless barbarian perpetrators of extreme violence of popular imagination. While violence and extortion were clearly part of the strategic package, they were carefully applied with stunning precision and effect.

The occupation of East Anglia

Tradition states that this force was commanded by Ivar the Boneless and Halfdan, the sons of Ragnar Lothbrok (Leather Breeches). The *Chronicle* entry for 866 provides no names for the leaders of the Danes, but *Æthelweard's Chronicle* clearly had access to other sources and names one of them as 'Igwar', a form of Ivar. This is confirmed by the *Chronicle* entry for 878, which records the defeat of an unnamed 'brother of Ivar and Healfdene' (Halfdan) and the capture of the Viking's raven banner.[6] The early twelfth-century *Annals of St Neots*, in recording traditions about this later battle, claimed that the banner was woven by the daughters of Ragnar Lothbrok. As a result, it is reasonable to assume that we have some idea of the names of these Viking leaders, even if some of the stories associated with them are the stuff of legend. What is interesting, given the later impact of this force on England, is that the later compiler of the *Chronicle* could supply no information regarding its size. Clearly, it was only when an attack had a direct bearing on Wessex that the record allowed for such detail and this reminds us of the very particular interest of the *Chronicle*. Nevertheless, the invaders were obviously large in number, hence the description '*micel*' (great/large). The fact that the section of this Viking force that was defeated in 878 was thought to have comprised 840 men gives us some idea of the scale of the earlier invasion. It is possible that the original army may have consisted of as many as 5,000 warriors by the time all its units had arrived.[7]

This growing army used East Anglia as its base, though its real target lay elsewhere. The *Chronicle's* account of the East Angles making peace with these unwanted arrivals says that the Vikings took up winter quarters there, adding significantly that, 'they were supplied with horses'.[8] Asser, basing his account on West Saxon sources, adds: 'almost the whole army was supplied with horses'.[9] This was a very ominous sign: horses gave the invaders mobility on land, coupled with their seaborne mobility, and indicates that they were set on a major incursion into inland England. The number of horses gathered, which so impressed Asser, suggests that the Vikings were set on turning themselves into a fully mobile army; and speed and range were to be major features of their strategies over the coming months and years. That they so quickly transformed themselves suggests that they came to East Anglia with a clear aim and purpose. And that purpose was the conquest of a different kingdom altogether: Northumbria.

The fact that East Anglia was not conquered reminds us of the flexibility of the Viking attackers. Outright conquest could be avoided if compliance delivered money and resources sufficient to support striking elsewhere. And, as we shall see, puppet rulers might be established in one kingdom in order to allow opportunities for a Viking force to target a different kingdom.

Clearly, there was no predetermined plan for each Anglo-Saxon kingdom, and we should not expect there to have been one. But, as the invasion continued, this initial, experimental phase would pass, especially if there were any signs of resistance or rebellion from once-cooperative and subservient Anglo-Saxons. Thus, while conquest might not have been formally decided on in 866, it was clearly amongst the options being considered and it rapidly became the policy of choice.

The destruction of Northumbria

From their base in East Anglia – and now mobile as a result of the supply of East Anglian horses – the Viking army struck north to York in the autumn of 867. Crossing the Humber, they seized and occupied this strategic northern city. This decision reveals three features of the tactics used by Viking raiders: firstly their 'nose for political weakness'; secondly, the connection between the twin tracks of trading and raiding; and thirdly, their exploitation of any opportunities provided by cultural activities on the part of their target populations.

The political weakness was apparent in an ongoing civil war in Northumbria. Internal disunity was often skilfully exploited by Vikings, as we shall see on a number of later occasions. In Northumbria, the ruler, Osbert, had been deposed by a rival, Ælle. Osbert had fought back in an attempt to regain his throne and, as a result, Northumbria was (in the words of the *Chronicle*) convulsed by 'great civil strife'.[10] Later writers saw this disunity and the swift destruction of the kingdom as signalling 'a people which has incurred the wrath of God'.[11] The Northumbrian crisis provided a golden opportunity for the Vikings, and now Osbert and Ælle faced a danger greater than that posed by their rival. However, their disunity and internal conflict had caused them to neglect the defences necessary to resist the external enemy. The same annal of the *Chronicle* notes that 'not until late in the year did they unite sufficiently to proceed to fight the raiding army'. The *Chronicle* and Asser imply this happened late in the autumn of 867, but the twelfth-century *History of the Church of Durham*, attributed to Simeon of Durham and based on northern traditions, gives the date as 21 March. A similar date of 23 March (Palm Sunday) is found in the mid-tenth-century anonymous *History of St Cuthbert* and in the early thirteenth-century *Flores Historiarum (Flowers of the Histories)*, written at St Albans by Roger of Wendover and drawing on some northern records otherwise lost. If these are correct then the battle may have occurred five months after the initial seizure of York. Whatever the exact date, the delay in uniting against the common enemy was to prove fatal. Although they succeeded in breaking into the city, both rival Northumbrian kings were killed, along with eight of their *ealdormen*, and their army was destroyed. In one swift action the *micel hæðen here* had conquered an Anglo-Saxon kingdom. Late ninth-century Northumbria might have been a shadow of its once mighty seventh-century self, but the achievement was still considerable.

In gaining this victory the Vikings had, no doubt, benefitted from the military intelligence gained from the long history of trading between Scandinavia and Northumbria. A long-standing relationship connected either side of the North Sea and, as with the first raid on Portland (Chapter 1) and the complex evidence for trading and raiding seen in the Bristol Channel (Chapter 2), this must have provided a useful source of information which could now be put at the disposal of ambitious Viking leaders.

The actual date of the earlier Viking attack on York is also very revealing. Simeon of Durham states that the seizure of the city took place on 1 November. It was All Saints' Day, a major event in the Christian calendar, and it was probably no coincidence that the attack coincided with an occasion which would have occupied the minds of the target population. While they prepared to worship and feast, the Vikings struck. In addition, the influx of people into York that would have accompanied such a major celebration would have provided an additional resource of wealth to plunder and slaves to seize. There is similar evidence of Viking raids in Ireland targeting monasteries on days of religious celebration and, later, in 878, Alfred was almost captured when a lightning raid on Chippenham (Wiltshire) coincided with the feast of Christmas.

With their political leaders annihilated, the Northumbrians had no choice but to make peace with the leaders of the Vikings. Roger of Wendover was probably drawing on authentic northern traditions when he later outlined the consequences of the battle at York: 'Then these most abominable victors, the Danes, ravaged the whole province of Northumbria as far as the mouth of the Tyne.'[12] This destruction was accompanied by new political arrangements. Roger also tells us that an Anglo-Saxon named Egbert was set up as a client-king under the victorious Vikings. The power relationship was clearly spelled out by Simeon of Durham (also probably drawing on authentic northern records): Egbert was king 'under their own domination' and his authority was restricted to the northern – Bernician – component of the kingdom of Northumbria, beyond the River Tyne.[13] The new Viking rulers kept York under their direct control and with it the wealthier part of Northumbria: Deira, with the wolds and the control of the Humber estuary. Conquest of a large part of Northumbria and the establishment of a puppet regime beyond the Tyne reveals how successfully the ambitions of the *micel hæðen here* had advanced since landing in East Anglia in 866. There is evidence that important sections of the elites of Northumbria now fell into line with the new political realities. Roger of Wendover tells us that, in 872, the Northumbrians rebelled (with only temporary success) against their Viking overlords and expelled not only the puppet king, Egbert, but also Wulfhere, archbishop of York (he later returned in 873). This implies that the archbishop was actively cooperating with the new regime. What may seem like treacherous behaviour was more understandable from the archbishop's perspective; by forging a working relationship with the new rulers he probably hoped to minimise the damage to churches and administration. And, for all he knew, this was the new permanent reality within which he would somehow have to operate. In fact, whilst considerable turbulence lay ahead, Viking dominance would endure and Anglo-Saxon rule would not again be securely established in Northumbria until the fall of Eric Bloodaxe and the collapse of the Norse kingdom of York in 954. Before this event, rival Viking leaders – Northumbrian Danes and Norse from Dublin – would contest the kingdom before finally giving way to West Saxon rule. When that eventually happened there is evidence that many in the north resented the imposition of rule from a southern dynasty (regardless of its Anglo-Saxon character) in place of a local king ruling from York (albeit a Scandinavian ruler). Local politics and regional identity was stronger than any sense of a national English community. It is in this light that we should evaluate Wulfhere's apparent cultural treason. However, at that time, the Viking rulers were still pagan and this may have made his cooperation seem more questionable than that of later northerners who lived under the rule of converted Viking kings.

The pagan nature of this rule and the shock to the system of living under such an administration is reflected in later – legendary – sagas of Viking actions in the aftermath of their victory. The Scandinavian *Tale of Ragnar's Sons* (*Þáttr af Ragnars sonum*) was not compiled until the thirteenth century and there is no evidence to suggest it draws on authentic ninth-century traditions but, despite this, it purports to explain the reason for the invasion of Anglo-Saxon England and especially for the conquest of Northumbria. The saga recounts the story of Ragnar Lothbrok, king of Sweden and Denmark, and his sons: Björn Ironside, Hvitserk, Ivar the Boneless, Sigurd Snake-in-the-Eye and Ubbe. According to this saga, Ragnar was captured after leading a raid on England and was killed by Ælle of Northumbria. The saga has Ragnar thrown to his death in a snake pit. Consequently, the Viking army which seized York was led by Ragnar's sons, with the express aim of avenging his death. They did this by subjecting Ælle to the pagan rite of the 'blood-eagle'. This involved either carving an eagle on the back of the victim or, even more horrific, hacking the ribs away from the spine, pulling out the lungs of the dying man and draping them over the victim to resemble an eagle's wings. Following this, the saga tells how Ivar became king over Northumbria. Later, his two sons, Yngvar and Husto, were responsible for the capture and torturing to death of King Edmund of East Anglia and the conquering of his kingdom. However, there is no evidence that such an atrocity as the blood-eagle was ever committed and the *Chronicle* and other English sources maintain that Ælle died in battle. The image is almost certainly fictional and the product of a twelfth- and thirteenth-century fascination with Viking savagery. In short: 'The ultimate begetter of the blood-eagle was not a sadistic bird-fancier but an antiquarian revival.'[14] Despite this, it remains in the popular imagination as an image of Viking savagery and barbarism. Strangely, these stories were not the product of Anglo-Saxon propagandists, but were from a much later generation of Scandinavian writers of Old Norse sagas.

What is clear, though, is that the subjugation of Northumbria was only the start of the policy of conquest. In 868 the Viking force moved south to Nottingham and the target this time was the Midlands kingdom of Mercia. However, if the plan was for a conquest similar to that of Northumbria, it was aborted. Burgred, king of Mercia, called on the West Saxons for assistance. In response, Æthelred, king of Wessex, accompanied by his younger brother, Alfred, arrived with the army of Wessex. What followed was a stand off in which the Vikings were contained in Nottingham, but refused to come out and fight; the besieging forces were also unable to break in. This reveals the pragmatism of the Viking leadership, in that they had no intention of risking battle with the combined military might of Mercia and Wessex. Consequently, the stalemate could only be ended with a peace deal, which saw the Vikings withdraw to Northumbria and the West Saxons return to Wessex. Although the *Chronicle* makes no mention of it, this was the same year (according to Asser) that Alfred married the Mercian noblewoman, Ealhswith. Following on from the marriage of Burgred to Æthelred's and Alfred's sister, Æthelswith, in 853, this further strengthened the Mercian/West Saxon alliance. Cooperation was also occurring on the economic front. Shortly after becoming king in 865, Æthelred appears to have sanctioned a form of monetary union with the Mercians. With the Mercian *Lunette-type* penny circulating in both kingdoms, cooperation on coinage issues was initiated and would continue into the reign of Alfred.[15] In the face of a strong unity, that which had been noticeably lacking in Northumbria, the ambitions of the *micel hæðen here* were frustrated.

But this may paint too optimistic a picture of Anglo-Saxon determination and purpose. Mercian relations with the withdrawing Viking army may have been less equal than this appears. When the Viking army returned to East Anglia and killed its king, Edmund, in 870, Burgred made no attempt to block their progress through Mercia. Similarly, in 871, he made no attempt to block the movement of a Viking army from East Anglia to Reading, where it threatened Wessex. It is also surely significant that when, in 872, the Northumbrians revolted and drove out the client-king Egbert and Archbishop Wulfhere, Roger of Wendover records that these exiles were received by Burgred, despite their history of cooperation with the Viking enemies of Mercia. Wessex would need a more resolute ally than Burgred if military success was to be maintained – but there was no other ally left in England.

The death of King Edmund of East Anglia

We do not know exactly why the relationship between the Vikings and Edmund of East Anglia shifted so dramatically in 870. It may have been that he had begun to act too independently. Alternatively, it may simply have been that the Viking agenda had moved on and that, following success in Northumbria and disappointment in Mercia, the obvious target for outright conquest was East Anglia. Whatever the reason, this next stage in the destruction of the Anglo-Saxon kingdoms unfolded with a rapidity to rival the humbling of Northumbria. Although the main manuscripts of the *Chronicle* do not say who led the Viking forces, the bilingual (Old English and Latin) *Manuscript F*, compiled *c.*1100, names the leaders of this attack as 'Ingware' (Ivar) and 'Ubba' (Ubbe), the sons of the semi-legendary Ragnar Lothbrok.

That winter Edmund swiftly went from 'king' to 'saint' and 'martyr'. Resisting the Viking army that was over-wintering in Thetford, he was swiftly crushed and he himself was killed. To the *Chronicle's* laconic description that he fought the raiding army, *Æthelweard's Chronicle* adds the note: 'for a short time'. Clearly, East Anglian resistance was quickly smashed. *Manuscript E*, also known as the *Peterborough Chronicle*, preserves an East Anglian tradition that the raiding army destroyed all the monasteries they came to; at Peterborough they killed the abbot, the monks and everyone they found there and burnt down the monastery. Things had changed dramatically since the cooperation of 866, when the *micel hæðen here* had first arrived.

We know very little about King Edmund, apart from brief references in the *Chronicle* and coins bearing his name. But his fame quickly grew after his death, as a Christian martyr killed by pagan savages. *Manuscript C* of the *Chronicle* simply describes him as 'King Edmund' but *Manuscript E*, written in East Anglia, calls him 'Saint Edmund' and reveals the transition from monarch to martyr which was clearly felt particularly keenly by a local chronicler as he continued to copy and update his copy of the *Chronicle*. In the later tenth century, Abbo of Fleury became Edmund's earliest biographer. The *Passion of St Edmund, King and Martyr* was written c. 985–87 and was translated into Old English by Ælfric of Eynsham. Abbo claimed he heard the story from Archbishop Dunstan, who himself had heard it when it was related to King Athelstan by a very old man claiming to have been Edmund's armour bearer. According to Abbo, Edmund was not simply killed in battle; instead he was captured and tortured by the Vikings. Abbo claimed that Edmund was scourged, tied to a tree and had arrows fired at him until he resembled a hedgehog, then his tormentors beheaded him. His body was left where it fell and his head was thrown into a wood, from where it was later retrieved as it was protected by an enormous wolf and cried out to those searching for it. Although written over a century after the events, it is possible that there is some truth to the claim that Edmund was executed.[16] While Abbo's *Passion of St Edmund* conforms to the expected hagiographical content of a martyr's death, the claimed provenance of the account of his death in the words of the armour bearer and the rapid rise to prominence of the king/saint, with his later shrine at Bury St Edmunds, may mean that accounts of his death were based on some historical evidence. On the other hand, the similarity of his death to that of St Sebastian may mean that the *Passion* imitated this more famous saint's martyrdom.

What is indisputable, though, is how popular a saint Edmund soon became. Ironically, even the newly converted Viking rulers of East Anglia minted coins, between 895 and 910, in honour of the martyred Christian king; a ruler martyred just one generation earlier by their fathers.

What is more puzzling is that, despite Edmund's death, some form of Anglo-Saxon rule continued in East Anglia. Coins issued by King Æthelred of East Anglia (870–80) reveal that a native dynasty continued to rule the kingdom until it was finally brought under the direct rule of the Viking king, Guthrum, in 880 (who ruled under the name Æthelstan II). The fact that Æthelred's name alliterates so closely with the names of other ninth-century East Anglian rulers (Æthelstan I, ruled 825–45; Æthelweard, ruled 845–55) suggests he was drawn from the East Anglian ruling family and was not a non-royal client-king imposed by the Vikings. Nevertheless, it is difficult to imagine that he had any real freedom of action. Why Edmund's defeat did not lead to outright conquest – which was delayed by ten years – is difficult to ascertain. Clearly, even the phase of conquest of the Viking Blitzkrieg was not as simple a process as it first appears.

The turn of Wessex

In 871 the Viking army crossed the frontier of Wessex and occupied Reading. This was a royal residence and so was a collecting point for taxes and the royal *feorm* (food rents). As such it offered an attractive proposition to the raiders. The Viking army was led by two kings: Bagsecg and Ivar the Boneless' brother, Halfdan. While two Viking *jarls* (high-ranking nobles) took a force further into Wessex to forage, the remaining invaders stayed at Reading and, according to Asser, fortified their camp by building an earth rampart between the rivers Thames and Kennet.

The West Saxons reacted swiftly to the occupation of Reading. Æthelwulf, *ealdorman* of Berkshire mustered the *fyrd* and attacked the foragers at Englefield (Berkshire), west of Reading and defeated them, killing a *jarl* named Sidroc. Four days later the *ealdorman* was joined by the West Saxon king, Æthelred, and his brother, Alfred. With their combined force they attacked the main Viking camp at Reading. In a ferocious battle the Vikings eventually gained the upper hand and the West Saxons retreated, carrying with them the body of *Ealdorman Æthelwulf*. It was a sharp reversal of the previous West Saxon success.

Within four days they were fighting yet another major battle. This time it was further west at Ashdown, on the Berkshire Downs. The exact location is difficult to ascertain but was probably overlooking the Vale of White Horse and on the line of the Icknield Way, a major routeway into central Wessex from the north-east. It seems that the Vikings reached the battlefield first, since Asser records that they held the high ground. The *Chronicle* explains that they assembled in two formations: one commanded by their two kings, Bagsecg and Halfdan; the other led by the *jarls*. Without giving much detail of the battle it goes on to say that King Æthelred fought against the Viking kings' troops, killing Bagsecg, while Alfred's troops faced the *jarls* and killed five of them. Both Viking armies fled before the victorious West Saxons. Asser – probably working from material provided by Alfred himself – adds the detail that Alfred began the battle first, since Æthelred had not yet finished attending Mass. The battle raged around a solitary thorn tree which Asser claimed to have seen. In a memorable phrase, Asser describes Alfred as charging the enemy 'like a wild boar'.[17]

Despite this resounding victory, and within two weeks of it, Æthelred and Alfred again faced the Viking army at Basing (Hampshire), but this time the Vikings won and the West Saxons were forced to withdraw. After this the pressure eased a little, but only two months later another major battle was fought at *Meretun* (the site is unidentified but was probably in Hampshire). There were a huge number of casualties and, once again, the Vikings emerged victorious. Amongst the West Saxon dead was Bishop Heahmund of Sherborne, with *Æthelweard's Chronicle* adding that he was buried at Keynsham; situated on the north Somerset border the location may have been chosen as a spiritual marker on the frontier of Wessex.[18] As if these were not troubles enough, the *Chronicle* informs us that a new Viking force, the '*micel sumorlida*' (great summer fleet) came up the River Thames to Reading, where they reinforced Halfdan. This may well have been the first appearance of the three Viking 'kings' Guthrum, Oscetel and Anwend, who are named in the *Chronicle* in its later entry for 875. Given reductions in the size of the *micel hæðen here* due to casualties and the necessary forces required to hold down York and East Anglia, these additional forces must have been very welcome for the Vikings; and the last thing the West Saxons wished to see arriving.

King Æthelred may have been seriously wounded at the battle of *Meretun* since, soon after Easter, he died and was buried at Wimborne (Dorset). By an arrangement that had been made between the royal brothers of the House of Wessex (see Chapter 7) the throne did not pass to one of Æthelred's young sons. Instead, it passed to Alfred. Wessex was in too great a danger for entering into minority rule and the potential instability that would have accompanied this. This shrewd piece of practical politics may well have been the major factor which saved the kingdom.

Within a month of his succession, Alfred faced a large Viking army at Wilton (Wiltshire) and lost. Asser says that an initial West Saxon advance at the expense of the Vikings was eventually reversed when the Vikings regrouped and turned on their pursuers. While the sources vary as to the exact number, it seems that perhaps nine major battles took place in 871. However, this does not take account of the many skirmishes against smaller groups of Vikings, foraging away from the main army, fought by groups led at various times by Alfred, his *ealdormen* and *king's thegns*. By the end of the year the Vikings made peace with the West Saxons and withdrew.

The end of Mercia?

The determined resistance of Wessex meant that the leaders of the Viking army turned their attention elsewhere over the next four years. In 872 the Vikings again occupied London and forced a peace treaty with the Mercians. In 873 they responded to the Northumbrian revolt against Egbert, their client-king, by returning to Northumbria to crush the uprising. That winter they returned to Lincolnshire and, once again, the Mercians made peace. This repetition of 'made peace' almost certainly implies that the Mercians came to terms with the Vikings, paid tribute and allowed them to stay in a base within the kingdom. Not a single battle is recorded as being fought by the Mercians. While the *Chronicle* gives a West Saxon view of events, this silence is still striking and suggests that the Mercian leadership lacked the will, or resources, to mount repeated campaigns against the Viking armies that intruded onto their territory.

The weakness of Mercia soon led to the end of its independent existence. In 874 the *micel hæðen here* occupied the royal centre of Repton (Derbyshire). Here was sited the mausoleum of the Mercian royal family, and the powerful eighth-century Mercian overlord of other kingdoms, Æthelbald, was buried in the crypt. Now this monument to Mercian political power and Christian holiness was turned into a pagan Viking camp with considerable devastation. The religious buildings were incorporated into the defences dug around the camp; two deep ditches were dug, curving round until they enclosed a D-shaped area of some 1.4ha (3.5 acres) between the abbey and the river. Major archaeological excavations took place here from 1974–88 and were directed by Martin Biddle, Birthe Kjølbye-Biddle and Dr Harold Taylor, and revealed a burial mound containing the inhumed (buried whole) skeletons of 200 men and 49 women, presumably wives or camp followers.[19] Another Viking cemetery has been excavated at nearby Ingleby, which was used for cremations rather than inhumations.

It is difficult to imagine a more vivid illustration of the humiliation of once-powerful Mercia as its royal centre was occupied and subverted. King Burgred – who may have attempted to stave off disaster by accommodating the invading Vikings in 872 and 873 – was now expendable. The *Chronicle* records that he was driven from his throne, fled abroad in the company of Æthelswith his wife (Alfred's sister), and died as an exile in Rome. In his place the Vikings installed a king named Ceolwulf (known to historians as Ceolwulf II). Looking back from the perspective of the 880s – when the resistance of Wessex had triumphed over Viking aggression – the Wessex-orientated *Chronicle* dismissively described him as 'a foolish *king's thegn*' and a traitor who would give up the kingdom to his new Viking masters 'on whatever day they wished to have it' and that, consequently, he was 'at the enemy's service'.[20] The negative tone continues in the annal for 877, when it recounts how Mercia was divided up amongst the Viking leaders and they 'gave some to Ceolwulf'.[21]

At the time, though, the situation may have been rather more complex than this later account suggests, as there is evidence that, in the late 870s, Alfred continued the coordinated monetary policy which had started in the reigns of Æthelred of Wessex and Burgred of Mercia. The major coinage issue, known as the *Cross-and-Lozenge* penny, has been dated *c*.878–85 and was minted by both Alfred and Ceolwulf in order to restore the silver content of the pennies they both issued. This was a remarkable cooperation with a king who was later so pilloried and dismissed. Similarly, in the period 875–78, the minor issue of the *Two Emperors* coinage was produced.[22] This carried a representation of two Roman emperors and was based on a Late Roman prototype: a late fourth- or early fifth-century gold *solidus* of a type found with some frequency in Britain. The unique surviving example of Alfred's coin was probably struck in London before the *Cross-and-Lozenge* issue and is very similar to the Roman original. It carries the title: *Aelfred rex Anglo* (Alfred king of the English). The unique Mercian example was struck from a less refined coin-die and carries the title: *Ceolvvlf rex* (Ceolwulf king).[23] The choice of the twin imperial portraits may have been intended to portray Alfred and Ceolwulf as brother rulers, although whether such a sophisticated use of the image really was intended, given the fact that the design had earlier appeared on gold shillings of the mid-seventh century, has been questioned.[24] Either way, Ceolwulf had not been regarded as a 'foolish *king's thegn'* at that point in time. Instead, even in his reduced state, he was clearly regarded by Alfred as an Anglo-Saxon Christian ally worth cultivating. But, following his death in 879, it was easy for the compiler of the *Chronicle* to dismiss Ceolwulf as nothing but a quisling (collaborator). The difference in titles, however, is intriguing and may have consciously communicated Alfred's senior role in the partnership when compared to the ruler of a weaker Mercia. And it may be an early indication of Alfred's presentation of himself as king of all Anglo-Saxons not under Viking rule.

Despite the *Chronicle's* account of a Viking attack on Mercia, the elevation of Ceolwulf may actually have been another example of the Vikings intervening in internal Anglo-Saxon conflicts. The removal of Burgred may really have been a coup engineered by Ceolwulf with Viking support. Burgred was a member of a Mercian royal line which had first held the Crown in 757. However, this line's rule had been contested several times in the ninth century by representatives of another royal line that was descended from Ceolwulf I (821–23). Ceolwulf II's name suggests that he was a member of this competitor royal family. In this scenario, the Viking camp at Repton may have been that of Ceolwulf's allies in a Mercian civil war.[25] If this was the case then Ceolwulf was of higher status than simply that of a *king's thegn* and the Viking invasion of Mercia, in 874, may have been more complex and nuanced that it initially appears.

Consolidation of gains and preparations for final Viking victory?

With Mercia subjugated and with Ceolwulf compliant with their wishes, the Viking army next moved to consolidate its gains. In 875 part of the *micel hæðen here* returned to Northumbria under the leadership of Halfdan and over-wintered by the River Tyne. If the previous interpretation is correct – that the client-king, Egbert, ruled beyond the Tyne while southern Northumbria was under direct Viking control – then that temporary division was now brought to an end. The *Chronicle*'s words that 'the army conquered the land'[26] suggests that direct rule was now imposed on all of Northumbria. In 876 this was put beyond doubt with the assertion that Halfdan 'shared out the land of the Northumbrians and they proceeded to plough and to support themselves'.[27] Viking invasion had turned to conquest; and now conquest had turned to settlement.

While this occurred, the rest of the Viking army moved to Cambridge under the leadership of Guthrum, Oscetel and Anwend, who are described as 'kings'. At first glance it might be imagined that they intended to bring East Anglia under their direct rule in the way that Halfdan was doing in Northumbria, but the time had not yet come for that. Instead, there was one major objective left and that was Wessex. The *Chronicle* says that the Vikings stayed at Cambridge for a year, and important preparations were clearly taking place because, in 876, the Viking army fell once more on the West Saxons. Evading defending forces, the Viking's occupied Wareham (Dorset). The selection of this location makes sense when we take into account the *Chronicle*'s reference to a Viking fleet wrecked off Swanage in 877. It seems that the attack on Wessex was a pincer movement involving land and sea forces, and probably envisaged using Poole Harbour (Dorset) as a base from which Wessex could be dismembered. The Latin of *Æthelweard's Chronicle* suggests a joining of forces when describing the movement of the land-based Viking army in 876 and so the arrival of the Viking fleet was almost certainly not coincidental.

Racing to contain the enemy, Alfred trapped them in Wareham. Here the near impossibility of negotiating with a Viking force, while its leaders thought they had any hope of turning a situation to their advantage, was revealed. As part of a 'peace deal', the Vikings gave Alfred senior members of their army as hostages and swore on their 'holy ring' that they would leave Wessex. Later Icelandic sagas refer to such rings, kept in pagan Viking sanctuaries and worn by a leader at community assemblies. The events at Wareham suggest that the Vikings were making every effort to communicate the sincerity of their negotiations. Asser was clearly uncomfortable with the memory of the whole arrangement and sanitised it from a Christian perspective with the words: 'they also took an oath, on all the relics in which the king placed the greatest trust after God Himself'.[28] Despite this, they broke the deal, killed their hostages and slipped out of Wareham under cover of darkness. Striking west, the Vikings then occupied Exeter (Devon). Frustrated by their betrayal – and probably after hanging all his Viking hostages – Alfred pursued them.

This time, though, events caused the Viking plan to unravel. A great storm wrecked their seaborne allies off Swanage and so, finally, the invaders came to terms. They again gave hostages and swore oaths, but this time they left Wessex. In 877, at the time of the harvest (Asser specifies 'August'), they returned to Mercia and shared out some of the land, giving the rest to Ceolwulf. Since the Vikings over-wintered in Gloucester, according to *Æthelweard's Chronicle*, it seems that they did so within the area of western Mercia which most historians believe remained under Ceolwulf's nominal rule.

However, they had not yet finished with Wessex. In midwinter and shortly after Twelfth Night, 5 January 878, they struck. Historians debate whether the rite of the blood-eagle was really enacted on Ælle of Northumbria; Alfred of Wessex was about to find out for himself.

5

ALFRED'S VICTORY

'*In this year* in midwinter after twelfth night the enemy army came stealth-ily to Chippenham, and occupied the land of the West Saxons and settled there…'[1], so the *Anglo-Saxon Chronicle* begins one of the most famous and iconic episodes in the history of England. The attack on Chippenham (Wiltshire) only narrowly failed to capture Alfred and sent him in desperate retreat into the marshes of Somerset, accompanied by only a small group of his personal household. This would provide the context for the famous episode of the burning of the cakes as Alfred sheltered in the hut of a peas-ant family and was lost in thought as he contemplated the disaster that had befallen him. From that nadir of his reign, when all seemed utterly lost, he would mount a guerrilla campaign of resistance which would eventually culminate in a decisive victory over the invading army of Danish Vikings; and would result in an historic treaty with their leader, Guthrum, and his baptism as a Christian. In addition it would see the invading Vikings with-draw from Wessex and see Alfred's transition from desperate royal fugitive to triumphant military resistance fighter, all in the space of one year. The *Chronicle*'s account magnifies the extent of this contrast by insisting that, following the winter rout, 'þæt folc hym to gebigde' (the people submitted to them) – 'except King Alfred'.[2] Clearly, all that followed was down to the king alone.

How dire was Alfred's situation?

Before we assess how and why Alfred survived, we need to look in more detail at the lightning Viking raid on Chippenham and the state to which Alfred was reduced. Neither the *Chronicle*, written in the 880s, nor Bishop Asser, writing in 893, actually say that Alfred was at Chippenham. However, it seems a reasonable inference that he was, since the *Chronicle* records that the attacking Vikings struck from their winter camp at Gloucester, and Chippenham, in north-west Wiltshire and close to the frontier of Wessex, would have made an ideal base from which Alfred could monitor the movements of his Viking enemies who were based in the Mercian town just 29 miles away. In addition, Chippenham was a royal estate and its status as a royal border settlement had caused it to be used for the marriage of Burgred of Mercia to Alfred's sister in 853. It was, therefore, well placed to guard the northern border of Wessex. If indeed Alfred was there when the Vikings attacked, the estate centre would also have been well stocked with provisions gathered in from the surrounding region as tax renders for the support of the royal household. The attack took place after Twelfth Night (5 January), so probably occurred on 6 January, the Christian feast of the Epiphany which celebrates the visit of the magi to the infant Jesus. As such, the attack bears resemblance to the Viking assault on York in 867, which coincided with All Saints' Day. On that day, the royal hall would have been well provisioned to celebrate the feast and its inhabitants' minds would have been focused away from warfare. Consequently, it would supply the Danes with ample food and drink as they contemplated what to do with the latest Anglo-Saxon ruler to fall into their hands. However, it was not to be, as Alfred eluded them and retreated into Somerset.

We have no idea how large the Viking force was which occupied Chippenham that winter. What we can say, though, is that it was not the same *micel hæðen here* which had landed in East Anglia in 866. Since then, units of the army had settled in Northumbria, in 876, and in (eastern) Mercia, in 877. This is not to diminish Alfred's achievement in 878, but it needs to be borne in mind when assessing its scale. Furthermore, there is evidence that Alfred and his small group of companions were not the only West Saxon forces holding out against the invaders, despite the explicit statement to this effect made by the chronicler as he looked back from the perspective of the later 880s. The later chronicler, Æthelweard, writing a Latin chronicle in the late tenth century which was based on the

Anglo-Saxon Chronicle and augmented with other West Country sources, tells us that Æthelnoth, *ealdorman* of Somerset, commanded another small force based in woodland. This was very possibly in Selwood, on the borders of Somerset and Wiltshire, but this can be no more than speculation. The tone of Æthelweard's statement seems to imply that Æthelnoth was not very proactive but, still, the existence of another West Saxon force capable of resisting the Vikings is significant and is ignored by the *Chronicle*. More importantly, a large force of West Saxon fighting men was based at Countisbury (Devon), probably in the refurbished defences of the Iron Age fort on Wind Hill. Interestingly, the *Chronicle* itself – in contradiction of its earlier claim that only Alfred remained to resist the Vikings – tells how this force defeated a large Viking army that had assaulted this part of Wessex at the same time as the other army was occupying Chippenham and the Viking raven banner was captured. *Æthelweard's Chronicle* names the victorious *ealdorman* of Devon as Odda, although confusingly goes on to say that the Vikings won. The leader of these Vikings was an unnamed brother of the Viking leaders, Ivar and Halfdan. A later source – Geoffrey Gaimar's *L'Estoire des Engles* (*The History of the English*), which translated sections of the *Anglo-Saxon Chronicle*, as well as using Latin and French sources, and was written *c.* 1136 – identifies the Viking leader as Ubba. Ubba (or Ubbe) was named as a son of the semi-legendary Viking king, Ragnar Lothbrok, in the thirteenth-century Scandinavian saga the *Þáttr af Ragnars sonum* (*Tale of Ragnar's Sons*) and in one manuscript of the *Chronicle* was named as one of the Viking leaders responsible for the murder of Edmund of East Anglia in 870. Whether Gaimar had access to a genuinely independent source or was just guessing, based on the other references, is impossible to decide. According to Asser, the Viking army that was defeated at Countisbury had crossed from South Wales where it had slaughtered large numbers of the Welsh population. Its defeat in Devon was very significant. The *Chronicle* numbers the Viking dead as 840, while Asser thought the number as high as 1,200 and Æthelweard recorded that 800 were killed. Whatever the number of Viking casualties, the victory was a considerable one and meant that Alfred – sheltering in Somerset – would only face the one Viking army based in Chippenham, rather than be caught between two invading forces. The *Annals of St Neots* adds the legendary information that the raven banner fluttered before victory and drooped before defeat.

Clearly, Alfred was not quite as isolated as the *Chronicle* suggests, though he was still in a vulnerable position. Large parts of Wessex had been overrun and, as Easter approached, there must have been many in Wessex who wondered whether Alfred could survive the disaster. It may have been at this point that some members of another branch of the West Saxon royal family began to collaborate with the Vikings. If so, it would be another example of the way in which Viking strategies were often interwoven with, and assisted by, political divisions within the Anglo-Saxon kingdoms. This occurred in Northumbria with Osbert fighting Ælle in 867; probably happened in Mercia when Burgred was ousted by Ceolwulf in 874; and may well have come close to occurring in Wessex in 878. The evidence for this is slim but telling.

In 901, Alfred's son, Edward the Elder, made a land grant and its preamble is very revealing. It says: 'grant of 10 *hides* [*cassati*] by the river Wylye [i.e., at Stockton, Wiltshire], forfeited by Wulfhere and his wife for treason'.[3] Wulfhere had earlier (c.883?) been deprived of his position as *ealdorman* of Wiltshire along with his lands at a joint meeting of the *witan* (council of the leading men of the kingdom) of Wessex and Mercia. This was a political decision of great importance and the occurrence of a joint meeting signals the gravity and sensitivity of the fall of a very powerful man and his wife. In his place was promoted a man whose daughter would later go on to become the second wife of Alfred's son, King Edward the Elder – clearly, an Alfred-loyalist. The charge against Wulfhere is not specified in detail but 'treason' at this time almost certainly meant collusion with the Vikings. It seems that he was defecting to the winning side, but was caught out by the changing circumstances as a result of Alfred's surprise victory. However, his treason may have been more nuanced. It has been suggested that Wulfhere was the uncle of the sons of Æthelred I, Alfred's brother,[4] and these two sons had been passed over when Æthelred died in 871, in favour of Alfred. If Wulfhere negotiated with the Vikings on behalf of his nephews it may have been because he felt that the throne was rightfully theirs, or because – with Alfred apparently finished – it seemed opportune to try to salvage an acceptable political arrangement which preserved at least some of the royal family's authority. In short, Wulfhere may not have been a traitor who struck at the low point of his king's life; instead he may simply have been a shrewd political operator who made his move too soon. That he was linked to divisions within the royal family at this critical point seems certain, and the granting away of one of his family's estates in 901 is revealing. In that year Edward the Elder had only recently put down a rebellion by Æthelwold, one of the sons of Æthelred I, who had grown up with a grievance. To choose that time as the moment to grant away one of Wulfhere's confiscated estates and to dredge up the matter of his treason was perhaps a way of warning a powerful family not to become entangled with conspiracy against Alfred's line again. It seems that, despite the decision by the joint *witan*, not all of Wulfhere's estates had actually been seized and a grandson had been able to inherit the title of *ealdorman* of Wiltshire. The action of Edward the Elder in 901 was, therefore, probably 'a warning shot' to this family.[5]

That Wessex was in danger of fragmenting in the dark days of 878 is revealed by the absence of the men of Dorset in the list of those who assembled to assist in Alfred's fightback. The *Chronicle* pointedly lists: 'all the people of Somerset and of Wiltshire and of that part of Hampshire which was on this side of the sea',[6] but there is no mention of Dorset. Given the fact that Alfred's brother, Æthelred I, was buried at Wimborne (Dorset) and that the later rebellion of his son, Æthelwold, against the accession of Alfred's son, Edward the Elder, was centred on Wimborne, it seems clear that a major part of Alfred's family was implicated in collaboration with the Vikings in 878. This drew in senior members of the West Saxon political establishment and denied Alfred the support of that family's base in Dorset; and this family and area continued to be a source of instability within Wessex, even as late as the accession of Edward the Elder in 899. Interestingly, when Æthelwold failed in his rebellion against his cousin in 899, he went over to the Vikings of Northumbria (see Chapter 9). This was, ironically, the culmination of a family tradition of collaboration that had started in 878 after Alfred fled from Chippenham.

Overall it seems fair to say that, while the *Chronicle* may have overstated the isolation of Alfred, the young West Saxon king was still in a desperate situation in the late winter of 877 and spring of 878. With his forces divided and the unity of the royal family beginning to splinter, Wessex could easily have gone the way of Northumbria, East Anglia and Mercia and fallen to the Viking Blitzkrieg.

The fightback

It was in such circumstances that Alfred launched his comeback. At Easter he established a fortified base at Athelney (Somerset). It was undoubtedly an area that he knew well from hunting and fowling in the marshes nearby.

The name itself means 'the island of the *æthelingas*' (princes)[7] and it was clearly a royal hunting lodge before it became a refuge for the fugitive king. It also provided Alfred with a well-protected base since the surrounding marshes were difficult to negotiate. Something of the extent of its isolation is revealed in the *Chronicle*'s description of the king fleeing 'in difficulties through the woods and fen-fastnesses'[8] and Asser's description of Alfred's base 'amid the woody and marshy places of Somerset'.[9] From here Alfred and his small group of followers raided both the Vikings and any West Saxons who had submitted to the invaders.

The site at Athelney consists of two low hills, rising above the Somerset marshes, commanding the junction of the rivers Parrett and Tone. The fort here probably consisted of little more than a ditch, bank and palisade, and in the mid-tenth century was still known as the '*eald henworth*' (old army enclosure). Nearby Burrow Mump, a sandstone hill rising above the wetlands, may also have been fortified at this time. At East Lyng Alfred built another fort, linked to Athelney by a narrow causeway which may have included a fortified bridge. The current lane, linking Athelney to East Lyng, follows the line of a twelfth-century drainage rhyne, which itself probably followed the line of the ninth-century causeway. The fort at East Lyng consisted of a large bank and ditch, which protected the promontory from attack on the western side. Traces of these defences can still be seen in the field behind the church at East Lyng.[10]

It was while Alfred was based in the Somerset marshes that the later legend claims he burnt the cakes and humbly accepted the scolding of the angry woman whose baking he had spoiled. The story is first found in the *Life of St Neot* which was written in the late tenth/early eleventh century and later incorporated into the *Annals of St Neots*. In 1574, Archbishop Matthew Parker oversaw the first printed edition of Asser's *Life of King Alfred* (written in 893) and popularised the legendary episode. Since Parker had wrongly assumed that Asser had written the *Annals*, the story of the cake-burning was lifted from the *Annals* and placed at the appropriate place in the *Life of King Alfred*. Although the legend and Asser's account have now been disentangled (the similarity in content was due to the later writer of the *Annals* taking material from Asser), the connection has remained prominent in the popular imagination. Like the legendary blood-eagle it has become another literary device now firmly fused with the history of the Viking Wars. The image of a king who humbles himself before God and accepts his reduced circumstances to the extent of putting up with the scolding of a swineherd's wife is a powerful one. But it is just that: a literary image and a legend. What is interesting, though, is that it is not unique in the portrayal of the king. The *History of St Cuthbert* contains a legend of Alfred sharing his fish with a stranger who turns out to be St Cuthbert. The saint then promises assistance against the Vikings. William of Malmesbury's *Gesta regum Anglorum* (*Deeds of the Kings of the English*), written *c.*1125, contains the fanciful legend of Alfred disguising himself as a minstrel and entering the camp of Guthrum the Dane in order to spy on his disposition prior to defeating him at the battle of Edington.[11] These legends tell us nothing about history, but they do give an insight into the high regard in which Alfred was held by later writers. He was presented as a model of Christian kingship, a combination of wisdom, humility, determination under duress and military prowess.

In 878 it was this military ability that helped turn events to a remarkable degree. According to the *Chronicle*, on the seventh week after Easter (Whitsun in the Christian calendar and celebrating the gift of the Holy Spirit to the Church at Pentecost), Alfred launched his comeback. The date was probably consciously chosen, both as an unmistakeable rendezvous time and as symbolic of the Christian fightback against the pagan Vikings. Riding to 'Egbert's Stone', he met the combined forces of Somerset, Wiltshire and part of Hampshire 'and they rejoiced to see him'.[12] The men of Dorset, however, were conspicuous by their absence. The site cannot now be accurately located but was probably somewhere in the vicinity of Alfred's Tower (Wiltshire), which is found above Bruton, a royal estate in the Late Anglo-Saxon period, and was completed in 1772 to commemorate the event.[13] After one night's rest he moved on to Iley. Located south of the royal manor of Warminster and now lost, later records reveal that Iley Oak (or the Hundred Oak) was the meeting point of two local *hundreds*: that of Warminster and Heytesbury.[14] After another night's rest he fell on the Viking army camped at Edington (Wiltshire).

The organisation that assisted Alfred in his fightback is implied in the sources but never explicitly stated. However, there are obvious clues: the two meeting points were near royal manors, with one located at a local government assembly point; and the mention of the forces of three shires indicates that the West Saxon administrative system of *ealdormen* and *king's thegns* had survived the Viking assault. Without this administrative network, the orders could not have been communicated and the muster points could not have been agreed. It was the efficiency and survival of the West Saxon local government administrative system that saved Alfred and Wessex as much as the resilience of the king himself. This is not to minimise Alfred's achievements, but it must also be taken into account when assessing why Wessex survived the events of 878.[15]

The assumption is that Guthrum and his Viking army was encamped within Bratton Camp, overlooking the steep scarp of the western edge of Salisbury Plain. Here, in Asser's words, the West Saxons fought 'fiercely with a compact shield-wall against the entire Viking army'.[16] After a prolonged conflict the Vikings broke. Alfred pursued them to Chippenham, killing all he found outside the defences and besieging those inside for fourteen days. At last the Vikings came to terms: they promised to leave Wessex and Guthrum promised to be baptised a Christian; and they gave hostages but Alfred gave none, so unequal was the victory. Alfred had come a long way since Twelfth Night.

Three weeks later Guthrum and thirty of his leading men were baptised at Aller (Somerset), near the West Saxon fortified base at Athelney. Alfred acted as Guthrum's sponsor. For twelve days he was entertained by Alfred at nearby Wedmore and honoured with gifts, and this was highly significant. Baptism, royal sponsorship and one-sided gift giving were all designed to bring Guthrum within the framework of Anglo-Saxon society under the overlordship of Alfred. Previously, it had proved difficult to find common ground on which to negotiate with Viking leaders, and through which to hold them to the terms of any treaties made. Time and again the sources talk of peace made and broken, treaties agreed and discarded, hostages given and then abandoned to their fate. This time, though, Alfred was attempting to establish a new context for dialogue and negotiation. A sign of this new beginning was the re-naming of Guthrum as 'Athelstan'.

The strategy appears to have worked. Guthrum left Chippenham and moved his army to Cirencester (Gloucestershire) and, although the *Chronicle* records the arrival of a fresh Viking fleet on the Thames at Fulham in 879, this did not prompt a renewed attack on Wessex, even though, as Asser records, the new arrivals joined Guthrum. Instead, in 880, Guthrum returned to East Anglia and shared out the land with his army and the other Vikings sailed for Ghent, in Belgium.

Reconstruction and consolidation

Wessex gained breathing space between the victory over Guthrum in 878 and the return of a large Viking force under different leadership in 892.

This did not mean, however, that there were no raids in this time period. From time to time other Viking raiders appeared off the coast and there was sometimes collusion with those living in Viking-run East Anglia. The *Chronicle* records a sea battle between West Saxons and raiders in 882 in which Wessex triumphed. In 883 an enigmatic entry records a West Saxon siege of London, without giving further information about what prompted this battle (perhaps this is a misplaced reference to Alfred's occupation of London in 886). In 885, another group of Vikings, fresh from Francia, besieged Rochester (Kent) until dispersed by a relieving army led by Alfred. So sudden was their retreat that they abandoned both their prisoners and their horses. That same year Alfred ordered a naval attack on East Anglia with mixed results: defeating one group of Viking ships but then being beaten by a second group. The reason for this foray into East Anglia is revealed in *Æthelweard's Chronicle*, where he says that the Vikings who besieged Rochester had received assistance from others in East Anglia. He also adds that a combined force of these newcomers and East Anglian Danes established a base at Benfleet (Essex), but the alliance broke up acrimoniously and the threat to Wessex receded.

It was in this period that a number of Welsh rulers accepted Alfred's overlordship and protection. Asser, a Welshman himself, records that this was done voluntarily as an act of self-defence, since a number of the Welsh kingdoms were threatened by other, more powerful Welsh princes and by the Mercians. At around this same time *Ealdorman* Æthelred of Mercia accepted the overlordship of Alfred. *Ealdorman* Æthelred had come to prominence following the death of the last Mercian king, Ceolwulf II, in around 879. Æthelred himself was not a king, although some Irish annals refer to him by this title and, curiously, *Æthelweard's Chronicle* calls him *'rex Eðered Myrciorum'* (King Æthelred of the Mercians) and differentiates him from other *ealdormen* who are titled *'dux'* (duke/general) in his account of a campaign against the Viking invaders in 893.[17] It is also intriguing that he appears in a surviving Mercian king-list and that Asser implies that he submitted to Alfred on the same basis as did the independent Welsh rulers. This, despite the fact that West Saxon documents only ever refer to him as *ealdorman*, *hlaford* (lord), *dux* (duke) or *dominus* (lord).[18] He himself, it appears, was careful not to use the royal title and in this he recognised the relative power relationship between himself and Alfred. The difference is revealed in charters in which they both appear, one as king and one as subordinate. For example, a charter of 889 uses the formula: 'Alfred, king of the English and the Saxons, and

Æthelred, *subregulus et patricius Merciorum*' (sub-ruler and nobleman of the Mercians).[19] Another of 898 or 899 contrasts Alfred's title of '*regem*' (king) with that of Æthelred as '*ducem partis regionis Merciorum*' (duke of a part of the region of the Mercians).[20] This realistic approach secured West Saxon support and approval. It was in the 880s that *Ealdorman* Æthelred married Alfred's daughter, Æthelflæd, thus sealing the alliance between Wessex and Mercia. They first witnessed a charter together as husband and wife in 888. This alliance would last until 918 when Alfred's son, Edward the Elder, annexed Mercia and removed Ælfwynn, the daughter of Æthelred and Æthelflæd, from power (see Chapter 9). As part of this increasingly close relationship between the two kingdoms, Alfred gave positions at his court and within the West Saxon Church to Mercian churchmen.[21]

This same period saw Alfred's focus switch to revitalising the Church and learning within Wessex by inviting in scholars from Wales, Mercia and the Continent. As well as sponsoring this educational programme, Alfred himself was closely involved in the translations of texts which he believed would improve the spiritual and governmental wellbeing of his kingdom (see Chapter 6).

At the same time, Alfred was seeking to create a defence-in-depth within Wessex. In order to have a standing army ready to repulse Viking attacks, he split the *fyrd* into two so that half were on service while half remained at home. This is recorded in the *Chronicle* entry for 893 but may have been implemented earlier. Alfred also oversaw a programme of fortification of some thirty *burhs* (defended urban sites). Strategically scattered across Wessex, some were existing settlements and others were new establishments, while some endured and others proved to be temporary arrangements. All had the same objectives: to provide places of refuge, marshalling points for armies, centres for royal administration and coinage, and the expansion of trade. During Alfred's reign the number of mints rose from two to eight and the quality of the silver pennies rose from a silver quantity of around 20 per cent to almost pure silver. Alfred's system was expanded by Æthelred and Æthelflæd in Mercia, and then again by his son Edward and grandson Athelstan as they conquered the *Danelaw* (see p. 86) in the tenth century. The system of *burhs*, as outlined in the early tenth-century *Burghal Hidage*, bears testimony to one of Alfred's most impressive administrative achievements. The law codes of Edward the Elder and of Athelstan made it compulsory that all trading should occur at one of these urban centres. This was based on Alfred's achievement and thus was a direct result of the Viking Wars.

Clearly, as the 880s progressed, Alfred's recovery from the Viking assault of 878 reached new heights, and part of the development of his power was the formal annexation of London in 886.

London: a case study in skilful diplomacy

The seizure of London in 886 ended a somewhat ambiguous period in the town's history. Prior to this, both Ceolwulf II of Mercia (died c.879) and Alfred of Wessex had minted coins in London. Two Mercian moneyers based there also struck coins for Alfred, and on two of Alfred's *Cross-and-Lozenge* pennies a Mercian moneyer accorded Alfred the title 'rex sm', which is likely to have stood for *rex Saxonum et Merciorum* (king of the Saxons and Mercians). This seems clear evidence that Alfred saw Mercia's troubles as paving the way towards a future annexation of the rival kingdom. In the same way, Alfred's grandfather Egbert (king of Wessex 802–39) had styled himself 'king of England' on a charter in 823 at the start of a decade which saw him temporarily conquer Mercia and overawe Northumbria.[22] All this suggests either that, since the 870s, Alfred had actually exercised authority in the Mercian town, or that 'London had become something of an "open city"'.[23] It is possible that, as soon as Burgred was deposed in 874, Alfred had increased his influence in London, or that Ceolwulf II had been forced to offer this in order to secure an alliance with Alfred. If so, the years of cooperation with the Mercians had not totally replaced the historic rivalries between the two kingdoms and the Viking impact on Mercia had given Alfred the opportunity to assert himself. And in the circumstances of the 880s, Alfred looked in a far better position to succeed where his warrior grandfather had failed and make this permanent – and all down to the Vikings.

Having taken the city, Alfred then entrusted its administration to his son-in-law, *ealdorman* Æthelred. This was a sensitive and sensible diplomatic move. London had been a Mercian city since they themselves had eclipsed East Saxon power there in the eighth century. By giving the city to his subordinate he showed a real awareness of Mercian sensibilities, while still maintaining his ultimate control.

Following the annexation of London, Asser claims that: 'All the Angles and Saxons – those who had formerly been scattered everywhere and were not in captivity with the Vikings – turned willingly to King Alfred and submitted themselves to his lordship.'[24] We may, however, question as to whether all Anglo-Saxons would have accepted Alfred in this capacity. After all, the concept of one king for all the Anglo-Saxons was novel and there would be many who would contest it right up until only one king remained in England after 954. In addition, there was still a legacy of deep rivalry between the once-independent kingdoms of Anglo-Saxon England. But the Viking Blitzkrieg had led to a situation that would have seemed impossible to imagine, even to a king as powerful as Alfred's grandfather, Egbert. There was now only one Anglo-Saxon king in England and that was a direct result of the Viking Wars.

From the time that Alfred adopted the title 'King of the Anglo-Saxons' to convey his rule over Wessex (Saxons) and Mercia (Angles), no other Anglo-Saxon ruler was ever called 'king' by the writers of the *Chronicle* or the compilers of charters within Wessex. This new royal title also appeared on some of Alfred's coins; '*rex anglox*' (king of the Anglo-Saxons) being the form used on the coins of his so-called *Two Emperors* issue.[25] His charters adopted the same approach and increasingly experimented with titles such as 'king of the English', 'king of the Anglo-Saxons' and 'king of the English and the Saxons'.

The recognition of the *Danelaw*

Sometime between 886 (Alfred's occupation of London) and 890 (the death of Guthrum), Alfred took more steps to regularise and formalise relations with the new Viking kingdom of East Anglia, which resulted in a formal treaty between the two.[26] The frontier ran 'up the Thames, and then up the Lea, and along the Lea to its source, then in a straight line to Bedford, then up the Ouse to Watling Street'.[27] This left Guthrum in control of East Anglia and eastern Mercia and became known as the *Danelaw*. Alfred, on the other hand, was in control of western Mercia and London, in addition to Wessex. The status of Essex is unclear from the treaty. At first glance it would appear to have been outside Alfred's sphere of influence, but it is hard to imagine him allowing this since it had been part of Wessex from the 820s. The treaty went on to establish parity of compensation for murdered Danes and Englishmen, and included arrangements for dealing with accusations of manslaughter. No slaves or freemen would be allowed to escape lordship by going over to the opposite side and arrangements were clarified to allow movement across the border for trading purposes. In short, Guthrum and his kingdom were brought into the legal framework of Anglo-Saxon England. It was a diplomatic conclusion to the process that had started at Aller back in 878. Guthrum the Viking was now Athelstan II, the king of an enlarged East Anglia. He began minting coins in his new name and imitated West Saxon coinage. The marauding sea king had become part of the Anglo-Saxon system. By the early tenth century many Scandinavian rulers of the *Danelaw* were minting coins in imitation of Alfred. The Viking 'cultural-chameleons' were beginning to change in keeping with their new socio-political surroundings.

The return of the Vikings

In 892 the Vikings returned. A large force crossed the Channel and proceeded to occupy parts of Kent. One group stormed an unfinished *burh* on the River Lympne; another, led by a Viking leader named Hæsten, sailed into the Thames estuary and set up a base at Milton, near Sittingbourne; and a third group made camp at Appledore. Hæsten is probably the same Viking leader of the same name who was raiding along the Loire in Francia in the 860s.

The arrival of this fresh wave of invaders was comparable to that of the arrival of the *micel hæðen here* in 866. The *Chronicle* talks of 250 ships, plus another eighty arriving with Hæsten and an unnumbered fleet arriving at Appledore. The *Annals of St Neots* talks of 350 ships. Whatever the exact number, the force was explicitly described as a *micel here* (great army). Furthermore, the arrivals destabilised the balance of power between Wessex/Mercia and the Viking kingdoms of the *Danelaw*. We hear again of raids by groups from Northumbria and East Anglia, and this would test Alfred's defensive system to its limits.

The king led his army to confront the danger and positioned himself, between the Viking army on the Thames and those to the south, beside the forest of the Weald. Alfred had forces both in the field and defending the *burhs*, and the *Chronicle* specifically refers to units from both sections of the army blocking incursions by roving Viking bands. This, of course, was exactly what the system was designed to do. After gathering what booty it could, the Viking army that was actively on campaign attempted to move north towards the middle Thames, but was defeated by the West Saxon field army at Farnham (Hampshire). Æthelweard adds that it was Alfred's son, Edward, who commanded this force in the field. The defeated Viking army crossed the Thames into Mercia where it was then besieged by Edward.

Since, by the terms of the reorganised *fyrd* system, these troops were near-ing the end of their period of service, it was now critical that they were replaced by fresh soldiers. However, *Ealdorman* Æthelred of Mercia brought up reinforcements from London (a fact added by *Æthelweard's Chronicle*) and the besieged Vikings agreed terms, gave hostages and withdrew.

Simultaneously, a seaborne force from Northumbria and East Anglia attacked the West Country in a coordinated attack, which threatened the north and south coasts of Devon and put Exeter under siege. This was clearly intended to wrong-foot the West Saxons and their Mercian allies who were, by this time, operating in Buckinghamshire against the remains of the army which had retreated after the battle at Farnham. Wessex had not faced a threat like this since the days of Guthrum.

The reorganisation of the West Saxon *fyrd* system was now demonstrated since the West Saxons and their Mercian allies kept up relentless pressure on the invading forces. Attacking their base at Benfleet (Essex), they cap-tured the family of Hæsten but returned these dependents because – in an unrecorded event – they had earlier been baptised. However, this aggressive policy had not defused the threat posed by Hæsten and neither did the gen-erous return of his family. While Alfred dealt with the Danish force besieging Exeter, Æthelred of Mercia and the other *ealdormen* chased down Hæsten (*Æthelweard's Chronicle* specifically mentions mounted Anglo-Saxon units) and besieged him at Buttington on the River Severn, far to the west of his Benfleet base. Defeated in battle, the remaining Vikings retreated to Essex, moved their families to the safety of East Anglia and then struck north-westward to Chester. In this they were assisted by friendly forces from East Anglia and Northumbria (the latter, according to Æthelweard, was com-manded by a Viking named Sigeferth). In 894, starved out of Chester and the Wirral, the Viking army returned to Essex via Northumbria and East Anglia – the distances travelled are truly astonishing.

In a further attempt to put pressure on their Anglo-Saxon enemies, they then sailed up the Thames and the Lea and, by 895, were camped 20 miles north of London, threatening the city. Alfred himself then supervised the protection of the bringing in of the harvest to London and began the con-struction of a linked set of fortresses – in effect, a fortified bridge of the kind built by the Franks – to trap the Viking ships further up the River Lea. Aware of the danger, the Vikings abandoned their ships, sent their families to East Anglia and shifted their base westward again, to Bridgenorth on the Severn. In 896, frustrated by the determination of the Anglo-Saxon resistance, the

Viking forces divided into three groups and headed for Northumbria, East Anglia and Francia respectively. Finally, despite further raids along the south coast, accompanied by a rather mixed performance by new warships designed by Alfred, the crisis was over. Alfred's system of defended *burhs*, the continuous availability of the *fyrd*, the use of the fortified bridges, and the availability of mounted troops, in contrast to the 870s, had triumphed.

Interestingly enough, Æthelweard made no mention of the great events of 895–96, which in the *Chronicle* is the culmination of Alfred's defence of Wessex. In contrast, Æthelweard provides more information about the contribution of Alfred's *ealdormen* to these victories over the Vikings, referring to: 'The famous *Ealdorman* Æthelhelm ... the generalship of Æthelnoth ...' And it is in this same version of the events of 893 that he talks of '*King* Æthelred of the Mercians ...' Æthelweard himself was an *ealdorman* and his downplaying of the role of Alfred and his upbeat account of the exploits of the *ealdormen* may have been his way of making the point that the West Saxon victories were possible because of the achievements of those who held the office of *ealdorman*.[28] It provides an interesting corrective to the dominant role of kings in the written sources and is a reminder that Wessex had been saved by more than just one man. It was its administrative systems and its experienced commanders – toughened in the crucible of war – that had contributed to victory, although of course refined and impressively led by the warrior-king.

The role, status and ambitions of Wessex had been transformed by the Viking Wars and, in the words of the *Chronicle*, Alfred had made himself 'king over the whole English people except for that part which was under Danish rule ...'[29] In October 899, Alfred died. However, even Alfred could not have imagined how this would develop under his son and grandson as they entered a new phase in the conflict with the Vikings.

6

WAR CORRESPONDENCE
OR PROPAGANDA?

The period of Alfred the Great's reign (871–99) is one of the best documented of the entire early medieval period within England, and for the first time we are presented with an Anglo-Saxon monarch who both supported and was heavily involved in literary production. However, although this has left us with an overwhelming amount of evidence when compared to earlier kings, we must be careful with the way that we use this evidence. The reign of Alfred presents an unusual problem, as all the sources are likely to have originated either from Alfred himself or from his immediate circle. This raises a number of questions. How far can the written evidence for the West Saxon fightback and the history of Wessex generally in the period 871–99 be trusted? Are we dealing with accurate war correspondence or West Saxon propaganda? And how far are these vital pieces of evidence products of the Viking Wars during which they were produced? As we briefly examine them, this last point will become clear in a number of surprising ways. In order to do this, it is necessary to assess all the written evidence for Alfred's reign: the *Anglo-Saxon Chronicle*; Asser's *Life of King Alfred*; Alfred's law code; Alfred's *Introduction to the Pastoral Care* and the other works within his translation programme; Alfred's *Will*; and the royal titles used in his charters and on his coins.

The *Anglo-Saxon Chronicle*

The *Anglo-Saxon Chronicle* is a collection of annals compiled in the late ninth century that begins with the Roman arrival in Britain and continues until after the Norman Conquest of England. It is the single most important source for the political history of England and, although complex, presents us with a framework of events for the entire Anglo-Saxon period. There are seven manuscripts and two fragments which have survived and these tell pretty much the same story up until the year 891. After this point, while many of the entries are the same, there are greater differences between the ensuing versions of the *Chronicle*. *Manuscript A* (or *Parker Chronicle*) is the oldest of these versions and was written up to the end of 891 by one person and seems to have been written at Old Minster, in Winchester. *Manuscripts B* and *C* are very closely related and seem to have been connected with Abingdon by the late tenth century. It is within these last two versions that the *Mercian Register* is found which covers the period 902–24 and is focused on Alfred's daughter, Æthelflæd. *Manuscripts D* and *E* also appear to be linked together and they form what is known as the 'northern recension' of the *Chronicle*. *Manuscript F* is a bilingual chronicle (Old English and Latin) produced in the late eleventh or early twelfth century by a scribe who used both *A* and *E* as templates. Finally, *Manuscript G* is a copy of *A*.

The *Chronicle* seems to have been composed by around 890 as Asser had a copy in 893, which was already two removes from the original text, and the *Parker Chronicle* also seems to have been similarly removed from the original so-called 'common stock'. Overall, most 'historians are in basic agreement that the original *Chronicle* extended to at least 890'.[1] Two of the leading experts on the *Chronicle*, Simon Keynes and Michael Lapidge, suggest that 'the return of the Vikings to England appears to have occasioned the publication, in late 892 or early 893, of the *Chronicle*'.[2] This original manuscript seems to have been copied and circulated to various churches – in much the same way as the products of Alfred's literary reform – where it was added to over time. After this point the different versions diverged in various ways, often due to local information and agendas.

The place of origin for the *Chronicle* has been much debated. It has been suggested that it was composed at Winchester as the earliest version appears to come from there; but, as this is not the original manuscript of the *Chronicle*, it may well have been sent to Winchester from somewhere else in Wessex. It has been argued that it was neither written under the patronage of the king, nor composed at Winchester, and that, instead, it was composed by an *ealdorman* in one of the south-western shires, most likely Somerset.[3] However, against this it has been asserted that the extent of the circulation of the *Chronicle* and the material that it contains are outside the scope of a local *ealdorman* and that the king may well have been involved in its production.[4] The fact that Asser rapidly gained access to a copy of the *Chronicle* and thought it was an appropriate basis for his royal biography supports the argument that it was 'a product of the court circle'.[5] This does not mean that Alfred himself was personally responsible for the *Chronicle*, but it does seem likely that the compiler was someone closely connected to him and that it was produced with royal support.[6] But compiled from what? And with what purpose?

The compiler of the *Chronicle* seems to have drawn on Bede's *Ecclesiastical History of the English People* (*c.*731), a few northern annals, some royal genealogies, regnal lists (lengths of reigns) and episcopal lists. It may have also used some earlier sets of West Saxon annals, one for the first half of the eighth century and another for the reign of Egbert (802–39) and the early years of Æthelwulf (reigned 839–58).[7] These sources inform the subject matter of the *Chronicle* and it is mainly concerned with the deeds and deaths of kings and bishops, though there are some more random entries, such as the reference to the 'great mortality of birds' in 671.[8] Although the *Chronicle*, up until the death of Alfred, mainly consists of brief, terse and to-the-point entries, there are also more detailed episodes, such as the Cynewulf and Cyneheard story in 757, and the latter years of Alfred's reign. After Alfred's death the *Chronicle* becomes even more diverse with poetry appearing at several points in the tenth century, including *The Battle of Brunanburh* in 937. The selection of most of its material was not arbitrary, however, and closer examination reveals that its purpose and content are largely due to when it was compiled (i.e., in the context of the Viking Wars).

The *Chronicle* is not simply a year-by-year account of the history of the West Saxons, however much it appears to be so, and, instead, it uses a selected body of evidence to create an historic myth of a united Wessex which demanded loyalty to one royal house in response to the national crisis caused by the Viking Wars. The chronicler was eager to create a foundation myth and a royal family based around its semi-legendary ancestors, Cerdic and Cynric. The preface to *Manuscript A* contains a regnal list and genealogy which recounts Alfred's descent back to Cerdic and Cynric, and then back again to the Old English pagan god, Woden. This is by no means the only time that this genealogical connection occurs; it is recounted back to Woden four times, descent from Cerdic is described five times and once the genealogy is taken back through Cerdic and Woden to Adam and Christ. This is in contrast to the way genealogies are used for the kings of other kingdoms, especially in Mercia. Two of the great Mercian kings, Æthelbald and Offa, also have their genealogies recorded and from these it can be seen that Æthelbald's great-grandfather and Offa's great-great-great-grandfather – Pybba – was a king of Mercia in the late fifth and early sixth century, although it is clear that Æthelbald and Offa represent quite different branches of the Mercian royal family. Indeed, one of the characteristics of Mercia is the lack of evidence for one royal bloodline, or even the same royal family, providing its kings. The supposedly tight family connections of the West Saxon royal house contrasted with the lack of unity shown by their neighbours. In reality, it seems highly unlikely that, in the 400-year period between Cerdic and Cynric's supposed arrival in England and the writing of the *Chronicle*, that this family line really remained so unbroken and unsullied. While the family tree from the reign of Egbert – in the early ninth century – does show a much more secure succession to the throne within a tight family unit than that seen in Mercia, it seems unlikely that we can project this all the way back continuously to the late fifth century. The truth is far more complex and a number of earlier kings of Wessex appear to have represented competing lineages.

Even the names of the founding fathers of the West Saxons show that something more complex was going on beneath the surface. The early history of Wessex, as described in the *Chronicle*, was defined by battles involving the Germanic newcomers against the Britons, through which the kingdom was carved out. The *Chronicle* tells us that the founders of Wessex were named Cerdic and, his son, Cynric.[9] However, Cerdic is a British name, while Cynric is Irish. This raises real issues about the ethnicity of the founders of Wessex. Although the British are airbrushed out of the *Chronicle*'s account of the migration period, the name of the founder of the dynasty sits uneasily amidst a tale of Germanic conquest. In addition, the fact that the brother of the West Saxon king Caedwalla was called Mul,[10] which means 'mule' (half breed), implies that there must have been at least the remnants of a British population within Wessex, and Caedwalla's name itself is Welsh. It was not, however, only the British who were censored out of the *Chronicle*. We are told by Bede that a group called the Jutes populated the Isle of Wight and Hampshire, but, apart from *Manuscript E*, there is no mention of the Jutes in the *Chronicle*, even when it reports that Cerdic and Cynric captured the Isle of Wight in 530.

The chronicler was keen to promote a single unified people, living under a single unified royal family since the late fifth century. Ethnic diversity was denied, just as rival royal lines had been, but, given how the Vikings exploited disunity within target kingdoms, this motive is readily explainable.

This theme of loyalty and unity is one which can be found throughout the annals created before 899. One such story, though, is a strange anomaly within the usually short entries for this period. This is a detailed account of the deaths of the king of Wessex, Cynewulf, and a rival prince of Wessex, Cyneheard. Cynewulf was murdered by Cyneheard; Cynewulf's men rushed to defend him, all being killed in the process. The next day, the rest of Cynewulf's men arrived, killing both Cyneheard and all of his retainers in retaliation for the deaths of their lord and kinsmen.[11] This is a tale of the importance of loyalty towards one's lord, as well as being a warning against internal family strife. This addition becomes less odd when viewed in the context of the Viking Wars, with the clear message that disunity within the royal family should be avoided at all costs. Given the evidence for the danger this posed when Alfred was at his lowest point in 878 (see Chapter 5), the chronicler's agenda is clear.

The idea of unity occurs again in 867 when the chronicler obviously felt that the Northumbrian failure to unite around their lawful king resulted in the Viking victory.[12] It is also interesting that the *Chronicle* makes no mention of the tensions there must have been amongst the West Saxon royal family during Alfred's reign, given his nephew's bid for the throne upon his death in 899 (see Chapter 9). Similarly, Alfred's *Will* seems to pick up on this theme of unity when it details the plan of succession between Alfred and his brothers.

The *Chronicle* also works by diminishing the role of other kingdoms and powerful kings. Despite the importance of kings who ruled during the Mercian supremacy, they are barely visible in the *Chronicle*. There are eight entries for Æthelbald – one of these is only found in *D* and another only in *F* – seven for Offa and four for Cenwulf, including those recording their accessions and deaths. What it does say is not overly hostile but it tends to concentrate on the bare facts of violence they perpetrated, such as Offa's execution of an East Anglian king in 794, or Cenwulf's suppression of the Kentish rebellion in 798. In contrast, the account of Egbert's West Saxon conquests after 825 is much more sympathetic.[13] This negative view of the Mercians can also be seen in the annal for 874, which describes the king of Mercia, Ceolwulf II, as 'a foolish *king's thegn*',[14] almost certainly because he came to an understanding with his Viking opponents (see Chapter 4).

However, a study of charters and coinage suggests that Ceolwulf was a successful king and held significant power. The fact that he was associated with Alfred in issuing a reformed joint coinage implies that Alfred cannot have thought as little of him as this remark would suggest.[15]

It is therefore clear that the *Chronicle* was a product of the Viking Wars. At this point in time the West Saxons were the last kingdom standing and, as such, had seen how destructive a lack of unity or contested succession could be. It promoted the idea of a single history, a single leadership and a single voice: a kingdom that deserved to survive due to its unity and loyalty to the West Saxon royal family. Although this message would have always been important in the early medieval period, the crisis of the Viking Wars brought it more firmly into focus.

Asser's *Life of King Alfred*

Although Asser's *Life of King Alfred* was based on the *Chronicle*, it seems to have served a different purpose. The *Life of King Alfred* was written by Asser in 893 and is the first biography of an English monarch. Asser was a Welsh monk from St David's and, in 885, he was invited by Alfred to join his circle of learned men, becoming the Bishop of Sherborne in 890. Although there has been some debate as to whether Asser actually wrote this work, Keynes and Lapidge argue that these arguments 'do not stand up to scrutiny and any lingering doubts should be laid peacefully to rest'.[16] This biography tells the story of Alfred from his birth in Wantage (Oxfordshire), up until 893 and, as well as translating the *Chronicle*'s annal entries into Latin, it also expands upon them. There has been much debate as to the intended audience of Asser's *Life of King Alfred*, but the most recent consensus seems to be that it was composed for a Welsh audience. Asser was clearly not writing for locals as he carefully explained the local geography of places he discussed and even provided an explanation in Welsh for some English place names: he tells us that Nottingham 'is called *Tig Guocobauc* in Welsh or *Speluncarum Domus* [house of caves] in Latin'.[17] In addition, Asser uses the Welsh idiom 'right hand' for southern Wales and refers to Offa as a 'tyrant', which would seem strange if the biography was intended for Alfred's court, given the large number of Mercians within it. Although the *Chronicle* does sometimes refer to the Vikings as the 'heathen army', it is also referred to as the 'Danish army'. Asser, however, consistently portrayed the Vikings as pagans, elevating the conflict to an epic battle between paganism and Christianity. This would have been a cause that the Welsh could more readily identify with than the plight of the English. Asser also tells us that, at the time he was summoned to Alfred's court, the kings of southern Wales had petitioned Alfred to protect them against both the Mercians and the Vikings. Asser probably wrote his biography in order to project a more positive image of Alfred back home and to soften views towards their English overlord.

The Alfred depicted by Asser is a sincere Christian, a man who overcame physical disability and illness to become an outstanding war leader, an upholder of the Church, a naval architect, an inspired educationalist and an earnest, painstaking scholar. The *Life* is divided into six sections: three of these are annalistic and are derived from the *Chronicle*; and these are intertwined with three sections describing aspects of the king's character and life. Asser's work seems to have been inspired by Einhard's *Life of Charlemagne*, which was in turn based on Suetonius' *Twelve Caesars*. In a similar way to both Einhard and Suetonius, Asser drew on themes such as Alfred's childhood, interest in the liberal arts, his building works and generosity to strangers.[18] The superiority of Alfred to his brothers and his perfection in all matters is a message that is revisited time and again. This is, however, at odds with Asser's continental models, which are not quite so adoring in their tone.[19] Although the extent of this praise for Alfred suggests that Asser really did believe that Alfred was an amazing man and king, this is undoubtedly an exaggeration. R.H.C. Davies wrote that Asser's *Life of King Alfred* reads like 'a report which every school boy would wish to write about himself',[20] while Barbara Yorke argued that Asser was not in 'the business of writing an objective account of Alfred's reign'.[21] Alfred is described as 'more comely in appearance than his other brothers', 'more pleasing in manner, speech and behaviour', to have a 'desire for wisdom' and a 'noble mind', as well as being 'an enthusiastic huntsman'.[22] Alfred comes across from Asser's account as an heroic saint. He is effectively portrayed as perfection personified: a warrior-king who charged into battle 'like a wild boar',[23] prayed for illness to prevent himself sinning, was a noble champion of learning and still found time to govern his country wisely. Alfred was presented as a figure of hope: a contrast for the Welsh to both the tyranny of the Mercians and the destructive force of the Vikings. Asser clearly saw Alfred as the only man capable of bringing the Christian peoples of Britain together in order to oppose the pagan/Viking threat. This agenda drove the composition and, although this does not undermine its value, this must be taken into account.

The royal titles of Alfred

This greater concentration on unity in the literary sources was accompanied, as noted earlier, by a change in the terminology of the royal title, and the changing use of these royal titles can be seen in the charters and coinage of the period. Charters, which are legal documents that typically grant land or record a privilege, are found in several different types, though the most important for these purposes are royal diplomas, which grant rights over land or privileges by the king. Traditionally, the West Saxon kings styled themselves as *rex Saxonum* (king of the Saxons) and Alfred's diplomas from the 870s and 880s show him continuing to use this style. However, from at least 899 he began to use *rex Anglo-Saxonum* (king of the Anglo-Saxons) instead, and this continued to be used into the reign of his son, Edward the Elder.[24] This is a change in terminology which can also be seen in Asser's *Life of Alfred*. Asser refers to Alfred as *rex Anglo-Saxonum* at the beginning of his biography, but it is not until the narrative for 882 that the title is used with any specific chronological reference and, afterwards, it appears five more times.[25] This change in the royal style seems connected to events of the mid-880s and, in particular, Alfred's capture and restoration of London and the submission of all the English people who were not ruled by the Danes to his overlordship. This period also witnessed the change of Mercia from a kingdom under its own king – Ceolwulf II – to a territory presided over by *Ealdorman Æthelred*, under the ultimate control of his father-in-law, Alfred.[26]

Although the coinage does not fit so neatly with this chronological pattern, it still shows a change in terminology. The *Two Emperors* coinage type for Alfred and Ceolwulf II in the 870s shows Alfred styled as *rex Anglorum* (king of the Angles or king of the English), while the *Gloucester* type from the early 880s styled Alfred simply as *rex*, even though it was produced in the heartland of *Ealdorman Æthelred* of Mercia's territory. The Viking Wars provided the opportunity for Alfred to extend his hegemony over the entirety of the English-speaking peoples. This was a deeply symbolic move, escalating him from the title of king of the West Saxons and allowing him to project a wider political identity. It mirrored the picture painted by Asser and complimented the sense of West Saxon destiny found in the *Chronicle*.

The law codes of Alfred

Alfred's law codes also show him projecting an image of himself as ruler of all the English-speaking peoples. Alfred issued two extant pieces of legislation and, of these, the *Domboc* (judgement book) is the longest of any of the pre-Conquest legal works. These laws show themes that run through all of the Alfredian texts, including the idea that the king is the centre of authority and the source of all wisdom.[27] Interestingly, there is also a focus on the laws concerning feuds and there is an attempt to defer violence and limit reprisals. This seems to echo the message of the passage in the *Chronicle* concerning Cynewulf and Cyneheard.[28] Alfred's *Domboc* starts with Mosaic Law, demonstrating that West Saxon law 'belonged from the outset to the history of divine legislation for humanity'.[29] Bede portrayed the English as God's chosen people and Alfred's law code harnessed this identity, allying themselves as the inheritors of God's kingdom who had survived divine punishment and could now enter their rightful inheritance.[30] The law code then goes on to claim precedents in the earlier legislation of Ine of Wessex, Offa of Mercia and Æthelbert of Kent. Alfred was thus expanding the interest and reach of his laws from the West Saxon heartland and into the entirety of English-ruled southern England.[31] The Viking Wars acted as a backdrop to this appeal to unity, made the idea of West Saxon domination more powerful and allowed the dreams of Bede to be forged into a reality by Alfred.

Alfred's literary programme

One of the most important bodies of evidence from Alfred's reign are the translations of Alfred's literary programme and, in particular, the personal prefaces to several of these works. Alfred's reign witnessed the first flowering of Old English prose and a large part of this was due to Alfred's translation programme, in which he set out to translate into Old English the books which were 'most necessary for all men to know'.[32] Three of these works attribute their authorship to Alfred in either the prose preface or the epilogue. These are: Gregory the Great's *Pastoral Care*; Boethius' *Consolation of Philosophy*; and Augustine of Hippo's *Soliloquies*. The Old English translation of the first fifty psalms have also been added to this collection, due to linguistic similarities in the translation between it and the other three texts.

There has, however, been some debate as to whether Alfred actually did compose either the prefaces or the rather free translations. Many scholars believe that, even though he may have had help interpreting the texts – and Alfred's prefaces admit as much – that the works themselves do reflect his language and his way of thinking.[33] These translations are very free, with Alfred adding a new book to Augustine's *Soliloquies* and turning Boethius' *Consolation of Philosophy* into a more explicitly Christian text. This means that the texts say very much what Alfred wanted them to say and all of them seem to be concerned in various ways with wisdom and, in particular, with building a spiritually wise existence.

There are several other texts which have also been added to the Alfredian canon, although these are opined not to be translated by Alfred himself. These are the Old English translations of Gregory the Great's *Dialogues*, Bede's *Ecclesiastical History of the English People* and Orosius' *History against the Pagans*. The combination of Bede with the *Chronicle* created a single narrative for the English-speaking peoples since their arrival in the British Isles, although, interestingly, the Old English Bede is compressed to three-quarters of its original length and the focus seems to be more on the miracle stories than the history passages. It seems, then, to have also been used as a moral exemplar. The same can also be said of the Old English *Dialogues* which contain many edifying moral tales. The Old English Orosius was heavily adapted for an Anglo-Saxon audience. Consequently, it is shorter, removes criticism of Germanic barbarians, expands and adapts the geographical lists and, while the original is an anti-pagan polemic, the Old English version is more concerned with the coming of Christianity, the Christianisation of the world and the transference of Christian sanctified power from one empire to another, creating an overall plan for history. Combined, these texts provide models for ways of Christian living and show how the scriptural and historical past can shed light on the eternal state of the universe and the place of the English within it. Philosophically they complement the other literary sources. Forged in the white heat of the Viking Blitzkrieg, Alfred and his advisers were setting forth both the divine justification for their success and a manifesto for a reformation of character that would ensure its survival and continuation. As a battle for hearts and minds, it has few precedents and is a direct product of the Viking Wars.

Texts that were products of their time

All these texts produced within Alfred's reign show the influence of the Viking Wars. There is a clear focus on unity, loyalty and the continued security of the Anglo-Saxons being reliant on their relationship with God. Alfred was not personally responsible for all of these texts and this reveals that the people around Alfred also bought into this political and spiritual philosophy. The programme is all the more impressive for this realisation. The Viking Wars were a period of crisis, both politically and spiritually, for the English-speaking peoples, and these texts show the West Saxons attempting to rise from the embers, create a united front and turn Bede's early eighth-century idea of a single English-speaking people into a ninth-century reality, with Wessex at its cutting edge.

How Great was Alfred 'the Great'?

When was Alfred 'Great'?

Alfred was born at Wantage (Oxfordshire), in 849, and was the fifth son of Æthelwulf, king of Wessex. The evidence concerning Alfred's succession is complex. However, it seems that – following the wishes of their father and by mutual agreement of the royal brothers – each of the surviving sons of Æthelwulf succeeded to the throne in turn, rather than pass the Crown to any of their immediate offspring.[1] Given the level of threat Wessex was facing from Viking raids this was a very prudent and politically astute policy, as it prevented a child inheriting the throne and thus weakening the royal leadership at this crucial time. Instead, it meant that experienced warrior succeeded experienced warrior and the kind of internal weakness and disunity that would have benefitted the Vikings was avoided. In time, however, this prudent policy would be tested as it left a number of so-called 'throne-worthy' candidates after Alfred's death in 899. This would make the accession of Alfred's son, Edward the Elder, turbulent, but, overall, the policy worked remarkably well.

The danger of internal disunity was demonstrated in 856 when Alfred's father, Æthelwulf, was effectively deposed by his son, Æthelbald. This followed a visit to Rome by Æthelwulf, who had travelled in the company of Alfred. It seems that Alfred made two pilgrimages to Rome, one at the age of 4, and one in the company of his father, in 855, following the death of Queen Osburh, his mother. On this second journey, Æthelwulf had left two of Alfred's elder brothers, Æthelbald and Æthelbert, to rule over Wessex and Kent respectively, and, upon Æthelwulf's return, a crisis ensued. Kent and the south-east were relinquished to him by Æthelbert, but Æthelbald refused to surrender Wessex. To avoid civil war at such a vulnerable time a compromise was hammered out, by which Æthelbald retained control of the western shires which formed the historic core of Wessex, while Æthelwulf ruled a rump state in the east, centred on Kent. This state of affairs, with the core and periphery of Wessex ruled separately, continued until Æthelwulf's death in 858. The crisis itself may have been caused by the fact that, as Æthelwulf returned from Rome, he married Judith, a Frankish princess. Æthelbald was probably concerned that this marriage might have resulted in the birth of heirs more throne-worthy than himself. After Æthelwulf's death, Æthelbald continued as the king of Wessex, while his brother, Æthelbert, again became king of Kent. Corroboration of the theory that the original revolt had been prompted by Æthelwulf's Frankish marriage is provided by the fact that Æthelbald married his father's widow, Judith, presumably to secure the continuation of the Frankish alliance and the prestige of a Frankish bride for himself. Later commentators in the 890s deplored this decision due to its contravention of Church law regarding marriage to family members. When Æthelbald died in 860 he was succeeded by Æthelbert, who himself died in 865. This later led to the accession of another brother, Æthelred I, who ruled until his death in 871.

During the short reigns of his brothers, Æthelbald and Æthelbert, Alfred is not mentioned in the documentary evidence. However, he came to prominence with the accession of Æthelred I. As a result of the innovative royal succession policy, Alfred became king of Wessex at the age of 21 on the death of Æthelred I. The date of the death of a fourth brother – Athelstan, the eldest son of Æthelwulf, who had been fighting Vikings off the Kentish coast in 851 – is unknown and he had probably died before the division of the kingdom in 855. Alfred reigned from 871 until his death, aged 50, on 26 October 899. There is some uncertainty about this date, however. The *Anglo-Saxon Chronicle* states the year as 901 and, when corrected for internal anomalies, this gives a date of 900.[2] However, *Æthelweard's Chronicle* says that Alfred's successor – Edward the Elder – was crowned on Whitsunday in 900, so this would mean Alfred died in 899 and this is the date taken by most historians.

In the sixteenth century, as interest grew in Anglo-Saxon England and in the collecting and preservation of Old English manuscripts, the title 'Great' first became applied to Alfred. His profile was raised higher during the nine-teenth century, as Victorian writers emphasised Alfred's role as a Christian gentleman-warrior, a champion of Anglo-Saxon virtues, a builder of the navy and proponent of education and the liberal arts. He was defender of the Christian Church, a codifier of law, a town planner, developer of the economy, an inventor of the horn-lantern and a new class of warships, and he was even something of an empire-builder as he expanded the rule of Wessex at the expense of the Vikings. In short, he was viewed as a civilis-ing force bringing order to barbarian chaos, and therefore someone very much like their own self-image. Alfred was as important as Arthur in the popular imagination; an irony since, though separated by centuries, the two warriors came from opposing cultural/ethnic groups. What is clear is that the cult of King Alfred developed remarkably and eventually included the erection of at least four public statues, more than twenty-five paintings, and the publication of over a hundred poems and books devoted to his achieve-ments, including works by famous authors such as Wordsworth. As early as 1852, J.A. Froude described Alfred's life as the favourite story in English nurseries. Alfred was truly 'England's darling'.[3]

By the end of the century his preeminent position amongst English kings was secure, and this is strikingly demonstrated by the heroic stat-ues erected in the market places at Wantage and Winchester. The statue at Wantage, Alfred's birthplace, was sculpted by Queen Victoria's cousin, Count Gleichen, and was unveiled in 1877 by the Prince and Princess of Wales. It sums up the Victorian image of the king; in his left hand he holds scrolls as proof of his commitment to education and law, and his right hand holds a mighty battle-axe as a symbol of his warrior status. The other, in Winchester, was the work of Hamo Thornycroft and this particular statue was commissioned in 1899 to mark the millennium of the king's death and was eventually unveiled in 1901. It is 2.5 times life size, is 4.57m (15ft) high and weighs just over 5,080kg (5 tons). The base is of Cornish granite, bear-ing the name 'AELFRED', and the whole monument stands 12.19m (40ft) high. It is an even more martial image than that at Wantage and depicts the king holding his shield and raising his sword aloft. Moreover, he holds the sword inverted, with the sword guard forming the shape of a cross, and so, even in warfare, his Christian character is affirmed. In the same year as this latter statue was unveiled, a national holiday marked the thousandth anni-versary of his death; it was organised by a committee including such famous names as Edward Burne Jones, Arthur Conan Doyle and Thomas Hughes.

The king's name continued to be linked to education as well as to military prowess: the current University College, Winchester, was originally named King Alfred's College between 1928 and 2004; and Alfred University, in New York State, USA (originating in an educational institution established in 1836), reputedly derives its name (via that of its home town) from the Anglo-Saxon king and a statue of the king stands in the centre of the university campus. It is reputed that when a commentator, inspired by the victory over the Nazi menace in the Second World War, once called Sir Winston Churchill the greatest Englishman ever. Churchill corrected him: no, the greatest was King Alfred. It is still possible to find assessments of King Alfred that reach heights the Victorian commemorators would have approved of:

> King Alfred stands out as the model king, the perfect knight, a dedicated Christian, a Protestant before Protestantism, soldier and scholar, rule maker and educator, author and reformer. He successfully fought against spiritual decay within the English Church as well as against the Viking invaders, creating the first English navy, authored English literature, ensured the survival of Christianity in England, and began the great process of converting the blood-thirsty Viking invaders to Christianity.[4]

And yet, in his home country, while the English relationship with King Alfred has never actually waned, the love affair cooled in the later twentieth century. Academic assessments became more critical and have questioned the impression given by the contemporary and near-contemporary sources; historical novels have chipped away at the image of the king and his values; a post-colonial society has been less comfortable with the imperial Alfred; a less deferential society has been more inclined to undermine the icons of previous generations; a more multi-cultural society has been more sympathetic to a religiously pluralistic ninth century that would have been unintelligible to Alfred and his advisors; the increasing ethnic complexity of the United Kingdom has meant that the ethnic diversity brought by the Viking Wars seems less a crisis and more a cause of celebration; and the rehabilitation of the Vikings as traders and contributors to English culture has transformed Alfred's enemies from heathen ravagers into international entrepreneurs. The academic world and the literati of the twenty-first century are less sympathetic to the Christian beliefs and norms than their Victorian counterparts. Alfred, the Christian warrior, sits uncomfortably in a modern context. Like the Victorians, this may hold up a mirror to modern society: less certain of itself; less sure of common values; and less committed to institutional religion. On New Year's Eve 2007, Alfred's statue in Wantage was vandalised, losing his right arm and his axe. On Christmas Eve 2008, the axe was again stolen. It is hard to imagine this happening in the heyday of the celebration of Alfred as hero-king.

All of this raises the question: how 'Great' was King Alfred? We have seen his achievements against the Vikings, and we have seen how the Viking Blitzkrieg and the West Saxon response to it (both militarily and in the battle for hearts and minds) created an image of kingship that has cast a very long shadow indeed. It might be said that this was one of the most enduring legacies of the Viking Wars. But how far is Alfred's reputation deserved? We may not subscribe to the heights of Alfredism as exemplified by the Victorians, but we do need to ask the question of whether the myth has completely overwhelmed the man and his achievements, or whether there is something peculiarly noteworthy about this most famous personality of the Viking Wars.

A well 'spun' king? Challenges to the iconic status of Alfred

Perhaps Alfred's greatest achievement is found in leading the fightback against the *micel hæðen here* which nearly drove him from his throne in the winter of 878.[5] This was the Viking force, under the supposed unified command of the sons of Ragnar Lothbrok – the legendary Viking leaders Ivar the Boneless, Halfdan and Ubbe – which destroyed the Anglo-Saxon kingdoms of East Anglia and Northumbria, and dismembered Mercia. From 865 until the 890s, the *Chronicle* consistently refers to the enemy force as '*se here*' (the army), which emphasises the unity of the force which threatened the communities of Anglo-Saxon England. Surely this was a 'Finest Hour' to rival Winston Churchill's in 1940? In fact, even more so, since Churchill and the 'Few' of the RAF had not had to face an enemy invasion force that occupied over half of England. Alfred's 'Finest Hour' surely stands above even this iconic image of defiant resistance in a time of national peril. No wonder Churchill deferred to Alfred. The form of blitzkrieg that Alfred faced in 878 was more threatening to national survival than even Churchill faced in 1940.

To challenge this assessment would seem to challenge a core feature of the Alfred myth, since the flight into the Somerset marshes, followed by the heroic resistance which snatched victory from the jaws of defeat and led to the crushing of Guthrum and the Viking army at Edington, epitomises Alfred's moral resolve and organisational skill. There is, though, persuasive evidence to suggest that the *micel hæðen here* that Alfred faced was not as large, organised or coherent as is sometimes suggested. Study of the *Chronicle* reveals that it used the term '*here*' to convey more of a sense of 'raiding army' than 'organised army'. When describing the Anglo-Saxon military units, it usually uses the term '*fyrd*', or occasionally '*folc*'. Later, in 917, when describing a campaign led by Edward the Elder, it consciously contrasts the '*gegadorode micel here*' (the assembled great army) of the Vikings with the '*gegadorode micel folc*' (the assembled great host) of the Anglo-Saxons.[6] In this book we have translated '*micel hæðen here*' as 'great heathen army' because this is the conventional form and no other term adequately conveys its meaning. But the writers of the *Chronicle* clearly intended to communicate something a little different: something akin to 'an army – but not like we Anglo-Saxons think of one'. The *micel hæðen here*, for all its threat and destructive power, was probably more an alliance of opportunistic pirate bands forming, breaking and reforming (as revealed in Frankish accounts of facing such an enemy in this same period). By the time it invaded Wessex, a number of its sub-units had already detached and Alfred was not facing the full might of the force that had landed in East Anglia in 866. His achievement, therefore, was perhaps not as impressive as it first appears.

Similarly, the case for the king as a fortress-builder may have been over-stated. Alfred is often hailed by contemporaries and later historians as the creator of a network of defended *burhs*, but urban renewal in Wessex parallels a wider process found across western Europe and the concept of the *burhs* had already been developed in Mercia.[7] Furthermore, the *burhs* were clearly designed not to thwart an attempt at conquest but rather to frustrate the raids of large Viking bands. As such they are part of the same evidence indicating that it was not a full-scale invasion that Alfred faced in 878, nor in the attacks of 892–96.[8] Consequently, Richard Abels has argued that, if we want an analogy for Alfred's resistance to the Vikings, 'it is not Churchill facing down a German invasion but George W. Bush desperately trying to objectify terrorism in order to deal with it in a proper military manner.'[9]

Even Alfred's relationship with the Church was more complex than the myth indicates for, in 877–78, Pope John criticised Alfred's ecclesiastical policy and threatened him with excommunication. This is almost certainly because, in the crisis of Viking attacks, Alfred took Church property back into royal hands, especially dynastic monasteries of rival royal houses and parallel lineages within Wessex, in order to strengthen his control over lands under his authority. There is evidence to corroborate this interpretation. In the tenth century, much of the land which had once belonged to Kentish royal monasteries ended up in West Saxon royal hands; at Abingdon, thirteenth-century tradition still remembered Alfred as taking land from the church there and compared him with being 'like Judas among the twelve'. Also, shortly after 900, Edward the Elder suppressed the religious community at Wimborne (Dorset) which was closely associated with the rival royal line of Alfred's brother, Æthelred (who was buried there), and with his surviving son, Æthelwold, who had used Wimborne as a base for his failed coup against Edward in 899. This reminds us that different branches of the royal family patronised different religious communities and these could be seen as part of their wider body of clients and supporters.

However, by 880, Alfred had repaired this breach and then demonstrated enthusiasm for raising the standard of the clergy. But this was not accompanied by lavish gifts to the Church; on the contrary, his *Will* emphasised gifts to royal family members and limited gifts to the Church. Even Shaftesbury and Athelney abbeys were not generously endowed, and Edward the Elder continued his father's policy of limited endowment. Alfred and Edward seem to have been determined to exploit all their resources, both lay and ecclesiastical, by building up a stronger military base for the West Saxon royal house in the face of the Viking threat. By way of contrast, this would be very different under Alfred's grandson, Athelstan, who emphasised relic collection and generosity to churches; especially ones associated with key saints (including royal ones). This change may be due to Athelstan's Mercian upbringing, fostered by his aunt, Æthelflæd, and her husband, Æthelred – Lady and Lord of the Mercians.

If Alfred's policy towards the Church was rather different to what we might expect, how much was government administration really reformed under Alfred? The answer seems to be: very little. His famous law code was no innovation and he himself made it clear that his achievement lay in collecting, editing and amending previous collections of laws, even paying tribute to earlier law codes, 'either in the time of my kinsman, King Ine, or of Offa, king of the Mercians, or of Æthelbert, who first among the English received baptism.'[10] Alfred was not a ground-breaking law-maker and it is instructive that the mid-tenth-century manuscript (*ms. Corpus Christi College Cambridge 173*) that contains the earliest complete copy of Alfred's law code, immediately follows it with a copy of the late seventh-century laws of King Ine. In a similar way, the governmental administration of the core shires of Wessex 'had been in existence throughout the ninth century, that is since the reign of Alfred's grandfather Ecgberht (802–39)' and may well have dated from the 750s.[11] It is also quite reasonable to assume that the procedures of law enforcement were already in place since they are not outlined in Alfred's law code. Clearly, Alfred did not reform government and certainly did not found the system of West Saxon government. For all his skills in kingship, the form of government under Alfred was far less sophisticated than that which carried England through a more terrible ordeal in a later phase of the Viking Wars, under Æthelred II, in the early eleventh century. Indeed, as one leading historian has reflected, 'there is an attractive informality about a king who corroborated the key judgement of one of his *ealdormen* in a dispute over a substantial estate at Fonthill while washing his hands in his chamber at Wardour [Wiltshire].'[12] And where we do see evidence for the creation of a common method of making land grants through literate churchmen operating in the royal household; it is a system that predates Alfred and one which he inherited.[13] In addition, very few charters survive from Alfred's reign, which suggests that even this inherited system was underemployed when compared with the flow of charters from the more sophisticated royal administration of tenth- and eleventh-century Anglo-Saxon kings.

Family relationships may also have been more complex than it first appears. The evidence in Asser's *Life of King Alfred* of an agreement between Alfred and his brother, Æthelred, in 868, that the line would go to and through the surviving brother and so not lead to a minority seems straightforward enough. Asser claims that Alfred was named 'heir apparent' in the same year.[14] However, the reality may have been more complex. That year Alfred married into a different Mercian royal family from his sister, who had married into the current ruling one in 853, and so Alfred may have been asserting his own distinct powerbase and not patiently waiting for the throne to devolve to him. In the same year, Æthelred's wife was termed 'queen' in charters, which is very unusual in ninth-century Wessex where 'king's wife' was the common term.[15] It is possible that Æthelred was staking a dynastic claim for his sons by naming her as a 'queen'. If so, he may well have been rethinking the previous arrangement he had made with his brother. The official view of a tidy succession from Æthelred to Alfred therefore hides a much more complex picture of intra-dynastic rivalry and family complexity.[16] As we saw in Chapter 5, Wulfhere, *ealdorman* of Wiltshire, was accused of treason against Alfred. As a probable relative, maybe an uncle, of Æthelred's sons, this may show division within the royal family in the face of Viking successes. It suggests that Wulfhere might have been negotiating with the Vikings for one of Ethelred's sons (Æthelhelm or Æthelwold) to replace Alfred as king.[17] If so, it long predated Æthelwold's revolt at Wimborne against the accession of Alfred's son, Edward the Elder, in 899. In essence, that Alfred was the focal point of West Saxon unity in the face of the Viking threat may have been more wishful thinking than political fact. Wessex may not have been as united under its heroic king as it appears in Alfredian written sources and there is a real possibility that eastern Dorset was consistently disloyal to Alfred, where he may have been regarded as a usurper.

If things could be delicate within Wessex then they could be even more fragile elsewhere, despite the *Chronicle* 'spin' which suggests that all Anglo-Saxons looked to Alfred as leader. There is evidence for ambiguity regarding the acceptance of Alfred's authority and his line in Mercia; he would have had little influence in East Anglia; the East Midlands were out of reach; and there was no Alfredian influence in Northumbria (where Wessex was seen as an intruder even when, later in the tenth century, it successfully united England). Alfred was careful to tread gently with Mercia and this was politically astute given the history of rivalry between the two kingdoms. After Alfred seized London in 886, he handed it over to his ally, Æthelred, Lord of the Mercians (married to Alfred's daughter, Æthelflæd, Lady of the Mercians), which suggests that his leadership of the whole Anglo-Saxon community could not be taken for granted.

Victorians hailed Alfred as father of the British navy, but this is simply not the case. Wessex had possessed naval forces well before Alfred's reign; for example, in 851 Athelstan, ruling as sub-king of Kent had – in collaboration with his *ealdorman* - defeated a Viking naval force off Sandwich (Kent) and captured nine Viking ships.[18] The *Chronicle* does, though, specifically claim that, in 896, Alfred himself designed warships 'neither on the Frisian nor the Danish pattern, but as it seemed to him himself that they would be most useful.'[19] These it claims were, at sixty oars or more, twice the size of the Viking vessels and were faster in the water and more stable. However, on their first deployment their success was rather mixed. Sent against a fleet of six Viking ships operating from the Isle of Wight, they all ran aground and four of the Viking ships escaped, although only after sustaining heavy losses.

The *Chronicle* never suggests a flaw in the design but it may well have been that the size of the new West Saxon warships made them more suscep-tible to beaching in shallow water than their Danish rivals, and this may also explain why the Viking ships were able to launch and escape before the beached West Saxon ships could be re-launched. The *Chronicle*, though, simply puts this down to the tide reaching the Viking ships before that of the West Saxons. Interestingly, the same *Chronicle* entry notes that a number of Frisian sailors (three of whom are referred to by name) died alongside the Anglo-Saxons in this engagement, suggesting that Frisian involvement may have been downplayed by the chronicler in the earlier part of the annal in order to raise Alfred's profile as sole designer of the new ships.

Finally, even later Anglo-Saxon kings did not have the exalted view of Alfred that the Victorians promoted. Æthelred II (ruled 978–1016) named his eight sons after just about every ruler of Wessex/England in the previous century or so. But it was not until his eighth son that he finally decided on 'Alfred'.

The case for the achievements of Alfred

Despite the above counter-arguments to challenge the Alfred-myth, there is still a case to be made for his impressive achievements. To start with, while Alfred did not invent the strategic use of *burhs*, his energy in extending the system was very important. He increased the role of defended towns, changing them from *emporia* (trading centres) to defended *burhs*, even if this continued a Mercian policy and was part of a European urban renewal. As a result of this policy, no part of Wessex was more than 20 miles from the safety of one of these *burhs*. Their size ranged from small forts such as Pilton (Devon) to large fortifications in well-established towns, with the largest being at Winchester (Hampshire). Not all were to prove successful settlements and some were only short-lived establishments, but the system gave Wessex defence-in-depth and denied Viking raiders the easy pickings in people, livestock and portable wealth that had fuelled their past incur-sions. As well as this, the garrisons of the *burhs* could threaten Viking lines of communication. Given that Viking tactics were geared to lightning strikes and then withdrawals, they were not equipped or provisioned for mounting a siege and so the *burhs* undermined a key element of their strategy.

The so-called *Burghal Hidage*, a document developed under Alfred and Edward the Elder, provides information regarding the manning of the *burhs* in Wessex and Mercia according to their size, the extent of their ramparts and the number of men required to garrison them. This was a system that expanded after Alfred's death and many of the tax assessments in *hides* that still dominated tax records as late as Domesday Book (1086) may have dated from the system devised to support the building and manning of the *burhs*. Alfred's system was well organised and had a long-lasting influence on both the defensive policies and the tax system of Wessex and of England.

Alongside the burghal system, Alfred, as we have seen, organised his army – the *thegns* and the existing militia of the *fyrd* – on a rota basis, so he could raise what we would now term a 'rapid-reaction force' with which to respond to incursions into Wessex. At the same time it was a sustainable long-term strategy as it meant that those not on duty could attend to their own business and to agricultural production. As the *Chronicle* notes under the year 893: 'The king had divided his army into two, so that always half its men were at home, half on service, apart from the men who guarded the boroughs [the *burhs*].'[20] It was such a system that, in that year, successfully resisted a massive Viking force – a second '*micel here*' – which had landed in Kent in 892. However, they did not capture a single completed *burh*, which is clearly a vindication of Alfred's military and defensive reforms.

Despite the reservations we have already addressed about the danger of attributing too much innovation in government to Alfred, it is still surely true to say that he had a significant impact on religious education, and the role of education generally, and on government administration, even if Asser and the *Chronicle* rather downplay the survival of pre-Alfredian West Saxon administration and government in order to emphasise Alfred's achievement. There is real evidence of a dynamic king with a real vision of Godly kingship striving to transform his kingdom. Without doubt, Alfred's reign, after he survived the Viking assault of 878, did see a quite extraordinary increase of royal educational activity. This was focused on inventive translations of key texts from Latin into Old English, with a number of these quite reasonably attributed to Alfred's own authorship or active involvement. As we have seen (see Chapter 6), analysis suggests that these different texts formed part of a unified programme to improve the way government and society were ordered. This process placed Alfred and his values at the heart of government authority. In this programme Alfred and his advisers draw on expertise and ideas from Frankish and other European sources.[21] At the same time, whilst Alfred was profoundly Christian, this campaign, accompanied as it was by the disruption of the Church brought by Viking attacks, led to a reduction in ecclesiastical power in contrast to a growth in royal power. This was one of the unintended and unforseeable consequences of the Viking attacks. And the law code itself, it has been argued, formed part of this literary programme.[22] If this is correct, we should see it not as written in the midst of battle, as claimed by the twelfth-century writer William of Malmesbury, but instead understand it as a product of the peace won by these victories, as Alfred sought to bring a new sense of order and purpose to government.

This policy of ordered government and the enhancement of royal authority is one of Alfred's most impressive legacies. This was particularly important with regard to royal control of land, since this was necessary in order to reward the growing military aristocracy required in the Viking Wars. In this, Alfred continued a policy (dating back to his grandfather, Egbert) of keeping royal land in the male line to avoid dispersal and to provide the line with the resources needed to function effectively. In this, he and his heirs were very successful; as late as Domesday Book only about 15 per cent of the royal land held by Alfred was no longer subject to royal control of some kind. This was a legacy of strong royal government that Alfred bequeathed to kings that followed him.

A similar grasp of strategic realities reveals itself in the way Alfred showed himself to be a skilful diplomat by using marriage alliances to strengthen his position with regard to the Viking threat. He married one of his daughters, Æthelflæd, to the *ealdorman* of Mercia, Æthelred; Alfred himself had, in 868, married Ealhswith, a Mercian noblewoman. She was the daughter of a Mercian *ealdorman* and her mother was a member of the Mercian royal family. This seems to have been part of a deliberate attempt by the West Saxons to create a strong alliance with a neighbouring kingdom that had once been a bitter rival. Furthermore, Alfred had wider horizons and had arranged for another of his daughters, Ælfthryth, to marry Baldwin II, the Count of Flanders. This was a significant move since Flanders was a strong naval power and provided a useful ally at a time when the Vikings were occupying eastern England and moving freely through the English Channel. And later, in the tenth century, when King Edgar was reforming coinage, his London halfpenny was a direct copy of Alfred's London Monogram penny.[23] Clearly, he felt his own rule and achievements were enhanced by association with his illustrious ancestor.

A balanced assessment

Alfred was a master of *realpolitik*. He resisted the Vikings but was prepared to buy them off too; he had more complex relationships with the northern kingdoms than is sometimes suggested, since Danish travellers were welcomed at his court; he did deals with Vikings and the treaty with Guthrum was probably designed to bring a Viking leader into the realm of regular diplomacy; and he made claims for himself as ruler of all Anglo-Saxons, going far beyond what many outside Wessex would have been comfortable with, whilst also handling Mercia sensitively now that the Viking annexation of its eastern areas had reduced it to a mere junior partner.

However, he did not lose sight of the way in which the position – and potential – of Wessex had been changed by the crushing of the other Anglo-Saxon kingdoms by the Vikings. As we have seen from an analysis of the titles Alfred used on his coins, he created the concept of 'King of the Anglo-Saxons' on the basis of the new relationship between Wessex and Mercia. It pointed towards a future possibility that one day the ruling house of the West Saxons might be dominant amongst all who were not subject to Viking rule.

Having said this, it must be stated that it was, of course, not Alfred but his son and daughter who launched the conquest of lands lost to Vikings in eastern England (the *Danelaw*). At the end of Alfred's life, Wessex was still just one kingdom amongst a number (even if it was the only surviving Anglo-Saxon one). But, it must be remembered, that without this survival the later conquest of the *Danelaw* would have been impossible. Alfred laid the foundations for this, although the realisation of it would occur in the generations after him. His greatest achievement, therefore, was the establishment of a West Saxon kingdom that was capable of resisting renewed Viking attack. When the Vikings returned in force, in 892, they faced a West Saxon kingdom that was defended by a reorganised and sustainable field army, and a network of garrisoned *burhs* which commanded navigable rivers and the road network and also provided a safe haven for local people and their valuables. Consequently, Wessex did not fall to them.

There is certainly a large measure of 'greatness' in these achievements, even when the limitations of Alfred's reign are taken into account. Alfred was a skilled manager of men, a proficient leader in battle, and an intelligent ruler who took a keen interest in government. We do not have to ascribe to Alfred such a degree of attributes and achievements as to suggest that he was the founder of every aspect of West Saxon government and administration. Neither do we have to assume that he uniquely innovated in every policy area that he applied himself to. As with every ruler, he deployed ideas and approaches that had been established by others, whilst developing them in ways appropriate to the demands of his time and the crises of the Viking Wars. Alfred's achievement was that he operated energetically and efficiently on a wide range of fronts, and had such a developed sense of kingship and the personal moral responsibilities of a ruler before God. These are impressive attributes in their own right without exaggerating them so much that they eclipse those who ruled before and after him. To survive the Viking Blitzkrieg and lay the foundations for West Saxon expansion were real achievements. After all, East Anglia and Northumbria had fallen, and Mercia had been emasculated. And even if the *micel hæðen here* was not the force that it had once been when it fell on Wessex in the winter of 878, it still came close to eliminating Alfred and inflicted such a humiliation on him during that winter that he might have abandoned his kingdom as Burgred did Mercia in 874. But Alfred did not allow that defeat to crush him; instead he became the one to dictate terms to the very invaders who had come close to destroying him. And he added to this a vision of transformative kingship which, as much as we might qualify it, still has the power to impress in the twenty-first century. Plus, he had an ability to reach beyond battle to hearts and minds, albeit in a way that suited the ambitions of his own line in one particular royal house. So, when all is said and done, we can still with some justification continue to employ that sixteenth-century title: Alfred 'the Great'.

The Impact on England of the First Phase of Viking Settlement

The Viking invasions led to a period of significant turbulence and change for Anglo-Saxon England, and this period of upheaval can be divided into two distinct phases. As we have already seen, the first encounter the Anglo-Saxon kingdoms had with the Vikings was in 789 when the *reeve* of the king of Wessex was killed at Portland after attempting to impose a tax on the Viking ship which had landed there.[1] The next significant appearance of the Vikings in the written record was the raid on Lindisfarne in 793 and this seemed to coincide with the escalation of raids across the whole of the British Isles, with the Irish annals reporting in 794 'the plundering of all the islands of Britain by pagans'; in 795 it also commented that the monastery at Rathlin was burned and those at Iona, Inishmurray and Inisbofin attacked.[2] However, despite the many raids that took place during the next fifty years, it was not really until the arrival of the *micel hæðen here* in 866 that large-scale invasion – and the resulting upheaval to society – really occurred. This period of invasion ran for roughly sixty years, until it came to an end in the 920s when the *Danelaw* was finally captured by the West Saxon kings and a single English kingdom began to emerge for the first time (see Chapters 9, 10 and 11). A second phase of Viking invasions occurred from the late tenth century until 1016, but we will consider this second phase later in our exploration of the Viking Wars (see Chapter 12). At this point, though, it is necessary to ask the question of just how much England was changed by the great upheavals that accompanied the first great phase of Viking activity?

It has traditionally been argued that this first phase of Viking invasion from the raid on Portland to the creation of a single kingdom of the English in the 950s and 960s brought with it a wide raft of changes and had a long-lasting impact on the English-speaking peoples. However, as always in the study of the Viking Blitzkrieg, the situation is more complicated than that.

The impact of the Viking Blitzkrieg:
the case for severe and widespread change

Initially, the evidence from the primary sources presents us with a scene of complete and utter destruction during the first phase of Viking invasions. The first reported attack on a monastery recorded in the *Anglo-Saxon Chronicle* describes how 'the ravages of the heathen men miserably destroyed God's church on Lindisfarne, with plunder and slaughter'.[3] These monks were then later forced to flee from Lindisfarne with the bones of their saints – the most important of these being St Cuthbert – in 875 due to the threat of further Viking raids. The monks were forced to wander for seven years, avoiding the Viking threat, before they were able to settle down in Chester-le-Street, which became the home of St Cuthbert's bones until they were threatened again by the Vikings in 995. Moreover, this picture of destruction is not just confined to the northern monasteries and the *Anglo-Saxon Chronicle* reports how later, in 865, 'Under the cover of that peace and promise of money the [Viking] army stole away inland by night and ravaged all eastern Kent'.[4] Asser expanded on this statement in his *Life of King Alfred*, explaining that they did this because 'they knew they would seize more money by secret plunder than by peace'.[5] Five years later, in the kingdom of the East Angles, the Viking army were not just content with destroying the land but also killed the king, Edmund the Martyr, and conquered the whole kingdom.[6] *Manuscript E* of the *Chronicle*, which had additional information added at Peterborough, unsurprisingly expands this local event and tells us how 'they destroyed all the monasteries they came to. In this time they came to Peterborough, burnt and destroyed it, killed the abbot and all the monks and all they found there'.[7] The invading Viking armies would definitely have been pagans – as Christianity did not really begin to take hold in Scandinavia until the late tenth century – and their destruction of Anglo-Saxon monasteries may well have made it appear as if they were attempting to destroy the Christian foundation upon which the Anglo-Saxon kingdoms were based.

It is little wonder then that the long-lasting impression of the Viking impact on England is one of devastation and pillage, and this is the image that still dominates the popular imagination.

This theme of destruction was continued by King Alfred, in his *Preface to the Pastoral Care* (see Chapter 6), when he claimed that: 'Learning had declined so thoroughly in England that there were very few men … who could … translate a single letter from Latin'.[8] He suggested by this that all centres of learning had been destroyed due to Viking raids. In support of Alfred's lament there are very few pre-Viking charters which survive, indicating a great loss to Church libraries and records, and therefore a consequent decline in the standards of literacy.[9] The charters which do survive also suggest that something catastrophic had occurred in the centres of learning. A charter, known as S344 and dating from 873 is found in the archive of Christ Church, Canterbury. This is a charter that has been described as having been written by a scribe who was 'barely able to read and write'.[10] The witness list has clearly been copied straight from an earlier charter with no attempt to update it, as the current king listed is Æthelwulf – Alfred's dead father – and the archbishop, Ceolnoth, who had died three years earlier. However, this does not represent the 'nadir of Lain scholarship in ninth-century charters' and Michael Lapidge, an expert in Anglo-Saxon charters, bestows this dubious honour on charter S287. This is a charter of 839 also found in the Christ Church, Canterbury archive and, according to Lapidge, is 'gibberish'.[11] This would certainly suggest that there was a decline at the Canterbury archive at the time of Alfred's accession to the West Saxon throne. It is also true that, while some significant manuscripts were produced in the late eighth and early ninth centuries, including the *Book of Cerne* and the *Tiberius Bede*, that there was a gap in production from around 825 until the Alfredian revival in the late ninth century. This seems to coincide with a decline in the organised Church, as demonstrated by this reduction in manuscript output and the disappearance of Church councils. Church councils were a common occurrence in the early ninth century, with seven occurring between 800 and 809, six between 810 and 819, three between 820 and 829, and three again between 830 and 839. However, in the 840s only one occurred – at London in 845 – and this was the last of the Church councils. It may be that there was a deal struck at the council of Kingston in 838 that Church business would now be conducted in a different way, but it does seem more likely that this is a symbol of decline.[12] Given the pressure caused by the Viking raids during this period, it seems natural to hold them responsible for this decline in learning and the disruption of Church organisation and government. Some bishoprics in the east and north vanished and huge tracts of Church land were lost to the land seizures by invading pagan Scandinavians.

It is also important to note that, while a lot of work has been done recently on rehabilitating the Vikings from raiders to traders, that we are dealing with trained fighters. The Viking armies were led by men who had grown to manhood in the vicious power struggles of Scandinavia, where the boundaries of kingdoms only really began to be definitively formed in the mid-to-late tenth century. In such a context of political flux, violence was virtually hardwired into the social system. These were men who appear in the Scandinavian saga and *skaldic* poetry tradition as violent and power-hungry warriors. In the poem *Eiriksmal*, which describes Eric Bloodaxe's welcome into *Valhalla* – the Old Norse afterlife for dead warriors – it states he was welcome:

> Because he has made many lands red
> with his sword', said Odin,
> And carried a bloody blade.[13]

All this suggests that the *Chronicle* was not simply the product of the feverish imagination of monks desperate to portray the Vikings in the worst possible light. Instead, it appears that defenceless monastic centres suffered heavily from premeditated acts of extreme violence and that, at the time, the monks had every right to feel that Christianity was under severe threat.

Sign posts, metal detectors and bits of brooches

The impact of the Viking raids was not only restricted to the destruction caused; there is also evidence of a great social impact on the population of eastern England. Until fairly recently the traditional view of a great influx of Scandinavian settlers, in the aftermath of Viking conquest, was dismissed by some experts as being an over-literal interpretation of the written primary sources and an over-emphasis on the presence of Scandinavian place names in eastern and northern England. These place names, it was argued, were in reality the products of an elite movement of new Viking lords into these areas, who seized control of Anglo-Saxon estates.

This minimalist view of Viking immigration, however, has been challenged by new archaeological discoveries.

The recent assessment of some 13,500 items of Viking and Anglo-Scandinavian metalwork, discovered by metal detectors, suggests that the impact of the Vikings was not just restricted to the destruction of Church property and the arrival of a minority of new landlords. The finding of 'poor quality, cheap, mass produced trinkets' in Lincolnshire supports the view that the first phase of invasions brought about profound change.[14] Kevin Leahy, while working as the archaeologist at the North Lincolnshire Museum and now as National Finds Adviser – Early Medieval metalwork for the Portable Antiquities Scheme,[15] has made a study of these low-grade brooches. He suggests that these 'are not the type of brooches you bring across to impress your English girlfriend', and instead that they are evidence for the mass migration of Scandinavian immigrant farmers into Britain and not just higher-status warlords.[16] This would challenge the view that there was no significant folk movement. In addition, comparisons of skeletons in the medieval cemeteries at York – the capital of the *Danelaw* – with skeletons from other areas of England and Scandinavia show that, in the early medieval period, skulls found in York were similar to ones from Oslo. This would suggest that York was heavily settled by the Vikings during the Viking Age.[17]

The evidence of changes to linguistics and place names can also be used to corroborate the argument for large-scale Viking settlement. In places such as the East Riding of Yorkshire, 48 per cent of place names were Scandinavian at the time of Domesday Book (1086), with Lincolnshire and Nottinghamshire also showing similar trends.[18] Many new place names also appeared in eastern and northern England, such as those with the Old Norse suffixes *-by* (village), and *-thorp* (dependent farm). There were also 150 Old Norse words adopted into Old English, including the key words *husband, fellow, thrall, outlaw, husting, wrong, call, egg* and *law*, to name but a few. These indicate Scandinavian influence at the lowest social levels, as well as higher in the social hierarchy. The Vikings also changed the use of administrative and landholding vocabulary with evidence of a new class of independent farmers known as *sokemen*; new units of tax assessment (*wapentakes* and *sulungs* in Danish areas) replaced the use of *hundreds* and *hides* in Anglo-Saxon areas; new titles for the nobility appeared (*jarl* instead of *ealdorman*); and new administrative areas were established (reflected in the *ridings* of Yorkshire and the *parts* of Lincolnshire). This is clearly evidence of profound change at all social levels.

In addition to social and cultural changes, there were also significant political consequences to the first phase of Viking invasions. The Viking wars helped to hasten the unification of England through the destruction of the old kingdoms. Although this process of consolidation had already begun with smaller kingdoms and territories being subsumed into the larger kingdoms, such as the kingdom of the Kent which become a sub-kingdom of Mercia in the eighth century, the Viking Wars accelerated this process and determined from which of these kingdoms the kingdom of England would grow. The pre-Viking make-up of England had often been more complex, but in simple terms there were seven main kingdoms: Northumbria, Mercia, East Anglia, Essex, Sussex, Kent and Wessex. This situation was changing even before the massive Viking-induced upheavals of the mid-ninth century since, in 825, Essex and Sussex were absorbed into Wessex. Nevertheless, by the mid-ninth century it was difficult to imagine one of the Anglo-Saxon kingdoms permanently dominating all the others.

By the end of the ninth century only one of these old kingdoms, Wessex, was still under the control of its own royal family. In 867 Northumbria became the northernmost Viking kingdom; in 870 the king of East Anglia was killed by the Vikings and from 880 the Vikings permanently settled there; in 877 the Vikings seized the eastern half of Mercia, leaving Ceolwulf II – the last king of the Mercians – to rule only the western half. Thus the map of political power in England was completely rewritten by the Vikings. The northern and eastern parts of the country became an Anglo-Scandinavian land dominated by the Viking capital at York (Norse *Jorvik*), while in the south and west of the country only Wessex remained as a unified kingdom. It was from this destruction of the old order that the tenth-century kings of Wessex were able to rise and to conquer the *Danelaw*, turning England into a united kingdom of the English (see Chapters 11).

This destruction of the kingdoms not only caused the removal of kings but also the dispossession of the Anglo-Saxon landlords of their estates. It really does seem that, with the Viking conquest of northern and eastern England, 'the fiscal system built up over the centuries by the English rulers was swiftly swept away'.[19] The Viking invasions also appear to have brought about profound change to England's economic structure, with their conquest coinciding with evidence of a huge increase in industrial production; increased use of wheel-thrown and glazed pottery; increased marketing and trade; and an upsurge in mass-produced metalwork. The trade stimulus provided by newcomers who had economic connections that stretched from Ireland to the Baltic and into Russia appears to have been hugely influential in this expansion of trade.[20] This was clearly seen in the case of Viking-conquered Northumbria. Before the Viking invasion of Northumbria, the kingdom was in a period of decline and, while all the other Anglo-Saxon kingdoms appear to have been making economic headway and were producing silver pennies, the Northumbrians were producing base-metal bronze 'stycas'. However, the Viking invasion and conquest of Northumbria facilitated a shift from bronze to silver coinage and, in doing so, re-energised the Northumbrian economy[21] and brought Northumbrian coinage into line with their major trading partners and competitors in southern England and in Francia.[22]

These developments also went hand in hand with an increase in the growth of urban centres across England. There was a huge growth in towns in Wessex such as at Canterbury, Exeter, Oxford, London, Winchester and Bath, and in the *Danelaw*, including York and Lincoln, during this period. The towns of Late Anglo-Saxon England do appear to have had a 'truly commercial market function'[23] and there occurred, by the early tenth century, a transition from the monopolistic regional centres of the Middle Saxon period towards ranked competitive markets.[24] It has even been argued that the tenth century witnessed something approaching an 'industrial revolution',[25] in which the Vikings 'provided both the stimulus and mechanism for it to happen'.[26] All of this suggests that 'we are left with massive evidence that the invasion opened a new chapter in English social history'.[27]

The impact of the Viking Blitzkrieg: the case for continuity and complexity

It seems that a great deal of evidence points towards widespread changes occurring as a result of the Viking invasions and settlement of the late ninth century. However, although the immediate impact of the invasions does appear to have been widespread, in the long term the changes brought about did not have nearly so great an effect as it may first appear. Whilst the breadth of change was considerable, the depth and profundity of that change can certainly be questioned.

One such piece of evidence is that, although the *Anglo-Saxon Chronicle* and Alcuin of York's account of the sack of Lindisfarne presents a scene of destruction, the event cannot have been quite as catastrophic as these sources would have us believe. As mentioned earlier (see Chapter 1), the fact that Alcuin was able to write a letter to the Bishop of Lindisfarne and his companions means that there must have been a community – of a large enough size to still be recognisable – left for him to write too. Clearly, they had not all been slaughtered. In addition, the fact that it was not until eighty years later, in 875, that the monks of Lindisfarne finally left the island in order to protect themselves and their relics, shows that their monastery cannot have been completely destroyed and that the buildings were still sufficiently intact to house a community. This raises questions about the nature of the destruction at other monastic sites, where we do not have the same quantity of evidence to allow us to chart the scale of decline as at Lindisfarne. In Ireland, according to the records in the Irish annals, repeated attacks on the same six churches made up a quarter of all recorded ninth-century Viking raids. The implication is that, despite the attacks, these communities continued and prospered sufficiently to make them targets of further raids. It seems likely that the situation may well have been similar in England. Despite the desecration of monasteries, Christianity continued to thrive at a grass-roots level and there appears to be little evidence for any pagan revival. This last point is particularly important because, despite modern archaeological discoveries, there have still been very few overtly pagan Viking burials found in England. This indicates both the vibrancy of native Christianity and the willingness of Scandinavian settlers to assimilate, which is rather different from the fire and the sword image of the wanton pagan destruction of Christian communities.

In addition, the impact on learning may not have been as severe as Alfred would have had us believe. Experts such as Simon Keynes argue that the Alfredian literary programme of the 880s and 890s did not come out of nowhere and must have involved an extraordinary amount of scribal activity.[28] This suggests that there cannot have been an educational wasteland to the extent which Alfred suggests, and that there must have been some significant level of literacy and learning left within Wessex. That Latin learning had not been obliterated is evidenced by the presence of learned Mercian and West Saxon clerics such as Plegmund, Wæferth, and Wulfsige in his court. While the charters of Canterbury from the ninth century make it clear that 'the metropolitan church [of Canterbury] must have been quite unable to provide any effective training in the scriptures or in Christian worship',[29] not all the charters from this period were quite so dire. The Mercian charters of the 840s are confident in their Latin and make use of spectacular language, reminiscent of the florid Latin of St Aldhelm in the early eighth-century golden age of manuscript production, before the Viking depredations. Although the West Saxon charters of the period are often terse and short, they are efficient and mainly accurate and, in the 840s, the so-called decimation charters of King Æthelwulf show an able scribe at work. In addition, while the Vikings may well have been partly to blame for the ending of the Church councils, it seems likely that this was also a result of internal decline. The Church appears to have become rather secular and inward-looking in its character, as can be seen in Asser's blaming of the decline on the Church's love of luxury: Alfred, in his *Preface to the Pastoral Care*, not only blamed the loss of books on Viking raids, but also on the monks who had failed to protect and make use of these books even before they were lost. The tenth century also witnessed the start of a reform movement in order to de-secularise the Church, which points to a deeper malaise affecting Church government and culture in the earlier ninth century. The ending of Church councils occurred under the rule of Archbishop Ceolnoth of Canterbury and it seems likely that a lack of leadership from this leading churchman was also part of the problem. It is therefore too simplistic to hold the activities of the Vikings solely responsible for the decline in learning. While there was undoubtedly a decline in learning in certain areas of the country, this was by no means universal. Furthermore, as has been seen from the educational initiatives in the reign of Alfred (see Chapter 6), even this decline in Latin resulted in a resurgence in the use of the vernacular and did not lead to the end of learning *per se*.

It seems likely as well that the attacks on the monasteries were attacks on undefended places of great wealth, rather than an outright attack on Christianity itself. The Vikings were by no means the first people to attack monasteries and, as has been noted earlier, even in the late seventh-century Aldhelm, abbot of Malmesbury (Wiltshire), was forced to negotiate a special arrangement with the kings of Mercia and Wessex in order to prevent them targeting his monastery. These two were both Christian monarchs and were certainly not attempting an attack on Christianity itself. Therefore, it may be going too far to attribute such a motive to the Vikings, even if they were pagans. Moreover, the Vikings quickly assimilated and converted, as can be seen in coins of the 890s where the grandchildren of Vikings who martyred King (Saint) Edmund of East Anglia began to mint coins in his honour.[30] Similarly, as we have seen, the assimilation of immigrants as measured by burial customs was rapid.[31] There is evidence for hundreds of

Scandinavian-style ornamentation on tombstones; however, all but thirty of these are within a Christian context. This suggests large numbers of people who were of Scandinavian identity but who were drawn from a community which was decreasing its ethnic signals and was adapting itself to Anglo-Saxon Christian burial customs at the expense of traditional pagan practices. By 1000 most of the northern pagans had become Christians and the Vikings appear to have rapidly adopted the lifestyle and beliefs of the numerically dominant people that they had conquered. In short, while the impact of Viking-associated change was dramatic, it lacked depth and profundity, and continuity won out over change in the long run.

Becoming Christian was not the only way in which the Vikings appear to have rapidly assimilated. There is virtually no evidence for Scandinavian-style buildings in England; even the houses excavated in the 1970s in Coppergate, in Viking *Jorvik* (York), are identical to Anglo-Saxon ones. This suggests a people who rapidly adapted and changed to fit in with the native culture, and there would have been little that actually looked Scandinavian in most 'Viking communities' of the *Danelaw*.[32]

Linguistically the impact was more complex than might appear at first examination. Although thousands of Scandinavian words are present in Middle English, there are little more than 150 intrusive words in Old English. These words were often significant and socially useful, but the number of words is really quite small. This suggests that Old English and Old Norse were both mutually understood and that, ultimately, despite some additions to English, it was the Norse language which was overwhelmed,[33] even where Scandinavian settlers may have been socially dominant.

The use of the Viking runic alphabet also quickly disappeared. This should come as no surprise given what occurred to the use of Old Norse on the Isle of Man. The Isle of Man had been ruled by the Norse since *c.* 900 (and possibly a little earlier) and was at various times part of a Norse sea community that stretched from Dublin and across the Hebrides to the west coast of Scotland. There are more pre-1100 Norse inscriptions on the Isle of Man than in any other area of Britain, or Ireland, which suggests that Norse was definitely the language of the elites and almost certainly the dominant language there.[34] Although it has been argued that Gaelic was retained as the language of the lower classes, the presence of a low-status house built in a Scandinavian style on the marginal land at Doarlish Cashen implies that the Norse settlement – like in Lincolnshire – was not just an elite movement.[35] This does not negate the survival of Gaelic, but does make it likely that

Norse managed to permeate into all classes of people on the Isle of Man. The dominance of Norse can be most clearly seen in place names, such as the -*by* ending to many Manx place names and in areas of the *Danelaw* in England. There are twenty-three place names recorded before the end of the Viking kingdom of Man in 1266 and, of these, twenty are Norse, leaving only three with a Celtic origin.[36] However, despite this initial dominance, the Manx place names reveal that Gaelic had gained the upper hand over Norse by 1266.[37] There are no Norse inscriptions from later than the twelfth century and, by this point, it is likely that Gaelic was widely spoken, with Old Norse dying out a generation or so after the end of the native dynasty after 1300.[38] If Norse could be completely replaced in a kingdom where Viking culture had been dominant for generations, then it should come as no surprise that it probably did not last beyond the third generation where Scandinavian settlement was less intense.

The Vikings were great 'cultural-chameleons' and seem to have quickly taken on the characteristics of the dominant social influences. This was a people who rode camels to Baghdad in order to trade with the Caliphate, became the personal guard of the Byzantine Emperor, merged with the Irish aristocracy, emerged as the Dukes of Normandy and became the mercenaries for the kingdoms surrounding the Irish Sea. It was not just the case that they assimilated culturally, as evidence from the comparison of skeletons from Wharram Percy (from 950 onwards) on the Yorkshire Wolds and medieval cemeteries in York suggests that, while in the early period the skulls from York can be most closely compared with those from Norway, in the later medieval period the skulls are broadly the same. Over time, therefore, the intermingling of the Anglo-Saxon country dwellers with the Viking city dwellers resulted in the genetic difference becoming 'diluted and eventually dissolved'.[39] Thus Viking DNA went the same way as Scandinavian building styles and the speaking of Old Norse: it was diluted, lost its distinctiveness and, eventually, could no longer be distinguished from those the Viking armies had conquered.

Politically, despite the traumatic short-term consequences, it probably made very little difference in the long term to the native farmers who ruled them. England was a rich and productive land and there was enough space within it for Scandinavian economic migrants to slot into the existing framework, and there appears to have been no mass killing of the Anglo-Saxon peasantry. As Julian D. Richards has put it: 'Viking settlers were not pioneers carving farmsteads out of a virgin landscape. The England they found was already intensively farmed, with few open expanses where new-comers could establish their own villages. For native farmers the Viking settlement probably just meant a change in whom they paid their taxes to'.[40] Evidence for this can be found in British place names, as, despite the large numbers of place names with Scandinavian origins in the north and east of England, the picture it presents may be more complex. The names given to places do not always denote the ethnicity of those that live there and is more likely to have been influenced by the aristocracy who con-trolled the community. Archaeological investigations of a number of villages on the Yorkshire Wolds with Scandinavian elements in their names, reveal they were originally Anglo-Saxon settlements. As well as the new land-owners who sought to legitimise their control by renaming the places they controlled, there also appear to be new place names dating from a second wave of colonists who moved into previously unused and less desirable land. This analysis suggests that colonisation on the best land was represented by Anglo-Saxon place names ending in -tun; those ending in -by repre-sented Danish settlement on rather less desirable land; and those ending in -thorp arose from even later Danish settlement on the least desirable land.[41] It therefore appears to be the case that Danish names are found on the least desirable land and were slotted into 'gaps' between Anglo-Saxon villages which continued to be occupied.[42] The -tun, -by and -thorp hierarchy has been questioned by more recent research which has combined linguistic and archaeological evidence to suggest that place names containing -thorp may actually represent a stage in the process by which dispersed farmsteads gave way to a landscape of nucleated villages.[43] Even with this proviso, there still seems sufficient weight within the earlier interpretation to suggest that these Scandinavian place names represented a Danish integration into the Anglo-Saxon countryside, even if that countryside was in a state of flux in terms of its settlement pattern.

In addition, the regional identities present before the Viking invasions were preserved under Viking rule, with regional Viking leaders simply replacing the previous Anglo-Saxon ones. Ironically, by the time the Danelaw was reconquered by Wessex, the Anglo-Saxons in the north would have felt more loyalty and kinship with the Danish 'invaders' than the West Saxon 'liberators'.

The Viking impact on the economy of England was also more compli-cated than it first appears. While it is tempting to attribute the renaissance in urbanisation to the impact of the Vikings, it is important to remember that this occurred not only in the *Danelaw* and in the Viking controlled area of Ireland, but also in the non-Viking areas in southern England as well.[44] This implies that the Vikings did not have a direct effect but were rather part of a general trend of increased urbanisation. A recent study of the development of coinage from 757 to 865 has concluded that historians should not overestimate Viking influence on later social and economic patterns due to the complex mix of causal influences.[45] Nevertheless, the Vikings clearly contributed to a revival of the economy in the north, since prior to their conquest the Northumbrian economy appears to have been in decline. Thus the Vikings were one of many factors affecting the growth of the economy in the tenth century and we must not attribute too much to their impact. For example, in Northumbria it is important to note that the Vikings were not town builders, but were well-connected traders who were able to re-start the flagging economy via their extensive trading contacts. And this did have wider consequences: it can be argued that this reinvigoration of the Northumbrian economy caused Wessex to increase its urbanisation in a significant way. Faced by an economic threat from the Viking north, the West Saxons responded to this in order to protect their economic prowess.[46] Economic competition, therefore, may have been as important as military necessity in the building of the *burhs* of Wessex.

Nevertheless, in addition to the economic threat, the military threat of the Vikings resulted in Wessex taking measures which would lead to a growth in urbanisation. For example, the trading places of the pre-Viking period, such as *Fordwich*, Sandwich and *Lundenwic* succumbed to both the fear and reality of Viking attack in the ninth century and were abandoned in favour of their nearby defended settlements of Canterbury, Richborough and *Lundenburgh* (later to be known as London).[47] It was in this ninth and tenth-century period that the Old English word '*burh*' shifted in meaning from that of a 'defending bank and ditch' to 'a town with trading rights and privileges'.[48] The creation of the system of *burhs* produced a series of towns which could be more easily defended and more effectively used to protect the inhabitants, trade and food sources from Viking attacks.[49] However, these defended centres of authority were also a product of the developing nature of extended regional kingship, with kings having greater access to resources and more need to use them. Consequently, these *burhs* were a characteristic response to the combined effects of developing royal authority, economic competition from a reviving Northumbria and the external threat of the Viking raids. They show 'a burgeoning royal authority which was developing its powers of taxation at the same time as having to assume responsibility for the protection of their people in the face of attack'.[50] Due to both economic and military reasons, the need to protect trade and the population became ever more pressing and, as such, urbanisation and the creation of defended towns offered a solution to both of these problems. Therefore, it can be argued that the Vikings did act as a stimulus for the growth of urbanisation, both in the north, where they can be seen as more directly responsible, and in the south, where it was more a reaction to the Viking threat. But, as with so much in the Viking Wars, simple answers do not do justice to the complexity of the evidence; the effect of the Vikings was but one factor, albeit an important one, in a cocktail of factors operating within England.

The impact of the Viking Blitzkrieg: making sense of the conflicting evidence

At first glance the evidence from this period appears to widely conflict; however, the reason for these wildly varying points of view is simply a matter of timing and perspective. For the ninth-century monkish chroniclers, the desecration of the monasteries would have felt like an outright attack on Christianity, although the reality on the ground was that, for those away from the main monastic centres, Christianity not only survived, it thrived. This destruction was also short-lived and, while it was devastating at the time, it did not continue for the entirety of Viking rule; nor was destruction and ravaging a feature that can solely be attributed to the Vikings. The evidence also seems to suggest that large numbers of Scandinavian men (and women in Lincolnshire) participated in the first phase of invasions and settlement but that, instead of maintaining their own ethnic identities, they quickly assimilated into key aspects of Anglo-Saxon culture. It is also important to note that, not only were the chroniclers monks, but they were also West-Saxons, keen to present the Vikings as invaders and Wessex as the liberator of England. So, while it is important not to dismiss what they have to say, these sources must be read with their agendas in mind. That said, it must also be remembered that, while there is little archaeological evidence for the widespread devastation common in the *Chronicle*, this does not take into consideration the effect of rape or emotional distress that leaves behind no visible archaeological trace.

Overall then, what can we say about the impact of the first phase of Viking invasions? Clearly, the initial impact destabilised much of society and had a particularly devastating impact on the kings and aristocrats whose kingdoms went under, and the monks whose monasteries were attacked. However, in the long term there was much less permanent cultural change, and what change that did occur cannot be attributed solely to the activity of the Scandinavian newcomers. Consequently, after the West Saxon re-conquest of the *Danelaw* in the first quarter of the tenth century, England emerged as a recognisably Anglo-Saxon state – albeit a state that was made possible by the Viking invasions of the ninth century and which, in the east and north, was now something of an Anglo-Scandinavian society.

9

BAND OF BROTHERS
– AND A SISTER

When King Alfred died in October 899, Wessex and its Mercian allies faced a Viking-dominated eastern England – the *Danelaw*. This division was the result of Alfred's treaty with Guthrum, which had recognised that these areas of England were now under Viking control. They constituted the territories of the old Anglo-Saxon kingdoms of Northumbria, East Anglia and eastern Mercia. Within these areas, Danish Viking settlement and cultural and political dominance was changing the nature of society and creating an Anglo-Danish community.

Within the next generation a new phase of the Viking Wars would see this balance of power completely transformed in favour of the West Saxons. This was largely down to a remarkable alliance of three people: Edward the Elder, king of Wessex; Æthelred, 'Lord of Mercia' and his wife; Æthelflæd, the 'Lady of the Mercians'. That these three are not better known to modern readers is largely due to the limited survival of written sources for their campaigns. For Edward, the only near-contemporary account of his reign is found in *Manuscript A* of the *Anglo-Saxon Chronicle* (also known as the *Parker Chronicle* and now in Corpus Christi College, Cambridge). Unlike Alfred, Edward did not have a biographer (as far as we know) and was not involved in the kind of educational revival that has allowed us to hear the 'voice' of Alfred. In a similar way, Edward's military achievements have been overshadowed by those of Alfred, and by those of his son, Athelstan. As a result, later medieval writers tended to downplay Edward's reign, especially since, as monastic writers, they were particularly focused on Alfred's devotion to learning. Similarly, Welsh chroniclers, such as those who wrote the *Annales Cambriae* (*Annals of Wales*) and *The Chronicles of the Kings*, were more aware of – since they were more threatened by – the military campaigns of his sister, Æthelflæd, and of his son, Athelstan. The later Anglo-Saxon chronicler, Æthelweard, makes little reference to the start of Edward's reign, since it involved crushing the rebellion of one of Æthelweard's ancestors, and is minimalist in his treatment of Edward's later victories. In contrast, Æthelflæd, the 'Lady of the Mercians', captured the attention of later medieval writers with her military victories.[1] Clearly the assertiveness of a woman intrigued them, while her commitment to the Christian cause against the pagans encouraged these later writers to overcome any reservations they might have felt about such a dominant female. In addition, her exploits are the focus of attention in a chronicle written in Mercia. The so-called *Mercian Register* contains annals for the years 902–24 and later compilers of the *Anglo-Saxon Chronicle* added these to *Manuscripts B* and *C* in a block and attempted to dovetail them into *Manuscript D*. What the *Mercian Register* provides is at least something of a Mercian take on events and, though not extensive or detailed, does give additional information about her exploits. Despite this, her modern reputation is still a pale shadow of that of the far less successful, and much earlier, female ruler and warrior, Boudicca.

Æthelflæd's marriage to the Mercian *ealdorman*, Æthelred, had sealed the alliance between Wessex and Mercia, and had established a situation in which Alfred's family and direct line were in control of the two remaining Anglo-Saxon kingdoms. This partnership with the old Mercian elite meant that the two kingdoms cooperated in a mutually beneficial way, even if it was clear that Wessex was the senior partner. What is so striking is that the military campaigning did not just involve Edward and his brother-in-law Æthelred – a fairly predictable Anglo-Saxon 'band of brothers' – but also his sister. It is noteworthy, though, that both Æthelflæd and Æthelred avoided using a royal title, although the realities of their power were such that one manuscript of the Welsh *Chronicles of the Kings* described her as 'Queen Æthelflæd' and *Æthelweard's Chronicle* referred to 'King Æthelred of the Mercians'. This prudent policy of West Saxon restraint and Mercian diplomacy fostered cooperation instead of the conflict that would almost certainly have been prompted by a direct West Saxon annexation of the remnant of the Anglo-Saxon kingdom of Merica. In time this would change and, by the time of Æthelred's death in 910 or 911, Æthelflæd's death in 918 and Edward the

Elder's death in 924, Mercia had been brought under direct West Saxon rule. There is evidence, which we will shortly examine, to show that encroachments on Mercian territory had been occurring since soon after Edward came to power. However, until Æthelflæd's death the relationship between the two territories was marked by careful diplomacy and by military and political cooperation, resulting in an expansion of territory at the expense of the newly established Viking communities of eastern England.

There is a tendency to describe this as the 're-conquest of the *Danelaw*',[2] but, as ever, the situation was rather more complex.[3] To start with, areas of eastern Mercia and Essex (lost in the 870s) were recovered in a 're-conquest', but, once campaigns were extended into East Anglia and further north into Northumbria, it rapidly became an expansion of West Saxon royal power into areas where the authority of Wessex had never formerly run. Indeed, this had started as early as the death of Æthelflæd in 918; from this point onwards it was a king of Wessex who was exercising authority over what was rapidly becoming 'Greater Wessex'. The movement towards the unification of England under descendants of Alfred was underway and this was one of the great unintended consequences of the Viking Wars. How this was viewed in East Anglia is unknown – since the survival of any kind of documentary evidence is thin from this area – and there is a strong possibility that not every Anglo-Saxon viewed West Saxon victory as 'liberation'. There is evidence, as we shall see, of mixed reactions in Mercia to the dominance of Wessex and the situation in Northumbria would be more complex still, as here the West Saxon rulers were very much in alien territory.

Æthelwold, 'king of the pagans'

Edward's reign started with the kind of dynastic turbulence that Alfred had sought to avoid. And it soon involved the Vikings, who were ever ready to fish in the troubled waters of another kingdom's internal divisions, although in this case they were invited to do so.

Between 899 and 902/3 Edward faced a rebellion led by his elder cousin, Æthelwold, son of Alfred's brother, Æthelred I, who had died in 871. Seen from the perspective of Edward and the West Saxon written source, although they give only minimal publicity to this rebellion, this act of treason jeopardised Wessex in the face of an ever-present Viking threat and undermined Alfred's arrangement with his brothers that whichever one of them survived longest would inherit the Crown. From Æthelwold's point of view, he was simply asserting his rights in the face of a novel and questionable arrangement which had robbed him of the Crown. However this is presented, his rebellion opened up a new chapter in the Viking Wars.

Æthelwold seized Wimborne (Dorset) and Twynham (Hampshire, now Dorset), which were royal manors and in an area where Æthelwold's branch of the royal family seem to have been based (his father was buried at Wimborne and Dorset had been slow to rally to Alfred's cause in the crisis of 878). Æthelwold then based himself at Wimborne. This was almost certainly not in the vicinity of the minster church, located in the centre of the settlement at Wimborne, but in a site whose ditches are still discernible near the modern Kingston Lacey house (the name 'kingston', from Old English *cyninges tun*, indicates that it was a royal manorial centre). Here he was in the company of a nun whom 'he had taken without the king's permission and contrary to the bishop's orders'.[4] This salacious cocktail of treason, sex and dysfunctional family relationships would rapidly gain a Viking ingredient.

Edward brought his army to the prehistoric hillfort of Badbury Rings in order to confront his cousin. Here he was in an ideal position to threaten the rebels in their defended *cyninges tun* a short distance away. The scene seemed set for a bloody confrontation of the kind the *Chronicle* celebrated in the story of Cynewulf and Cyneheard who, in 757, had both died in a conflict over the throne which had also involved the siege of a defended residence. But it was not to be. Æthelwold slipped away by night, leaving the nun behind. It was at this point that West Saxon intra-family feuding drew in the Vikings, as Æthelwold went north 'to the Danish army in Northumbria, and they accepted him as king'.[5] This reference is found in *Manuscript C* of the *Chronicle* but not in *Manuscript A*, the oldest surviving version; clearly the matter was initially too contentious for inclusion. Just why Æthelwold was acceptable to the northern Vikings remains unexplained, but the likelihood is that they calculated that, under his overlordship, there was the possibility of undoing the work of Alfred and gaining control of the whole of Anglo-Saxon England. This came close to fulfilment. In 902 Æthelwold made his move and, accompanied by a Viking fleet, he landed in Essex. Once again *Manuscript A* seeks to minimise the scale of the threat by simply recording his arrival, but *Manuscript C* (which clearly had access to a less guarded tradition) adds: 'and submission was made to him in Essex'.[6] This was an explosive turn of events. Æthelwold had been accepted by a region that had been ruled by the West Saxons since the 820s. While it had been lost to Viking control by Alfred's treaty with Guthrum, Essex was part of the expanded Wessex of the ninth century. Reading between the lines it looks as if Æthelwold was creating an alliance of Danish Vikings and Anglo-Saxons in support of his bid for the throne. The *Annals of St Neots*, which had access to East Anglian traditions, describes him as 'king of the Danes' and 'king of the pagans', adding that he arrived with 'a great fleet'.[7] While later West Saxon sources sought to deny this rebellion any publicity, it was significant as it seemed set to alter the whole trajectory of English history.

Æthelwold next drew the Viking communities of East Anglia into his plans, persuading them to break their peace treaty with Wessex. In place of *Manuscript C*'s comment that he 'induced the army in East Anglia to break the peace', *Manuscript A* more negatively substitutes 'seduced' for 'induced'.[8] Like the Vikings of Northumbria, the Vikings of East Anglia clearly thought that Æthelwold's actions opened up dramatic opportunities. Together they invaded Mercia and then Wessex, probably in the autumn of 902 (903 in the *Chronicle* which began its year on 24 September).[9] They then drove into Wiltshire, via Cricklade, which was a *burh* and royal centre of Wessex and a crossing point over the River Thames. Similar to the seizures of Wimborne and Twynham, and like the Viking assault on Chippenham in 878, this followed a familiar pattern of targeting royal centres. This had the multiple attractions of seizing products collected at these centres as tax renders (*feorm*) to the king, denying resources to royal opponents, disrupting royal government, and dominating centres which 'mattered to contemporaries and signified the performance of royal power.'[10]

Having struck at Mercia and Wessex and thus rewarded his allies, Æthelwold turned back towards East Anglia. This appears to have been a strategic mistake as it avoided a decisive confrontation with Edward. As a result, Edward – who had taken time to gather his army – pursued them and 'harried all their land between the Dykes and the Ouse, all as far north as the fens'.[11] This retribution fell on Cambridgeshire and the Anglo-Danish (since it is reasonable to assume it was more than just a Viking force) communities who had given allegiance to Æthelwold. A battle ensued, which the *Mercian Register* names as the battle of the Holme, and a section of Edward's army was defeated; the Kentish contingent was slow to respond to Edward's order to withdraw and suffered heavy casualties when it was overtaken by Æthelwold's army. However, it proved a disaster for Æthelwold's Anglo-Danish adventure. The *Chronicle* records that the battle resulted in the deaths of King Eohric (we presume the Viking king of East Anglia), Æthelwold himself, and Brihtsige, son of the *ætheling* (prince) Beornoth, along with the *holds* (a Viking nobleman whose *wergild* — compensation value in the event of death or injury — was twice that of an Anglo-Saxon *thegn*) Ysopa and Oscetel. Besides providing an intriguing insight into how much the West Saxons knew about their enemies, this suggests that Æthelwold's rebellion was even more significant than it already appears, since Brihtsige and the *ætheling* Beornoth are otherwise unknown from West Saxon sources and were probably members of one of the royal family lines of Mercia. This may explain why Æthelwold's campaign began in Mercia before turning south into Wessex.

Had he won and then defeated Edward, Æthelwold would have succeeded in uniting the Viking forces of Northumbria and East Anglia with the Anglo-Saxons of Essex and parts of Mercia under his overlordship, before extending this rule to include Wessex/Mercia. This counter-factual, but very possible, scenario would have established a quite different trajectory for the Viking Wars and the ensuing history of England. England could have 'been united in a different manner, involving much less warfare than ultimately proved to be the case'.[12] It would have been completed a generation earlier than it was initially united under Athelstan and two generations before it was finally united following the death of Eric Bloodaxe, king of York, in 954. Instead, Æthelwold became no more than a curious footnote to the Viking Wars. At his death, in 902, *Manuscript A* once more downplays Æthelwold's significance by referring to his kingship over the mixed Viking forces as the one who 'enticed' the East Anglian King Eohric into the war.[13] Instead of Æthelwold, therefore, it would be Edward the Elder, king of Wessex, Æthelred, 'Lord of Mercia' and his wife, Æthelflæd, the 'Lady of the Mercians' who would lay the foundations for a later united kingdom of England.

The conquest of the *Danelaw*, 909–17

The relationship between Edward, and his allies in Mercia, with the Viking forces beyond their borders is unclear in the four years following the battle of the Holme and the death of Æthelwold. It must have been tense since the rebellion of Æthelwold had brought to the surface the ambitions of the rulers of the *Danelaw* concerning Wessex and western Mercia, and had revealed how vulnerable the remaining Anglo-Saxon areas were to attacks launched from the *Danelaw*. However, the crushing of Æthelwold and the death of Eohric of East Anglia must have given Viking leaders pause for thought.

In that year a treaty was agreed at Tiddingford, near Leighton Buzzard (Bedfordshire), between Edward and the Viking rulers of East Anglia and Northumbria. Tiddingford is on the later shire boundary of Bedfordshire and may have been on the boundary of the land controlled by the Viking army settled around Bedford. Why it was not negotiated on the line of the boundary agreed between Alfred and Guthrum is unclear. This treaty suggests that the years since 902 had been marked by border hostilities. The *Chronicle* suggests that in this treaty Edward again asserted himself against the threat from the east and north-east by claiming that the treaty was 'just as King Edward decreed'.[14] However, this may have been West Saxon 'spin'. *Manuscript E*, the *Laud* or *Peterborough Chronicle*, which was later copied in East Anglia with additional information of interest to an East Anglian readership, notes that Edward established the peace 'from necessity'.[15] The *Mercian Register* notes the restoration of Chester in 907 and this may be further proof of tension on the border which caused the Mercians to refurbish the decayed defences of the old Roman town against a Scandinavian threat, probably from the direction of the Wirral where place names suggest Viking settlement.[16] The *Chronicle* gives little information about Viking settlement in this area, but Irish and Welsh sources refer to a settlement of Dublin Vikings, under the leadership of Ingimundr, who had been expelled from Ireland in 902 following an Irish victory over the Dublin Norse. The significance of this event, though, is that it introduced a new ingredient into the volatile political situation in northern England. Until this period, most Viking activity in England had been enacted by Danes. The newcomers were Norwegians and their arrival led to conflict with Danish Vikings who had been established in the north for over a generation. Eventually, in 919, Danish rule in York would be replaced by that of Norse rulers. These Irish-Norse, or Hiberno-Norse, rulers would also bring under their overlordship the independent Anglo-Saxon state ruled by the hereditary *high reeves* of Bamburgh – what was left of the old Northumbrian sub-kingdom of Bernicia that had escaped Viking conquest. The tensions and conflicts amongst Danish and Norse groups would roll on through the tenth century and would lead to some surprising situations in which established Danish Viking communities in eastern England would look to Anglo-Saxon kings for protection from Norwegian newcomers.

In 909 the campaign against the *Danelaw* began in earnest, with West Saxon and Mercian forces invading Northumbria in a five-week campaign. The fact that the *Chronicle* talks about large numbers of cattle killed, alongside the human casualties inflicted, indicates that economic warfare was going on as well as conflict between armed warriors. This ravaging was typical of warfare between earlier Anglo-Saxon kingdoms and reminds us that once Viking raiders turned into settlers they were as vulnerable to attack as their victims had once been.

A Viking counterattack was defeated at Tettenhall (in the West Midlands) in 910. The *Chronicle* explains that this occurred while Edward was in Kent and the northern raiders thought they could take advantage of this. In the battle two Viking kings were killed – Eowils and Healfdene – along with two earls and five *holds*. In the twelfth-century *Chronicon ex Chronicis* (*Chronicle of other Chronicles*), John of Worcester (once designated as Florence of Worcester) added that the two kings were brothers of 'King Hinguar', by which he meant Ivar. Earlier, *Æthelweard's Chronicle* had cryptically noted that, at this battle, 'Ivar lost his sovereignty and hastened to the court of hell.'[17] Exactly who these 'kings' were and how they divided Northumbria between them is difficult to say, though evidence suggests that there was a loose confederation of Viking 'kings' operating north of the Humber who cooperated in alliance against Wessex/Mercia. Whatever the exact situation, this was a decisive battle which broke the power of the Viking kingdom (or kingdoms) of York. Following this battle, Edward and Æthelflæd began a piecemeal annexation of the *Danelaw* south of the Humber.

The campaign was waged by brother and sister because Æthelred, 'Lord of Mercia', was now dead. The main manuscripts of the *Chronicle* date this to 911, while *Manuscripts D* and *E*, along with *Æthelweard's Chronicle* date it as occurring in 910, and Æthelweard adds that he was buried at Gloucester. Variously described as 'Lord of the Mercians', or '*ealdorman* of the Mercians', he had clearly been a loyal ally to Edward, and that role was continued by his wife.

The Viking communities of the Five Boroughs (Derby, Leicester, Lincoln, Nottingham and Stamford) now faced concerted pressure. While the motivation for burying coins and treasure is open to interpretation, the fact that coin hoards from the period 895–965 are concentrated in eastern England suggests that communities under stress were protecting their movable wealth.[18] By adopting a forward policy that did not overreach itself, the combined West Saxon and Mercian forces were able to overwhelm the

Viking forces they targeted in each movement. The process was clear: consolidating threatened areas of Wessex and Mercia with *burhs*; then building new *burhs* on the frontier zone; and finally moving into Viking-held areas and building new *burhs* to hold down the newly annexed region. The final stage was marked by a policy of allowing Viking settlers to keep their land in return for submission to the new *status quo*. As a result, most chose to do so; especially given the fact that every attempt to dislodge a newly established *burh* failed. This process of conquest was assisted by Anglo-Saxon lords purchasing land within the *Danelaw*,[19] and there seems to have been official encouragement of this before campaigns of conquest, in order to increase Anglo-Saxon influence in border regions.[20]

Mercian and West Saxon policy was clearly coordinated in these slowly advancing lines of influence, although the Mercians also faced the need to strengthen their frontier with the Welsh at the same time. The *Chronicle* and the *Mercian Register* record the progress of this creeping encroachment on the *Danelaw*: in 912 Edward constructed a *burh* at Hertford (Hertfordshire) and one at Witham (Essex), while Æthelflæd did the same at the otherwise unknown *Scergeat* and Bridgenorth (Shropshire); in 913 Æthelflæd built *burhs* at Tamworth and Stafford (both in Staffordshire); in 914 Edward built a double-*burh* at Buckingham (Buckinghamshire), while Æthelflæd built *burhs* at Eddisbury (Cheshire) and Warwick (Warwickshire); in 915 Edward occupied Bedford and built a *burh* there and Æthelflæd built *burhs* at Chirbury (Shropshire), the unidentified *Weardbyrig* and Runcorn (Cheshire); in 916 Edward built a *burh* at Maldon (Essex); in 917 Edward had *burhs* built at Towcester (Northamptonshire) and the unidentified *Wigingamere*, and Æthelflæd captured Derby (Derbyshire), although 'four of her *thegns*, who were dear to her, were killed within the gates';[21] in 917 Edward captured Tempsford (Bedfordshire) and killed the Viking king of East Anglia, and later erected a stone wall at Towcester and repaired the defences at Colchester (Essex); in 918 Edward built the *burh* at Stamford (Lincolnshire) and captured Nottingham and oversaw the repair of its defences. These annals, which record the extending boundaries of Edward's kingdom, read almost like the boundary points of land charters and, like them, declare the extent of 'legitimate' control of territory.[22]

The amount of effort expended in the fortifying of these *burhs* is well illustrated from recent research at Bedford (Bedfordshire). This has led to the conclusion that it involved the building of a massive weir across the River Ouse (which can still be identified in the modern river), in order to divert flowing water down the defensive ditch and around the southern part of Bedford, later known as the King's Ditch.[23] When this kind of effort is added to the number of *burhs* constructed, the achievement is astonishing.

After 917, with the Viking king of East Anglia dead, organised resistance to Edward collapsed. In a chain reaction, the isolated Viking armies still holding out in the *Danelaw* surrendered, as the defeats of other groups left them dangerously exposed. It was a rapid culmination of what had, until this point, been a slow advance. West Saxon power was now extended into East Anglia and the Viking communities of the East Midlands. The conquest of the *Danelaw* had taken just seven years. For a brief moment it looked as if Northumbria, too, would fall and a united kingdom of England be created before the end of the second decade of the tenth century. In 918 the Northumbrians (lacking strong leadership since the battle of Tettenhall) submitted to Æthelflæd but she died before this achievement could be consolidated. While Edward was incorporating Mercia into Wessex, the power vacuum north of the Humber was filled by a Norse Viking chief from Ireland named Ragnald. It would be ten years before Edward's son, Athelstan, drove the Irish-Norse Vikings from York and established himself as king over all England; a feat which had so narrowly eluded his father.

Following Æthelflæd's death, Edward moved to annex Mercia. This was not such a revolutionary step and needs to be seen in the context of the fact that Edward's title of 'King of the Anglo-Saxons' used on his charters, his minting of coins in Mercia and his taking of Oxford and London on the death of Æthelred, always presupposed he was the ruler of a composite kingdom that Alfred had created. Similarly, prior to 906, he had annexed Bath into Wessex.[24] He then went on, in 918 and 919, to consolidate this position:[25] first he occupied Tamworth, the ancient centre of Mercian royal power and the place where Æthelflæd had died; next, the Mercians submitted to him; and finally he put an end to any possibility of Mercia developing an independent political existence by arresting Æthelflæd's daughter in 919. The *Mercian Register* tersely records an event that is unmentioned in the main manuscripts of the *Chronicle* (the exception being *Manuscript D*, which contains northern material): 'The daughter of Æthelred, lord of the Mercians, was deprived of all authority in Mercia and taken into Wessex, three weeks before Christmas. She was called Ælfwyn.'[26] She was probably held in the nunnery of Shaftesbury (Dorset), or Wilton (Wiltshire). Mercian independence may have ended, but its vital contribution to the development of the English nation should not be underestimated. As Simon

Keynes has put it: 'Mercians had vital parts to play in Alfred's inspirational "Kingdom of the Anglo-Saxons", Æthelstan's visionary "Kingdom of the English", and in Edgar's realisation of the same.'[27]

The overlordship of Edward the Elder, 920–24

In 920 the Northumbrians, the Scots and the Strathclyde Welsh submitted to Edward. Earlier, in 918, the Welsh kings had also submitted to him. Therefore, in a decade he had conquered the *Danelaw*, annexed Mercia and been accepted as overlord by all the other kings and rulers in Britain. The submission of 920 has been interpreted in one of three ways: a genuine submission implying full respect for Edward's territory and agreement to ally with him against his enemies; an anti-Irish-Norse coalition of fairly equal rulers; or an alliance between equals recognising spheres of influence (particularly with regard to Ragnald of Northumbria and Constantine of Scots). If this was a 'real' submission then there is none of the supporting evidence that exists for the submission to Athelstan in 927, and it is possible that the *Chronicle* over-emphasises Edward's domination of his neighbours.[28] The pointed avoidance, in all versions of the *Chronicle* except the northern *Manuscript D*, of calling Ragnald 'king' ignored the fact that this was his title and that Edward was not strong enough to conquer Northumbria.

In 924 King Edward died at Farndon (Cheshire), in Mercia. The location of his death, far from his heartland in Wessex, may suggest he was present there to keep a reluctant Mercia in order.

What had been achieved by the time of Edward the Elder's death?

By the time that Edward the Elder died in 924, the next phase in the Viking Wars that he had overseen had changed the character of England yet again. Mercia was now firmly under West Saxon control and, while on at least two later occasions it looked as if Wessex and Mercia might again be governed separately (facing division between Edward's sons Ælfweard and Athelstan in 924, and again in 957–59, when the kingdom was briefly divided between Eadwig and Edgar), there would never again be a Mercian state ruled by Mercian royalty. Those days were over and, at the points of stress in the future, the competition would be between rival members of the West Saxon royal family; and these times of stress passed without a lasting division of the newly unified kingdom.

In the southern *Danelaw* (East Anglia and the East Midlands), the new Viking elites had come to terms with Edward. While some Viking leaders emigrated (such as *Jarl* Thurcytel of Bedford), most accepted Edward's rule in return for his acceptance of their land ownership and customs. Since no attempt was made to 'ethnically cleanse' the area of its Danish settlers, or to abolish their systems of land ownership and governance, there was no reason to leave. This seems to have been formally recognised in Edward's second law code, where the phrase 'peace writings' presumably refers to specific treaties made with *Danelaw* landholders,[29] thus creating an Anglo-Danish landowning class whose rights were protected by the West Saxon kings.

In such a context, trade and commerce could flourish and, by the mid-tenth century, the area of the southern *Danelaw* was one of the most prosperous in the country. This was a situation that would last into the eleventh century and beyond. Town life and a coin-based economy developed at a faster pace than in other areas of England; population increased and colonisation of the Fens expanded; small landowners enjoyed a considerable degree of freedom and prosperity in a region where the landholding power of the Church had been greatly reduced by the first phase of the Viking Wars in the ninth century and by the Danish colonisation which followed.[30] New units of taxation (*geld*) and terms for local government (*carucates* and *wapentakes*) replaced Anglo-Saxon arrangements in *hides* and *hundreds*. And in their uneven occurrence across the East Midlands and East Anglia, the patchwork of these terms represents 'a bundle of disconnected regional communities' with mixed Anglo-Saxon and Danish origins whose one unifying factor was its acceptance of Danish law;[31] and now, through the efforts of Edward the Elder, Æthelred and Æthelflæd, the overlordship of the West Saxon Crown. Such communities might experience mixed emotions when later Scandinavian rulers once again intervened in England. On the one hand there were common ethnic ties which could be appealed to by these newcomers, but on the other hand the newly established Anglo-Danish elites had a lot to lose if the *status quo* was seriously threatened.

A lot had changed since the death of Alfred in 899. Mutual respect and a growing unity within the conquered *Danelaw* territories had been surprising outcomes of the campaigns fought by Edward and Æthelflæd. In addition, the decisive – though ruthless – action of Edward in 919 had finally united

Mercia with Wessex. Alongside the recapture of Essex, the expansion into East Anglia and the conquest of the southern *Danelaw*, the 'Kingdom of the Anglo-Saxons' (balancing the sensitivities of both Mercia and Wessex) that Edward had inherited from Alfred the Great was on its way to becoming the 'Kingdom of England'. On Edward's death its northern border lay on the River Humber, and in 918 it had come close to advancing beyond that, but circumstances had frustrated Edward's ambitions. This would change in the next phase of the Viking War and a 'Kingdom of England', uniting all of England, would finally emerge. But before that happened, there would be crises that seemed set to undo all that Edward had achieved, and a war that brought all the peoples of Britain into conflict.

10

EMPEROR OF BRITAIN

Between 924 and 939 the achievements of Edward the Elder in his campaigns against the Viking communities were surpassed by those of his son, Athelstan. His reign would see a West Saxon king annex Viking Northumbria, invade Scotland and finally defeat a huge alliance of Viking forces, Scots and Welsh. During his reign the new royal title of *rex to (tius) brit (anniae)* (King of all Britain) appeared on his coinage, along with the first representation of any English monarch wearing a crown. Athelstan made himself king of a united England and was, in effect, Emperor of Britain as he had become overlord of the whole island. With good reason a recent biography of the king was entitled '*Æthelstan: The First King of England*'.[1] Athelstan achieved a political domination of the island of Britain that had not been seen since the end of the Roman Empire. His kingdom of England was one that included Anglo-Saxons, Danish and Irish-Norse Vikings, and whose authority overshadowed the neighbouring kingdoms of the Scots and the Welsh. It was an achievement forged in wars that were fought on a scale dwarfing those of previous phases in the Viking Wars. But it was a reign that started in circumstances which suggested that Edward the Elder's 'Kingdom of the Anglo-Saxons' was actually about to fragment. And it was a reign that, in modern consciousness, is not accorded the fame it deserves.[2]

The succession of Athelstan

Athelstan was raised in Mercia, in the household of his aunt, Æthelflæd, the 'Lady of the Mercians', and her husband Æthelred, 'Lord of Mercia'. Although he was the eldest son of Edward the Elder, his succession was threatened by a new son born to Edward's latest wife. A later account of Athelstan's boyhood, the *Gesta regum Anglorum* (*Deeds of the Kings of the English*), written in the early twelfth century by William of Malmesbury (who claimed he had access to a near-contemporary poem detailing the reign of Athelstan), asserted that Edward the Elder had explicitly named Athelstan as his heir and that his grandfather, Alfred, had recognised his claim to the throne with a gift of a scarlet cloak, a jewelled belt and a sword with a gold scabbard. Despite these later claims it seems that, in reality, by the 920s, Athelstan's position as inheritor of a joint West-Saxon/Mercian throne was in jeopardy. By this time Athelstan's greatest rival was his half-brother Ælfweard, although Athelstan had the strongest claim as the eldest son.

As a result of this, when Edward died in 924, his newly unified kingdom looked set to break apart into its constituent units of Wessex and Mercia. How far this was what Edward intended we do not know; he may have actually intended that Ælfweard would inherit the entire kingdom; or, alternatively, he may have intended to partition his realm, and this is certainly what occurred. However, the division that followed may have been as much due to where the two *æthelings* found themselves in the summer of 924, rather than a prearranged plan.[3] *Manuscript A* of the *Anglo-Saxon Chronicle* simply records the death of Edward and the accession of Athelstan. This annal was later added to *Manuscripts E* and *F* likewise. However, the *Mercian Register* – a document that gives a peculiarly Mercian view of events – gives a much fuller account. Given the fact that Athelstan may, by this time, have been viewed as a Mercian *ætheling*, this is not surprising. In this account, we learn that Athelstan was initially chosen as king by the Mercians, and he only succeeded to Wessex because his half-brother, Ælfweard, died 'very soon after' Edward the Elder.[4] Another manuscript of the *Chronicle* (*Manuscript D*, also known as the *Worcester Chronicle* and probably constructed from earlier sources in around 1060) had access to a more detailed tradition and states that Ælfweard only outlived his father by sixteen days. Had he lived, it seems likely that he would have ruled Wessex; and Mercia would have been taken by Athelstan. As it happened, Ælfweard was buried alongside his father in Winchester. The fact that Athelstan was not crowned until September 925 suggests that he may have had to overcome some opposition to his taking control of Wessex in addition to Mercia. Perhaps he was seen as something of an outsider to the Winchester-based elite and this may be why he chose to be crowned at Kingston (Surrey) on the River Thames. Like his father, who was also crowned there, its location on the river boundary between Wessex and Mercia drew the two kingdoms together. Today, the so-called 'Coronation Stone', an ancient and irregularly shaped stone block, still stands next to the Guildhall in Kingston upon Thames and claims to be the very stone used in the coronations of Edward the Elder, Athelstan and five later Anglo-Saxon kings (Edmund, Eadred, Eadwig, Edward 'King and Martyr' and Æthelred II).

The *Chronicle* says nothing about resistance to Athelstan's succession, but William of Malmesbury asserted that Athelstan was opposed by a group who claimed that the new king was born of a concubine and lacked legitimacy. William went on to claim that this clique had attempted to seize Athelstan at Winchester and blind him, thus rendering him unfit for kingship. Whatever the truth of this report, the community of monks at Malmesbury in William's day claimed that some of their estates had been granted to them by Athelstan from the lands forfeited by those who had taken part in this failed attempt to stop his succession to the throne.

Relations with the Viking kingdom of York

What is clear is that Athelstan moved swiftly to establish amicable relations with the Viking kingdom of York. In 926 he met with King Sihtric of York, at Tamworth (Staffordshire), the old royal centre of the Mercian kings. Here Athelstan gave his sister in marriage to Sihtric, who, according to the early thirteenth-century account written by Roger of Wendover, became a Christian. King Sihtric – also known as Sihtric *Cáech* (squint-eyed) – had ruled in the Irish-Norse kingdom of Dublin before extending his authority to York in 920 or 921, following the death of its previous Irish-Norse king, Ragnald. Back in Dublin, Sihtric's kinsman (possibly his brother) Guthfrith became king.

With a Viking king of York now the brother-in-law of the Anglo-Saxon king, the possibility of conflict with the northern Vikings was greatly reduced. However, later sources suggest that the marriage did not go well. Roger of Wendover, in his *Flores Historiarum* (*Flowers of the Histories*), written in St Albans and drawing on some northern records otherwise lost, claimed that Sihtric soon abandoned both his wife and Christianity and reverted to paganism.

Sihtric died the following year and Athelstan moved swiftly to annex Northumbria. Irish sources indicate that he was not the only one keen to move into the power vacuum caused by Sihtric's death. According to the Irish annals, Guthfrith, the Viking king of Dublin, led a fleet in a bid to capture the kingdom of York. Whether he succeeded, only to be ousted by Athelstan, is unclear. The Anglo-Saxon sources simply record Athelstan's succession to the kingdom of Northumbria, and if Guthfrith did briefly occupy the throne there he was not in possession of it long enough to mint any coins.[5] As we shall see, when he does make an appearance in the annals of the *Chronicle*, it is as an unsuccessful rival who attempts to unseat Athelstan as ruler of York.

No previous West Saxon king had ruled in York and the extension of his border northwards was truly astonishing. Just as his father had brought the Danish settlers of the East Midlands under his authority, now Athelstan had done the same for the Danes of Northumbria and the new Irish-Norse communities who had also settled there. The *Chronicle* records Athelstan's annexation as if nothing particularly out of the ordinary had happened. It simply uses the usual formulation that he: '*feng to Norðhymbra rice*' (succeeded to the kingdom of the Northumbrians).[6] However, what the Anglo-Saxon communities of Northumbria felt about this is open to question. From later events (see Chapter 11) there is every reason to believe that they did not all regard his arrival with enthusiasm. In place of a local king ruling in York (whatever his ethnic origins), they now had a ruler whose political centre of gravity lay far to the south. This hardly placed his new Northumbrian subjects at the centre of political decision-making and we may guess that the local elites (Anglo-Danish or Irish-Norse) viewed the turn of events with less than enthusiasm. Study of the locations from which Athelstan issued charters reveal that he mostly remained in the south and, in particular, within Wessex.[7] Clearly, with the exception of major campaigns in the north, he made only a limited attempt to act like anything other than a southern king who had now subjugated the northern regions. Furthermore, the continuity of settlement locations demonstrated by archaeology and the continued existence of Anglo-Saxon elites in Viking-held areas, as demonstrated by documentary evidence, reveals that many Vikings established their new territories within existing systems of landholdings, trading arrangements and alliances. In such situations, Anglo-Saxons who cooperated could prosper under the new regime; the last thing they would want was the arrival of an alien ruler with his own network of patronage and allies to reward.

William of Malmesbury added the detail that Athelstan levelled the walls of York, which suggests that he anticipated possible future trouble in the region and did not intend to leave behind him a defensible base for someone who would later contest his rule. William says that Athelstan also defeated a rebel with the Anglo-Saxon name of Ealdwulf. This may well have been a member of the family which acted as *high reeves* of Bamburgh (a region north of the River Tyne and beyond direct Viking control) and who ruled there as virtual kings; a privilege they may well have felt was as much threatened by a new ruler from the south as it had once been by Viking warriors based in York. The politics of the north were, therefore, anything but simple.

The impact of Athelstan's annexation of Northumbria

What is certainly clear is that the annexation of Northumbria radically altered the political *status quo* of Britain and shifted the balance of power considerably. *Manuscript D* goes on to record that the event was rapidly followed by Hywel, king of the West Welsh (the Cornish); Constantine, king of the Scots; Owain, the Welsh king of Gwent and Ealdred of Bamburgh (the Anglo-Saxon *high reeve*), meeting with Athelstan at Eamont (Cumbria). There, 'they established peace with pledge and oaths ... and renounced all idolatry and afterwards departed in peace'.[8] William of Malmesbury appears to have had access to a tradition which adds that Owain, king of the British (Welsh) kingdom of Strathclyde, was also present at this meeting. According to the mid-tenth-century *History of St Cuthbert* (which contained both legendary material and some authentic information), Ealdred of Bamburgh had earlier been driven into exile by the Irish-Norse leader, Ragnald. Fleeing into exile in Scotland, he had returned alongside Constantine, king of the Scots, only to be defeated by Ragnald in battle at Corbridge. While both Constantine and Ealdred survived the battle, it might explain why they were ready to accept Athelstan's overlordship in 927. As well as being the new power in the north, Athelstan may have seemed a more amenable overlord than an Irish-Norse king based in York. After all, Athelstan would eventually return to his home territory south of the River Humber and this may have offered scope for Constantine and Ealdred to increase their influence once more. As we have seen, William of Malmesbury enigmatically claimed that the annexation of Northumbria was accompanied by the expulsion of an otherwise unknown Ealdwulf. This Anglo-Saxon had a name reminiscent of 'Eald-red' of Bamburgh and, as we have seen, he may well have been a relative and member of the Bamburgh elite.

Athelstan's powerful position brought him some surprising allies. Later Scandinavian sources tell us that, as a young man, Hákon the Good, son of King Harald Finehair of Norway, was sent to the English court, where Athelstan acted as his foster-father. In these accounts, Hákon is described as '*Aðalsteinsfóstri*' (fostered by Athelstan). At the English court, Hákon became a Christian and later ruled as the first Christian king of Norway. When, in the mid-930s, Hákon launched a bid to claim his throne from his half-brother, Eric Bloodaxe, these same sources claim that he was offered military assistance by Athelstan. There is a striking irony in this image of the king of England intervening in the troubled dynastic politics of Scandinavia; Alfred the Great would, no doubt, have appreciated the turn of events that had led to such a reversal of roles.

Following the annexation of Northumbria and the submission of the other rulers in Britain, Athelstan's new authority was reflected in the titles used on his coins and in his charters. A new style of coin – the so-called *Circumscription Cross* type – carried, in variously abbreviated forms such as *rex to brit*,[9] his new title of *rex totius Britanniae* (king of all Britain). The same grandiose titles also appear in his charters; for example, when he granted land at Bremhill (Wiltshire) to the monastery at Malmesbury, the charter declares: 'I, Æthelstan, king of the English, through the favour of the Almighty raised to the throne of the kingdom of the whole of Britain, have bestowed as a perpetual right a certain parcel of land on the venerable community of Malmesbury.'[10] The later coinage, known to numismatists as the *Bust Crowned* type, shows Athelstan regally crowned instead of wearing the diadem usually worn on previous royal coin portraits. A number of these coins also carry the *rex to brit* title.[11] In contradiction of the view sometimes expressed that Athelstan's grand titles were not as closely adhered to in Mercia as in other areas of his realm, it should be noted that the same title also appears on a series of coins issued in the Mercian centres of Chester, Hereford, Shrewsbury, Stafford and Warwick.[12] These innovations in royal titles and royal portraiture reveal how important Athelstan's seizure of Northumbria and his control of York had been. The Viking kingdom was now firmly in the grasp of a West Saxon king and the previous humiliations suffered by his grandfather in the earlier Viking Wars had been completely reversed.

In this period, Athelstan also actively intervened abroad in order to secure key areas for allies and to deny these areas to Viking raiders. In 936 he gave military assistance to his godson, Alan 'Twisted beard' of Brittany, who that year returned to Brittany from exile at Athelstan's court. His exile had been caused by the Viking attacks that had forced his father – Mathuedoi, the count of Poher and the son-in-law of Alan the Great, duke of the Bretons – to seek refuge in England with Athelstan. Alan had participated in a failed attempt in 931 to regain the duchy from its Viking occupiers. However, within a year of the start of the second attempt, Alan had reconquered most of Brittany and had driven the Viking invaders back to the valley of the Loire. Clearly, Athelstan's support had been significant and revealed a strong strategic motivation, as well as a desire to assist a client who was also his godson. With a grateful ally ruling Brittany, the Vikings had lost a base on the eastern shore of the English Channel from which they could menace England. For the same reason Athelstan supported the Norwegian prince, Hákon, who had been fostered at his court, when he made his successful bid for the Norwegian throne in 934. As with Alan in Brittany, a friendly ruler on the throne of Norway denied that country as a base to hostile Viking bands. These foreign interventions indicate the extended reach that Athelstan developed following the submission at Eamont.

Challenges to Athelstan's rule

However, Athelstan's position, although impressive, was not accepted by everyone since, soon after the acknowledgement of his overlordship in Britain, the Irish-Norse king Guthfrith left Dublin and made a bid for control of York, just as Sihtric had successfully done in 920. But Guthfrith failed and was driven out by Athelstan. William of Malmesbury later claimed that this Viking warrior eventually made his peace with Athelstan, was richly rewarded for this and so returned to Dublin, where he died in 934 and was succeeded by his son, Olaf Guthfrithson. This would not be the end of attempts by the Irish-Norse kings of Dublin to unite their kingdom with that of York, but for now the strategy had been thwarted.

It looks as if the Viking leader, Guthfrith, was not the only person challenging Athelstan at this critical time. *Manuscript E* is alone in recording, laconically, for 933: 'In this year the *ætheling* Edwin was drowned at sea.'[13] Edwin was Athelstan's half-brother and there was apparently more to this tragedy than meets the eye. William of Malmesbury records a tradition – apparently based on early twelfth-century popular songs – that Edwin was accused of plotting against Athelstan, was exiled in an old boat without oars and with only one companion, and drowned at sea in a storm. Whatever the truth behind this unlikely folk tale, a conspiracy against Athelstan may well have existed amongst the Winchester establishment, who were not reconciled to his rule, at a time when he was facing a threat from Irish-Norse Vikings in alliance with others of the neighbouring kingdoms who felt threatened by him.

During the mid-930s this discontent over Athelstan's domination of Britain grew amongst the neighbouring kingdoms who had been forced to recognise his authority at Eamont in 927. In 934 Athelstan invaded Scotland, accompanied (according to John of Worcester) by a great fleet and many mounted men, causing considerable damage. On his way north, according to the mid-tenth-century chronicler Simeon of Durham in his *History of the Church of Durham*, Athelstan visited the tomb of St Cuthbert at Chester-le-Street (Durham). Here the king asked for St Cuthbert's assistance from heaven and the king gave rich gifts to honour the saint and to support the community of monks. Athelstan's gifts included two beautifully decorated manuscripts; one of these (now held in Corpus Christi College Library, Cambridge) contains the earliest surviving portrait of an English ruler. The picture shows Athelstan, with his crown, bowing his head and presenting a copy of Bede's *Lives of St Cuthbert* to the saint. St Cuthbert stands at the doorway of his church, raising his right hand in blessing. To a genuinely devout king such as Athelstan, such saintly support was crucial as he embarked on a major military campaign. Later medieval accounts claim that he also honoured the shrines of John of Beverley (died 721) and St Wilfrid at Ripon (both in Yorkshire). Confident of heavenly support, Athelstan then struck north. John of Worcester added the information that the attack was so severe that Constantine was forced to give up a son as a hostage to Athelstan. The reason for the attack on Scotland is unknown, but it seems that Athelstan had gained intelligence of an alliance building against him because, in 937, a storm broke over his newly minted empire. An enormous army of the Scots, the Irish-Norse from Dublin under Olaf Guthfrithson, and the Strathclyde Welsh invaded England.

This invasion was later referred to by Æthelweard as 'the great war' and its climactic battle led to the deaths of five kings and seven earls among Athelstan's enemies. The Irish *Annals of Ulster* called it 'a great, lamentable and horrible battle'.[14] This battle should be as famous in British history as Hastings or Bosworth, since its outcome had an immense impact on the history of the island. Yet, ironically, it is not well known outside of students of the period and even the location of the battle site of *Brunanburh* is uncertain. Æthelweard called it '*Brunandun*' and Simeon of Durham called it '*Wendun*' or '*Weondune*'. While many modern historians have located it on the Wirral, John of Worcester stated that the Irish-Norse component landed in the mouth of the River Humber, which throws the possibilities wide open. All of this makes a geographical fix difficult, but it clearly occurred in the north and probably in the north-west; the Wirral is a distinct possibility and a recent study has again suggested the vicinity of Bromborough (Cheshire) which has been a frequently named candidate.[15] What is beyond question, however, is the tremendous victory that Athelstan achieved there.[16]

The writers of four manuscripts of the *Chronicle* recorded it in alliterative verse. The poem celebrates the heroic exploits not only of Athelstan but also of his younger brother Edmund, who fought alongside him. In the words of the poet they 'won by the sword's edge undying glory in battle ... for it was natural for men of their lineage to defend their land, their treasure and their homes, in frequent battle against every foe.'[17] How far the invaders had penetrated inland from their ships is a little unclear. The poem insists that: 'The whole day long the West Saxons with mounted companies kept in pursuit of the hostile peoples ...'[18] This gives the impression of an extended rout since the poem later suggests this drove the invaders to their ships and some escaped to their vessels, including 'the prince of the Norsemen', Olaf Guthfrithson. Those Vikings who survived fled back to 'Dublin across the deep water, back to Ireland humbled at heart.'[19] The Scots, too, fled for their lives.

Behind lay the carnage of battle and the dead included the son of Constantine, king of the Scots. As the victorious West Saxons and Mercians, both specifically mentioned by name, left the battlefield: 'They left behind them the dusky-coated one, the black raven with its horned beak, to share the corpses, and the dun-coated, white-tailed eagle, the greedy war-hawk, to enjoy the carrion, and that grey beast, the wolf of the forest.'[20] The poet sought to set the victory in a wider context and insisted that it was the greatest slaughter 'since the Angles and Saxons came hither from the east, invading Britain ... and won a country.'[21]

A Viking take on the battle is found in the thirteenth-century Icelandic work known as the *Saga of Egil Skalla-Grímsson* (or *Egil's Saga*).[22] In this account, a battle called *Vinheiðr* is generally considered to be a reference to the battle of *Brunanburh*. However, it is difficult to be sure what credence to give to this account. While it may contain genuine tenth-century traditions, it is fundamentally a literary work that tells us more about how the past was remembered, understood and elaborated in an Icelandic society that was far removed from the events described and which was greatly motivated by Viking nostalgia. Nevertheless, it may give a glimpse into some aspects of the context of the battle, even if a confused and manipulated one. In the saga, Athelstan is opposed by 'Olaf, king of the Scots', which is clearly a reference to Olaf Guthfrithson and confuses the king of Dublin with that of the Scots. It also mentions that Athelstan's hold on Northumbria is threatened by Danes, Norwegians and Scots, all of whom considered they had a legitimate claim to the region, and this certainly seems to be an echo of tenth-century realities. The saga goes as far as claiming that Olaf had secured control of much of Northumbria before being challenged by Athelstan, who takes some time to marshal his forces and bring them north. In the battle, the Viking hero, Egil, fights alongside Athelstan's army and loses a brother, Thorolf, in the conflict. This too, though short on details of the personalities involved, may reflect a complex reality in which Scandinavians and Anglo-Saxons fought on both sides in this great battle. The battle itself, as described in *Egil's Saga*, lacks the gritty brutality of the description in the *Chronicle's* poem. It feels more ritualistic with the mutually agreed site on a moor marked out by hazel stakes; Egil's wily strategy caused Athelstan's army to camp in such a position so as to appear larger than it really was; and the treacherous deployment of Olaf's army outside the agreed battle site led to the death of Egil's brother. This seems more in keeping with the motifs of folk tales than an actual account of the battle.

The Icelandic compiler of *Egil's Saga* was not the only later writer to offer an imaginative account of the battle. William of Malmesbury, writing in the early twelfth century, recorded an unlikely account of the Viking 'Anlaf' (Olaf), disguised as a harpist and spying on the Anglo-Saxon camp. This mirrors William's equally unlikely story about King Alfred similarly spying in the camp of Guthrum the Dane in 878. Despite shifting the camp, Athelstan still falls victim to a night attack by his enemies. In a similar way to the account in *Egil's Saga* we see the use of the literary motif of the treacherous enemy who is thwarted; in this case by divine intervention.

Athelstan cries out to God and to St Aldhelm to assist him and finds a miraculous sword appears in his scabbard. With this he inflicts a crushing defeat on Anlaf (Olaf) and his allies, the Scots. Clearly, William was determined to promote the cause of the saint most closely associated with his monastic house of Malmesbury.[23] In a second account of the battle, within the same overall narrative relating to Athelstan, William puts the Anglo-Saxon army at an improbable 100,000 men. Clearly, William had no more accurate a source concerning the battle than did the Icelandic writer of *Egil's Saga*.

Nevertheless, these later and fanciful accounts give us an impression of the shock waves of the battle. Its ripples ran far and wide, finding its way into later sources, both historical and literary, though there were few contemporary detailed accounts of the battle. Closer to the events, tenth-century chroniclers did record the battle's significance. From Ireland, the *Annals of Ulster* referred to the huge number of casualties and the *Annals of Clonmacnoise* reported how the 'Saxons' faced both the Danes of Dublin and the Danes of England, who were united in a hostile alliance. In Scotland the *Chronicle of the Kings of Alba* and the *Pictish Chronicle* both recorded that this battle had seen the son of the king of Scots killed. The Welsh *Annales Cambriae* (*Annals of Wales*) referred to the '*Bellum Brune*' (Battle of *Brune*), and the *Armes Prydein* (*Prophecy of Britain*) may even give us a preview of the battle, though not all modern experts agree on its date of composition, with its account of a great alliance of confident Welsh, Scots, Irish and Irish-Norse against the *meirion mechteyrn* (stewards of the great king) of *Iwys* (Wessex); and Æthelweard dated the subservience of the Scots to the English as a product of their defeat at the battle.

Clearly, the significance of Athelstan's victory at *Brunanburh* was immense. With his combined enemies crushed, no other king dared fight against him. But had he lost, then the achievements of his reign, and also those of Edward the Elder, would have been undermined. With a victorious Irish-Norse king once more triumphant in York, then Mercia and the whole of the *Danelaw* would have been open to invasion from the north. And how might the Danish Viking communities of the *Danelaw* have reacted to this? The Irish *Annals of Clonmacnoise* claim that the invaders were supported by English Danes. Whether these were from communities settled in Northumbria or in the *Danelaw* is not known, but it seems that the invasion had the potential to upturn the entire arrangement that had been carefully constructed since Alfred's death in 899. Furthermore, William of Malmesbury quoted a source which suggested that the Northumbrians sided with the 'other side' at *Brunanburh*. It seems that the 'kingdom of England' constructed by Athelstan lay in the balance and, had it collapsed, it could even have caused the downfall of the 'kingdom of the Anglo-Saxons' (Mercia and Wessex) that had been constructed by Edward the Elder on the foundations laid by Alfred. *Brunanburh* was therefore a pivotal point in the Viking Wars.

Two years later, in 939, Athelstan died in Gloucester and, according to John of Worcester, was buried at Malmesbury. A border monastery, set between Wessex and Mercia, Malmesbury had long been in contention between the two kingdoms.[24] It was rather fitting that a king who had not quite fitted in with the Winchester establishment of Wessex was buried at such a location. According to William of Malmesbury, the monastery had earlier benefitted from the patronage of the king through gifts of land and holy relics.

Athelstan had not married and was succeeded by his brother, Edmund; the same companion who had triumphed with him at *Brunanburh*. Within a few months of Athelstan's death, new Viking adventurers were threatening the kingdom that he has passed to his brother. And this was a challenge to Athelstan's achievement which was all the more potent due to the active cooperation of Northumbrians with the Irish-Norse of Dublin. The Viking kingdom of York was about to be reconstructed and with it came a direct challenge to the West Saxon kings who aspired to be rulers of all England.

THE ROAD TO A UNITED KINGDOM OF ENGLAND

The kingdom of England that Athelstan had created proved remarkably fragile. Within a matter of months the Northumbrians had chosen Olaf Guthfrithson, from Ireland, as their king. The return of the Viking Irish-Norse to the north undid all that Athelstan had achieved there, and the fact that the *Anglo-Saxon Chronicle* draws no distinction amongst those who chose him suggests that this decision involved both Anglo-Saxon and Scandinavian Northumbrians. The situation was clear: the feeling in the north was that it was better to have a local king ruling from York than an intruder from the south.

The revival of the kingdom of York

Olaf Guthfrithson's return threatened to undo more than just the annexation of Northumbria; it threatened to unravel the whole enterprise that had begun under Edward the Elder. The *Chronicle* entry for 942 contains a poem, written in alliterative verse, which extols the virtue of Edmund (Athelstan's brother) for regaining control of the *Danelaw*. This is evidence that, prior to the recovery of the *Danelaw*, Olaf Guthfrithson had rolled back the frontier to retake the Five Boroughs. *Manuscript D*, under the annal for the year 943 which actually looks back to events that had unfolded since 940, refers to Viking forces from York storming the old

Mercian centre of Tamworth. Simeon of Durham, in his twelfth-century work *Historia Regum* (*History of the Kings*), explicitly states that the attack on Tamworth occurred under Olaf Guthfrithson, and the fact that he drew on northern sources to construct his work makes his account rather more persuasive than the more imprecise and chronologically muddled entry in *Manuscript D* of the *Chronicle*.

What is certainly clear is that this campaign south of the River Humber occurred with the active support of Wulfstan, the Anglo-Saxon arch-bishop of York, for the *Chronicle* records that both Olaf (Guthfrithson) and Wulfstan were both besieged at Leicester when Edmund led the southern fightback. This shows that the Northumbrian ecclesiastic had been an active supporter of the return of the Irish-Norse. Their paganism appears to have been less significant than the re-establishment of a Northumbrian polity based in York. However, the willingness of Church leaders to come to terms with the new Viking rulers was nothing new. As early as the late ninth cen-tury, according to the anonymous *History of St Cuthbert* (which was itself written in the mid-tenth century), the abbot of Carlisle was responsible for the selection and public proclamation of a new Viking king.[1] This event, which appears to have occurred in the 880s, is in the great tradition of saints' lives, with St Cuthbert appearing in a vision to the abbot, and it claims that the whole territory between the rivers Tyne and Wear were placed under the special authority of St Cuthbert. This seems to suggest that a pagan royal inauguration rite was made legitimate by the presence of the relics of St Cuthbert. This legendary account gives an intriguing insight into the relationship between the Church and the Viking army, which is a long way removed from the image of the latter as despoilers of churches and suggests that some political interaction occurred between the native Northumbrian community and Scandinavian newcomers.[2]

Returning to Wulfstan's involvement with Olaf Guthfrithson, Simeon of Durham puts Wulfstan's role in a more positive light by giving him the role of mediator between the protagonists, along with Oda, archbishop of Canterbury. Interestingly, Oda was the son of a pagan Viking settler who had converted to Christianity and his life reveals the astonishing speed at which many Scandinavians assimilated.[3] As a result of this mediation, Watling Street was once again a boundary between an Anglo-Saxon and a Viking kingdom, albeit briefly.[4] Soon after, though, the eastern *Danelaw* had been prised from the control of the king of York by Edmund's fightback and this boundary had been erased once more.

With regard to Edmund's retaking of the Five Boroughs, the *Chronicle*'s comment that 'The Danes were previously subjected by force under the Norsemen, for a long time in bonds of captivity to the heathens ...' may be more than just a West Saxon spin on events.[5] Just as Anglo-Saxon Northumbrians may have acquiesced in the return of a Viking ruler from Dublin, the Danish communities of the East Midlands may have looked favourably on a return of a king from Wessex. A generation after conversion to Christianity, under Edward the Elder's rule, the return of a pagan ruler such as Olaf Guthfrithson may have been unacceptable. If so, it underlines the extent to which Viking settlers had fitted into Anglo-Saxon society. In addition, they may have looked on a ruler from York as no less alien than one from Winchester. Indeed, the latter may have seemed preferable to a northern ruler, since he was a known quantity and accommodations had been reached with such West Saxon kings in the past, following the conquest of the *Danelaw* under Edward the Elder.

Olaf Guthfrithson did not have long to enjoy the triumph denied to his father for he died in 941. He was succeeded by another member of the Irish-Norse dynasty from Dublin, his cousin Olaf Sihtricson, also known as Olaf *Cuaran*, or Olaf the Red. This was the son of the king of York who had married Athelstan's sister, although his rapid repudiation of her and the Anglo-Saxon tradition that she remained a virgin makes it clear that the new King Olaf was not descended from that marriage.[6]

York subdued once more ... and revived

In 943 the restored power of Edmund was revealed in the baptism of Olaf Sihtricson, with Edmund as sponsor. Their relative roles indicated that Edmund was the overlord, just as Alfred had stood sponsor to Guthrum in 878. This was followed by the same process with regard to another member of the Irish-Norse dynasty of Vikings, Ragnald Guthfrithson. It seems that both he and Olaf Sihtricson were somehow sharing the kingdom of York since both are referred to as 'king' in the same annals (943 and 944) of the *Chronicle*.[7] But within a year, in 944, Edmund had expelled them both from Northumbria. The tangled state of northern politics is revealed in the fact that, according to *Æthelweard's Chronicle*, he was assisted in his recovery of York by an alliance of the *ealdorman* of the Mercians (unnamed) with Wulfstan, archbishop of York. Clearly, Wulfstan had detected a change in the political and military tide and had jumped ship.

With York secured, Edmund went on to attack Cumberland in 945 and then granted it to Malcolm, king of the Scots, on condition that the Scots acted as allies in the future. Just who was being targeted in Cumberland is not known. The name of the area reveals it as being British, derived from the Welsh word *Cymry*, a Welsh collective term for the Welsh community, although it seems to have experienced significant Viking settlement as evidenced in the place names of the Lake District. As such, it had become part of the Irish Sea community of Scandinavian settlers which had united communities on both sides of the Irish Sea. In the mid-tenth century the term 'Cumberland' may also have included the land otherwise described as the British (Welsh) kingdom of Strathclyde.

Edmund was murdered at Pucklechurch (Gloucestershire) in 946 while attempting to save one of his *thegns* from a robber who had broken into the royal residence. He was buried at Glastonbury (Somerset) and succeeded by his brother, Eadred.

In 947–48, Eadred moved to subdue Northumbria, which suggests its loyalty was once again in doubt, and the Scots recognised him as overlord. He was supported in this by Archbishop Wulfstan, who led a Northumbrian delegation to Tanshelf (near Pontefract in west Yorkshire) to offer pledges and oaths of loyalty. However, the *Chronicle* says they soon broke these, and it was then that the northern elites – Anglo-Saxons, Danes and Irish-Norse – gave their allegiance to yet another adventurer who offered them the chance of a more locally based ruler. This was the dramatically named Eric Bloodaxe.

'He wasn't called Erik Bloodaxe because he was good with the children'[8]

Eric Bloodaxe was the son of Harold Finehair, king of Norway, and he came to England as an exile from Norway. Interestingly, Simeon of Durham wrongly describes Eric as 'Danish'. Eric became king of western Norway after his father's death; however, he lost the throne to his younger half-brother, Hákon I 'the Good', who had been fostered at the court of Athelstan in England and who seized the Norwegian Crown with the support of Athelstan in 934. William of Malmesbury records the existence of diplomatic links between Athelstan and Harald Finehair, and this corroborates the saga tradition.

As a result of Hákon's success, Eric moved to the British Isles where he raided Scotland and established himself in the Irish Sea region. His nickname 'Bloodaxe' appears in later Old Norse sagas that looked back to what was perceived as an heroic Viking Age from the safe distance of thirteenth-century Iceland. Other saga writers developed equally chilling names for their 'heroes', such as 'Thorfinn Skullsplitter' of Orkney. These later sagas present Eric as a henpecked husband, a description that sits incongruously with his nickname. Other sources for his life are equally late and are in the form of two late twelfth-century Latin accounts of the lives of the kings of Norway. The sagas may draw on some of the material found in these 'Lives', but the 'Lives' themselves only offer brief accounts of events and lack the dramatic content of the later sagas, some of which purport to tell the stories of the great kings of Norway. There is also a reference to Eric in the 'Life' of a Scottish saint, Caddroe. This was probably written in the late tenth century and in it Caddroe is said to have visited Eric and his wife in York; possibly around 940–41. However, the *Chronicle* made no mention of Eric in York this early and, instead, only mentions the activities of Olaf Guthfrithson and Olaf Sihtricson at this point.

The picture we gain from these complex sources is of a ruthless and ambitious man who eventually gained the Norwegian throne by a policy of murdering his four older brothers. One of the Latin texts actually names him '*fratris interfector*' (brother-killer) and he is presented as a harsh and unpopular king, who was eventually ousted by his one surviving half-brother, Hákon. The sagas claim that, following his loss of the Norwegian throne, he was welcomed by Athelstan because Harald Finehair had been an ally. The claim, though, seems unlikely given the Scandinavian tradition that Athelstan had earlier supported Eric's half-brother Hákon in driving Eric out of Norway. This version of Eric's career is found in *Egil's Saga*, which refers to historic characters of the tenth century and incorporates earlier material and traditions. In it we hear how Eric was made sub-king of Northumbria by King Athelstan as 'protector of the land for King Athelstan against the Scots and the Irish.'[9] However, there is no support for this in the English and Irish sources and the saga also misplaces the events of Eric's life, since he did not make his move in England until after the death of Athelstan. *Egil's Saga* also contains a dramatic but fictional account of the confrontation between the poet (Egil) and his bitter enemy, Eric, in York. In this story, Egil saves his own life by composing and reciting a *drápa* (a Norse praise poem) in honour of Eric. Recited before the king, Egil is allowed to leave the northern kingdom unharmed.

What is clear is that, once installed as king, Eric adapted his rule to the context of Northumbria. His first coinage imitated standard Anglo-Saxon types used by kings Athelstan, Edmund and Eadred; his second coinage, with the words *eric rex* above and below a sword, copied earlier Scandinavian coinage issued from York. The sagas recount that, once Eric was established in York, he used it as a base to raid Scotland and areas around the Irish Sea. In this he may have been attempting to wrest the region from the influence of the Irish-Norse of Dublin, assisted by controlling the influential asset of York itself.

Jorvik (York) in the mid-tenth century

By the reign of Eric Bloodaxe, York was a thriving commercial hub. Originally the Anglo-Saxon city of *Eoforwic*, its name became adapted to appear as *Iorvík* as the original Old English name gave way to an Old Norse variant under Viking rule. In later Old Norse this became *Iork*, which was later adopted by the English as York.[10] It is today remembered in the form *Jorvik*. To many modern visitors to this northern English city, its Viking period history is now best known through the Jorvik Viking Centre, which is situated on the very site where the excavations by archaeologists from York Archaeological Trust, between the years 1976 and 1981, revealed houses, craft workshops, alleys and backyards of the Viking city which flourished there in the tenth century.[11] The dig area covered 1,000 square metres of the city known as the Pavement and Coppergate, and benefitted from up to 9 metres of archaeological layers, most of which dated to the Viking Age. A remarkable state of preservation occurred here because damp conditions meant that the organic remains of timber buildings, textiles and leather survived. In addition, the recovery of seeds, animal bones, insects, plants, pollen and even human parasite eggs meant that archaeologists have gained a remarkable insight into the environment and sanitation of the city that Eric Bloodaxe ruled. In all a total of 20,000 objects were recovered.

The Viking Age city saw a remarkable expansion between *c*.900 and 935. New streets were established, lined with timber houses and workshops. Evidence for the far-flung trading network that met at *Jorvik* is found in the wide range of artefacts and raw materials discovered there, including: silk from the Far East; coins from the Central Asian centre of Samarkand, which were familiar enough in trade to prompt counterfeiters to copy

The Lindisfarne tombstone, showing advancing warriors who are often interpreted as Vikings. However, it dates from about a generation later than the 793 attack on the monastery. © *Bridgeman Art Library*

Defences of the *burh* of Wareham (Dorset), showing the height of the surviving western rampart. © *Authors' collection*

Westbury White Horse (Wiltshire). Alfred won the battle of *Ethandun*, 878, on the downs above here. © *Authors' collection*

Alfred and the Viking wars continue to influence English culture. Here the commemoration combines a version of the statue of Alfred from Winchester with the battle of *Ethandun*, on the village sign at Edington, Wiltshire. © *Authors' collection*

Reconstruction of a *Jorvik* street scene, from the Jorvik Viking Centre, York. © *Jorvik Viking Centre, York*

The causeway to Northey Island, crossing the river Blackwater, Essex. The site of the battle of Maldon, 991. © *The Battlefields Trust*

The Cuerdale Hoard. Probably buried *c.*905, by a Viking army passing through Lancashire. It is a mixture of over 8,000 objects, including coins, hack-silver and other silver objects.
© *The Trustees of the British Museum. All rights reserved*

Medieval tomb of Athelstan at Malmesbury Abbey (Wiltshire). © *Authors' collection*

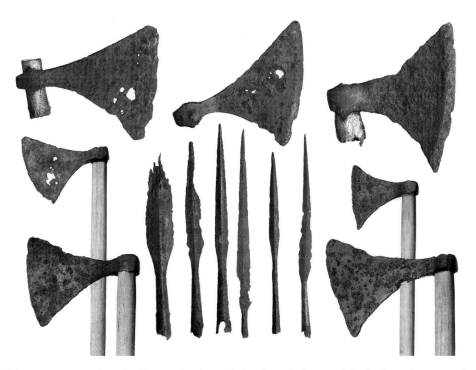

Viking-age weapons from the Thames foreshore. Dating from the late tenth/early eleventh century, they remind us of how London was targeted by Viking raiders on numerous occasions. The axe was a weapon particularly associated with Scandinavian warriors. © *Museum of London*

The church of St Laurence, Bradford on Avon (Wiltshire). Constructed *c.*1000 as part of a refuge from Viking attacks for the nuns of Shaftesbury Abbey and their relics of Edward King and Martyr. © *Authors' collection*

Agnus Dei coin. Featuring the Lamb of God, these coins were minted under Æthelred II as part of his strategy for enlisting the assistance of God in repelling the Vikings. © *The Trustees of the British Museum.*

Eleventh-century Viking tombstone, found in St Paul's churchyard, London. An inscription on it reads: 'Ginna & Toki had this stone put up.' It reminds us of the increased Scandinavian influence under Cnut (1016–35).
© *Museum of London*

The church of St Martin, Wareham (Dorset). The present church was constructed in the 1030s to replace one destroyed by the great Viking raid up the river Frome, in 1015.
© *Authors' collection*

Cnut giving a cross to the church at Winchester. The act and the illustration remind us of Cnut's aim of portrying himself as a Christian monarch. © *The British Library Board*

the coins; amber from the Baltic; and cowrie shells from the Red Sea. The Scandinavian trading system that extended into Russia and down its great rivers to Byzantium meant that *Jorvik* was connected to a vibrant and expanding system of international exchange. Local crafts included: jewellery making in gold, silver, copper and jet; other metal working; an antler comb industry; leather work; the dying of textiles; weaving; and wood working.[12]

A specialised pottery industry was developing through the tenth century and the city became a centre for work in precious metals and copper that hitherto had been largely confined to rural high-status sites. At Coppergate, two tenements were occupied by metal workers and around 1,000 crucible fragments were unearthed, which illustrates the extent of this expanding urban industry. Viking Age York also saw a huge increase in the variety of foodstuffs consumed compared with the earlier Anglo-Saxon city. While staple meat species remained similar in both periods, the Viking city saw a remarkable expansion in the consumption of animals such as pigs, geese and chickens, along with intensive exploitation of river and woodland resources. It seems as if the Viking Age traders and craftspeople enjoyed far greater freedom of operation compared with their Anglo-Saxon predecessors, who seemed to have been much more tightly constrained within a system of food rents run by the local elites.[13]

This thriving entrepreneurial environment was dependent on an active monetary economy. And in the design of coins there was a striking eclecticism which drew on both Christian and pagan motifs. Under Sihtric (921–27), one coin issue carried a sword on the obverse with a reverse design of a cross, while a similar issue carried a Thor's hammer in place of the cross; and under Olaf Guthfrithson (died 941), the raven of Odin was displayed on the obverse, while the reverse carried a small cross. Earlier in the tenth century, rulers of York had issued coins which did not carry the name of the king, but instead were issued in the name of St Peter. Some related coins from this series even carried images of Thor's hammer on the reverse.[14] It seems that the rulers of York were seeking to appeal to both Christian and pagan elements in their population. By the late tenth century, 75 per cent of the moneyers in York bore Scandinavian names. Whilst this does not prove ethnic origins, it is surely some indication of the way in which the Viking community had adapted to and exploited the coin-using economy that they inherited from the Anglo-Saxon rulers of ninth-century Northumbria.

It was not just *Jorvik* that seemed to benefit from Scandinavian rule. New finds are revealing just how prosperous and sophisticated this

Anglo-Scandinavian society was. The 'Huxley Hoard' of silver arm rings (discovered in 2004) shows a thriving economy using fixed weights of silver in transactions;[15] the 'Vale of York (or Harrogate) Hoard' (discovered in 2007) was the most important Viking find for 150 years and contained artefacts linking the hoard to Afghanistan, the Carolingian Empire (in modern France and western Germany), Ireland, the Middle East, Russia and Scandinavia.[16] A similar picture of widespread trading links is revealed in the 'Silverdale Hoard' (Lancashire, found in 2011) which dates from the early tenth century (*c*.900–10). It contained twenty-seven coins, ten arm rings, two finger rings and fourteen silver ingots, a fine wire chain and 'hack-silver' (cut pieces of jewellery), which had been protected by a lead container. The arm rings and fragments of brooches were of types found around the Irish Sea, in Scandinavia and in central and northern Russia. The coins, similarly, revealed the extent of Viking trading connections with examples from areas of England under Anglo-Saxon and Viking control, as well as Frankish and Islamic examples. One coin, bearing the ruler's name '*Airdeconut*' (possibly Harthacnut), alludes to an otherwise unknown Viking king in northern England. On the reverse the letters *dns* (*Dominus*) *rex* were arranged in the shape of a cross, suggesting that the Viking king had either converted to Christianity, or wished to appeal to Christian subjects. Another coin bore the name '*Alwaldus*' and was probably issued by Alfred the Great's nephew, Æthelwold, who had gone over to the Northumbrian Vikings in 899 (see Chapter 9). Another hoard called the 'Furness Hoard' (Cumbria, also discovered in 2011) was probably buried *c*.955–57, although possibly as late as 965), and contained silver fragments, silver ingots and seventy-nine coins. These coins were mostly Anglo-Saxon or Anglo-Scandinavian, although there were also two Islamic *dirhams*. The concentration of finds from the 940s and 950s probably reflects the revival of Scandinavian power in the kingdom of York under Eric Bloodaxe. The deposition of the hoard itself probably dates from immediately after the ending of this resurgence, on the death of Eric in 954. As such, the late date for the burial of this particular hoard differentiates it from most other Viking hoards, although this may be explained by the fact that Cumbria remained beyond the control of Anglo-Saxon kings even after the suppression of the kingdom of York.[17]

The death of Eric Bloodaxe and
the end of the kingdom of York

In 948 Eadred, furious at what he regarding as Northumbrian betrayal in accepting Eric as king, marched north and campaigned far and wide in Northumbria. Striking at the social and economic base of the northern elites, his invasion caused widespread damage. Even the great minster at Ripon (North Yorkshire) was destroyed. An ancient centre of Christian worship in the north, it had served its local area since the seventh century. The great church was founded by St Wilfrid and was dedicated in 672. St Wilfrid had brought stonemasons, glaziers and plasterers from France and Italy to build his basilica and, in doing so, he founded one of the first stone-built churches in Anglo-Saxon England. A contemporary account by Eddius Stephanus gives us insights into the impressive appearance of the early church. The Anglo-Saxon crypt of the present church is one of the oldest in the country and is the only part of Wilfrid's original church that remains. But in 948 it was not Viking marauders but an Anglo-Saxon king who had it burnt to the ground. This shocking act – clearly designed to over-awe the Northumbrians and remind the archbishop of York of the vulnerability of his assets – is a striking example of how Vikings were not the only marauders to target Christian churches.

On the way south from this incursion Eadred's army was severely mauled at Castleford (West Yorkshire) by a Northumbrian force from York. Incensed, Eadred resolved 'to march back into the land and destroy it utterly.'[18] In panic the northern elites deserted Eric and paid compensation to Eadred.

If Eadred thought he had solved his 'northern problem' he was soon to realise that the matter was far from over. In 949 Olaf Sihtricson (aka *Cuaran*) once again made a play for the Northumbrian throne. Whatever his previous relationship with the Northumbrians had been, this time his intervention soon ran into opposition. The political and strategic manoeuvrings that lay behind his denouement are now difficult to unravel, but within three years, in 952, he had been expelled by the Northumbrians, and Eric Bloodaxe had once again been accepted as king. The *Chronicle* informs us that in this same year an exasperated Eadred arrested Wulfstan, archbishop of York, and held him prisoner in the unidentified fortress of *Iudanbyrig*. Identification of the fortress is problematic due to the possibility of textual corruption of *Manuscript D* at this point. What is clear is that Eadred had finally lost patience with the political intrigues of Wulfstan, although quite where the archbishop stood with regard to the rival ambitions of Olaf and Eric is difficult to say. The coincidence of his arrest with the return of Eric Bloodaxe does perhaps suggest that he had thrown his considerable political and economic weight behind the candidature of the Norwegian exile.

Following his expulsion by Eric Bloodaxe, Olaf Sihtricson returned to Ireland where, after initial success against the Irish, he was, in 964, himself defeated at Innistiogue by the men of Ossory. However, in the tangled web of Vikings and competing Irish kingdoms he fought back and, in 970, in conjunction with the Leinster Irish, he plundered the great monastery at Kells. That same year he defeated Domhnall O'Neill, over-king of Ireland. Following other victories over the Irish in 978 and 979, he was eventually crushed at the battle of Tara in 980. Viking Dublin was, as a consequence, occupied by the Irish. Olaf's son, Ragnall, was killed at Tara, and Olaf himself retired to the Scottish monastery at Iona, where he died in 981.

Back in Northumbria, Eric Bloodaxe was no more successful. In fact, his achievement in regaining Northumbria was soon brought to a shuddering halt. In 954, in a complex series of events, Eric was expelled from York by the Northumbrians and killed in battle. The circumstances behind his death are hard to unravel and were clearly rooted in the complex politics and rivalry of the northern kingdom and its neighbours. In the early thirteenth century, Roger of Wendover, writing his *Flores Historiarum* (*Flowers of the Histories*), offers a sympathetic view of Eric's death: 'King Eric was treacherously killed by Earl Maccus in a certain lonely place which is called Stainmore, with his son Haeric and his brother Ragnald, betrayed by Earl Oswulf.'[19] The Norse sagas claim that Eric was accompanied to his final battle by five kings from the Hebrides and the two earls of Orkney. The identity of Eric's fatal opponent, Maccus, is uncertain, but the name appears in the dynastic lists of the Viking rulers of the Isle of Man and it may well have been that he was acting as an ally of Eadred of Wessex. The mention of Earl Oswulf, the Anglo-Saxon *high reeve* of Bamburgh, suggests that there was a high-level conspiracy against Eric. The fact that Eadred was the main beneficiary of Eric's death should not obscure the fact that the elite family ruling the enclave of Bamburgh would have greatly increased their own freedom of action now the threat of an ambitious king at York had been removed. And, no doubt, Eadred was grateful and less likely to interfere in the day-to-day exercise of power, patronage and influence in the north-east. In short, Eric Bloodaxe had fallen foul of northern political intrigue as well as that of southern ambitions.

The Norse *skaldic* poem *Eiríksmál* (*Eric's Story*) was probably composed shortly after 954 and was traditionally thought to have been commissioned by the Norwegian queen, Gunnhild, in honour of her slain husband, Eric Bloodaxe. It is preserved only in *Fagrskinna* (*Fair skin*); one of the so-called Viking 'kings' sagas', a compilation which dates from *c.*1220. The name *Fagrskinna*, probably written in Norway or Iceland, is derived from one of the manuscripts in which it was later preserved and means 'Fair skin or leather'. The poem, which is dedicated to Eric Bloodaxe, is incomplete but recounts the arrival of the recently slain Eric in the hall of the pagan Norse god, Odin. There Eric is greeted:

> Hail to you, Eric,
> welcome here!
> Enter the hall, wise king;
> I must hear
> what warriors follow you
> fresh from the fight.[20]

The death of Eric was a momentous event, as the kingdom of York had fallen and would never rise again. As Simeon of Durham reminds us: 'Here the kings of the Northumbrians came to an end, and henceforward the province was administered by earls.'[21] From this moment onwards there would be no rival king to the House of Wessex until the conquest of England by a fresh wave of Viking invaders in the eleventh century. Until then, occasional divisions of the kingdom would only be as a result of internal divisions within the dynasty. And although England would be temporarily partitioned between Cnut and Edmund Ironside in 1016 (see Chapter 12), from this moment onwards it is realistic to talk of one king of a united kingdom of England. What had temporarily occurred at previous periods under Athelstan and his immediate successors was now finally established with the death of Eric Bloodaxe. Whilst we will still refer to 'Anglo-Saxons', we can now with increasing confidence also call them 'English', for one English state and people was really emerging out of the Anglo-Saxon and Scandinavian communities.

England after Eric Bloodaxe

Eadred finally reoccupied Northumbria in 954 and, incidentally, Wulfstan was released and allowed to take up his position as archbishop again. A year later, in 955, Eadred died at Frome (Somerset). He was succeeded by his nephews, the sons of his brother, Edmund, who had been murdered at Pucklechurch (Gloucestershire) in 946. These two brothers – Eadwig (or Edwy) and Edgar – divided the recently united kingdom between them for a short time. This did not happen immediately and, at first, Eadwig appears to have inherited a united kingdom; however, in 957, his brother succeeded to the kingdom of Mercia and England was divided along the River Thames (and presumably also along the line of the Bristol Avon). This division reflected internal political factions within the court but did not become a long-lasting division because, in 959, Eadwig died and 16-year-old Edgar reunited the kingdom.

All of this political infighting took place when Scandinavian interference in England was minimal. Had it occurred a generation earlier, it is likely that it would have encouraged the kind of devastating intervention that had caused such problems in the 860s, or had almost overturned Alfred's political settlement in 899 when Æthelwold had been briefly accepted as 'king of the pagans'. But the absence of Viking raids meant that this did not occur when Eadwig and Edgar were in competition for influence in the 950s. In fact, the only information we have of Viking raiding at this time is from 966, when a leader named Thored ravaged Westmoreland, but we know little else about this event. In 973, Edgar was crowned at Bath and later his overlordship was recognised at Chester by neighbouring kings, including the king of Scots, the British (Welsh) king of Cumbria (Strathclyde) and the Viking ruler, Maccus Haraldsson, 'king of many isles',[22] who seems to have ruled the Hebrides and was active in the Irish Sea region. Memorably, Edgar was rowed along the River Dee by eight kings while he took the tiller. The Anglo-Saxon dynasty of Wessex had come a long way since Alfred was almost captured at Chippenham in the winter of 878.

But dark clouds were again on the horizon. Edgar died in 975 and was succeeded by his son, Edward. In 978, Edward (later known as 'Edward King and Martyr') was murdered at Corfe (Dorset) and replaced on the throne by his half-brother, Æthelred II (later known as 'Æthelred *unræd* '). In 980, Viking raiders sacked Southampton (Hampshire), and Thanet (Kent) and Cheshire were also ravaged. A whole new Viking Blitzkrieg was about to strike England, and the scale and ferocity would rival the devastation caused by the *micel hæðen here* of the 860s. A whole new chapter in the history of the Viking Wars was beginning.

RETURN OF THE VIKINGS

The Viking attacks on Anglo-Saxon England fell into two phases. The first phase, as we have seen, started in the late eighth century; escalated during the ninth century; reached a crescendo in the period between 866 and the 890s; declined in the face of the victories of Edward the Elder; challenged Athelstan but then met a dramatic defeat at his hands; and finally ended with the death of Eric Bloodaxe in 954. From 954 until 980, it seemed as if all this was in the past. England was finally a united kingdom under one dynasty, the West Saxon, and, under the rule of Edgar (959–75), achieved political stability, with an efficient system of coinage and taxation, and a strong fleet with which to deter Viking raiders.[1] The return of the Vikings, therefore, was all the more shocking, and the intensity of raids equalled those of the ninth century in their violence and disruption. So great was the impact of these new raids that the failure of the contemporary ruler to successfully resist them led to Æthelred II (978–1016) later being accorded the unflattering nickname of *unræd* ('no counsel/wisdom', or perhaps 'ill-advised'), as a bitter contrast to the meaning of his actual name, 'royal counsel/wisdom'. He has popularly been remembered as 'Æthelred the Unready'.[2] Whether this dismissive judgement is really justified will be explored later, but before this can be attempted it is necessary to explore the evidence regarding this second phase of the Viking Wars and explain the reasons why it occurred.

Factors leading to the resumption of Viking attacks

Archbishop Wulfstan of York was in no doubt as to why the Viking attacks had resumed: they were God's punishment on the sins of the English. Wulfstan was a major player in the government and Church under both Æthelred II and his successor, the Viking ruler Cnut (1016–35). Wulfstan was bishop of London from 996 to 1002, then archbishop of York from 1002–23, and also bishop of Worcester until 1016. (It should be noted that he was a different ecclesiastic to his namesake mentioned earlier (see Chapter 11) who is sometimes called Wulfstan I.) In addition to being a leading figure within the Anglo-Saxon Church, he was also extremely active in government and was responsible for drafting much of the legislation under both Æthelred II and Cnut.[3] He is most famous for a dramatic sermon that he preached in 1014; its title translates from the Latin original, *Sermo Lupi ad Anglos*, as *The Sermon of the Wolf to the English* and was a play on his name, which meant 'wolf-stone'. This famous declaration survives in five different manuscripts, which represent three editions of the text, and was preached at a time of acute crisis in the English state; Æthelred II had been driven into exile by Scandinavian invaders late in 1013 and the nation was in turmoil.

Looking back over the previous generation, Wulfstan recorded a great catalogue of sins that stood against the English nation. Payments to God had been withheld, monks and nuns were treated without respect, churches were robbed, widows forced into marriage, the poor defrauded and sold abroad as slaves, little children had been enslaved for minor thefts, the rights of freemen and slaves had been denied them, and family loyalties had been betrayed. Others were political crimes: the first was the murder of Edward King and Martyr in 978, a royal killing that had not been avenged; the second was the failure of the English elite to prevent Æthelred II from being driven into exile. These were mingled with moral outrages that are so specific that they almost certainly derived from real life events known to Wulfstan. Groups of men had bought women and used them as sex slaves until they finally sold the poor women abroad. Wulfstan angrily denounced this treatment of fellow human beings, especially women who were precious to God but abused by men. And family members had even sold relatives into slavery. As a result of this, Wulfstan reminded his readers: 'God's anger violently oppresses us.'[4]

As Wulfstan neared the climax of his sermon he turned to the matter of the Vikings, and it is one of the relatively rare examples of the term 'Viking' being used in Old English literature. A slave deserted his master, Wulfstan wrote, and 'becomes a viking'; then when he killed a *thegn*, no compensation (*wergild*) was paid, but the Viking army demanded compensation for the run-away who had joined them if he was killed by an Anglo-Saxon. This upturning of the social order clearly disturbed Wulfstan, but he felt that these Viking successes had only occurred because God had allowed them as judgement. Wulfstan was shocked at the inability of the English to defend their families and themselves from heathen assault. He stated how, 'we pay them [Viking marauders] continually and they humiliate us daily; they ravage and they burn, plunder and rob and carry on board; and lo, what else is there in all these events except God's anger clear and visible over this people?'[5] If the English would not repent of their sins, Wulfstan concluded, they would lose their land as the Britons long before had lost theirs to the invading Anglo-Saxons. The warning was a bitter reversal of the conclusion drawn at the end of the poem *The Battle of Brunanburh* when, at a time of victory over Vikings, its author had concluded that it was the greatest slaughter 'since the Angles and Saxons came hither from the east, invading Britain … and won a country.'[6] Now roles had been reversed and England seemed to be slipping out of the grasp of its once-victorious inhabitants. Wulfstan's warning was taken almost *verbatim* from Alcuin's letter, written after the 793 sack of Lindisfarne to, ironically, another Æthelred, then king of Northumbria (see Chapter 1). The warning of judgement on a nation's sins, which had heralded the start of the first Viking Blitzkrieg, was now sounded again as the second phase of Viking attacks ground down Anglo-Saxon defences.

The resumption of Viking raiding has produced different theories from historians and archaeologists. From around 965, the Arab trade routes into Russia and beyond began to suffer from an acute shortage of silver, due to the exhaustion of the silver mines that had previously supplied the Islamic world.[7] This was a major problem, as the availability of Arab silver had fuelled a far-flung trade network in which the products of eastern and northern Europe, including slaves, were exchanged for Arab coins. These became the silver armbands and ingots that supported gift-exchange, tribute and the rewarding of Viking warriors.[8] At the same time that the supply of Arab trade-silver faltered, the growing power of the Kievan Russian state made it more difficult for Viking adventurers to seize precious metals as booty. The decline in the eastern trade routes may also help explain the presence of Swedish Vikings in the new phase of Viking attacks on England, since they were no longer benefitting from the eastern trade that they had previously dominated. This shutting off of the silver supply from the east was simultaneously accompanied by more silver becoming available in western Europe, due to the discovery of new silver sources in the Hartz Mountains in the 960s; this caused Viking raiders to target western Europe again, to compensate for the lack of silver moving into Scandinavia from the east.

The ability to restart this aggressive action was strengthened by the growing centralisation of power in the Scandinavian kingdoms; a process which was also being seen in the Viking Earldom of Orkney and the Kingdom of Man. In this early stage of kingdom-building, the increasing expense of centralised kingship was not yet met by a correspondingly sophisticated taxation system. Adventures abroad were a convenient means by which kingship at home could be financed. Amongst the more far-flung Viking communities – such as those of Orkney, the Western Isles and the Isle of Man – this policy of raising revenue by means of piracy rarely developed a long-term political objective. During the tenth and eleventh centuries it was the emerging kingdoms of Denmark and Norway whose larger resources meant that piracy could develop once more into conquest.

A more unified Danish state began to emerge in the early tenth century, under King Gorm, and this trend was accelerated when Harald Bluetooth extended Danish rule into Norway in the 960s. This increase in the centralisation of power in Denmark was probably the major factor which led to the construction of the military barracks complex at Trelleborg on Zealand. Here, geometrically laid-out buildings within a circular fortress probably date from around 980 and indicate the growing military and organisational power of the Danish monarchy. One of four such complexes, they were probably built late in the reign of Harald Bluetooth as military camps to bolster royal authority against threats both internal and external. Harald became a Christian and oversaw the conversion of the Danes. Harald Bluetooth has left a strange legacy in that his unifying achievements are, in the twenty-first century, remembered in 'Bluetooth' technology, an open wireless technology which can connect several devices. Created by the Swedish telecommunication and data-communication-systems company, Ericsson, in 1994, its logo is formed from the runic alphabet initials of Harald Bluetooth. It is a strange legacy that a tenth-century Danish ruler should be remembered in the field of electronic networking.

In Norway, after the decisive naval battle of Hafrsfjord in 872, Harald Finehair came to dominate a generally united Norwegian kingdom, even if northern regions remained beyond his control. After Harald Finehair's death, the unity of Norway fragmented and it was ruled, at times, by direct descendants of Harald and, at other times, with political power being held by earls who accepted a Danish overlordship. In the late tenth century, Olaf Tryggvason (died *c.*1000) aspired to hold the Norwegian throne independent of Denmark and briefly achieved this; however, following the death of his successor, Olaf Haraldsson (St Olav) in 1030, the Danish king, Cnut, reasserted Danish control. Following Cnut's death in 1035, Olaf Haraldsson's son, Magnus the Good, took the throne, and he was himself succeeded by Harald Hardrada, who died at the battle of Stamford Bridge in 1066. What is significant is that the ferocity of the second phase of raids was increased by the fact that the more unified Viking kingdoms of Denmark and Norway could focus far greater military resources on their attacks on England than were previously available. In this, two rulers rapidly came to prominence: Olaf Tryggvason and Svein Forkbeard.

Olaf Tryggvason was king of Norway from 995–*c.*1000 and was the grandson of Harald Finehair (father of Hákon the Good and Eric Bloodaxe), who had ruled Norway until 930.[9] As such, he came from a Norwegian royal family who had an interest in, and a knowledge of, England. Olaf Tryggvason played an active role in promoting the Christian conversion of Norway, but historical information about his life and activities is limited. Apart from brief mentions in the *Anglo-Saxon Chronicle*, the only other near-contemporary account is found in Adam of Bremen's *Deeds of Bishops of the Hamburg Church*, written in about 1070. In the late twelfth century he featured in two Icelandic sagas,[10] one being *Ólafs Saga Tryggvasonar* (*Saga of Olaf Tryggvason*). This, the earliest independent life of Olaf Tryggvason, was compiled in the monastery of Thingeyrar in Iceland, in the late twelfth century. But the most extensive description of his activities was written *c.*1230, again in Iceland, by Snorri Sturluson in *Heimskringla* (*Circle of the world*), which is a history of Norway from prehistoric times to 1177. In these saga accounts we read of Olaf Tryggvason gaining his first military experience in the Baltic, raiding the Slavs and Balts who were living on the southern and eastern shores of the Baltic Sea. Large numbers of Arabic silver coins have been found here and testify to the fact that the West Slavs (the Wends) were well integrated into the trade routes which stretched through Russia and into the Middle East. This made them a lucrative target for Viking raids. Whatever role Olaf Tryggvason played in the Baltic, we are on firmer historical ground when tracing his impact on England. Anglo-Saxon sources first record him as raiding Folkestone (Kent) in 991 with a fleet of ninety-three ships, before he was bought off with £10,000. This would not be the last time that Anglo-Saxon communities raised huge sums of money in taxation to pay off marauders, and it later became known as *Danegeld* (Dane-tax).

At the same time that Olaf Tryggvason began his raiding, England was also targeted by Svein Forkbeard, king of Denmark. Svein Forkbeard ruled Denmark between 985 and 1014 and he briefly ruled England for five weeks before dying in 1014. Like Olaf Tryggvason, he appears in the *Chronicle*, albeit in a greater number of annals, as well as in Adam of Bremen's account and in *Heimskringla*. In addition to these sources, we have rather conflicting accounts of his later life in the *Encomium Emmae Reginae* (*In Praise of Queen Emma*), which is an eleventh-century account (*c.* 1040–42) written in honour of Emma, Cnut's queen, and in the *Chronicon ex Chronicis* (*Chronicle of other Chronicles*) written by John of Worcester and compiled up until *c.* 1141. According to the thirteenth-century Icelandic *Jómsvíkinga Saga* (*Saga of the Jómsvíkings*), Svein was raised among the *Jómsvíkings*, a semi-legendary group of Viking mercenaries. This saga claims to recount the dealings between the *Jómsvíkings*, a colony of Viking warriors based in the southern Baltic coastal town of Wolin, with Harald Bluetooth of Denmark and the Norwegian *earl*, Hakon of Lade. But this is a literary composition, representing later legendary retellings of earlier events and cannot be taken as an historical source.

Svein Forkbeard was the son of Harald Bluetooth, who had earlier unified Denmark, and became king after he deposed his father in 985. In 994 he teamed up with Olaf Tryggvason in an extended campaign of attacks on England; in fact, Svein made a highly lucrative career out of attacking England. In the future, tensions would develop between these two rulers over influence in Norway, but in the early 990s their attention was jointly focused on raiding England.

Archbishop Wulfstan would not have recognised these factors as a reason for a new Viking onslaught, but both he and modern historians have identified one common factor that may have made England more vulnerable to new Scandinavian interventions in the 980s. And this is that the death of Edgar, in 975, led to dynastic weakness that may have encouraged Viking opportunism. The murder of Edward King and Martyr, at Corfe (Dorset) in 978, may have led to more turbulence than we now give it credit. It was a year before his successor, Æthelred II, was crowned, which suggests lengthy political manoeuvring taking place and, as he was the main beneficiary of the murder of his half-brother, the real possibility of opposition to his reign. Modern investigation into the way in which the murder was perceived at the time has shown that there was remarkably little by way of contemporary accusations of guilt aimed at Æthelred or his mother, who was identified in later sources as a wicked and murderous step-mother.[11] Nevertheless, the beginning of the new phase of Viking attacks in 980 coincides remarkably with the aftermath of the murder and the early – and possibly contentious – years of the reign of Æthelred, who was only in his early teens. This combination of dynastic instability and a young king may have encouraged the kind of Viking activity which had earlier sought to exploit Anglo-Saxon political infighting in the 860s and 870s.

The Viking assault on England

The *Chronicle* offers a particularly detailed account of the escalating crisis that assailed England under the rule of Æthelred. In 981, south-west England was targeted for attack and St Petroc's monastery at Padstow (Cornwall) was sacked. In 982 Portland (Dorset) suffered a heavy raid and London itself was burnt. There was then a brief respite until Watchet (Somerset) was devastated in 988. The number of West Country references suggests that these early raids were conducted by Irish Sea Vikings. This interpretation is supported by the evidence of Anglo-Saxon coin dies – from the mints at Bath (Somerset), Watchet (Somerset) and Lydford (Devon) – being used to strike Viking coins in Dublin from c. 995.[12]

The scale of the raids changed in 991 with the first great campaign of Olaf Tryggvason targeting Folkestone and Sandwich (Kent). From there the raiders moved north and landed at Maldon (Essex). Here occurred one of the most famous battles in Anglo-Saxon history when the *ealdorman* of Essex, Byrhtnoth allowed a Viking army to cross the causeway and lost the subsequent battle in heroic fashion. The wisdom of this action has been hotly argued ever since, and even at the time was a matter of debate. Line 89 of the contemporary poem, *The Battle of Maldon*, describes his decision as stemming *'for his ofermode'* (i.e., is it was due to either his 'confidence' or his 'pride'). The Old English word *ofermode* can bear both translations and so we are left wondering whether the poet thought the decision a brave and honourable gamble, to prevent the raiders harrying elsewhere, or an act of folly. Either way, we have a picture of English warriors laying down their lives around the body of the fallen *ealdorman* in heroic self-sacrifice.[13] One old retainer sought to rally the troops with the memorable exhortation: 'Thoughts must be the braver, heart more valiant, courage the greater as our strength grows less.'[14] That same year a great payment of £10,000 was made to persuade the Viking army to leave. All in all it had been a highly successful campaigning season for Olaf Tryggvason.

Heroic as the sacrifice was at Maldon, it was victories that Æthelred needed, not heroic defeats. And victory was less attainable when there was political treachery at work. One of the recurring themes of the *Chronicle* is of a lack of loyalty and resolve amongst certain key figures within the English political establishment. In 992, we hear of *Ealdorman Ælfric* of Hampshire warning a Viking army, which consequently escaped an ambush and inflicted defeat on two units of the naval force sent against it. In 993, a large English army was sent against a Viking force, operating around the Humber estuary, but was betrayed by its three leaders who fled from the battle. John of Worcester adds bitterly, 'because they were Danes on the father's side.' This opens up the possibility that the arrival of new and victorious Scandinavian forces was increasing ethnic tensions in the *Danelaw*, which many must have thought had long been resolved. The anger of Æthelred may be revealed in his decision that year to have the son of *Ealdorman Ælfric* blinded.

The year 994 started badly for the defenders of England, as it witnessed the first recorded allied attack of Olaf Tryggvason and Svein Forkbeard, when their joint army unsuccessfully attacked London. Although they failed to take the city, they did cause immense damage and then over-wintered in Southampton. However, political manoeuvring on Æthelred's part appears to have divided this alliance, since Olaf Tryggvason was confirmed at Andover (Hampshire) with Æthelred as his sponsor and he promised to end his attacks. By *c.*1000 Olaf was dead and the initiative had passed to Svein Forkbeard.

In the disasters that followed, the *Chronicle* provides a relentless account of Viking assaults, English suffering and the betrayal of the king by leading members of the English elite. Huge damage was done to Devon in 997; and in 998, it was the turn of Dorset since 'as soon as they [the English forces] were to have joined battle, a flight was always instigated by some means, and always the enemy had the victory in the end.'[15] The same bitter lament of the lack of resolve, the betrayal of men and defeat in battle occurs in the entries for 999 and 1001. Another huge *Danegeld* of £24,000 was paid in 1002 and it was following this that Æthelred ordered a savage purge of suspect Danes.

Retribution

The annals of the *Chronicle* give us the impression of a suffering English population that was the subject of violence and extortion. Yet this passive view of the English response to the Viking attacks does not tell the whole story. Between 2008 and 2009, Oxford Archaeology worked along the line of the Weymouth relief road (Dorset), which was being built as part of the preparations for the 2012 Olympics. In 2009, on the line of the Ridgeway, between Dorchester and Weymouth, a remarkable discovery revealed that Anglo-Saxon communities could, at times, strike back at their oppressors. A pit dug into the chalk was found to contain fifty-four headless bodies and fifty-one skulls. The skulls all had at least one cervical vertebra, which is typical of a head severed by a sharp blow. Many showed signs of trauma affecting other vertebrae, the clavicle and jawbone, which is consistent with beheading as a result of multiple blows. Some had cuts to their hands, which suggests that these men, at least, were not bound and had raised their hands in a futile attempt to defend themselves. The layering of bodies and skulls suggests a prolonged act of execution in which bodies fell into the pit before others were executed and fell on top of them. All the bodies were male, young, tall and healthy, and the killing represents a single event. None of the bodies were accompanied by buckles, pins or any other evidence of clothing, which indicated that they had been stripped naked before being killed. Since a number of skulls were missing it is possible that these had been taken away as trophies.

Using radiocarbon analysis the event was dated, with 93 per cent probability, to 970–1025. Clearly, the most likely time of death was around the turn of the millennium, *c.* 1000. Most revealing of all was that isotope analysis of sample teeth all indicated an origin in Scandinavia, so the most likely explanation is that this represents the execution site of a Viking crew, or crews, captured by the men of Dorset.[16] Any attempt to link the execution to a specific historical event is not possible but, in its anonymous brutality, it offers an insight into the realities behind those events that are known to us from the historical sources.

One retaliatory event that is dated by the *Chronicle* is commonly known as 'The Massacre of St Brice's Day' on 13 November 1002. Not that we should attempt to forge any link between this event and the anonymous mass execution that occurred on the Ridgeway. The *Chronicle* simple states: '... the king ordered to be slain all the Danish men who were in England – this was done on St Brice's day – because the king had been informed that they would treacherously deprive him, and then all his councillors, of life, and possess this kingdom afterwards.'[17] William of Malmesbury, writing in the twelfth century, claimed that the victims included Svein's sister, her husband, Pallig, and their child. The *Chronicle* recorded that, in the previous year, Pallig had betrayed an alliance he had made with Æthelred. There is only one other early reference to this ethnic cleansing and that is from a replacement document issued by Æthelred to the church of St Frideswide, Oxford, as a result of their original document being destroyed when the church was burnt during the massacre of the Danes. The replacement document is dated 7 December 1004 and describes how, 'all the Danes who had sprung up in this island, sprouting like cockle [a weed] amongst the wheat, were to be destroyed by a most just extermination.'[18] The document then goes on to recount how the Danes living in Oxford barricaded themselves in St Frideswide's church but died when the townspeople set fire to the building.

Taken as it stands, these references are hard to believe. A total ethnic cleansing of all the Danes in England would have been quite impossible, as Danish settlers had been established in eastern England since the ninth century and, since the reign of Edward the Elder, had been increasingly intertwined with Anglo-Saxon society and its ruling class. To kill all the Danes in England was as undesirable as it was impossible; much of eastern and northern England constituted an Anglo-Danish society. And yet the evidence of the *Chronicle* and the renewal document is insistent; something very significant was attempted in 1002, as a result of growing anger at the renewed Viking assaults and the awareness that a significant minority in the population had loyalties that were, at best, questionable. The most likely scenario is that, in 1002, Æthelred ordered the deaths of prominent and recognisably distinct Danish settlers who had arrived in England during the previous decade. Many of these were probably merchants whose activities meant that they were connected with communities living either side of the North Sea. Or it might have involved the elimination of Danish mercenaries.[19] However, we may safely discount the idea that the English state was able, or willing, to remove everyone with Danish origins. Indeed, the massacre may have been confined to a handful of prominent towns, such as Oxford, where these newcomers constituted a recognisable social group. It may be relevant that, in 2008, the bodies of thirty-seven people were excavated in Oxford; most were apparently fit males, aged 16–25, who had eaten a great deal of seafood over the years, as revealed by analysis of their bone collagen.

It is always difficult to link such discoveries to historical events, but there is a strong likelihood that these were Scandinavian mercenaries and their deaths may well have been linked to the events of 1002,[20] though it is hard to imagine anything of this kind happening in the *Danelaw*. In the same year, Æthelred married Emma of Normandy; clearly part of an alliance designed to deny Viking armies friendly bases in the region.

'When they were in the east, the English army was kept in the west …'

In 1003 the *Chronicle* specifically refers to the return of Svein Forkbeard, which is the first mention of him by name since 994. The chronicler recounts that Exeter was captured by Svein due to treachery and that, later, *Ealdorman* Ælfric feigned sickness 'and began retching to vomit'[21] and so failed to attack. Why he was allowed to remain in post is not explained. The next year, Svein devastated Norwich and Thetford (Norfolk). In 1005 a great famine struck England and may have been related to the economic disruption caused by the Viking attacks; John of Worcester later claimed that, as a result of this famine, Svein returned to Denmark. Svein may well have been disappointed with the success of his 1003–05 campaign compared with the campaigns of 994, 1002 and 1003, when he does not appear to have been personally campaigning in England.[22]

However, a detailed annal for 1006 refers to so much damage that 'they [the Viking army] had cruelly left their mark on every shire of Wessex with their burning and their harrying.'[23] As a result, a truce was negotiated and, in the next year, a massive *Danegeld* of £36,000 was paid. It seems that the year 1006 marked a decisive moment in the war; from this point onwards, invasions and internal disputes undermined English resistance.[24] In the face of these disasters Æthelred ordered a refurbishment of the navy with a new ship paid for from every 310 *hides* of land but, in 1009, internal disputes culminated in a section of the fleet rebelling, under Wulfnoth Cild of Sussex, and harrying the south coast. To make matters worse, a huge Danish army landed that summer under the leadership of Thorkel the Tall, one of the semi-legendary *Jómsvíkings*. Attempts to contain its ravaging movements through southern England were undermined – deliberately in the opinion of the *Chronicle* – by Eadric Streona, *ealdorman* of Mercia from 1007 and preeminent amongst Æthelred's *ealdormen* by 1012.[25] Things were clearly slipping out of Æthelred's control. In 1010, after devastating East Anglia, Oxfordshire and Buckinghamshire, Thorkel's army returned to their ships. It was after this that the chronicler recorded the bitter conclusion that: 'When they were in the east, the English army was kept in the west, and when they were in the south, our army was in the north'[26] as no policy was followed through and each shire looked to its own defence. A common purpose appeared to have vanished.

From a modern perspective, the switching of sides during the war appears as treachery but, at the time, the major players may have felt that they had the right to independently make new alliances in a volatile political context.[27] Either way, the result fuelled the turmoil. In 1011 the Viking army stormed Canterbury (Kent) and took the archbishop, Ælfheah, as hostage. The contemporary account, by the German chronicler Thietmar of Merseburg, claimed that Ælfheah attempted to raise his own ransom but failed, and that Thorkel the Tall offered to pay it himself but Ælfheah would not allow anyone else to buy his life. The same refusal to pay is found in the slightly later account in the *Chronicle*. The twelfth-century version of the event, written by John of Worcester, claimed that the Vikings demanded an additional payment of £3,000 for the archbishop's life. The next year (1012), despite receiving a massive *Danegeld* of £48,000, the Vikings murdered the archbishop, pelting him with bones and ox-skulls and striking him on the head with the back of an axe.[28] They were, according to the *Chronicle*, 'greatly incensed against the bishop because he would not promise them any money, but forbade that anything should be paid for him. They were also very drunk, for wine from the south had been brought there.'[29] The detail found in the *Chronicle* that he was killed with the back of an axe is supported by the term used in the account – *yr* – to describe the weapon. The same word is used elsewhere for a blunt tool used to crush bones.[30] It suggests that the chronicler was drawing on eyewitness accounts and not simply following the stock phrases expected in a hagiographical account of a saint's martyrdom. This killing clearly shocked even some within the Viking army and Thorkel the Tall defected to the English.

The price of defeat

Paying Viking armies to go away did not originate with the policy of Æthelred, but its scale and impact had never before been so huge. To the Viking armies sailing to England it became a way of life and a highly lucrative one at that. The total amount of *Danegeld* paid between 991 and 1014 was enormous. Adding together the figures recorded in the *Chronicle* gives a total of £158,000, which, in modern terms, would have amounted to billions of pounds drained out of the English economy. To give some idea of the scale of the sums raised, it is necessary to express it in the terms of the tenth and eleventh centuries. In the mid-tenth century a fully grown pig cost 6 pence (with 240 pennies in each £1); in the 1060s the four mills of the Abbey of Ely at Hatfield turned in a combined yearly profit of £2, 6 shillings and 4 pence; while the combined value of all the estates of Glastonbury – the wealthiest abbey in 1066 – was in the region of £820. Valued against these figures, the total *Danegeld* was the equivalent of 6,320,000 pigs, or 272,806 mills, or 192 abbeys of the value of Glastonbury. Somewhere in the region of 37,920,000 individual silver pennies were shipped across the North Sea. In the late tenth century, England had become the first western kingdom to successfully re-institute a taxation system, with attendant record keeping (last experienced in the Roman Empire). And this began as *Danegeld* but was regularised over time into an working tax system.

In Uppland, Sweden, a memorial stone records in runes that 'Áli had this stone put up in his own honour. He took Knútr's *danegeld* in England.'[31] As well as revealing the way in which Viking warriors used the wealth of England as an investment at home, this rune stone also reveals the presence of Swedish Vikings in the army of Cnut of Denmark. Another rune stone from Uppland records how Ulf 'took three payments of *geld* in England. The first was the one that Tosti paid, then Thorkel, then Cnut'.[32] Tosti was a Swedish Viking whose daughter married Svein Forkbeard. English coins in hoards from Scandinavia increase to 'nothing less than a flood' in the period 978–1035 and, in total, some 35,000 such coins have been discovered in Scandinavia to date.[33]

This is testimony to the great wealth of Late Anglo-Saxon England and to the efficiency of the government tax collecting system which levied and collected this huge amount. It is no wonder that those who plundered England came to see the attraction of ruling the country themselves.

Conquest, 1016

In 1013 Svein of Denmark again took command of the Viking forces invading England, and this time it was clear that outright conquest was his goal.

Landing in the Humber estuary, he quickly received the submission of the Northumbrians, parts of Lincolnshire, the Five Boroughs and the Danish set-tlers in the *Danelaw*. The chronicler's specific details indicates that he certainly thought there was an ethnic pattern to this chain of events; Svein had come into an area where many in the population had some affinity with Denmark. Acting swiftly, Svein soon secured the submission of Oxford, Winchester and Bath, where the western *thegns* submitted. Only London held out because Æthelred was there, but the scale of the collapse was unmistakable and he fled into exile in Normandy. Svein of Denmark was now king of England.

He did not enjoy his triumph for long, however; he died on 3 February 1014, to be replaced by his son, Cnut. At this point the English elites switched sides and sent messengers to Æthelred, asking him to return. Furious at this turn of events, Cnut mutilated those given to him as hostages – cutting off their hands, ears and noses – and put these victims ashore at Sandwich (Kent). One of those mutilated, Æthelwine, the grandson of Leofwine who was later Earl of Mercia, was still alive in 1066. Following this atrocity, the Viking army took payment of £21,000 and left – but not for long.

The year 1015 started with more political turbulence. The closing years of Æthelred's reign saw the royal court divided into a faction around Eadric Streona and a faction around the *aethelings* Athelstan (died 1014) and Edmund Ironside. These latter were sons of Æthelred by a previous marriage, before his marriage to Emma of Normandy, and they, no doubt, feared that the succession would now go to one of the sons from that later marriage. The *aetheling* faction included Leofwine of the *Hwicce*, who had earlier lost control of Mercia to Eadric Streona. In this bitter struggle, Æthelred seems to have backed Eadric Streona, despite the fact that he had earlier betrayed the English cause. To compound this, Eadric Streona had rivals from the *Danelaw* murdered during an assembly at Oxford. This seems to have been with the agreement of Æthelred, who seized their property and ordered the widow of one of them to be brought to Malmesbury (Wiltshire). In this he was suddenly and actively challenged by his son, Edmund Ironside, who married the woman and rallied the *Danelaw* against the king. At this critical juncture and – probably in response to this infighting – Cnut returned. His army included Norwegian as well as Danish Vikings, for a rune stone from Galteland in Norway reads, concerning a man named Biórr, that: 'He was killed in the guard when Knútr [Cnut] attacked England.'[34]

With Æthelred incapacitated by sickness, the newly arrived Viking army harried Dorset, Wiltshire and Somerset. Edmund found himself betrayed by Eadric Streona, who went over to Cnut, and Æthelred refused to lead the army himself, fearing betrayal. As English government faultered, *Ealdorman* Uhtred of Northumbria submitted to Cnut but was later murdered. *Manuscript C* claims that it was done on the advice of Eadric Streona; however, John of Worcester later claimed that the murder was committed by a Yorkshire landowner whose family was locked in a feud with Uhtred.[35]

In April, Æthelred died. Edmund succeeded to the kingdom but had to fight a series of battles against Cnut. These included battles fought at Penselwood (Dorset) and Sherston (Wiltshire). According to John of Worcester, the battle at Sherston lasted two days and Eadric Streona attempted to panic the English army by spreading the false news that Edmund had been killed. In addition, John claimed that Eadric had defected to Cnut with a contingent of men from Southampton and Wiltshire. However, although Edmund had been unable to defeat the invaders and their English allies, Cnut had failed to deliver a knock-out blow and withdrew eastward to besiege London. After more inconclusive battles, Edmund was eventually reconciled with Eadric Streona, who then betrayed the king at the hard-fought battle of Ashingdon (Essex). Following this, Edmund and Cnut met at Alney (Gloucestershire) and agreed to divide England; Edmund took Wessex and Cnut took Mercia. Within a matter of months, Edmund Ironside was dead – possibly from wounds sustained at Ashingdon – and Cnut took the kingdom. Within a year he had executed the treacherous Eadric Streona, along with three other members of the English elite. To further secure his position, Cnut married Emma, the widow of Æthelred; she prudently sent her sons by Æthelred (Edward and Alfred) to Normandy for their own safety. Edmund Ironside's surviving brother, Eadwig, and Edmund's wife and sons fled abroad. Eadwig was murdered when he returned to England but Edmund's sons were safe in Hungary, beyond Cnut's reach.

Had there been no Norman Conquest, then 1016 would no doubt be better known, since it would not have been overshadowed by the crushing end of Anglo-Saxon England which occurred exactly fifty years later. In 1016, though, the change was profound. The old Anglo-Saxon dynasty had been replaced by a Danish one and England was now part of a Viking North Sea Empire.

13

HOW 'UNREADY' WAS ÆTHELRED?

Before we examine the aftermath of the Viking conquest of 1016 and the subsequent reign of Cnut, we need to pause and ask: was the conquest a result of fatal flaws in the leadership of Anglo-Saxon England? And, in particular, how far was King Æthelred responsible for the Anglo-Saxon defeat at the hands of the Viking invaders?

Æthelred II is perhaps the most infamous of all the Anglo-Saxon monarchs and the one most associated with unmitigated failure and disaster. The image of Æthelred the Unready is one which has firmly imprinted itself onto the public psyche, and the view of Æthelred's reign as a long series of defeats and inactivity in the face of Viking attacks has become deep rooted. However, Æthelred, whose name meant 'royal-counsel/wisdom', was never actually called 'the unready' by his contemporaries and the original epitaph given to him was *unræd*. This does not mean 'unready' and was, instead, a pun on his name, creating the juxtaposition: Æthelred *unræd* or, in modern translation, 'royal-counsel/wisdom', 'ill-advised'. Although this was the original nickname, even this name was not contemporary and was not used until the twelfth century. This means that the view of Æthelred as the unready king was not one which was associated with him in the primary sources or even one which was associated with him soon after his death. In addition, the negative force of this twelfth-century nickname was not actually aimed at Æthelred at all, but instead at the ineffectiveness of his counsellors. Despite this, it has to be admitted that we do gain a very negative view of Æthelred from the primary sources and, in particular, the *Abingdon Chronicle* of the *Anglo-Saxon Chronicle* and from Bishop Wulfstan's *Sermo Lupi ad Anglos* (*Sermon of the Wolf to the English*). It is from these sources that our opinions of Æthelred have been largely formed.

The nature of the case against Æthelred

The most damning piece of evidence concerning Æthelred's failure as a king has to be his inability to firmly secure the succession for his children. Despite all the upheaval and stress that the Viking Wars had put upon the West Saxon royal line, up to 1016 there had been an unbroken line of members of the house of Cerdic (the legendary founder of Wessex) on the throne of Wessex and, from the mid-tenth century, this family had also ruled England. This by no means meant that the succession had always been straightforward and there had been significant tension between members of this family at various points; but, before the reign of Æthelred, the throne had not passed out of West Saxon hands. However, upon the death of Æthelred the country was in the midst of an invasion by a prince of Denmark and, despite a brief period of joint rule between Edmund Ironside and Cnut of Denmark, England became a part of an Anglo-Danish empire which, at times, also encompassed Norway and Sweden. It is this break from the rule of the house of Wessex, lasting twenty-six years, which more than anything else has prompted Æthelred's negative reputation.

Æthelred is also widely associated with 'ineffective military activity',[1] and the closing years of his reign 'witness a military collapse'.[2] The fact that Æthelred failed to 'survive the Viking onslaught' and seemed incapable of stemming the Viking raids and preventing Danish conquest have all contributed to his image as a failed king.[3] The continued buying-off of the Vikings can also be seen as a 'serious indictment on his military capabilities'.[4] This view can be seen in the changing way that the paying of *Danegeld* was reported in the *Chronicle*. The first accounts discussing this practice in Æthelred's reign referred to the paying of *Danegeld* in the same neutral way that the *Chronicle* had referred to Alfred paying off the Vikings. However, by the end of the reign of Æthelred, the details given about the tribute appear to show disillusionment after years of bitter experience.[5] In 994 the *Chronicle* states, without moral comment, that 'they were paid 16,000 pounds in money', whereas in 1014 it reports that 'on top of all these evils, the king ordered 21,000 pounds to be paid to the army'.[6] The military failure, coupled with the failure of Æthelred to successfully pay off the Vikings, gave the impression of Æthelred as a king who was incapable of defending his kingdom and was powerless to stop the Viking attacks. This is summed up particularly well in the entry for 1011 in the *Chronicle*, which wearily states: 'All these disasters befell us through bad policy, in that they were never offered tribute in time nor fought against; but when they had done most to our injury, peace and truce were made with them.'[7] In short, the inability of Æthelred to protect his people either through military force or through buying the Vikings off was made particularly evident by the events of 1016 and the coming of Cnut to the English throne. Many other kings of Wessex and kings of England had suffered setbacks and defeats when confronted with Vikings – and Alfred, of course, had also, like Æthelred in 1014, lost his kingdom for a time – but, despite this, no other monarch seems to have been perceived as so disastrous and as out of control of events as the *Chronicle* would have us believe about Æthelred.

Another way in which the *Chronicle* presented Æthelred as having been out of control, albeit in a personal sense, is the image of him as a perpetrator of vicious and spasmodic acts of violence. These sudden fits of 'spite, paranoia and rage'[8] provide fuel for accusations against the moral character of the king.[9] The most noticeable of these apparently wilful acts of violence were the ravaging of Rochester in 986, the blinding of Ælfgar, son of Ælfric, in 993, and the massacre of the Danes on St Brice's Day.

The blinding of Ælfgar was traditionally thought of as an act of vengeance visited on an innocent son for the crimes of his father as, in the preceding year, *Ealdorman* Ælfric had warned the Viking army of an impending battle and fled by night from the army.[10] In addition, the evidence from Æthelred's charters suggest that the Danes who were murdered on St Brice's Day were not a group of Viking raiders who had entered Oxford but, instead, were the unfortunate victims of ethnic hatred (see Chapter 12). The atrocity appears to have been carried out against first generation, ethnically distinct Viking traders and, as such, shows Æthelred's order for the massacre of all the Danes as not so much a royally executed order but rather an exploitation of ethnic hatred.[11] All of this gives the impression of an unstable king, of a violent disposition, and who failed to act within the appropriate bounds of kingship. By allowing himself to use this underlying ethnic hatred for his own purposes, Æthelred failed to unite his kingdom and, instead, deliberately exploited the ethnic differences within it. This has led at least one historian to argue that Æthelred strayed across the line of strong, royal government and into open tyranny, and that the sanctioned use of assassination and mutilation undermined confidence in his regime.[12] The importance of St Brice's Day lay not so much in the awful events of the day, but in the way it helped to alienate the Scandinavian people living within Æthelred's kingdom, and that it further deepened the rifts within the fabric of society.

Consequently, one of Æthelred's greatest failures lay in his inability to reconcile regional divisions. England was a country which had only very recently been united and, as such, its unity was centred on, and symbolised by, the king and his personality.[13] As such, the actions of the king were vital to the promotion of national unity. However, once Æthelred achieved his majority he seems to have supported western or northern Mercian leaders at the expense of the East Anglian elites, and by doing so he further exacerbated regional tensions. By alienating these nobles, Æthelred threw them into the arms of the Danish Vikings and helped to significantly weaken his own kingdom. In times of peace these disputes may have remained local, but the pressure resulting from the new Viking raids helped to translate these disputes onto the 'stage of national politics'.[14] It has been further argued that the pursuit of these feuds and the developing history of the relationships between these key figures and rival claimants for the throne led to the volatile, and apparently treasonable, behaviour of many of the major players of this period.[15] Although Æthelred cannot be blamed for the Viking invasions, he can be held accountable for his policy of being 'incapable of presiding over regional rivalries with the necessary degree of circumspection to avoid driving one party to take desperate measures'.[16]

Therefore, it is necessary to conclude that the invasion and conquest of England by Svein in 1013 and Cnut in 1016 were made possible because of the support of the *Danelaw* and Northumbria.[17] The conquest of the north by the kings of Wessex had been a hard-fought affair and it was only when the people of the north had decided that they would rather be ruled by Wessex than by the Norse that any permanent headway was made. This meant that there were still many in the north who may well have felt that rule by a Viking king was preferable to a southern one, particularly if the southern one was unable to fully represent their interests. Throughout his reign, Æthelred failed to unite England and many of his actions can be seen as divisive. This meant that Æthelred failed in one of the most fundamental areas of kingship: to bring his country together. His failure to do this in the face of prolonged Viking attack had disastrous consequences, since those leaders and *ealdormen* that he had alienated found that, in the Viking leaders Svein and Cnut, they had an alternative option for kingship.

Æthelred not only succeeded in dividing the country, he also succeeded in creating division within his own family at a time of national crisis. His insistence that his adult sons should stand aside in favour of his younger family, by his second wife Emma of Normandy, divided the dynasty and alienated these elder sons from his previous marriage. The divisions that Æthelred had created within the country meant that his eldest sons naturally found supporters within the provincial rivalries of the day. In consequence, the disadvantaged East Anglians and eastern Mercians rallied around Athelstan, Æthelred's eldest son, in the hope of creating a regime more favourable to themselves.[18] The question of succession is another example of Æthelred's lack of political astuteness as, by alienating his own sons during a period of sustained Viking threat and, further exacerbating the existing political and regional divisions that he had already created, Æthelred demonstrated a monumental failure of judgement. By creating an avoidable succession crisis in the middle of a very turbulent period, Æthelred revealed that he was unable to grasp either the consequences of his actions or the severity of the situation. Given the fact that Æthelred's own succession had been made turbulent through his own father's lack of clear planning, it might have been expected that Æthelred would have been far more prepared when it came to the succession of his own sons.

Æthelred also seems to have been a remarkably poor judge of men. There are numerous complaints in his charters of the 980s which refer to men who had led him astray, and the *Chronicle* seems to suggest that his military leaders had an 'alarming tendency to run away'.[19] But perhaps his greatest and most disastrous failure of judgement was the misguided trust he placed in Eadric Streona, *ealdorman* of Mercia from 1007 to 1017. The unreliability of Eadric and his tendency to betray those who trusted him massively contributed to the downfall of his own country, as his defection in the middle of a 'highly charged domestic situation effectively undermined English resistance'.[20] However, it was not just Eadric but also Æthelred's dependence on a small clique of noblemen which antagonised many of his more important subjects.[21] Once again, Æthelred's lack of political astuteness came to the fore. By supporting the ambitions of a small group of men, many of whom, like Eadric, could not be trusted, at the expense of his other nobles, Æthelred succeeded in further alienating many important people.

Had Æthelred chosen to favour men who were competent and loyal, this favouritism would not have been so great an issue, but his failure to surround himself with men of this type shows his failure to grasp what the kingdom needed. The fact that, in 1017, Cnut ordered the execution of Eadric, despite his defection to him in 1015, because he could not trust him, is an indictment of the kind of man that Eadric was. Overall, Æthelred's reign was not a sustained period of uniform degeneracy but one undermined by both the Vikings and the internecine conflict between those in a position to influence the king.[22]

Æthelred the Unready, the case for the defence

However, as always with history, the situation was not as simple as it first appears. Although Æthelred's reign was one of sustained Viking attack, twenty-five years out of his thirty-eight-year reign were peaceful. It is also interesting to note that, despite the incredibly negative tone of the *Chronicle*, it reserves specific criticism for and bemoans the conduct of military executives such as *ealdormen* Ælfric and Eadric Streona of Mercia, rather than the king himself.[23] The chronicler even declared sympathetically, when Æthelred died, that the king 'had held his kingdom with great toils and difficulties as long as his life lasted'.[24] This suggests that the chronicler felt that, despite the many and various military defeats of his reign, that Æthelred had wrestled with impossible circumstances.

It is also true that Æthelred faced a very different kind of threat from that which had previously been seen. It has been convincingly demonstrated that Æthelred faced an army of two to three times the size of that faced by Alfred the Great in the late ninth century.[25] Further analysis supports this argument by suggesting that, not only was the Viking army significantly larger, but it was also a different type of army to the ones which had previously been seen and thus was a new sort of threat. The Viking armies had by now had two centuries of fighting experience, and Æthelred did not face a band of raiders but, instead, was confronted with a highly trained army of professional soldiers whose purpose was not to colonise but to fight.[26] Æthelred was also facing an army which, for the first time, was commissioned and commanded by the king of Denmark. Given the size of this threat, Æthelred and his advisors did attempt to respond to the Vikings in a number of different ways via resistance, complex negotiation, *Danegeld* and alliance-building with Normandy.[27] The paying off of the Viking army was not a new technique and, in contrast to the wearisome tone in which the *Chronicle* describes the paying of *Danegeld* by the end of Æthelred's reign, at the beginning it was accepted as a perfectly acceptable solution.

Æthelred was also adept at turning the leaders of the Viking army against each other and exploiting the complicated political situation in Scandinavia against the invading king of Denmark. At the end of the tenth century, Norway was being ruled by the Earls of Lade (important northern Norwegian lords) under the overlordship of the kings of Denmark. In 994 the *Chronicle* tells us that Olaf Tryggvason and Svein of Denmark attacked London together. However, later in the year Olaf met with Æthelred at Andover and Æthelred acted as his sponsor at his confirmation, with the promise that Olaf would not return to England (see Chapter 12). The following year Olaf returned to Norway and proclaimed himself the king of Norway. It seems likely that Æthelred was involved in funding Olaf in his attempt on the Norwegian throne in order to destabilise Danish control in the region and reduce the Danish pressure on England. It also seems likely that Æthelred used this tactic again in 1015. After the death of Olaf Tryggvason in 1000, Norway had reverted back to Danish control until the arrival of Olaf Haraldsson in Norway in 1015. Olaf Haraldsson had been in England in 1009, where he had fought on the side of King Svein Forkbeard of Denmark, and was also there, in 1012, when he received part of the largest *Danegeld* of all time: £48,000 in silver. It's very possible that it was his share of this treasure that funded his bid for the throne.

The political situation in England, however, was unstable and many men switched sides more than once. After 1013, Olaf Haraldsson deserted Svein and fought on the side of Æthelred. Like Olaf Tryggvason, it seems that it was from Æthelred that he received encouragement and the resources to pursue his claim to the Norwegian throne. Clearly, Æthelred could be a shrewd operator.

The two Olafs were not the only Viking leaders to change sides and, after the murder of Archbishop Ælfheah in 1012 by his Viking captors, Thorkell the Tall – in disgust at his men's actions – defected and fought for Æthelred. The fact that seasoned warriors such as Thorkell and Olaf Haraldsson were prepared to fight for Æthelred suggests that he was capable of commanding at least some respect. Morover, Æthelred was also the subject of a highly prestigious Scandinavian-style praise poem of a type referred to as *skaldic* verse.[28] The Icelandic *skaldic* poet Gunnlaug Serpent-tongue supposedly arrived at the English royal court and delivered a *skaldic* poem in honour of Æthelred. It is unclear whether this actually occurred, as it is only recorded in the late thirteenth-century saga about his life. However, what matters is the acceptance of Æthelred within the same sphere as that which the heroes of saga society inhabited. This would suggest that, at least in the thirteenth century, Æthelred was viewed as an impressive northern European king on a par with his Viking Danish, Norwegian and Swedish counterparts; this view of him may well also have prevailed during his actual reign.[29]

It is also interesting to note that the *Chronicle* entry for the year 1000 describes the king going into the British kingdom of Strathclyde and ravaging it.[30] This shows that Æthelred was capable of leading his army, even if it seems that he did not personally lead his army against the Vikings. It is hard to understand why Æthelred chose to lead a raid into Strathclyde but, unlike his predecessors, not against the Viking invaders. The Vikings had always been very adept at smelling out weakness and it may have been felt that the possibility of Æthelred dying in battle and leaving behind a child heir was too great a risk to take. The attack on the kingdom of Strathclyde may, in contrast, have been considered less of a risk and therefore safe for the king to lead.

In addition, although modern interpretations focus heavily on the military aspect of Æthelred's defence of the realm, this was not the only way that Æthelred attempted to protect his people. The Viking raids had for a long time been seen as divine retribution for the sins of the nation and, in the writings of Wulfstan of York, the killing of Æthelred's half-brother, Edward King and Martyr, by persons unknown in 978 was described as: 'A full, the greatest treachery there is in the world' and was viewed as the catalyst for the Viking attacks.[31] Within a fundamentally religious kingdom, it would have seemed only natural that a crime as great as regicide should have taken on a larger dimension and been viewed as leading to worsening attacks.[32] It may well have been that Æthelred and his advisors felt that the best way for the nation to atone for the death of Edward, even though they personally were not directly accused of complicity in it within contemporary society, was to recognise his saintly status and to promote his cult. In the *Chronicle, Manuscript D*, the fact that Edward's death was not avenged seems to have been regarded as being as large a crime as the killing itself and, as Æthelred was Edward's closest kinsman, the later promotion of his brother's cult may have been his attempt to correct this error; although, as Æthelred was only a child at the time of his brother's murder, he was unable to avenge his death at the time. God had taken on the role of avenger and, therefore, the recognition of Edward as a saint showed that the leading men appreciated the depth of both the original sin and also how it had been compounded by a lack of retribution.

This recourse to a religious solution for a political and military problem is not only witnessed in Æthelred's embracing of the cult of his brother. The arrival of a new army under the command of Thorkell the Tall in England in August 1009 initiated a new wave of increased Viking attacks and the immediate response to this threat seems to have been the law code known as *VII Æthelred*. This code was an attempt to gain the mercy of God through a programme of national penance, which involved fasting, alms giving, confession and abstinence from wrong doings.[33] The next response to the crisis was also a devotional one and seems to have been the minting of the *Agnus Dei* coins which had the Lamb of God on the obverse and a dove on the reverse. Only twenty-one of these coins have so far been discovered and their rarity has led to questions over their exact purpose, although it seems likely that they were linked to the law code *VII Æthelred*.[34] This was by no means the first time that kings had turned to prayer when faced by the Vikings: in 854 King Æthelwulf enacted the decimation of all of his land, along with a special programme of prayer every Sunday; Alfred found inspiration through translating the first fifty psalms; and Edgar issued a special law code to deal with the famine of 962–63.[35] As such, Æthelred's attempt to find a religious solution to a military problem should not be seen as a weakness but rather as indicative of the world in which he lived. To his people and counsellors this would have been as real a strategy as armed combat.

In addition to all the ways in which Æthelred attempted to defend his kingdom, it is important not to view his entire thirty-eight-year reign as a series of defeats because, if the whole of Æthelred's reign had been so militarily disastrous, it is highly unlikely that he would have been able to reign for those thirty-eight years. Ultimately he was unsuccessful, but many of his policies would have appeared sensible at the time and we must not allow the events of 1016 to overshadow his earlier achievements.[36] It is also important to note that the cumulative effect of thirty years of raiding would have been enough to demoralise a population and it is no wonder, in this environment of disillusionment, that resistance to the Vikings crumbled towards the end of Æthelred's reign. Æthelred was therefore not as incompetent a leader as is often assumed. Despite the fact that his reign would end in defeat, it is important to remember that he did survive as king for thirty-eight years and this – given the scale of the threat – was an impressive achievement. Also, the epitaph of 'unready' is entirely unfair, as he did actually adopt a variety of different strategies in attempting to resist the Viking attacks.

The military failure of Æthelred's reign can also be blamed on the divisions, rivalries and treachery of his own noblemen. Although Æthelred did little to reconcile the divisions within England during his reign, it must be remembered that, when Æthelred ascended the throne, England as a single, unified nation-state was barely twenty years old. Too much talk of unity conceals the dependence on kinship and regional lordship, and by 'indulging in these fantasies' of unity we create the unreasonable expectation that the kingdom was strong enough to survive the Danish onslaught.[37] It is also pertinent to remember that Æthelred could not take for granted the loyalty of the Mercians, the Northumbrians, or those living within the *Danelaw* and, due to this, he was very dependent on the local leaders of those areas. This may have held together in times of peace, but in times of threat 'the fragile edifice threatened to come apart at the seams'.[38] Moreover, the struggle for political dominance between east and west Mercia reflected wider social and cultural issues which related not to the failings of Æthelred but to the unresolved problems arising from Edward the Elder's 're-conquest' of Mercia at the beginning of the tenth century.[39] Æthelred was also thwarted by the constant treachery of the English magnates and, in particular, by the defection of Eadric of Mercia.[40] The defection of Eadric in the middle of a very turbulent domestic situation effectively undermined English resistance, and the fact that Cnut executed Eadric within a year of becoming king shows just how little Cnut believed that he could be trusted. With friends like Eadric, Æthelred had no need for enemies.

It is also important to consider Æthelred's apparently unprovoked acts of violence within the military and political context of the time. The ravaging of Rochester occurred only after a three to four-year dispute with the bishop of Rochester; Ælfgar's blinding was squarely within Anglo-Saxon law and was most likely due to his own crimes during Æthelred's minority; and lastly, St Brice's Day was aimed at mercenaries and traders whom the king was probably right not to trust and who could easily have been sending information home to the Danes. It was also carried out by men who had suffered from thirty years of unprovoked Viking attacks so, whether it was just or not, they had every reason to hate the Danes.[41] The fact that the massacre is recorded as having occurred in Oxford, which was never part of the *Danelaw*, suggests that the massacre was carried out not against the Danes from the first phase of Scandinavian colonisation, who had assimilated into Anglo-Saxon society, but first generation Danes who had close links with Denmark.[42] In fact, however reprehensible the events of St Brice's Day were, they do show a confident, active ruler who was well aware of the national mood and the general resentment and ethnic hatred felt towards the Danes.[43] Whether he was morally right to use this hatred is an entirely different matter to whether it shows him to be a perceptive king who was able to manipulate the public mood for his own benefit. Similarly, the chronicler did not recall this event with the disgust that we tend to view it with today. This suggests that, at the time, these 'acts of spasmodic violence' were not seen as such and that, given the general violence of the period, these acts were not viewed as anything particularly unusual. This means that these actions cannot really be used to show Æthelred as an ineffective monarch and, instead, can be seen more as a king using – what appears to us as – extreme measures in a time of high tension.

The rehabilitation of Æthelred

Æthelred's reign also witnessed impressive advancements in legislation, coinage and the development of the medieval state. The shire, sheriff and royal *writ* (written government orders) were all either perfected or make their first appearance under Æthelred.[44] The evidence from royal diplomas shows that there existed a royal secretariat which acted on the authority of the *witenagemot* (royal council) and who were also responsible for drawing up administrative communication from the king to his subjects.[45] This shows that Æthelred had at his disposal an office which was competent enough to perform the written business of government, and secure enough not to crumble under the pressure of the escalating Viking incursions. The administrative system and economy also managed to cope with the heavy demands made upon it, with the system under Æthelred responding effectively to the turbulence of his reign[46] and the economy managing to sustain the huge *Danegeld* payments culminating in a sum of £82,000 in 1018.[47] This means there must have been an extensive network of state machinery in order to produce the number of coins necessary for the economy to function, revealing a country that, despite a second phase of Viking invasion and conquest, still maintained a stable and thriving economy capable of responding to these huge demands. It also shows a king with enough power and control to impose high taxes upon his people and 'able to extract every last drop of wealth from his subjects'.[48] The picture from the administrative and legislative side of Æthelred's reign does not, therefore, show a man who was a failure as king. Instead, we see well-conducted domestic affairs prospering under the management of an effective ruler, who faced challenges which would have swiftly overwhelmed a less organised state.

An explanation for the negative image of Æthelred

It is necessary to remember when considering Æthelred's reign that the primary source of evidence for the period is not as objective as one would wish. It is all too easy to take the *Chronicle* account of his reign at face value and to accord it the respect due to contemporary authority, but it was not a set of annals drafted year by year. Instead, critical examination has revealed that its 'Æthelred-annals' form a retrospective account, written by one man, probably in London, during the early years of Cnut's reign.[49] The narrator allowed his own feelings 'to permeate his presentation of events' and he abandoned the brevity associated with the *Chronicle* and instead adopted a more literary style.[50] As these particular *Chronicle* annals were written after the end of Æthelred's reign, they were very much coloured by the events of 1016, and by concentrating on the Danish invasions the chronicler 'telescopes the reign' and created the impression that this was the only theme worth discussing.[51] Furthermore, the chronicle failed to mention the military resistance of the reign in the form of Byrhtnoth's last stand at Maldon, or the valour of Ulfkell Snilling of the East Angles, who resisted Thorkell the Tall at the battle of Ringmere in 1010. He also failed to mention the great scholars of the period, such as Ælfric of Eynsham and Byrhtferth of Ramsey, and the unknown monks who produced some of the most notable illustrated manuscripts of the entire Anglo-Saxon period.[52] Their achievements indicate that these people were able to work relatively undisturbed in a society which the chronicler would have us believe was in chaos. The *Sermo Lupi ad Anglos* (*Sermon of the Wolf to the English*) also gives the impression of chaos. However, it is important to remember that this, too, dates from the last part of Æthelred's reign, when England was finally overwhelmed by the formidable force led by the Danish kings and, therefore, however applicable it was to the situation when it was preached, it cannot be used to describe Æthelred's reign as a whole.[53] This means that, although the primary evidence is useful in giving us a view of the end of Æthelred's reign, it should not be used to judge his reign as a whole.

Æthelred 'the unready'?

Even the most sympathetic and impartial historian would find it difficult to completely rehabilitate the reputation of Æthelred. Æthelred ultimately failed militarily against the Vikings, he failed to reconcile the regional divisions within England and he created divisions within his own family. However, given the combination of circumstances which faced him, it is hard to imagine how any ruler would have emerged unscathed. Æthelred confronted a professional, trained army and was troubled by treacherous magnates who put their own interests before that of Æthelred and the kingdom. It is also important not to over-exaggerate the importance of the primary evidence when assessing this period, as it was written at the end of Æthelred's reign and, as such, shows him in his weakest position and telescopes the whole of his long reign in the light of those truly disastrous few years. Æthelred was not without serious flaws but, given the massive Viking attacks on England, he was not as 'unready' as history has judged him.

14

'One Nation ... Divisible'?

How ethnically and culturally divided was England in the early eleventh century? This is a pressing question to answer given the influx of a new wave of Scandinavian influence and personnel in the closing years of the tenth century and the first three decades of the eleventh century. We have already explored the impact of Viking settlement as a result of the first phase of Viking colonisation (see Chapter 8), but what occurred in the second phase was equally crucial and eventually led to a period of time when Scandinavian influence apparently reached new heights with a king – Cnut – who ruled both Denmark and England. The political and military impact of that North Sea Empire (see Chapter 15) and its long-term consequences (see Chapter 16) will be explored later, but in this chapter we will be exploring the effects on the cultural unity of England from the renewed upsurge of Scandinavian influence.[1]

Cultural apartheid in Anglo-Saxon England?
A tale of two law codes

One of the clearest pieces of evidence often cited for the way in which the second phase of Viking attacks opened up the ethnic divisions latent in England is in the promulgating of separate law codes for different parts of England by Æthelred II. In 997 he issued his so-called 'Wantage law code', which included a great deal of Scandinavian terminology and seemed designed for use in the *Danelaw* region. Issued at Wantage (Berkshire), it gave royal sanction to the local court customs which were operating in the Five Boroughs of the East Midlands. According to this law code's provisions, the twelve leading *thegns* who lived in each *wapentake* (the Danish equivalent of the local government area of the *hundred*, operating in southern England) were to swear on holy relics not to accuse an innocent man, nor conceal a guilty one. In the absence of a unanimous verdict, the agreement of eight *thegns* would suffice.[2] This is the earliest reference in English law to the existence of a sworn jury. To what extent this was an institution unique to the Five Borough is unclear from the code, but it certainly seems to have been associated with the way that justice was carried out there.

At about the same time he issued his 'Woodstock law code', which was thoroughly Anglo-Saxon in its terms and approach. As if to emphasise this, it specifically states that it was promulgated 'according to the law of the English'.[3] The phrase in its prologue – '*æfter Engla lage*' – was clearly meant to differentiate it from the '*Dene laga*' (Danish Law) of the Wantage Law Code, although the actual phrase does not appear in the prologue of the Wantage code.[4] Within approximately two decades this contrasting pair of phrases had become established within law making associated with Archbishop Wulfstan, under both Æthelred II and Cnut.

The conclusion seems obvious: the arrival of a new wave of Scandinavian immigrants had unsettled the careful fusion of cultures which had been painstakingly created, under West Saxon rule, in the earlier tenth century. Cultural differences, which had become diluted over time, were now very much back on the agenda and apparent to all. As one historian has commented: 'Not all of Athelstan's successors would be such strong leaders and, before long, cultural tensions would begin to flare.'[5] This certainly seems to have occurred with regard to these new law codes and would seem wholly consistent with a new influx of Danish landlords in the early eleventh century.[6] Not surprisingly, ethnicity has become one of the key ways in which early medieval society is defined and understood.[7]

The evidence for unity, as opposed to ethnic divisions, in eleventh century England

These two law codes, therefore, seem to suggest a distinctive cultural character to the *Danelaw*. This seems consistent with a trend which had started in the mid-tenth century, under Edgar, when his fourth law code (*c.* 962–63) allowed for the exercise, in Danish areas, of 'good laws as they can best decide on.'[8] However, this conclusion needs a little more consideration.

It is common practice to describe the area of Viking settlement as the *Danelaw* and the term is used in this study, as it is in most others that examine this period of history. However, this may actually accord the region too distinctive and homogenous a character. The term itself does not actually appear in any document prior to a later law code of Æthelred II in 1008. It then occurs throughout the eleventh and twelfth centuries to distinguish an area where it was thought that Danish law, as opposed to Mercian and West Saxon laws, prevailed. But the significance of this can be easily overstated. In reality, there is little in this 'Danish law' that looks particularly Scandinavian, beyond the use of some Danish terminology.[9] And many of these terms were simply the renaming of existing institutions and practices.[10] Furthermore, the different law codes were probably designed for political rather than cultural reasons. For Edgar, it made a southern king appear more sensitive to northern sensibilities, regardless of ethnicity.[11] Closer analysis of his law making shows a king who insisted on some laws being applied across the whole kingdom – such as the use of one coinage – whilst others were subject to local variation. Far from suggesting that the *Danelaw* was autonomous, this suggests a situation in which Crown authority was enhanced by Anglo-Danish gentry having some local freedom of action, whilst still being very much under royal administration.[12] In addition, such ethnic labels were more likely to have been used as regional identifiers and they reveal more about how outsiders sought to categorise an area than about how inhabitants of that area viewed themselves.[13] In short, the ethnic labels in the law codes say more about regionalism than about ethnicity.[14] At other times, different regional labels were used to define the areas in question, such as 'Northumbria', 'East Anglia' and '*Norðleoda*' (North people). When the 'Danish-ness' of the area was referred to, as it was in the law codes of Æthelred II, and later under both Cnut and Edward the Confessor, it was probably because it was a useful way to recognise regional identity within the overall kingdom of England.[15]

Where 'Danes' appears as a label in other written sources, it was not a term used to describe the descendants of those Viking colonists who had arrived in the late ninth century; instead it was used to denote 'recent arrivals: the Danish raiders, merchants and nobles who arrived from the mid-tenth century'.[16] These were more likely to be urban merchants than the more numerous and well-established rural inhabitants of the *Danelaw*.[17] These former were 'recent Danes',[18] whose commitment to England was as questionable as their long-term residency. This makes sense of the Massacre of St Brice's Day, which could never have come remotely near to the targeting of all those with Viking ancestry. In the same way, the early eleventh-century condemnations of Anglo-Saxons for following Viking fashions almost certainly picked on a fashion feature associated with newly arrived and upwardly mobile immigrants who were resented as intruders. Those English who imitated them were accused of 'abandoning the English practices which your fathers followed, and in loving the practices of heathen men who begrudge you life ... [you show] that you despise your race and your ancestors ...' The practice that so disturbed this particular clerical correspondent was the copying of 'Danish fashion with bared necks and blinded eyes ...'[19] This seems a fairly innocuous practice, but was clearly disapproved of precisely because it was so easily identified as being associated with a distinct and alien social group. These people would certainly not have been the descendants of Viking settlers of the ninth century, but rather those Scandinavian newcomers who were associated with the problems facing England in the early eleventh century. In exactly the same way, the cleric Alcuin had written to the Northumbrian king in 793 condemning the 'trimming of beard and hair, in which you have wished to resemble the pagans'.[20] It is instructive that in 1066 – as evidenced by the Bayeux Tapestry – Normans affected just such an extreme hairstyle, with the back of the head shaved, and were making 'a conscious statement about their origins, however bogus',[21] which proclaimed their supposed Viking ancestry.

Another attempt at identifying newcomers via unfamiliar and suspect social practices lay behind the accusation, by the chronicler John of Wallingford (died *c.*1258), that Viking men had seduced married English women and persuaded the daughters of English nobles to be their mistresses through the questionable habits of bathing every Saturday, frequently changing their woollen clothes and regularly combing their hair.[22] Revealingly, his description of this seductive cleanliness was associated with his account of the Massacre of St Brice's Day. This is consistent with the sociological phenomenon of stereotyping the suspect 'other' and, in the context of the eleventh century and in myths that outlasted this period, was clearly prompted by the arrival of a new and distrusted social group. At the same time, reading between the lines of these condemnations suggests that the fashion characteristics so roundly condemned were actually being appreciated by – and copied by – significant numbers of people beyond this target group of newly arrived immigrants. So, even in this respect, what was being described was not a Viking ethnic signal and this tells us nothing about a distinct and ethnically recognisable mass of people living in the *Danelaw*. These established settlers were not the target of the anxieties of clerical letter writers and later chroniclers.

This does not mean, however, that there was no sense of Danish character in the well-established communities of the east and north. Svein Forkbeard's strategy in 1013, of reserving 'the greatest damage that any army could do' for the area he entered after 'he had crossed Watling Street',[23] suggests that he may have felt more affinity with the inhabitants north and east of that old frontier line. Nevertheless, the overall evidence does not suggest a deep cultural and ethnic division within Late Anglo-Saxon England.

Instead, it has been argued that, by the early eleventh century: 'Political lordship and allegiance rather than Anglo-Saxon, Celtic, Danish or Norse race were the determining factors'[24] in defining identity. In fact: 'Despite the [new] influx of Danes and the social and legal peculiarities they sustained, the inhabitants of England in the eleventh century were as conscious as they had been in Bede's time that there was a land called England whose inhabitants could be described as Englishmen.'[25] A contrasting view challenges this belief in growing national unity and, instead, argues in favour of older, regional identities being more important to most people in the eleventh century. But even this challenge still insists that 'Danishness/Vikingness' was irrelevant, although its conclusion is reached from a different standpoint since: 'When England split again in 1035, it was the older pattern of Mercia and Northumbria against Wessex which reasserted itself. Few people actually felt English ... and the identity of Mercians, Northumbrians and West Saxons was arguably more important than that of Danes.'[26]

Indeed, counterintuitively, Scandinavian influence increased in the law codes under Æthelred II, even though fewer Anglo-Scandinavians appeared at court. This may reveal a desire to both 'distance himself from those of Scandinavian descent', in a period of renewed Viking attacks, while 'trying to placate these subjects' who were descendants of the first phase of immigration.

Despite this complication it seems that, generally, 'cultural traits became shared and over time ethnic boundaries became blurred.'[27] As a consequence, it was an 'Anglo-Scandinavian state' which emerged during the early eleventh century, in which newly arrived immigrants quickly became integrated into the English system, which was flexible enough to adapt in order to accept them. In a detailed study of the relationship between the Fenland abbeys of Ramsey and Thorney (Cambridgeshire) and local Danish lords in the 1020s, revealed in written monastic sources, there is evidence for both anti-Danish sentiment and the integration of these same Danes into the system of patronage which supported these establishments.[28] Clearly, the matter of ethnicity was complicated and, at times, sensitive in the turbulent context of renewed Danish raids and eventual conquest, but it still allowed for these Danes to become an influential and integrated part of East Anglian society.

In the same way, even at the height of Æthelred's attempts to resist Viking attacks he was employing Scandinavians in his armed forces. In 994 his successful effort to separate Olaf Tryggvason from Svein Forkbeard was based on a financial relationship which provided a large sum of money, along with gifts and provisions, and was clearly sufficient to buy Olaf. In this case the arrangement did not cause Olaf to act as a mercenary captain in England but, instead, he shifted his operations back to Norway where he caused trouble for Svein until his death at the battle of Svold in 1000. Æthelred probably felt that it was money well spent. A more obvious example of the employment of Viking mercenaries was when Thorkell the Tall and forty-five ships switched sides to support the English in 1012. In fact, the term *Danegeld*, though commonly applied to all tribute payments to Viking marauders, was strictly speaking actually the term used to describe the annual *here-geld* (army tax) instituted from 1012 to pay Thorkell's mercenary fleet. So, at times there were Viking forces operating on both sides in the conflict. The Scandinavian term *liðsmann* – a member of the fleet – is first recorded in *Manuscript E* under the year 1036, but the force seems to have been in existence since the time of Æthelred II. And this practice was not new: the late tenth-century chronicler Æthelweard (probably writing *c.* 978–88) referred to Viking fleets operating in English waters under treaty arrangements. Clearly, from the rule of Edgar onwards, Viking mercenaries provided experienced warriors in the service of the king of England and could be deployed against other Vikings who were operating outside of the royal system of mercenary employment. These experienced military professionals may actually have proved more effective than the more *ad hoc* forces which were being raised by the king and the *ealdormen*. In short, Vikings may have been both part of the problem and part of the solution in the defence of Anglo-Saxon England.

Therefore, it seems that the evidence of the two law codes is more complex than at first sight. The separation of Anglo-Saxon from Scandinavian was not what characterised Late Anglo-Saxon England; on the contrary, even as kings such as Edgar and Æthelred II were involving more Scandinavians in the workings of the royal court (in the case of Edgar) and recognising Scandinavian terms and practices in law codes (in the case of Æthelred II), they were actually also enforcing their own authority across the whole of England to an unprecedented degree.[29] And many of the Scandinavians they employed were well integrated into the workings of English society and government. Late Anglo-Saxon England was actually becoming more, not less, united; and this occurred even as Viking pressures and influence increased in the second great phase of attacks and eventual conquest.

Artistic developments and the influence of Viking art forms in the eleventh century

'Scandinavian art-forms and social customs were to dominate English life in the tenth and eleventh centuries.'[30] In this process the reign of Cnut and the close association of England with Denmark, in the period 1016–42, had a noticeable impact on artistic styles. The most obvious example is the use of the Scandinavian *Ringerike* style, found on objects manufactured in England which were influenced by the art styles associated with the new ruling elite. *Ringerike* style consists of animals elaborated with extensions of foliage tendrils.[31] It was a style that was itself inspired by Anglo-Saxon and Frankish art forms and, when reintroduced to England, was readily incorporated into the use of acanthus fronds which was already a popular form of decoration.[32] Perhaps the most famous example of pure *Ringerike* style is found on a stone panel discovered in the vicinity of St Paul's churchyard, London.[33] This depicts a running mythical beast caught in the coils of a serpent-like animal. Close examination of the stone reveals that its surface received a gesso-like treatment, formed from a mixture of an animal glue binder and white pigment (often using chalk or gypsum). This formed the base for a striking colour scheme, whereby the beast was painted black with white spots, with some details picked out in brownish-red, and the serpent was painted brownish-red. A runic inscription on the side of the slab reads: 'Ginna and Toki had this stone set up'.[34] The names emphasise its Scandinavian character. A number of other *Ringerike*-style objects have been found in the vicinity of London, including another stone from St Paul's, a fragment of a stone from All-Hallows-by-the-Tower and small finds of metal and bone decorated in the style. Another example of *Ringerike* style decorates a copper-gilt strip found at Winchester (Hampshire). This probably originally formed part of a casket and is decorated with a mixture of engravings and punched animal ornament. Aspects of its decoration (the use of acanthus foliage, popular in Late Anglo-Saxon art), suggests that it was probably made in England.[35] A stirrup from Mottisfont (Hampshire) was also decorated in the style.

Alongside and incorporating Anglo-Saxon decorative motifs, the style appears on a number of eleventh-century manuscripts. In the *Winchcombe Psalter* (now in the University Library, Cambridge) a number of the decorative initials are striking examples of the style's use in the decoration of an Anglo-Saxon manuscript. The stag-like beast decorating an initial 'd' on *folio 37v* is very reminiscent of the running beast from the St Paul's churchyard stone. It is also similar to a crude stone slab from Bibury (Gloucestershire). Another manuscript showing the use of the style is the *Junius II Cædmon Bible* (now in the Bodleian Library, University of Oxford). Mixed Anglo-Saxon and *Ringerike*-style decorations are also found on a silver disc brooch discovered on the Isle of Ely (Cambridgeshire). Its Old English inscription indicates that it was owned by a woman named Ædwen.[36] Despite the obvious stimulus to the use of this artistic style from a Viking king – Cnut – ruling a North Sea Empire, the total number of such objects is modest from the south of England and even rarer in the north.[37] The Otley Slab – with fine quality *Ringerike*-style tendrils – from the parish church at Otley (Yorkshire) is one of the few northern examples.[38]

The continued taste for Scandinavian-inspired art forms reveals itself in the appearance of objects decorated in the later *Urnes* style after *c.*1050. This style consisted of extensions to the foliage-like tendrils of the *Ringerike* style until these ceased to resemble vegetation and instead became asymmetrical interlace.[39] These sinuous, snake-like creatures appear as fighting beasts on the copper-gilt Pitney Brooch, found in Somerset, which is a notable example of the art form. There is evidence that this style may have been introduced from Dublin by Scandinavian traders who were operating through the Bristol

Channel,[40] while the Pitney Brooch was probably manufactured in England. Another example of *Urnes* style produced in England can be found in the animals depicted at the feet of a figure of Christ in the church at Jevington (East Sussex). A bronze plaque found at Hammersmith (London) appears to combine aspects of *Urnes* and *Ringerike* styles. Even after the Norman Conquest the *Urnes* style was still deployed to decorate the church doorway at Kilpeck (Herefordshire), though the style was not used in any manuscript decoration until after the Norman Conquest.

Overall, the fact that the Scandinavian *Urnes* and *Ringerike* styles of artwork are more commonly found in central and southern England, than in the old Viking strongholds in the north, reveals the attraction of court fashion rather than ethnic identities.[41] As such, its distribution pattern was a product of politics affecting fashion in southern England, rather than indicating the actual presence of Scandinavians. *Ringerike* style in particular is also usually found on high-status objects and seems to represent a fairly short-lived fashion amongst aristocrats 'embracing Scandinavian fashion as a gesture to the new political leadership'.[42] And its southern bias may indicate the geographical area to which Cnut accorded the most attention; he himself was never recorded north of Oxford after he took the Crown.[43]

The impact of the second phase of Viking raids and Viking conquest on religious beliefs

While the second phase of Viking attacks might have been expected to stimulate a pagan revival, this was not to be the case. In fact, quite the opposite was true with increasing numbers of the invaders having been converted to Christianity in Scandinavia, or converting once resident in England. Far from the arrival of new Vikings undermining the Christian character of England, it was Christianity which rapidly became the cultural norm to which the newcomers aspired. A number of the new wave of Vikings were Christians on arrival and this certainly differentiated them from the earlier invaders and made eventual assimilation into English culture much easier. Cnut's father, Svein Forkbeard, had actually converted to Christianity in Scandinavia and went on to promote the faith in both Denmark and Norway. This followed a youth which was far from Christian and which may have been a reaction against the Christianity of his father, Harald Bluetooth. If this promotion of a possible 'pagan party' was a feature of his youth,[44] it was certainly not the religious position of the mature Svein. In maturity he banned the practice of pagan beliefs and the worship of idols, and ordered the adoption of Christianity in Norway. Even the earlier 'pagan period' may have been more anti-German than anti-Christian, and may have been more concerned with attempting to restrict the influence of the archbishops of Hamburg-Bremen in the affairs of Denmark. This is a very real possibility since later, on Cnut's death in 1035, there was significant conflict between his successor in Denmark – Harthacnut – and the archbishop of Hamburg-Bremen. The evidence for Svein's early paganism comes largely from the German monastic chronicler Adam of Bremen (writing in the second half of the eleventh century), who was promoting the influence of Hamburg-Bremen and whose account is therefore suspect. This suspicion is reinforced by the fact that Adam, as well as recounting Svein's paganism, also reports his promotion of Christianity. On balance then, the evidence suggests that when Svein Forkbeard conquered England in the winter of 1013–14, he did so as a second-generation Christian king of Denmark. When his son, later known as Cnut the Great to differentiate him from similarly named but less powerful monarchs, completed the Danish conquest in 1016, he did so as a third-generation Christian Danish ruler, or at least a semi-Christian. It is also likely that Cnut was baptised before he succeeded to the Crown of England. This was a major departure from the first phase of Viking conquest in the late ninth century and it had huge repercussions for the kind of religious settlement that occurred in England following this conquest. It helps to explain why Cnut so readily adapted to English culture (see Chapter 15); why he cooperated with Archbishop Wulfstan in legal encouragement of Christianity and suppression of pagan practices; and it helps explain why, in 1019, he was comfortable in writing from Denmark to promise the English that he would be a good Christian king, would uphold Edgar's law code and exhorted the recipients of the letter to keep the Sunday fast, honour the saints, confess their sins and look forward to attaining 'the bliss of the heavenly kingdom'.[45] As a consequence, the raiding and stealing that despoiled English monasteries in the late tenth and early eleventh century was due to brutal economic exploitation; it had no anti-Christian component whatsoever.

This meant that the pagans in the Viking armies which troubled and eventually conquered the England of Æthelred II had a great incentive to convert to Christianity. In so doing, they brought themselves firmly into line with their supreme commander and with the influential English elites.[46]

Even warriors as prominent as the Norwegian Olaf Tryggvason were drawn into explicitly Christian alliances in England; in 994, he was confirmed at Andover (Hampshire), with King Æthelred II as his sponsor. This was clearly designed to separate him from Svein Forkbeard, by making him Æthelred's ally and subordinate, but it was not Christianity which differentiated Olaf from Svein, since both were now officially Christians. Adam of Bremen, writing c.1080, seemed uncertain of whether Olaf had died a Christian, but this was possibly because Adam wished to suppress information which revealed Scandinavian religious indebtedness to England rather than to Hamburg-Bremen. Certainly, mid-thirteenth-century Icelandic saga tradition was confident that Olaf became a committed and active Christian and, in 999–1000, it was Olaf Tryggvason who actively encouraged the conversion of Iceland.[47]

It is noticeable that, despite the troubled times, there was actually an expansion of church building in the eleventh century. And the style of churches was the same in all areas of England; there was no significant Scandinavian style in buildings, just as there is no evidence of paganism having an impact to any significant degree. The impact of the so-called 'Tenth Century Reformation', with its revival of monasticism and more elaborate church architecture and liturgy, is seen across England. The only significantly different church, architecturally speaking, is the wooden 'stave-constructed' church at Greensted (Essex), which is similar in style to church buildings found in Scandinavia (often termed *stavkirke*, stave-churches). The church itself has been heavily restored but its construction has been dated by dendrochronology to 1063–1108. Built from half trees, hewn flat on the inside and stripped of sapwood and rounded off outside, the construction used massive quantities of timber.[48] It is considered to be the oldest wooden church still in existence.[49] However, as an example of Scandinavian architectural influence it is as unrevealing as it is unique. Built too late to be seen as a product of early eleventh-century Viking culture, it is also much older than the surviving *stavkirke* in Scandinavia. Consequently, it casts little light on Scandinavian influence.

More revealing is the dedication of Kirkdale church (North Yorkshire). The church, known as St Gregory's Minster, is famous for its external sundial, which carries the inscription: 'Orm, son of Gamal, bought St Gregory's church when it was completely ruined and collapsed, and he had it constructed recently from the ground to Christ and St Gregory, in the days of King Edward and in the days of Earl Tosti [Tostig].'[50] The inscription can therefore be dated to the period 1055–65. This remarkable Romanesque church, with its inscription reminiscent of Classical Roman forms reveals just how fully Scandinavians had become part of the culture and patronage of Christian England by the mid-eleventh century.[51]

This does not mean that there were no pagan aspects to society, however. As we have seen, Scandinavian art forms influenced jewellery and carvings; furthermore, pagan literary motifs influenced poetry, which was later preserved in Iceland. In a poem, *Knútsdráper* (*the Drápa of Cnut*), probably written for recitation at Cnut's Christian English court, the imagery of the northern pagan world was still deployed to convey the ideas of the poet, Hallvarðr. The poet used *kennings*, complex figures of speech which employed circumlocution to express meanings. Three times Cnut is described in a *kenning* based on the name of a pagan god; two references are made to *Miðgarðsormr*, the world-serpent; a reference is made to Óðinn's horse, the gallows; and there are references to *valkyries*, the mythical beings believed responsible for choosing who would die in battle. At the same time Cnut's power is described as coming from the Christian God.[52]

Another poem, *Liðsmannaflokkr* (*the Flokkr* – poem without a refrain – *of the men of the fleet*), surprisingly survives with all ten verses preserved in their correct order in a late fourteenth-century Icelandic manuscript, *Flateyjarbók* (*Flat-island Book*).[53] It purports to have been written, as a victory poem, by the warriors who fought for both Thorkell the Tall and for Cnut, and was clearly written in/for an English context, as it specifically refers to women of London and to swords 'reddened with blood on the bank[s] of the Thames.' Its exact attribution and date of composition remain uncertain. Like the poem, *Knútsdráper*, its *kennings* employ pagan Viking motifs with references to gods, including Óðinn, goddesses and a *valkyrie*.[54] There is, though, very little surviving of this literary evidence which can definitely be dated as coming from the court and context of Cnut's England, and what there is only survives in later Icelandic collections. This is not surprising given the limited survival of written sources from the period and the fact that a Christian editor in southern England would have been unlikely to preserve such material. The evidence for reintroduced pagan beliefs that appear in tenth-century place names and picture stones, for example, is in contrast to the very little impact of paganism on native English imaginative literature of the late tenth and early eleventh centuries.[55] Even if some experts are correct in their suggestion that the famous poem *Beowulf* was actually written as late as *c*.1000, due to a resurgence of pagan influences, the poem still carries distinct Christian overtones and would have been written down by a Christian monk.[56]

The limited evidence for active paganism in contrast to the dominant influence of Christianity is striking. This means that the 'pagan' motifs and designs found on brooches, in artwork and in literature should not be misinterpreted. Despite the appearance of apparently pagan symbols on eleventh-century artwork and references to pagan motifs in poetry, the overall evidence suggests that these should be interpreted as remnants of what has been termed 'cultural paganism',[57] divorced from beliefs in the old gods and their religious cults. As such, they were references to pagan origins and Scandinavian roots, rather than evidence for active pagan beliefs. On the other hand, law code evidence,[58] containing prohibitions of heathen practices, suggests that in the 1020s, and particularly in the north, there was official concern at increased occurrences of heathen practices amongst ordinary country people. At this social level there seems to have been a continuation of some pagan practices which gave rise to concerns amongst these law makers. That these laws were promulgated under Cnut shows that there was a real desire amongst the newly empowered Scandinavian elites to put a distance between themselves and anything remotely resembling pagan practice. And they were keen to condemn its practice when this occurred, often by people lower down the social hierarchy. All of this led to a 'light pagan colouring' to Late Anglo-Saxon England; but the evidence is clear that it did not lead to anything like a pagan revival.[59] Given the disapproval of the new Scandinavian rulers, who had either come to England as Christians or had rapidly assimilated to Christian culture, this is not surprising.

Given the massive impact of the second phase of Viking attacks and eventual conquest, it might have been expected that severe cultural changes would have ensued. However, this does not seem to have been the case. While Scandinavian culture, including the continued use of pagan artistic motifs, influenced a number of aspects of life in Late Anglo-Saxon England, it did so in a way which integrated into Christian Anglo-Saxon society and which rapidly accepted the dominant religious and cultural norms of that society. Overall then, it seems that, in the face of Viking upheaval and change: 'Unity had triumphed over the forces of disintegration and ethnic division.'[60]

CNUT: VIKING EMPEROR
OF THE NORTH

Although the Danish Viking, Svein Forkbeard, had briefly held the throne of England until his death in February 1014, it was really in the reign of his son, Cnut, that Viking power in England reached its crescendo. With the English ruler Edmund Ironside dying in November 1016, Cnut united the kingdoms of England and Denmark to form an Anglo-Danish North Sea empire which, at times, also included the kingdom of Norway and extended its influence into Sweden. It was everything that the Viking invaders of the ninth and tenth centuries had failed to do. However, despite the victories of Danish Viking armies, the creation of this single Anglo-Danish kingdom was by no means a foregone conclusion and, indeed, was seemingly not the design of his father, Svein Forkbeard. Svein had two sons and divided up his empire between them: Harald, the eldest, was given Denmark; while Cnut was given the much less certain, but wealthier, inheritance of the kingdom of England.

As we have already seen (see Chapter 12), after Svein's death Cnut unsuccessfully attempted to maintain the Danish hold on the English, but was forced to return to join his brother in Denmark. It is unclear exactly what Cnut expected to happen on his return home, as he had ordered coin-dies cut in England as if he expected to issue coins in his own name in Denmark. According to the author of the *Encomium Emmae Reginae* (*In Praise of Queen Emma*), Cnut wanted to rule Denmark jointly with his brother, but Harald refused.[1] The *Encomium* was composed by a cleric in St Omer (now in

France) during the later reign of Cnut's son, Harthacnut (1040–42), and is a text about the life of Cnut's queen, Emma. It was commissioned by Emma in the politically delicate period at the end of the Anglo-Danish rule. Given the issues of that time, when Cnut's death had led to a power struggle between his two sons, the matter of brotherly power sharing may have influenced the writer's take on the earlier dynastic dispute.

What is clear is that Cnut's apparent ambition was frustrated by his brother's reluctance to cooperate. Given Harald's refusal to share power, it seems likely that Cnut had two options: he could either fight his brother for control of Denmark, or he could claim England. He chose the latter and, in 1015, he launched his invasion of England, becoming sole king after the death of Edmund Ironside in 1016. As with much of the early history of Denmark, very little is known about the reign of Cnut's brother, Harald, and his death is not actually recorded. It seems likely, though, that he died at some point in 1018, as in 1019 Cnut returned to Denmark and became king of Denmark as well as of England, uniting the two kingdoms into an Anglo-Scandinavian Viking empire of the north.

Cnut's consolidation of power in England

On Cnut's formal accession to the entirety of the kingdom of England in 1017, following Edmund Ironside's death in 1016, he divided the kingdom into four major earldoms: Wessex, Mercia, East Anglia and Northumbria. He kept Wessex as royal land – although this would later be given to Earl Godwin – Mercia went to Eadric Streona, East Anglia to Thorkell the Tall and Northumbria to Eric of Hlathir, a Norwegian nobleman. However, these roles were not to last long and, later in the same year, the double-crossing Eadric Streona was killed on Cnut's orders, even though he had finally chosen the Danish side in the conflict. In *Manuscript F* of the *Anglo-Saxon Chronicle* we are told that he was 'very rightly' killed, while John of Worcester reports that his corpse was thrown over the city walls of London and left unburied.[2] It seems that Eadric Streona's frequent swapping of allegiances had finally caught up with him.

Eadric was not the only nobleman to be caught in the purge that occurred at the start of Cnut's reign. The *Chronicle* also tells us that Northman, son of *Ealdorman* Leofwine, Æthelweard, son of Æthelmaer the Stout (*ealdorman* of the western provinces) and Brihtic, son of

Ælfheah of Devonshire were killed. Given this purge it is interesting that Leofwine would later lead one of the most powerful families in England under Cnut. This was not the end of the purge, however, and in 1020 *Ealdorman* Æthelweard was outlawed and the following year Thorkell the Tall suffered the same fate – although he was reconciled with the king a year later. It has been argued, with justification, that this was just the tip of the iceberg, as the *Encomium* states that many English leaders were killed at the same time as Eadric Streona, and the later *Evesham Chronicle* reports that many of Eadric's soldiers were killed with him.[3]

The royal family was not immune from this purge and, in 1017, the *ætheling* Eadwig (brother of Edmund Ironside) was exiled and later murdered on Cnut's orders.[4] The little children of Edmund Ironside (*æthelings* Edward and Edmund) were also at risk and the 1057 entry in the *Chronicle* tells us that Cnut had them banished to Hungary. This story is expanded on by John of Worchester, who informs us that they were first sent to the king of Sweden for him to kill but, reluctant to do so, he instead sent them to Solomon, king of the Hungarians for him to bring up in his court.[5] John of Worcester also adds that it was the treacherous Eadric Streona who advised Cnut to murder the children of Edmund Ironside.[6] Another man exiled was the enigmatic Eadwig 'king of the peasants'. Given this odd title in the *Chronicle* entry for 1017 (in Old English *ceorlacyng*) and by the twelfth-century historians John of Worcester and Henry of Huntingdon (in Latin *rex rusticorum*), we know nothing else about this noble, or why he was given this enigmatic title.[7] What is certain is that Cnut was a ruthless man who was well aware of the various threats posed to his rule. The combination of the large number of men slain at the battle of Ashingdon in 1016, with the purges at the beginning of his reign, must have had a devastating effect on the English ruling classes and eased the transition from the Cerdic royal line to that of the Danes.

Another way in which Cnut appears to have eased the transition was through his marriage to the widow of Æthelred and daughter of the Duke of Normandy, Emma. Cnut already had a wife 'in the Danish fashion', Ælfgifu of Northampton – effectively a mistress – with whom he had two sons, but in 1017 he ordered that Emma should be fetched from Normandy as his wife.[8] Despite the age difference between them – Cnut was a young man while Emma must have been approaching middle age – and the fact that Cnut's taking of the throne had led to the exile and loss of birthright of her two sons by Æthelred, this marriage seems to have worked well and resulted in the birth of another son, Harthacnut. It seems likely that one of the main purposes in marrying Emma was to neutralise the threat posed by her two sons by Æthelred and prevent them from mounting a bid for the throne with Norman assistance.[9] Emma was a politically astute woman and, due to her commissioning of the *Encomium Emmae Reginae*, is one of the few early medieval women whose life we know much about.

The acceptance of Cnut as king did not result in an immediate end to the payment of *Danegeld* and, in 1018, a tribute was paid all over England of £82,500 to Cnut's army; resulting in only forty ships remaining with Cnut while the rest returned to Denmark. However, this was to be the last of the *Danegeld* payments and there were to be no more Viking raids during Cnut's reign. This payment is paired in the *Chronicle* with a reference to the English and the Danes meeting at Oxford and coming to an understanding. In a document produced after the meeting, by Archbishop Wulfstan of York, it was claimed that all differences between the two sides were set aside and that peace and friendship was established. These two sources imply that this was a truly significant meeting which finally cemented the position between the two sides. Cnut managed to bring peace to England and the fact that ordinary people were being ruled by a Dane meant very little given that it had ended the trauma and threat they had experienced during Æthelred's reign. In short, a Viking victory had, at last, brought an end to the Viking-induced turbulence.

This accord did not immediately end all political tension, however. The fact that Cnut's temporary return to Denmark in 1020 witnessed the exile of *Ealdorman* Æthelweard of Wessex suggests that Cnut's absence had led to some level of unrest in England, although not enough to threaten his position as king. In the same year, Cnut was also to found a church at the site of the battle of Ashingdon and it may well be that the monks of Bury St Edmunds were installed in the same year.[10] The unrest in England during his first absence cannot have been too great though as, by 1023, he was once again back in Scandinavia making terms with a Viking rival and one-time ally, Thorkell the Tall. Cnut was not in Denmark for long and returned to England later in the year, with Bishop Gerbrand of Roskilde brought for the archbishop of Canterbury to anoint. Cnut's devotion to Christianity can be seen later in the same year with the translation of St Ælfheah – the archbishop of Canterbury that Cnut's countrymen had murdered during Æthelred's reign – from St Paul's in London to Canterbury (Kent). Clearly, Viking rulers had come a long way in their religious journey from paganism to Christianity.

In the later 1020s Cnut travelled several times to Scandinavia and, in 1027, he journeyed to Rome in order to witness the accession of the Holy Roman Emperor, Conrad II. The letter that Cnut wrote on his return to his English subjects states that he visited Rome in order to pray for the forgiveness of his sins and the security of his subjects, as well as to negotiate a decrease in the amount that English archbishops had to pay when they journeyed to Rome to collect their *pallium* (symbol of office). This visit to Rome appears to have been a political success and in the Old Norse *skaldic* poem *Knútsdrapa* he is described as being 'dear to the emperor, close to Peter'.[11] In 1031 Cnut was back in England, visiting Scotland and receiving the submission of three kings: Malcolm II, Mælbæth and Ihemarc. Cnut was now firmly in control of his English kingdom and its borders. Unfortunately for Cnut, he was not to enjoy this security for long and on 12 November 1035 he died in Shaftesbury (Dorset), the most powerful king that England had ever known.

Cnut's Scandinavian Empire 1019–22

Although there is a relatively large amount known about the rule of Cnut in England, we know surprisingly little about his rule in Denmark and Scandinavia in general. The advent of written sources very much coincides with the arrival and conversion to Christianity in the early medieval period. While in England conversion had occurred in the late sixth and early seventh century, in Denmark it was not until the reign of Cnut's grandfather, Harald Bluetooth, that this occurred. This means that we have very few Scandinavian sources for this period and that much of our information therefore derives from abroad, or from much later works. Despite being the king of Denmark, Cnut spent very little time in the country and only visited Denmark four times during his reign. Despite this, the military support he was able to muster for his campaigns against Norway must mean that he still had significant power there.[12] It does seem clear, though, that Cnut was an Anglophile and that, despite his Scandinavian origins, it was England and not Scandinavia that was his first priority. Given the relative wealth of the two countries and how much more sophisticated England was economically, politically and socially, this should not really come as a great surprise.

One of the main issues regarding Cnut's rule of Denmark is how he organised its government. Was a regent elected in the same way in which the government of England had been entrusted to Thorkell the Tall during his visit to Denmark in 1019? Or were multiple earls appointed in imitation of the way in which he had split England into four earldoms?[13] The *Chronicle* informs us that Thorkell the Tall was tasked with overseeing Denmark in 1023, but after this point he completely disappears from the records and he may well have never actually taken up this position. It is possible that Cnut took this opportunity to free himself from this powerful and trouble-some figure.[14] This would be by no means the first time that Cnut had rid himself of subjects he saw as a threat. A new Danish deputy does appear in the sources and, *c*.1024, Cnut appointed his brother-in-law, Úlf – who was a member of a powerful Danish family and had been involved in his conquest of England – as his regent. Adam of Bremen tells us that Úlf was a 'duke' in England, and some modern scholars have supposed that he was therefore English, but it seems highly unlikely that that was the case as none of his rel-atives have English names: his father was named Thorgils; his brother Eilif, his sons Bjorn and Svein; and his sister was named Gyda. It is far more likely that Úlf was, in fact, Danish but had been granted land in England by Cnut. Adam of Bremen was a late eleventh-century monk from the bishopric of Hamburg-Bremen (modern Germany) who wrote a history of the Church there, entitled *Gesta Hammaburgensis Ecclesiae Pontificum* (*Deeds of Bishops of the Hamburg Church*). Hamburg-Bremen had been given responsibility for the conversion of Scandinavia and this led to Adam including some infor-mation about Scandinavia in his work. Úlf's rule of Denmark was, however, to be short lived, and in 1026 he joined forces with the kings of Norway and Sweden against Cnut, presumably hoping to become king of Denmark in his own right, rather than as the regent for Cnut's young son, Harthacnut. Cnut responded by bringing an army from England and fighting a battle, the outcome of which has been the subject of controversy.

In order to gain an understanding of this battle – the battle of Holy River – it is necessary to look back over Cnut's relationship with the other two Scandinavian kingdoms of Norway and Sweden. After Cnut had gained control of Denmark he became concerned with Norway, Sweden, the German Empire and the Slav peoples east of the River Elbe. After the death of Olaf Tryggvason in Norway in 999, the kingdom had been ruled by the Earl of Lade – the most powerful magnate in Norway whose lands lay in the north of the kingdom – under the sovereignty of Svein Forkbeard. However, the defeat of the Earl of Lade by Olaf Haraldsson at the battle of Nesjar in 1015 meant that Cnut lost the control over Norway that his father had enjoyed.[15] Cnut suffered another serious setback in Scandinavia with the death of the Swedish king, Olaf. Cnut counted King Olaf of Sweden as an ally and Adam of Bremen tells us that Cnut had intended to conquer England and Norway with support from Olaf.[16]

The next major incident to occur in Scandinavia was the battle of Holy River in 1026. This battle appears to have been the culmination of a joint venture on the part of the kings of Norway and Sweden who felt threatened by the strength of Cnut.[17] The *Chronicle* reports that Cnut's enemies won, whereas contemporary Scandinavian skaldic poetry has been cited as evidence that Cnut was victorious. One thing that seems clear is that Úlf was killed. The late twelfth and early thirteenth-century Danish historian, Saxo Grammaticus, alleges that 'Úlf was assassinated in a church at Roskilde,' but it is unclear if this is true or not.[18] However, although the outcome of the battle of Holy River is disputed, it left the opponents of Cnut still able to negotiate a peace treaty, meaning that they had not been reduced to the acceptance of a settlement dictated by Cnut. However, Cnut was able to travel immediately to Rome so they were also not in a strong enough position to capitalise on any gains they may have made.[19] In the letter that Cnut wrote home to his English subjects, he claimed to be king of all England, Denmark, the Norwegians and some of the Swedes; if this is genuine then it means he had already taken Olaf of Norway's throne.[20] It is reported by John of Worcester that Cnut heard that the Norwegian magnates were discontented in 1027 and so he sent them gold and silver to secure future support.[21] However, it seems likely that – as Olaf Haraldsson was still on the throne – this claim does not really have any foundation. The significance of the Swedish claim in Cnut's letter written in 1027 is also unclear. It cannot have been a hereditary claim based on Svein's position of superiority over King Olaf, as Olaf was undoubtedly king of the Swedes. The runic evidence suggests that, instead, the Swedes over whom Cnut claimed to be king were those who had served in his army.[22] There is a small group of coins struck in Sigtuna (Sweden) which carry the legend *cnvt rex sw* (*Cnut rex Swevorum*), but the fact that these were all struck by the same die makes it more likely to have been an adaption of a coin of Cnut, rather than evidence for him being king of Sweden.[23] This would imply that, although Cnut was by far the most dominant of the three Scandinavian kings even after the battle of Holy River, he did not exercise any real political power over the other kingdoms. He may have held a loose overlordship, but both Norway and Sweden retained their independent dynasties. And this contrasts with the political power of his father, Svein Forkbeard, especially with regard to his overlordship of Norway.

However, Cnut returned to Scandinavia again in 1028 in order to reassert his authority over the Norwegians. King Olaf of Norway's position had already been weakened due to pagan reactions to his firm, Christian-orientated rule and Cnut undermined this further through generous bribes and promises of greater freedom. Cnut was accepted by the major magnates within Norway and appointed Earl Hakon of Lade as his governor. Hakon died soon after, in 1030, and this gave Cnut the opportunity to provide an inheritance for his son, Svein, who was named king of Norway with the support of his mother, Ælfgifu.[24] However, the reign of Svein and Ælfgifu was to prove to be a failure once the Norwegians realised that they had simply swopped a native king for a foreign ruler, who attempted to exert greater control over the Norwegian people in terms of taxation and punishment. This led to widespread resentment. This – combined with the growing cult of King or St Olaf Haraldson – led to the Danish position in Norway becoming untenable and, eventually, Svein and Ælfgifu were forced out of Norway in 1034.[25] By attempting to impose a Danish ruler onto the Norwegian population, Cnut demonstrated that he exercised significant political authority in Norway, but it also alienated the Norwegian people. They then reacted against this control and, ultimately, Cnut was forced out of Norway and out of his position of political influence there. The Viking Emperor of the North had overplayed his hand.

Cnut and the waves: the image of a pious Viking king

Perhaps the most powerful image which we have today of Cnut is his attempt to hold back the tide. However, this was not a contemporary tale and it first appears in the writings of Henry of Huntingdon, a twelfth-century chronicler. He relates how Cnut set his throne by the seashore and commanded the tide to halt and not wet his feet and robes. Yet:

> continuing to rise as usual [the tide] dashed over his feet and legs without respect to his royal person. Then the king leapt backwards, saying: 'Let all men know how empty and worthless is the power of kings, for there is none worthy of the name, but He whom heaven, earth, and sea obey by eternal laws.'

He then hung his gold crown on a crucifix, and never wore it again 'to the honour of God the almighty King'.[26] This incident is usually misrepresented by popular usage as an example of Cnut's arrogance,[27] but is actually the complete opposite and shows Cnut's insignificance compared with the power of God.[28] It may well be that Henry of Huntingdon's story was an expansion of a tale by the eleventh-century writer Goscelin of St Bertan. In his writings he instead has Cnut place his crown on a crucifix at Winchester one Easter, with no mention of the sea, 'with the explanation that the king of kings was more worthy of it than he'.[29] The fact that neither of these stories are mentioned in the contemporary *Encomium Emmae* makes it highly unlikely that they actually occurred, given that the *Encomium Emmae* is at great pains to display Cnut as a pious and devoted king it would seem odd for it not to include this tale if it actually occurred. The story of the tide was often repeated by later historians and, within these adaptations, most have adjusted the tale so that Cnut is more clearly aware that the tides would not obey him, and stages the scene to rebuke the flattery of his courtiers. A curious survival of the legend is in the Latin name of the wading bird, the knot (*Calidris canuta*), so named because it feeds along the shoreline.

Even though the tale itself is unlikely to be true, it does say something very interesting about the legacy of Cnut. King Cnut was clearly viewed by the historians of the later middle ages to have been a pious Christian king, and this is likely to have been influenced by the lavish gifts that he gave to the Church. In the *Liber Vitae* of the New Minster Winchester, Cnut and his queen, Emma, are depicted presenting a cross to the minster, while an angel places a crown on Cnut's head. He also ordered a gold shrine to be made for St Edith at Wilton Abbey and donated the gold- and silver-encased arm of St Cyriacus to Westminster Abbey. As we have seen earlier, he also patronised the cults of Ælfheah of Canterbury and St Edmund of East Anglia. It is undoubtedly significant that both of these Anglo-Saxon saints were killed by Scandinavian warriors. Viking-English history placed Cnut in a difficult position as, although he himself was a Christian, he came from a kingdom which was not completely Christianised and a people who had terrorised the English Church for several hundred years. It was no doubt astute political sense, as well as actual devotion, that led to Cnut's lavish gifts to the Church and to his particular choice of saintly recipients. Despite the atrocities committed by Cnut in the early years of his reign, he seems to have managed to avoid any later associations with this violence and, instead, to have reinvented himself as a Christian, peaceful and humble monarch.

The sons of Cnut

When Cnut died in Shaftsbury (Dorset) in 1035, there was once again a complicated succession. Cnut had two adult sons: Harthacnut, who was his son by Emma of Normandy; and Harald Harefoot, who was his son by Ælfgifu of Northampton. Both had strong claims to the throne. The *Encomium Emmae* claims that, when Emma agreed to marry Cnut, part of the deal was that it would be her offspring who would take the throne, and this does certainly seem to have been the case in Denmark where Cnut sent the 8-year-old Harthacnut to reign in his absence.[30] In addition, given that one of Cnut's key aims in marrying Emma was to neutralise the threat of her sons by Æthelred, it does appear plausible that this would have been part of the marriage contract. However, 'the best laid plans of mice and men oft go astray' and when Cnut died in 1035, Harthacnut was in Denmark dealing with the fallout of his half-brother, Svein, being expelled from Norway by King Magnus the Good. This left the path to the throne open to Harald Harefoot – Svein's brother – who was in England at the time of Cnut's death.

Immediately after Cnut's death, there was a meeting of the noble councillors in Oxford in order to decide upon the next king. At this council Earl Leofric of Mercia and many of the northern *thegns* took up Harald's cause, whereas Godwin of Wessex favoured the absent Harthacnut. This division serves to highlight the regionalism still inherent in eleventh-century England, and the continuing rivalry between Wessex and Mercia and the two great families of these earldoms. It seems likely that it was a combination of Harald's half-Mercian blood – his mother was Mercian – as well as the chance to get one over on Godwin that led to Leofric's support. Godwin, on the other hand, would have been very keen to preserve the *status quo* and probably felt that an absent king in Denmark would allow him to effectively rule England on his behalf. There also seems to have been some issue over the paternity of Harald, with the C, D and E *manuscripts* of the *Chronicle* all casting aspersions on Harald's claim to the throne.[31] However, despite these concerns over Harald's paternity, at the Council of Oxford it was Godwin's side which lost out and a compromise was reached, with Harald Harefoot recognised as king north of the Thames and Harthacnut recognised as king in Wessex, with Emma of Normandy remaining in Winchester (Hampshire) as regent for him. However, despite this compromise, Emma was unable to prevent Harald from seizing the royal treasure and, in the continued absence of Harthacnut, effectively ruling the entire kingdom.

Although there is little in the written record about how this division of the kingdom worked out in reality, the numismatic evidence can give us more of an idea. There were pennies issued by both kings in circulation until 1037 and these were comparable coins, simply struck with the two separate names. These coins were originally minted in the areas where they were supposed to be in control but, as 1036 and 1037 progressed, Harald's coins began to be struck south of the Thames, while there was no equivalent movement on the part of coin distribution for Harthacnut. The numismatic evidence therefore suggests that, in 1036, Harald became recognised in Wessex, whereas Harthacnut failed to make the corresponding progress in the north.

In 1036 another challenge to Harald's kingship was to emerge in the shape of Emma's sons from her previous marriage to Æthelred. It is unclear exactly what prompted Edward and Alfred to return to England, but the *Encomium Emmae* claims that Harald's faction wrote a letter to them, pretending it was from their mother and enticing them to return. Whether or not this was true, they returned and attempted to meet up with their mother in Winchester. However, at this point, Godwin – who had previously been a supporter of Emma – switched allegiances. Godwin was a man who had been 'made' under the Anglo-Danish regime and would therefore have been much more comfortable with the idea of Harald as king, rather than Edward or Alfred. Godwin, consequently, stopped Alfred's progress to Winchester, captured him and blinded him, which resulted in Alfred later dying of his injuries. The *Chronicle* condemns these actions and tells us that 'no more horrible a deed was done in the land since the Danes came and peace was made'.[32] This act was to have long-term consequences for Godwin and, as we shall see, greatly embittered his relationship with Edward the Confessor.

The following year, 1037, Harald was declared king over the entirety of England and Emma was driven out of the country. He is thus remembered as King Harald (or Harold) I, to differentiate him from Harold II, Godwinson, who reigned in 1066. Harthacnut had been away for too long and Godwin had decided to throw in his lot with Harald's faction instead. It is a testament to the power of Godwin that his support for Harald seems to have enabled Harald to gain recognition across England. Once in power, Harald seems to have been a fairly unremarkable king and he left no charters or any evidence of activity during his brief reign until his early death in 1040.

On the death of Harald, Harthacnut – who had in the previous year come to visit his mother in exile in Bruges, in Flanders – landed in England and claimed the throne for himself. Harthacnut seems to have got off on the wrong foot with the English people from the start when he imposed a very heavy tax upon his arrival, in order to pay for his ships and soldiers. The fact that this tax was highly resented can be seen in Worcestershire where the inhabitants killed two of Harthacnut's *huscarls* (royal household troops) who attempted to impose it. This led to an angry reaction from Harthacnut and the county being ravaged. The *C* and *D manuscripts* of the *Chronicle* tell us that 'he did nothing worthy of a king as long as he ruled' and in 1041, in order to bolster his unpopular regime, he was forced to recall his half-brother, Edward the Confessor, son of Æthelred, from his exile in Normandy.[33] Harthacnut was not to reign for very long and, in 1042, he died while 'standing at his drink'.[34] The Anglo-Danish period was at an end and the house of Cerdic, under Edward the Confessor, was once again at the head of the English nation. But, if Viking rule was over, its repercussions were by no means past and would influence key features of Edward's reign and lead to the end of Anglo-Saxon England.

16

THE ROAD TO HASTINGS

Edward the Confessor was king of England from 1042 until January 1066, and his reign brought with it the reassertion of the royal house of Wessex after almost thirty years of rule by kings of Danish descent. This return to the line of the descendants of Alfred was, though, to be short lived. At the end of Edward's reign the throne was first seized – seemingly without opposition – by the Anglo-Danish earl, Harold Godwinson, and then later in the same year – after the momentous events of the battle of Hastings – by the Norman duke, William, with an attempt on the throne by the Norwegian king, Harald Hardrada, occurring shortly before William's successful bid for the Crown.

Edward was 47 years old when he came to the throne and had spent most of his life in exile at the Norman court due to his connection with the dukedom through his Norman mother, Emma of Normandy. This meant that Edward had far greater foreign connections, allegiances and influences than any other 'English' king of Anglo-Saxon England before him. It also meant that he was politically very inexperienced and had been out of the English 'political loop' for over twenty-five years; consequently, the situation he found himself in as king was very different to the English political system his father had experienced. Given how quickly Anglo-Saxon England unravelled upon the death of Edward, it seems impossible to separate the events of his reign from the events of the year following his death. However, should the net be cast back even further? And should the Viking Wars also be held responsible for the eventual conquest of the kingdom of the English by the Normans? The evidence suggests that this indeed was the case, and that the end of Anglo-Saxon England in 1066 was one of the unintended consequences of the Viking Wars.

The Viking legacy: the destabilisation of the Anglo-Saxon political system

There were several long-term factors that arguably led to the destabilisation of the English political system and ultimately contributed to the events of 1066. The Viking attacks and the conquest of England by the Danes under Svein Forkbeard and then his son, Cnut the Great, led to the weakening of the royal house of Wessex. The traditional features of a lawful succession were eligibility by birth, designation by the late king, recognition by the leading elites and consecration by the Church. Normally it was the eldest son of the previous king who succeeded, although English politics had become so confused that a king could well nominate different men as his heir at different points, the different regions within England could make different choices and sometimes consecration was dispensed with. For example, the *Anglo-Saxon Chronicle* does not mention the coronation of any of the Anglo-Danish kings, although it does discuss those of Æthelred II and Edward the Confessor.[1] The murder of Edward King and Martyr and the treachery and weakness of Æthelred II's reign, as well as the rule by Anglo-Danish rulers since 1013 (and especially from 1016), undermined the support base of the house of Wessex. The leading English nobles had become accustomed to having a role in the choosing of kings and while they had supported the kings presented to them, they seem to have felt that they still had a role to play.[2] In short, the events associated with the rule of Viking Danish kings from 1013 until 1042 had raised the expectations of the English political elites regarding their own role in the succession. Furthermore, the 'rapid succession' of kings after Cnut's death in 1035 also created a 'long-term fragility of the royal kin and the breakdown of its monopoly of kingship'. The succession of a non-royal to the throne before the reign of Cnut would have been almost impossible, but this fragmentation of the English royal line (from 1035 to 1042) eventually meant that Harold Godwinson, rather than the rightful king, Edgar *ætheling*, was able to take the English throne in January 1066 and therefore set in train 'the dramatic events of the remainder of the year'.[3]

In the previous century, despite the minority of both Æthelred II and his half-brother, Edward King and Martyr, they had still been anointed as kings; however, Edgar *ætheling*'s minority led to the acceptance, in January 1066, of someone completely outside of the royal line. This was clearly an unintended but direct consequence of the chain of events set in motion by the Viking conquest of England in 1016 under Cnut.

The period of Scandinavian conquest caused many alterations in political society and these had far-reaching consequences, deeply disturbing to the Anglo-Saxon *status quo* that had developed during the tenth century, leading to unrest and socio-political instability. In contrast, Edward's reign was a period of consolidation and of growing Anglo-Danish concord. It seems likely that it was this increased unity that prevented the disintegration of England after the Norman Conquest. If Edward had presided over an ineffective and divisive government then the effects of that conquest would probably have been a lot deeper and even more far-reaching than they eventually were.[4] Consequently, the weakening of the English state by fifty years of inconsistency and turmoil meant that the infrastructure was more likely to give way under pressure, but did not by itself lead to the events of 1066. This is evident in the way in which Edward the Confessor, for all his faults, successfully managed the turbulent twenty-four years of his reign. It would take a combination of these long-term effects with other, more specific factors to create the momentous events of that year.

Clearly, the Viking Wars had a great impact on royal succession and, in a similar way, the Viking invasions and Danish rule during the first half of the eleventh century also resulted in a huge upheaval within the English political elite. England was a political and social community which had been put under enormous strain through 200 years of Viking raids. In addition to the vast economic cost incurred from the last months of Æthelred II's reign to the beginning of Cnut's rule, the three most important earls in the kingdom, Uhtred of Northumbria, Eadric of Mercia and Ulfcetel of East Anglia, along with Ælfric of Hampshire and Godwin of Lindsey all died. The *Chronicle* records that seven important *thegns* also died in battle, through assassination or execution.[5] This meant that, although many of the magnates under Cnut were Anglo-Saxons, very few of these were from the same families who had previously ruled regions of England. A historic continuity of regional government, with all its attendant self-confidence and web of patronage and obligation, had been shattered by the Viking Wars. The whole process of the second phase of Viking attacks had worn down the Anglo-Saxon ruling class, but none more so than the battle of Ashingdon in 1016 in which, according to *Manuscript E*, perished 'all the flower of England'.[6]

The Viking legacy: over-mighty subjects

However, from this wreckage the Earls Godwin, Leofric and Siward emerged. These earls were the political, but not the actual, descendants of the powerful *ealdormen* who had administered Anglo-Saxon England since the ninth century. Until the reign of Edward the Elder (899–924) these *ealdormen* had administrative responsibility for a single *shire*, but after the conquest of the *Danelaw* their role expanded to cover a group of *shires*. From the start of Cnut's reign in 1016, their title was replaced by that of *earl*, which was related to the Norse word for a senior nobleman, *jarl*. These new *earldoms* did not have fixed boundaries and different ones were sometimes combined. By the mid-eleventh century any combination of *shires* might be combined to form an *earldom*. During the reign of Edward the Confessor there were usually nine *earldoms* in operation at any one time, although sometimes they were without an earl.

What is so important about the earls under Cnut is that the Viking conquest of 1016 led to major changes in the political landscape of English regional government and the political balance of power generally. Firstly, while Siward and Leofric held the 'old' regional powerbases of Northumbria and Mercia, Godwin was in the unprecedented position of being the first Earl of Wessex since, as Cnut was the first king of England not to be descended from the West Saxon kings, he had no special attachment to Wessex. Secondly and most importantly, all of these men were 'made' by Cnut. Godwin is not mentioned in English sources before Cnut's reign and it seems his father, Wulfnoth Cild of Sussex, was the rebel who fought against Æthelred II mentioned by the *Chronicle* in 1009;[7] Leofric, son of *ealdorman* Leofwine, who died c.1028, owed his accession to the death of his brother in the early months of Cnut's reign; whereas Siward was a Scandinavian import who owed his position solely to Cnut.[8] This created a new class of elites who both owed everything to the king and yet also wielded huge amounts of unprecedented power. It also meant that, when Edward returned to England in 1042, the area which had been the heartland of his ancestors was now presided over by a new Anglo-Danish magnate family – Godwin had married Gytha, the sister of the Danish earl, Úlf, who in turn was married to Cnut's sister, Estrid.

This was a process which had started under King Athelstan, with the rise of powerful local men such as Athelstan Half-King (*ealdorman* of East Anglia), and continued under Æthelred II, with the rise to influence of Eadric Streona. However, the Godwin family, in particular, were to be mightier subjects than either of these earlier figures. And this was an innovation directly attributable to the reign of Cnut and his sons. By the reign of Edward, the house of Godwin – and, to an extent, that of Leofric – had created for themselves a place of enormous power within society, and this was a power that the previously exiled Edward found difficult to challenge in any serious way. When he married Godwin's daughter, Edith, in 1045, it further bolstered the power of the house of Godwin and it is difficult to be certain how much choice Edward had in the matter. However, that he resented the situation can be clearly seen in the events of 1051. In this year Edward's brother-in-law, Eustace, the Count of Boulogne, had a violent encounter with the people of Dover. Godwin was ordered to punish the people of Dover but he refused to do so and thus went against the orders of his own monarch. This led to the exile of not only Godwin but also Godwin's sons. And, at the same time, Edward sent his wife, Edith, to a nunnery. The events of this year are described in detail by the *Vita Ædwardi Regis* (*Life of King Edward*). This is a text that was commissioned by Edward's widow after his death and, as she was the daughter of Godwin and sister of King Harold Godwinson, is often favourable to the house of Godwin. This tells us that when Earl Godwin sent to Edward to ask him for peace, 'the malice of evil men had shut up the merciful ears of the king'; the implication of this is that the king was glad to be finally rid of Godwin and was enjoying the absence of his over-mighty subject.[9] But the king's weakness is illustrated by the fact that he could not enforce the exile of Godwin and his family. By 1052, Edward had been forced to restore Godwin's earldom to him, as *Manuscript C* records: 'unconditionally and as fully and completely as he had ever held it, and all his sons all that they had held before.'[10] Edith was restored to her position at the same time. The situation which Cnut had created, of powerful but insecure elites, had evolved into one, under Edward, in which these same elites were impossible to suppress. This was a direct result of the kind of government created by Cnut, in combination with Edward's exile.

The relative power of the English earls compared to that of the king can also be seen in the revolt against Tostig in 1065. A younger son of Godwin and seemingly Edward's favourite member of the house of Godwin, he had been made Earl of Northumbria following the death of Siward in 1055. While he ruled it for some years, he never seems to have been a popular ruler. The situation came to a head in 1065 when the *thegns* of Yorkshire descended on York, outlawed Tostig and sent for Morcar – a member of the house of Leofric. In this incident Edward was powerless in the face of a Northumbrian and Mercian conspiracy against Tostig and was required to dismiss Tostig in favour of Morcar.[11] Harold Godwinson refused to back his brother, earning Tostig's bitter resentment and leading to Tostig's support for Harald Hardrada in 1066.

Clearly, the destruction of large elements of the Anglo-Saxon elite during both the Viking Wars and the first few bloody months of Cnut's reign led to the creation of a new class of nobles who, particularly in the case of the house of Godwin, became over-mighty subjects. Due to Cnut's North Sea Empire, both Cnut and Harthacnut, his son by Emma of Normandy, were often absentee rulers. This was a new concept to the English political system and meant that these Viking rulers by necessity had to lean more heavily on their earls than would otherwise have been the case. These powerful earls were consequently so entrenched into the political system that, by the time Edward came to the throne, he was unable to exert any real control over them. As we have seen, Edward was probably forced to marry Godwin's daughter and was unable to permanently oust the house of Godwin, despite attempting to exile them in 1051. This meant that the Viking Wars' destabilisation of the political elite made it easier for the house of Godwin to challenge Edward and eventually to take the throne in 1066. However, while this process may have helped to set the stage for 1066, it did not write the entire script.

The creation of this new layer of over-mighty subjects also led to factions and tensions within this top layer of English society. The rivalry between the earls of Mercia and the house of Godwin was a continuing feature from Cnut's reign up until the Norman Conquest and, although there were periods when they did cooperate, this rivalry was a significant factor in English politics from 1035 to 1066. The anonymous author of the *Vita Ædwardi Regis* was not exaggerating when he alluded to '*odia veteri*' (old hatreds) between the earls of Mercia and the house of Godwine. This '*odium*' constitutes essential background for a reading of the mid-eleventh-century annals in *Manuscript C* of the *Chronicle*, because it helps explain their agenda: they are anti-Godwinson precisely because they were written in Mercia by annalists whose political sympathies lay with the earls of

Mercia.[12] The mid-eleventh-century annals in *Manuscript C* contain nine annals displaying anti-Godwinson views and four that are concerned with the affairs of Abingdon – an important Mercian religious house. They also contain fifteen annals concerned with Mercian affairs generally, and seven which are specifically interested in the family of Earl Leofric. These annals in *Manuscript C* therefore display three distinctive characteristics: antipathy towards the family of Earl Godwin; interest in Mercian affairs generally; and sympathy for the earls of Mercia in particular.[13] Since the families of Godwin and Leofric were political rivals, these characteristics were almost certainly closely related. In contrast, *Manuscript E* contains nine pro-Godwinson annals, four annals concerned with the affairs of St Augustine's in Canterbury and eight concerned generally with southern affairs. This is probably because it was written at a location with greater sympathy and affiliation to Godwin. A slightly less partisan approach can be seen in *Manuscript D*, which contains three annals concerned with the family of Edward the Exile, fifteen which deal with Mercian affairs and twelve concerned with northern and Scottish affairs.[14] It seems then that the manuscripts of the *Chronicle* can roughly be summarised as: *C* being pro-Mercian, *E* being pro-Godwin and *D* pushing a more neutral, royal agenda. Together they illustrate the divisions that threatened the English establishment in the years preceding 1066.

The closing decades of Anglo-Saxon history can therefore be followed in three sets of annals whose 'political prejudices were partly a function of the very politics they describe',[15] though it is significant that they all continued to draw on a common base text. The fact these annals appear to show such obvious biases tells us something of the divisive nature of these powerful earls, who were not only competing against each other but were also causing factionalism amongst the population as a whole.

Ironically, the strength of the English magnates led to yet a further weakness in the English system and one with a direct connection to Scandinavia. It was the rivalry between the two houses that led, in 1065, to the expulsion of Harold Godwinson's brother, Tostig, in favour of Edwin and Morcar, after Northumbria had risen up against Tostig's heavy-handed rule as earl. Following this, Tostig joined forces with Harald Hardrada of Norway and so opened the door to a Norwegian Viking invasion in September 1066.[16]

However, despite the rivalry between the houses of Godwin and Leofric, Edwin and Morcar were still capable of determinedly fighting Harald Hardrada, when faced with a common Norwegian threat – which alarmed and united all the English elites – at the battles of Gate Fulford and Stamford Bridge in the autumn of 1066. Moreover, the magnates continuously seem to have stepped back from the brink of civil war and so it was, in 1065, that Harold Godwinson backed Edwin and Morcar against his own brother rather that plunge the country into internal conflict. This, at least, they had all learned from their common history; for it was through such internal divisions that Scandinavian adventurers had profited in the past. This raises the crucial issue of the way in which the Scandinavian interventions in England in the first half of the eleventh century had affected the relationship of England with its neighbours.

The Viking legacy: foreign claimants to the English Crown

Although the Viking invasions of the eleventh century were to have important implications for internal stability, they also had massive consequences in terms of foreign relations. It was the Danish reign of Cnut which created the Scandinavian connection that led to the unsuccessful invasion of England by the Norwegian king, Harald Hardrada, in September 1066. Harald Hardrada was a brutal ruler and a seasoned warrior who had fought from Scandinavia to the Mediterranean, where for a time, while in exile, he had served in the *Varangian Guard* of the Byzantine emperor. Cnut's son, Harthacnut, had made an agreement with Harald Hardrada's brother, Magnus the Good, whereby if either of them were to die childless then the other would inherit his kingdom. Harthacnut did die childless but the kingdom of England went not to Magnus but to Edward the Confessor. Nevertheless, Magnus did become king of Harthacnut's other kingdom, Denmark, from 1042 to 1046, in addition to Norway which he had ruled since 1035. This meant that, as Magnus' eventual successor and half-brother, Harald Hardrada believed that he had a right to the English and Norwegian throne and this could never have occurred if an English king had been on the throne for the entirety of the eleventh century. It is also significant that both the *Chronicle* and *Heimskringla* (*Circle of the World*) – an Old Norse history of the kings of Norway written *c.* 1230 – indicate that Magnus the Good also considered an invasion of England in 1045, in order to make good his claim to the throne. If successful, this would have made him ruler of Norway, Denmark and England, in imitation of the empire forged by Cnut the Great. Significantly, the *Chronicle* states that Magnus was prevented from invading due to his warfare with Svein Estrithson in Denmark, while *Heimskringla* claims that Edward wrote a letter begging the Norwegian king not to invade and to which he acceded after his saintly father (St Olaf of Norway) appeared to him in a dream. This is clearly legendary and from a much later source than that of the *Chronicle*. Interestingly, Godwin was also involved in this complicated manoeuvring in the 1040s. He advised Edward to send assistance to Svein Estrithson who, having previously accepted a position as Magnus the Good's deputy in Denmark, declared independence in 1045. This was astute advice from Godwin, since Magnus was the greater threat to England and the longer he could be kept embroiled in a northern war the better. However, Edward opted for a policy of neutrality and Magnus prevailed over Svein Estrithson. Fortunately for both Edward and Svein, Magnus died in 1046.[17] This, though, then raised the possibility of an intervention in England by Svein Estrithson, who was no longer threatened by Magnus.

The years of Danish rule had also introduced another possible contender for the English throne and, as the nephew of Cnut the Great, Svein Estrithson (king of Denmark from 1046 to 1074) felt that he had a right to inherit Cnut's North Sea Empire.[18] There is also a possibility that Edward the Confessor made an offer of the succession to Svein in the 1040s, in order to placate him and remove him as a threat.[19] It may be significant that it was Svein's actions in 1045 that prevented Magnus the Good from invading England and it may have been that Edward, like his father before him, was more active than our sources suggest and was, in reality, encouraging this contender to one of the Scandinavian kingdoms (Svein in Denmark), in order to distract a more threatening power (Magnus, king of Norway). In the tangled world of Scandinavian politics, Svein Estrithson turned his mind to his own invasion of England once the threat from Magnus the Good had been removed, but was prevented from implementing his plan because he soon faced renewed war with Norway, under Magnus the Good's successor, Harald Hardrada. However, Svein would not completely forget his English connection and unsuccessfully attempted an invasion of England in 1069–70, allied with Edgar *ætheling*, as did his son in 1075.

Perhaps the most important foreign connection that was introduced courtesy of the Viking Wars was the Norman connection. Æthelred II was married to Emma, the daughter of the Norman duke and Æthelred, and Edward both spent periods of time in exile in Normandy due to the Viking invasions of England. And the Normans who gave them shelter were, ironically, themselves descendants of Vikings. Despite their adoption of Frankish characteristics, they remained conscious of their northern roots and, as such, were drawn into the eleventh-century diplomacy of Æthelred II and remained 'participants in the maritime culture of the world of the northern seas'. [20] In fact, Edward's long exile in Normandy was to have a significant impact on his rule. As a result of this exile, there were many Normans in England before 1066: the archbishop of Canterbury, Robert of Jumièges, and the bishops William of London and Úlf of Dorchester were major players in the crisis of 1051–52 when Godwin was exiled and then returned; there was a 'Norman colony' in Herefordshire in the 1050s; and Robert fitz Wimarc was a leading figure at court and attended the king at his deathbed. The Norman presence and influence was particularly apparent at court and this can be seen as a precursor to the events of 1066. [21] The marriage of Emma of Normandy to Æthelred II and then to Cnut can be seen as the first time that Norman influence filtered into England, and it was this that led to Duke William's dynastic claims and thus to the battle of Hasting in 1066. [22] However, focussing on these major figures can distort the picture, as the Normans at court were unrepresentative of Normans in England as a whole. The typical Anglo-Norman of Edward's reign was not a powerful figure at court, or in the Church, but a landowner of modest means. [23] It is also important to remember that the Norman aspect of court politics appears to have much more significance because the Normans later went on to conquer England. At the time it was just 'one strand in a complex web of court intrigues'. The crisis of 1051–52 should be viewed not as a vital turning point in Norman involvement in politics at Edward's court, but instead just one phase in which the Normans came to the fore. [24]

However, whatever the nature of the Normans at Edward's court, the source of the Norman faction at the court was very much down to Edward himself. It would be a mistake, though, to attribute this solely to his maternity, as Harthacnut was also half-Norman but was not regarded as particularly pro-Norman. Clearly, Edward's pro-Norman outlook had more to do with his growing up in Normandy and this was solely due to the actions of Cnut in 1016. As a result, Edward was culturally Norman in terms of habits, preferences and in his world view. The English court under Edward definitely had a 'French accent', even if it was not specifically Norman. They were also not the only foreigners in Edward's court and there were priests and clerics from Germany, particularly Lorraine, and the

English elites themselves had links to Flanders, Denmark, Wales and Ireland. To divide Edward's court into English and Norman is to take far too simplistic an approach.[25] However, the fact is that no other previous king had had such strong connections with the Normans and, even if his court was a cosmopolitan one, he was the only king whose death could have ushered in a Norman invasion.

The Succession crisis and the events of 1066

'It would take a careful detachment that bordered on perversity not to treat the reign of Edward as a prelude to the Norman Conquest.'[26] One of the main reasons for this was not only the connection he had with the Normans, but also the disputed question of the succession. There was, as we have seen, chronic dynastic instability and there had been a crisis of sorts at the death of every king since Edgar in 975 – and many kings before him. In many of these crises foreign powers had intervened in order to further their own ends; since the ninth century these had always been Viking or of Viking extraction. And 1066 was to be no exception. In fact, it was simply the latest example of Scandinavian opportunism combining with Anglo-Saxon opportunities. The reign of Edward would always have been difficult, not only due to the dynastic ambitions of the great families but also due to inherent structural weakness.[27] If it is true that Edward had already chosen celibacy before his accession to the throne then the problem of the succession would have been at the fore from the first day of his reign.[28] It is likely that Edward had named William as his heir before the crisis of 1051 and this may well have been one of the causes of this crisis rather than an unintended consequence of it. A Norman historian, William of Poitiers, tells us that Robert of Jumièges told William of the offer of succession as he passed through Normandy on his way to Rome to collect his *pallium* in 1051. This suggests that the idea was already in Edward's mind even before Robert was in his post as archbishop of Canterbury.[29] It would seem then that *Manuscript D*'s mention of a visit by William to England in 1051 represents a visit by William as heir-apparent rather than the time when the offer of the throne was made. At this time there may well have been a desire for friendship, as Edward was looking for security and William for prestige. Also, in the absence of an obvious claimant to the succession, William, as an able soldier and a ruler of a duchy, made a suitable candidate and one capable of checking the power of the Godwin family and of aggressive Scandinavians, such as Svein Estrithson of Denmark who clearly thought that he should have inherited on the death of Harthacnut and had not relinquished his claim since then. Even if Edward had nominated William as his successor, it is not certain that it was intended to have the importance that it ultimately did. In 1051, Edward still had fifteen years to live and, as such, probably expected to be able to repeatedly play the diplomatic succession card in a similar way to Elizabeth I playing the marriage card in the sixteenth century.[30] However, Edward massively confused the issue of the succession by refusing to consistently name a successor: he appears to have named William in 1051; he may well already have made promises to Svein Estrithson in the 1040s; but then he nominated Harold Godwinson for the role on his deathbed. This meant that, although Harold had been promised the throne, according to *Manuscript E* and the *Vita Ædwardi Regis*, which are both pro-Godwin sources, William believed that he was the true heir in keeping with Norman legal custom. And, in direct competition, so did Svein Estrithson; although William of Poitiers makes the unlikely claim that Svein accepted the superiority of William's right to the throne.[31] However, the custom was different in England and, as such, Harold's final nomination was also legal. Since Edward must have been familiar with both systems this means that he shoulders a large amount of the responsibility for the confusion that occurred.[32] Therefore, the great political difficulty of the succession was left unanswered on his death. As a result of Cnut's conquest in 1016, Harthacnut's diplomacy and Edward's indecision after 1042, there were two Viking kings, of Denmark and of Norway, one Norman duke and an Anglo-Danish earl who all thought that they had a legitimate claim to the English throne.

The situation was further complicated by the 'Edward the Exile policy'. Edward the Exile was the son of Edmund Ironside, Edward the Confessor's older half-brother, who had been in exile in Hungary during Danish rule. Edward the Exile was recalled back to the English court in 1056. This may have been a temporary strategy of Edward the Confessor's, or it may have been forced on him by factions within the court, hence his apparent refusal to meet the returning exile. This would have provided an undisputed succession and a continuation of the West Saxon line but, unfortunately, Edward the Exile died soon after landing in England. He was survived by his son, Edgar *ætheling*, but he was only a child and the political situation was too volatile for a minor to safely be the heir to the throne.

Despite all this confusion, when Edward died on 5 January 1066, the thirty-nine men who were present at Edward's Christmas court and then acclaimed Harold Godwinson as king – he was rapidly crowned on 6 January – were thoroughly representative of the various voices of the land and included foreign as well as native elements. This means the decision can be viewed as the voice of the nation.[33]

The actions of Edward can clearly be seen to have led to the Norman invasion in 1066, and his close connections to Normandy and the promise of the throne to William seem to have made William's play for the throne inevitable. However, the events of 1066 constituted far more than just the Norman invasion and, while Edward's decisions seem to have contributed to this Norman invasion, he cannot be held responsible for the Norwegian invasion of Harald Hardrada which preceded it. In short, Edward made the Norman invasion almost inevitable, but not the Norman Conquest. And in this context, the Norwegian invasion, which was to prove so strategically important in the events of the autumn, was to prove decisive in wrong-footing Harold Godwinson.

In September 1066, Harald Hardrada of Norway made his move.[34] He arrived in the Humber estuary, in the company of the exiled Tostig, who had earlier (in May) unsuccessfully raided England with the assistance of Orkney Vikings. The invaders were opposed by Earls Morcar and Edwin at the battle of Gate Fulford on 20 September, where the combined English armies of Mercia and Northumbria were heavily defeated. As a consequence, Harold Godwinson was forced to march north. Although he comprehensively surprised and defeated the Norwegians at the battle of Stamford Bridge on 25 September – killing both Harald Hardrada and his rebel brother, Tostig – the Normans were able to land unopposed on 28 September while Harold Godwinson was occupied in the north.

In many ways the failed Viking invasion of Harald Hardrada secured victory for William of Normandy. When, in mid-October, Harold Godwinson attempted the same kind of rapid advance to battle that had earlier caught Harald Hardrada and his Viking army by surprise, he found the Normans far from being taken unawares. The march north that had cost the English men, and time had also allowed the Normans a crucial breathing space in which to secure their bridgehead. Whilst less than convincing in other areas of his account, the later Norman historian, Wace, may have been correct when he claimed that the English forces had been severely weakened by the conflict in the north against the Danes and Tostig.[35] John of Worcester similarly referred to the loss of key English warriors in the northern battles.[36] Even so, it was only after a hard-fought day, on Saturday 14 October, that Harold Godwinson was killed. And he died amidst his personal bodyguard of *huscarls*, the fighting force that Cnut had bequeathed to his successors, wielding that peculiarly Scandinavian weapon, the two-handed battle-axe.[37] There was, therefore, much that was influenced by the Vikings in the defeat on Senlac Hill that day.

The specific events of 1066 were not inevitable, but that there would be some form of crisis was obvious; and Edward the Confessor bears a large amount of the responsibility. The lack of an obvious heir and Edward's refusal to make a firm decision about the succession until he was on his deathbed put the kingdom in an unstable position where it was vulnerable to foreign attack. This was exacerbated by his earlier willingness to back any candidate likely to split the Godwin family, whatever the consequences. This caused him to side with Tostig; a man whose later alliance with Harald Hardrada would cause one of the most significant events leading to Harold Godwinson's defeat at Hastings. However, in the longer term, the English state had already been weakened by years of Viking attacks and the effects of Danish rule, and many of the factors peculiar to the succession crisis under Edward actually had their roots in these earlier events.[38] The 'road which led to 1066' had started in Scandinavia.

17

THE END OF THE VIKING WARS

The death of the English king, Harold Godwinson (Harold II), on Saturday 14 October 1066, may seem a fitting end to the Viking Blitzkrieg, which had impacted on English history since the first raid on Portland in 789. After all, in the autumn of 1066, the last great Viking invasion, which threatened to repeat the success of Cnut in 1016, had been decisively defeated at the battle of Stamford Bridge. On that day the political ambitions of Harald Hardrada of Norway had been cut down, along with a large part of his army. Then, on Senlac Hill, the descendants of Viking adventurers, albeit highly assimilated to French language and culture, had killed the last Anglo-Saxon king of England in a battle that would be named from the nearby settlement at Hastings. The Norman Conquest, therefore, might be seen as the last great act in a process of Scandinavian intervention in English affairs that had dominated over two and a half centuries of Anglo-Saxon history.

The Viking impact on England, however, did not end in 1066. In fact, in the generation after Hastings, the threat of Viking intervention would hang over the new Norman rulers; it would, ironically given earlier sufferings caused to England, encourage and enable English resistance to the new Norman regime; and it would influence one of the greatest documents created in the Middle Ages.[1]

The Vikings as allies of the defeated Anglo-Saxons

Following the failure of a revolt at Exeter (Devon) against Norman rule in 1068, Harold Godwinson's mother, Gytha, shifted her base of anti-Norman operations to the island of Flatholme in the Bristol Channel. This had earlier been used as a base by Viking raiders in the ninth century and it is ironic that the relatives of the last Anglo-Saxon king were imitating the tactics of those who had been the enemies of Anglo-Saxon England two centuries earlier. Reduced to raiding their former country, this loose alliance of disaffected English nobility was operating very much in the mould of the Vikings. The parallel became even more apparent after Harold Godwinson's sons by Edith Swan-neck sought assistance from King Diarmait of Dublin and returned to England, later in 1068, with a force of Irish-Norse mercenaries in fifty-two ships. Revealingly, *Manuscript E* uses the Anglo-Scandinavian word *lið* (seaborne military) to describe both the forces of Harold Godwinson's sons and those of Svein Estrithson of Denmark who invaded England in 1069–70.[2]

The first attack by Harold Godwinson's sons was on Bristol, where 'the citizens fought against them fiercely';[3] this clearly indicates that they were seen as Viking-style raiders rather than as liberators. When repulsed, they raided the coastal settlements of Somerset. After defeating a local defensive force and killing its commander, Eadnoth the Staller, who had earlier served their father and had now transferred his allegiance to William I, they returned to Ireland. In 1069, these Anglo-Irish-Norse adventurers returned and again raided the South West. But by the end of the year they had been defeated by the Normans, who then went on to establish strongholds in the South West.[4] There was apparently no popular support for these Anglo-Norse invaders and it seems that they were simply regarded as raiders.[5] After failing to secure a bridgehead in Somerset, the base on Flatholme was abandoned; the women found refuge with a relative by marriage, the count of Flanders, and the surviving sons of Harold Godwinson travelled to the court of King Svein Estrithson of Denmark. Here they were in friendly territory, since Svein Estrithson was Harold Godwinson's cousin. Furthermore, in the 1040s, Godwin of Wessex (Harold's father) had urged Edward the Confessor to assist Svein Estrithson in his struggle for independence from Magnus the Good, king of Norway.[6] This had further enhanced the connection between Godwin's family and the king of Denmark. How the request for aid against the Normans was received is unknown since, seeking assistance at this court of a Viking king, they vanish from history after Svein's death in 1074.

It is likely that their request for help was turned down since Svein Estrithson had discouraging experiences of intervention in post-conquest rebellions. Prior to the arrival of the sons of Harold Godwinson, he had intervened in England in an attempt to secure the English throne for himself, even though, in 1066, he had provided some diplomatic support for the Norman Conquest. Clearly he did not feel that his own claim was diminished by the Norman success.[7] As part of this unsuccessful attempt he had given assistance to English anti-Norman rebels such as Waltheof, Earl of Northumbria, and his northern allies, and to Hereward the Wake (the 'watchful') in the Fens of East Anglia.

In 1069, Svein Estrithson had invaded northern England and had been seen as an ally by those English nobles who wished to expel the Normans. The most prominent of these were Earl Waltheof and Edgar *ætheling*. Edgar was the last surviving male of the royal house of Wessex and the grandson of Edmund Ironside. As such, he was the rightful king of England but had been passed over in 1066 due to his youth and the political supremacy of Harold Godwinson. Before returning to England during the reign of Edward the Confessor, Edgar had grown up in Hungary where his father, Edward the Exile had fled to escape the agents of Cnut the Great, after Cnut became king of England in 1016. But, whereas Edward the Exile had been forced to flee from the hands of a Viking king of Denmark, his son – in the late summer of 1069 – looked to Denmark for assistance. Earlier that year Edgar *ætheling* had returned from exile in Scotland when a major revolt had broken out against Norman rule in northern England. However, after the revolt was crushed by William I, Edgar retreated to Scotland. But by then, late in the campaigning season, Svein Estrithson of Denmark had launched a new Viking bid for the English throne. The fleet reputedly numbered 240 ships and was commanded by Svein Estrithson's son, Cnut (later called Cnut IV the Holy). Arriving first at Dover (Kent), the fleet then sailed north along the eastern coast of England, landing at Sandwich (Kent), Ipswich (Suffolk) and near Norwich (Norfolk). In none of these places was there sufficient English support for a major uprising. It finally arrived in the Humber estuary, as so many other Viking fleets had done in the past. Here the Danish army was soon joined by Edgar *ætheling* from Scotland and this alliance of the Viking king of Denmark, the rightful king of England, and the northern English crushed the Norman forces at York and seized control of Northumbria. The Normans responded with characteristic vigour, but the Anglo-Danish army refused to be drawn into a decisive battle and

William I was distracted by an English revolt that had broken out in the Midlands.[8] Only once that was settled, in November 1069, was he able to focus again on the alliance that opposed him in the north.

Quite how the ambitions of Svein Estrithson and Edgar *ætheling* would have been reconciled is difficult to imagine; perhaps they envisaged a division of the kingdom such as had occurred between Cnut the Great and Edmund Ironside in 1016. Whatever the possible solution to their mutual ambition was, it remains unknown as William and his Norman forces moved north and succeeded in retaking York in December 1069, driving his opponents to the Humber estuary. William then began the systematic destruction of opposition in an episode known as the 'Harrying of the North' in the winter of 1069–70. The aim may have been as much to render the area unattractive to the Danish Crown as to punish the rebels.[9] Despite this, Svein Estrithson joined his son in the Humber estuary in the spring of 1070 and, in June, a section of the Danish fleet sailed down the coast where they assisted another English rebel – Hereward the Wake – in sacking Peterborough (Cambridgeshire).[10]

Hereward held lands in Lincolnshire and was probably from an Anglo-Danish family,[11] revealing the ethnic complexity of East Anglia resulting from the Viking Wars. By the 1070s a man with recognisably Danish ancestry could leave a legacy as an 'Anglo-Saxon' resistance hero. He appears to have left England some time after 1062 and may have been banished as an outlaw; but what is certain is that he later reappeared, in 1070, plundering the abbey at Peterborough. *Manuscript E*, which was compiled at Peterborough in the 1120s to replace a lost original, states that a Danish contingent of Svein Estrithson's army arrived in nearby Ely and that the local English rose up in support of them. This united front of East Anglians – ethnic Danes and Anglo-Saxons – in their alliance with Svein Estrithson illustrates the way in which English-Danes had become well integrated into English society during the eleventh century.[12]

News reached Peterborough Abbey that its own tenants were planning to plunder the abbey since they had heard that it was to be given to a Norman, Thorold. Quite why these tenants considered that sacking their local abbey was an appropriate response to the imposition of an unpopular abbot is not explained. Clearly, they seem to have felt that an attack on the abbey was an attack on him, and it is a reminder that the looting of religious houses was not just the *modus operandi* of Vikings. The *Chronicle* records that, among those planning the attack, was 'Hereward and his following', who are also described as 'outlaws'.[13] Hereward was accompanied by members of the Danish army, who drove out all the monks, except for one who was ill in the infirmary, before most of the settlement was burned. Even given the partisan outlook of *Manuscript E*, the looting of the church that followed is difficult to justify in terms of a revolt against Norman rule. Later Peterborough monastic tradition adapted the story to present Hereward as seizing the monastic treasure in order to prevent it falling into Norman hands. At the time, though, the attack was regarded less favourably by the Church, as the *Chronicle* records that, following the attack, the Anglo-Saxon bishop Æthelric excommunicated those responsible.

However, it was at this point that the limited commitment of Svein Estrithson to his English ambitions was revealed. With English resistance fading, as a result of the Norman counter-attacks, he was bought-off by the Normans. Consequently, the Danes left Ely with their loot and the revolt became a solely English affair. As revolts failed elsewhere, it was to Ely that a number of other rebels headed. These included Morcar (Earl of Northumbria until replaced by William I after Harold Godwinson's defeat in 1066), Bishop Æthelwine and Siward Barn (a rebel northern *thegn*), along with several hundred supporters. However, by the end of 1071, the revolt at Ely had collapsed in the face of a twin Norman attack by sea and land across a causeway bridge constructed specifically for the purpose of reaching the rebels' base on the island of Ely. All the rebels surrendered, with the exception of Hereward and his immediate supporters; he continued to resist the Normans and his eventual end is uncertain. The fact that a landowner named Hereward was recorded as holding land in 1086 on the Warwickshire/Worcestershire border has led to the suggestion that the East Anglian Anglo-Danish rebel eventually came to terms with the Normans, but this is likely to have been a different Hereward. From these brief references in the *Chronicle* – and additional references in Domesday Book to land held on the edge of the Lincolnshire fens, from the abbeys at Crowland and Peterborough before the Norman Conquest, by Hereward – has grown the folk tale of 'Hereward the Wake'. The legend developed quickly, being found in accounts written as early as the 1140s. What is clear is that Hereward's revolt was heavily dependent on Danish support; it was only after the arrival of a Danish force that the *Chronicle* records the start of the revolt and, once that support had been withdrawn, the revolt quickly collapsed. Heroic though his continued resistance in the Fens appears, it offered little real threat to Norman rule. It was only Viking assistance that could have changed that and this was not available to Hereward beyond 1070.[14]

With the main English rebels defeated, Edgar *ætheling* himself was forced to flee once more to Scotland. Following a final, unsuccessful anti-Norman expedition in 1074, Edgar was reconciled to William and died shortly after 1125. However, despite the failure of 1069–70, the events of that year had demonstrated that Viking interest in England was far from over.

Five years later, in 1075, Cnut of Denmark returned once more, and this time came with a Danish-Norwegian fleet of 'two hundred ships'.[15] The intervention was prompted by 'push-factors' from Denmark, as well as 'pull-factors' from England. In Denmark the death of Svein Estrithson in 1074 had led to a disputed succession from which his illegitimate son, Harald (who ruled as Harald III), eventually emerged victorious.[16] Unsuccessful in his bid for the Danish Crown, but allied with Olaf III 'the Peaceful' of Norway, Cnut seems to have refocused his energies on gaining the English throne. On this occasion, the 'pull factor' from England was provided, not by rebellious English elites, but instead by disaffected Norman earls who invited his intervention. However, by the time the Danish fleet arrived, the revolt had ended and Cnut's activities were confined to landing on the Humber and sacking York. As with the failed invasion of 1069–70, what had started as a grand political intervention had ended as a Viking plundering raid that would have been recognised by Æthelred II almost a century earlier.

The threat of Viking invasion and the commissioning of the Domesday Inquiry, 1085

In 1080, Cnut finally succeeded his brother, Harald III, as king of Denmark (as Cnut IV). Five years later, in 1085, he began preparations for another invasion of England. Ever since the campaigns of Svein Forkbeard, the dynastic ambitions of the kings of Denmark had been intertwined with events in England. As a result, Cnut IV now prepared for the last great Viking invasion of England. This time, though, the strength of the Norman defences seriously deterred the Danish elites whose support was crucial to the success of the enterprise. Disputes in Denmark also challenged the royal plans. The fleet never sailed and, in 1086, Cnut IV was assassinated. The last great Viking threat had passed.[17]

The plans of Cnut IV to repeat the achievements of Svein Forkbeard and Cnut the Great may have come to nothing, but they stimulated one of the most striking achievements of the Middle Ages. For it was as a response to the threat of Viking invasion that William I commissioned the Domesday inquest in 1085.

There were many reasons why, in late 1085, William I ordered the vast enterprise that became known as the Domesday inquest and which culminated in Domesday Book. Clearly, one of its roles was to establish the titles to land, given the great upheaval in land ownership that had occurred since the Norman Conquest in 1066.[18] The vast collection of data also gave the Crown a detailed record of who was liable to pay *geld* (tax) and the tax value of all estates; it allowed the Crown to identify exactly what land was held by the king's vassals and its value; it also had the legal purpose of settling the disputes over land ownership which had characterised England since 1066.[19] In addition, according to the historian Orderic Vitalis, writing in the 1120s, it aimed to define the nature of knight-service owed to the Crown, 'ready to be mustered at a moment's notice in the king's service whenever necessary'.[20] But the context, as Orderic reminds his readers, was that 'Cnut the younger, king of Denmark was then preparing a great fleet, and making arrangements to invade England, conquered in earlier times by his ancestors Swein [Svein Forkbeard] and Cnut [the Great] and claim his right.'[21] Despite the fact that the compiler of the *Chronicle* and most other twelfth-century historians did not make this direct connection between the crisis of 1085 and the Domesday inquest[22] – and saw the inquest solely as aiming to produce the document we know as Domesday Book – it seems clear that the crisis had in fact caused the inquest to occur.[23] That both the Domesday inquest and Domesday Book may have had a number of important functions need not be doubted, but the trigger cause was clearly the threat of yet another Viking invasion. A radical interpretation has separated out the actual writing of Domesday Book from the inquest that preceded it. In this reappraisal of the two processes, Domesday Book appears as a land register drawn up for administrative purposes following the revolt against William II (Rufus) in 1088. In contrast, the Domesday inquest was rooted firmly within the context of the threat of Danish invasion in 1085, which highlighted weaknesses in the national system of taxation and of defence. As a result, it was necessary to review and, where necessary, renegotiate what *geld* and knight-service was owed by landowners.[24] Even if the more radical aspects of this interpretation are questioned,[25] we are still left with a monumental survey that was a direct product of the Viking Wars.

As such, the Domesday inquest joins such major institutional achievements as the creation of a unified English state and the establishment of a national system of taxation; these were also direct outcomes of the Viking Wars and had a major impact on the development of the English nation and its government.

The last of the Vikings?

The Scandinavian connection with England in the aftermath of 1066 was curiously intertwined with the survival of a son of Harold Godwinson by his second marriage, whose later career became linked to the ambitions of Viking adventurers. Harold Godwinson had, for over twenty years before 1066, been married *more danico* (in the Danish manner) to Edith Swan-neck. This was an arrangement that was not considered legitimate by the Church and the term used for it illustrates the influence of Viking practices in England. The term implies an on-going and fairly stable relationship that had not been formalised by marriage. While such a woman might be described as a 'mistress' rather than a 'wife', the case of Harold Godwinson and Edith Swan-neck reveals that it could be far from casual. For members of the elite it allowed them the option of a relationship based on love and personal attraction, while still leaving them free to contract political marriages whose 'legitimate' offspring would have unquestioned rights of inheritance and, in the case of kings, would be worthy of the throne. It is a curious reminder of the many different ways in which Scandinavian culture and mores impacted on England. Harold Godwinson had a number of children with Edith Swan-neck and the older of these, as we have seen, went on to unsuccessfully attack Norman England following the death of their father in 1066. However, in January 1066, Harold Godwinson contracted a political marriage as part of the consolidation of his weak claim to the English throne. At that time he married Ealdgyth,[26] daughter of Ælfgar, the old Earl of Mercia, and the widow of the Welsh prince, Gruffydd ap Llywelyn. She was the sister of Edwin, the current Earl of Mercia, and Morcar, the Earl of Northumbria. The marriage created a close political alliance between these powerful English nobles and clearly bolstered Harold Godwinson's position. Despite this, it was Edith Swan-neck who identified Harold Godwinson's body after Hastings by signs that only she would know from a lifetime of intimacy. Nevertheless, it was a son by his second wife, Ealdgyth, who would take his father's fight into another generation and who would intertwine it with the last major intervention by Scandinavians. This son was Harold Haroldson.

According to John of Worcester, writing *c.*1140, after the defeat at Hastings the pregnant Ealdgyth was taken to Chester by her brothers.[27] It was here that Harold Haroldson was born, in 1067. The connection of the family with Chester left a strangely garbled tradition which was recorded in 1188 by the Welsh cleric, Gerald of Wales. This tradition maintained that Harold Godwinson had survived Hastings, although badly wounded and blinded by a Norman arrow, and had escaped to the vicinity of Chester. Living there in disguise as a hermit his 'real' identity was only revealed in his deathbed confession.[28] It seems that the presence of Harold Haroldson in Chester, albeit as a baby, had given rise to this twelfth-century folk tale which confused the son with his more famous father.

Following the failure of the northern uprisings against William I and the 'Harrying of the North', Ealdgyth fled with her son to Dublin. In time, Harold Haroldson travelled on to Norway, where he was well received by Harald Hardrada's son, King Magnus II Haraldsson (king of Norway from 1066 to 1069, jointly from 1067 with his brother Olaf Kyrre). This was, according to the twelfth-century historian William of Malmesbury, because King Harold Godwinson had shown mercy to the Viking survivors of the battle of Stamford Bridge.[29] In 1098 there is the last reference to Harold Haroldson, who was by then active in the Irish Sea region, fighting against a Norman army in North Wales. At this time he was a member of a Viking fleet led by the new king of Norway, Magnus III Barelegs (ruler of Norway from 1093–1103 and ruler of the Kingdom of Man and the Isles from 1099–1103). His curious surname was gained from his favouring of Gaelic fashion, with legs bare from the knee downwards.

This Magnus was son of King Olaf Kyrre and, therefore, a grandson of Harald Hardrada who had died at Stamford Bridge. In 1098 Magnus Barelegs launched the last sizeable Viking expedition into the Irish Sea area. His objective was the conquest of the Viking Kingdom of Man and the Isles. This kingdom had been growing since the military campaigns of Thorfinn the Mighty, Earl of Orkney (*c.*1020–65). As well as ruling Orkney and Caithness, Thorfinn had extended the rule of his earldom to Ross, the Shetlands and the Isle of Man; he also campaigned in Galloway and Ireland. In 1042 he raided north-western England at the head of a combined army of Norse, Scots and Irish. He was truly a 'sea-king' in all but title, while still being nominally under the authority of the Norwegian Crown. After his death in 1065, the Hebrides and the Kingdom of Man became united in a Scottish-Viking sea kingdom by Godred Crovan of Islay, until his death in 1095. In 1098 the campaign of Magnus Barelegs was designed to bring this sea kingdom under the control of the kingdom of Norway. Never before had Norwegian power in the Irish Sea region been so absolute. The Norwegian fleet captured Dublin, took tribute from Galloway and the island of Anglesey, and sacked Bangor. William of Malmesbury claimed that Magnus Barelegs intended to go on from here to invade England. In this last area of operations, in North Wales, the Norwegians fought two Norman earls, who opposed their landing on Anglesey. At the battle of Menai Straits, Harold Haroldson made his last appearance in the historical record; a point recorded only by William of Malmesbury amongst the medieval chroniclers of this battle.[30]

William of Malmesbury commented that, at the battle of Menai Straits, Hugh of Montgomery, the Norman Earl of Shrewsbury, fell while charging with his knights through the surf, shot with an arrow from one of the Norwegian ships.[31] This sounds very much like a conscious reworking of the later accounts of the battle of Hastings and may have been carefully constructed in order to imply God's judgement on the Norman earls, just as earlier accounts had portrayed Hastings as God's judgement on the sins of the English. Following this, the Viking fleet withdrew and, in 1104, Magnus Barelegs was killed in battle in Ireland. Consequently, the battle of Menai Straits – which ironically brought together in battle Norwegian Vikings, the descendant of the last Anglo-Saxon king of England and the Norman knights – provides an appropriate end to the Viking Wars. The blitzkrieg of attacks that had started in 789 and had radically transformed England had come to a close. And, by 1100, the Danes themselves were the victims of escalating raids by the Wends, a Slav tribe of the southern Baltic coast. In the face of these attacks, the Danes were no more successful in defending their coastal settlements than the Anglo-Saxon kingdoms had been in the early ninth century.

The ghosts of Vikings past

The Viking Wars had ended by 1100, but there were still odd echoes of these conflicts which continued into the twelfth century before they finally died away. In 1153, King Harald Eystein of Norway led the last ever recorded Norwegian Viking raid on England. That year he attacked Hartlepool (Durham), Whitby (North Yorkshire), Scarborough (North Yorkshire) and raided as far down the east coast as the Wash. There was no political purpose in this and his aim seems only to have been to seize plunder.[32] On the periphery of English territory, however, Viking influence lingered longer. In 1156, Somerled, an Argyll chieftain of mixed Norse and Scottish ancestry, defeated the king of Man, Godred II, in a mid-winter battle, fought by moonlight. Two years later, in 1158, Somerled devastated Man but continued to recognise the overlordship of the Norwegian king. The Isle of Man would remain under the formal authority of the kings of Norway until 1266. Only at that late date did the Norwegian king, Magnus VI, cede it to Scotland, along with the Hebrides, in return for 4,000 *marks* and a yearly payment of 100 *marks* (a *mark* being a denomination equivalent to two-thirds of a pound sterling).

The *Orkneyinga Saga* (*Saga of the Orcadians*), also known as *Jarla Saga* (*Saga of the Earls*), which was compiled in Iceland between 1192 and 1206 as a 'history' of the conquest of Orkney by Norway and the subsequent history of the earldom of Orkney, tells the tale of the man who may have been the last Viking of all to raid English territory.[33] According to the saga, Svein Asleifarson, or Asleifsson, lived in the Orkneys but raided the Hebrides, Wales and Ireland and mounted what was probably the last ever Viking raid on England when he plundered a monastery on the Scilly Isles. He was killed while raiding Dublin in 1171.[34] Despite the fictional nature of parts of the story, at least some of the account of Svein's career was probably based on sources of evidence from Orkney regarding actual events.[35] In the memorable words of the saga, he conducted two Viking exploits a year. The first he called his 'spring trip', which began after he had sown his crops and this lasted until mid-summer; the second was his 'autumn trip', which started once the harvest was completed, and this lasted until his return to Orkney in mid-winter. With such a piratical example of plundering free enterprise, history had come full circle to the character of the first raids on Portland and Lindisfarne. But *Orkneyinga Saga* is more a literary composition than a work of history and with its tales of Svein Asleifarson the historic Viking Age was finally over.[36]

ON REFLECTION

How can we sum up the importance and impact of the Viking Blitzkrieg – the series of raids, wars and colonisation – that racked England, and indeed Britain, from the late eighth century until the late eleventh century? In the amusing and highly informative *British History for Dummies* by Seán Lang, we see something of the problem in finding a simple answer. On one hand: 'Horned helmets, great longboats, and plenty of rape and pillage', and on the other hand: '… the Viking raids helped to bring the different peoples of Britain closer together, because they all suffered together.'[1] And this brings us to the counterintuitive conundrum of the Vikings Wars, for, despite all the destruction and mayhem, kingdoms that were more united arose in response to the challenge, since 'battling the Norsemen was not only an objective in itself … but also a means to an end: consolidating power and creating nations.'[2] The Viking Wars are therefore, and understandably, very hard to sum up in one simple sentence.

Images of the Viking wars

Our modern images of the Viking Wars are a triumph for the compilers of the Anglo-Saxon written sources. Even twenty-first-century inhabitants of Britain who have never read the *Anglo-Saxon Chronicle*, Asser's *Life of King Alfred*, Æthelweard's *Chronicle*, the *History of St Cuthbert*, the *Annals of*

St Neots, the *Encomium Emmae Reginae*, the *Vita Ædwardi Regis*, or Henry of Huntingdon's *Historia Anglorum*, will carry mental images of burning churches and villages, dead monks and enslaved civilians, Alfred and the burnt cakes, and Cnut at the seashore whenever the Viking Wars are mentioned. When, in 2002, the BBC conducted a poll of the '100 Greatest Britons', Alfred the Great came in fourteenth – not a bad achievement for a ruler who died in 899.[3]

Furthermore, even without an awareness of *Eiríksmál*, *Heimskringla*, *Liðsmannaflokkr* or the *Saga of Egil Skalla-Grímsson*, modern people will have had their visual images of axe-wielding warriors reinforced from the (mostly much later) Old Norse sources which appear to revel in tales of feud and ancestral bloodshed. Indeed, the twelfth- and thirteenth-century Icelandic sagas were products of a later antiquarian interest in Viking ancestors. And many today will have heard of Erik Bloodaxe, even if they have no idea of when or where he lived and what he did.

There may, though, be some antidotes administered to this fever of violence and destruction. Those who have visited the Jorvik Viking Centre in York will have a balancing set of mental images that focus more on trade, crafts and urban life. And those who have carried their metal detectors across the Wolds of Lincolnshire and Yorkshire will have contributed – via their finds of copper alloy buckles, brooches and strap-ends – to a more homely concept of the Scandinavian presence. While those who marvel at road signs with names such as Wetwang Slack, Fangfoss, Fridaythorpe and Whipmawhopmagate – all these examples are found in Yorkshire – will realise that a Scandinavian presence has changed the maps, road signs and street names of eastern and northern England.

As a result, our mental images are conflicting ones of horror and heritage, of destruction and northern distinctiveness – better, after all, to be a northern descendant of Vikings than a soft southerner! At this point it should be noted that the authors are southerners, each bears a medieval surname derived from an Anglo-Saxon personal name, live in what was once Wessex and were raised on stories of how Alfred saved us from the northern Viking marauders.

This collage of conflicting images is readily explainable. For a start, the Viking Wars lasted a long time. In the three centuries between *c.*800 and *c.*1100, many different interactions occurred within Anglo-Saxon society. Different leaders on both sides of the conflict worked to different agendas and in different combinations of enemies and allies. The Viking Blitzkrieg was, consequently, a series of different events and this was just from the

Scandinavian perspective: small-scale raids; large-scale raids; mass attacks based on conquest; settlement; offensive capabilities blunted by colonisation and turning to the defensive needs of settled Scandinavian communities; integration and cooperation with existing Anglo-Saxon communities and then assimilation; conflict and cooperation with the kings of Wessex; large-scale invasions led by a newly revived and centralised Danish kingdom under a new dynasty; extortion as a way of life; conquest; creation of an Anglo-Danish North Sea Empire under a surprisingly anglophile monarch; disintegration of that empire; reassertion of claims to the English throne by continental powers whose claims were products (direct and indirect) of the Viking Wars; defeat at the hands of more unified and capable Anglo-Saxon and then Norman rulers; a reversion to partially successful raiding on behalf of firmly established Scandinavian kingdoms; and a fizzling out of raids because Scandinavian rulers could now benefit from settled and effective taxation structures at home that promised more rewards than a hazardous campaign against strong Anglo-Norman resistance. In such a drawn-out affair it would be unrealistic to expect one 'experience' to dominate. Instead, we find a complex tangle of outcomes.

Secondly, the three centuries offer different perspectives based on different class experiences. The true 'Viking' worked to a different agenda, compared with that of the Scandinavian trader at *Jorvik*. And, even among the true 'Vikings', a small-scale adventurer on the make in the 830s had a different set of expectations and prospects compared to a powerful magnate operating semi-independently in the army of Svein Forkbeard, *c.*1000, or in the semi-imperial context of Cnut in the 1020s. Similarly, the local (and newly established) Danish landlord and landlady in the *Danelaw*, *c.*900, had a different set of life-experiences compared to a lower-class contemporary female peasant follower, who partook of the poor copper alloy brooches found today in northern Lincolnshire. These ambitions could sometimes work to mutual advantage and sometimes lead to conflict. The same political minefield of competing and sometimes conflicting ambitions also occurred amongst Anglo-Saxons. So much so that, if an eleventh-century ruler such as Æthelred II seemed unable to establish political stability, an Anglo-Saxon magnate such as Eadric Streona could feel free to hack out his own path through the jungle of competing factions, setting off chain reactions of conflict with other, slighted, Anglo-Saxon earls. And *æthelings* such as Athelstan (died 1014) and Edmund Ironside (died 1016) could feel their dynastic ambitions were sufficiently threatened to see as much danger in the power of rival Anglo-Saxon magnates as in the threat posed by Vikings such as Svein Forkbeard and Cnut.

This does not allow for ethnic tensions between tenth-century Danes, settled in Lincolnshire and Yorkshire, and incoming Irish-Norse expelled from Dublin and looking for new opportunities in England. In such a situation, a Dane from the *Danelaw* could suddenly look quite favourably on an alliance with an accommodating West Saxon ruler who was keen to win friends in newly annexed territory. The same contrasting experiences were mirrored on the Anglo-Saxon side and this included the tensions felt between West Saxon monarchs set on 'liberating' the *Danelaw* and Northumbrian nobles who had worked out a manner of living with the Scandinavian conquerors, such that things were working out rather well – before a West Saxon intruder upset the political applecart.

No wonder the images and impressions of the Viking Wars are complex and difficult to reconcile at times. But that is the nature of history and it is that which makes this particular period of history so fascinating, dynamic, significant and intriguing.

The long-term significance of the Viking Blitzkrieg

All this said, what can we identify as the long-term significance of the Viking Wars? One abiding legacy must be a sense of English identity and destiny forged in the crucible of conflict. It is no surprise that the national epic of the *Anglo-Saxon Chronicle* was created in the heat of the Viking Wars and promoted the supposed unity of the royal house of Wessex at a time of national crisis. Alfred's image may have been the projection of West Saxon propaganda, but it was effective and it has been long lasting – remember the BBC survey of 2002. It created a sense of God-given and providence-blessed national identity that was no ephemeral creation. It can, arguably, be traced through the Middle Ages to modern-day ideas of national significance. No wonder that Alfred was so beloved by nineteenth-century imperial gentlemen; his blend of muscular Christianity inspired more than just his contemporaries in Wessex. Not surprisingly, in *1066 and All That*, he was described as: 'the first Good King, with the exception of Good King Wenceslas'.[4]

Allied to this is the unification of England. Given the balance of power that had become established by the early ninth century, it is easy to imagine a dominant Wessex, but hard to imagine one king of a unified England.

The Viking Wars changed all that; eclipsing all rivals to Wessex and then presenting the West Saxons with the propaganda advantage of being able to present themselves as the only viable Christian alternative for Anglo-Saxons across England (whatever grumbles persisted in Northumbria). England's advance towards an early and precocious nation-state was undeniably possible due to the opportunities presented to, albeit motivated and gifted, West Saxon rulers in the tenth century. A united England is a rather impressive legacy, even if an unintentional one. Without the Vikings it is difficult to imagine the imperial figure of Athelstan in the 930s and the settled power of Edgar in the 970s.

With this unity came the urban and industrial expansion of the tenth century and the centralised organisation of the magnificent coinage and unified taxation system of Late Anglo-Saxon England. This made England into a prize so desirable to invaders as different as Svein in 1013, and William of Normandy in 1066. It is going too far to solely credit the Vikings with this, but quite reasonable to accord them the status of being one of the most important factors in making this possible.

The desirability of England combined with another unintended Viking legacy, the Norman Conquest, to set the trajectory of medieval England both in its continental and insular dimensions. The whole tangle of events that brought William to southern England in 1066 was a product (direct and indirect) of the Viking Wars, even if by then the Normans were more French-men than North-men. And, as if to underscore this Viking connection, it was the arrival of a real Viking in the Humber estuary that autumn that so wrong-footed Harold Godwinson and was, arguably, the biggest factor in making the Norman Conquest possible.

That the Norman Conquest was a product of the Viking Wars is a justifiable claim. As if that was not enough, the most important medieval survey in western Europe, Domesday Book, was itself a product of yet another set of Vikings on the horizon.

There is always the danger of over emphasising any past phenomenon that is the subject of an historical study. However, while allowing for the huge importance of other factors and processes, it still seems fair to identify the Viking Blitzkrieg as the most significant formative factor in English history between 800 and 1100. And one whose legacy echoed far into the Middle Ages. Long after the 'earthquakes' of the Viking attacks were over and even when the 'time-epicentre' was long past, the 'aftershocks' were still affecting England and its neighbours – they still do.

ABOUT THE AUTHORS

Hannah Whittock graduated with a 'First' in Anglo-Saxon, Norse and Celtic from Pembroke College, Cambridge University, in 2011. In 2012 she completed her Masters at Cambridge, researching the relationship of the Bradford-on-Avon charter of 1001 to the development of the cult of Edward King and Martyr. She is currently working with the Welsh devolved government. Her publications include: 'Why does the north-western boundary of Wiltshire ignore the River Avon?', in *The Wiltshire Archaeological and Natural History Magazine*, vol. 105 (2012); 'The annexation of Bath by Wessex: The evidence of two rare coins of Edward the Elder', *British Numismatic Journal*, vol. 82 (2012).

Martyn Whittock graduated in politics from Bristol University in 1980 and since then has taught history at secondary level for over thirty years, currently teaching history at a Wiltshire secondary school. At A-Level his specialist subject is Late Roman Britain and Anglo-Saxon England, *c.* 350–1066. He is the author of thirty-seven school history textbooks and adult history books, the latter including: *A Brief History of Life in the Middle Ages* (2009), and *A Brief History of the Third Reich* (2011). He is the author of articles on the Anglo-Saxon royal estate at Keynsham (north Somerset), and the strategic significance of the West Wansdyke earthwork (in north Somerset). He has acted as an historical consultant to the National Trust and English Heritage. He is currently writing *A Brief Guide to Celtic Myths and Legends*.

BIBLIOGRAPHY

Abels, R., *Alfred the Great, War, Kingship and Culture in Anglo-Saxon England* (Longman: London, 1998).

Abels, R., 'Alfred the Great, the micel hæðen here and the viking threat' in T. Reuter (ed.), *Alfred the Great* (Ashgate Publishing: Aldershot, 2003), pp.265–80.

Abram, C., *Myths of the Pagan North: The Gods of the Norsemen* (Hambledon Continuum: London, 2011).

Adams, J. and Holman, K. (eds), *Scandinavia and Europe, 800–1350: Contact, Conflict and Coexistence* (Brepols: Turnhout, 2004).

Arnold, M., *The Vikings: Culture and Conquest* (Hambledon Continuum: London, 2006)

Balbirnie, C., 'The Vikings at Home', *BBC History Magazine*, vol. 13, number 9 (September 2012), pp. 22–8.

Ballin Smith, B., Taylor, S. and Williams, G. (eds), *West Over Sea: Studies in Scandinavian Sea-borne Expansion and Settlement Before 1300* (Brill: Leiden, 2007).

Barlow, F., *Edward the Confessor* (Yale University Press: New Haven and London, 2nd edn, 1997).

Barlow, F., *The Godwins* (Pearson: Harlow, 2002).

Bates, D., 'In search of the Normans', *BBC History Magazine*, vol. 13, number 8 (August 2012), pp.30–5.

Baxter, S.D., *The Earls of Mercia: Lordship and Power in Late Anglo-Saxon England* (Oxford University Press: Oxford, 2007).

Blackburn, M.A.S., Dumville, D.N. (eds), *Kings, Currency, and Alliances: History and Coinage of Southern England in the Ninth Century* (Boydell Press: Woodbridge, 1998).

Bolton, T., *The Empire of Cnut the Great: Conquest and the Consolidation of Power in Northern Europe in the Early Eleventh Century* (Brill: Leiden, 2009).

Bradbury, I., *The Battle of Hastings* (Sutton Publishing: Stroud, 1998).

Brooks, N., 'Alfredian government: the West Saxon inheritance', in T. Reuter (ed.), *Alfred the Great* (Ashgate Publishing: Aldershot, 2003), pp.153–74.

Brown, M.P., *Manuscripts from the Anglo-Saxon Age* (The British Library: London, 2007).

Cameron, K (ed.), *Place-name Evidence for the Anglo-Saxon Invasion and Scandinavian Settlements* (University of Nottingham: Nottingham, 1975).

Cavill, P. (ed.), *The Christian Tradition in Anglo-Saxon England* (D.S. Brewer: Cambridge, 2004).

Cooper, J. (ed.), *The Battle of Maldon: Fiction and Fact* (Hambledon Continuum: London, 1993).

Cowie, R., 'Mercian London', in M.P. Brown and C.A. Farr, *Mercia: An Anglo-Saxon Kingdom in Europe* (Continuum: London, 2001), pp. 194–209.

Crumlin-Pedersen, O., 'The Vikings and the Hanseatic merchants, 900–1450', in G.W. Bass (ed.), *A History of Seafaring* (Thames and Hudson: London, 1972), pp. 182–207.

Crumlin-Pedersen, O., 'Large and small warships of the North', in A. Nørgård Jørgenson, B.L. Clausen (eds), *Military Aspects of Scandinavian Society in a European Perspective, AD1–1300* (PNM: Copenhagen, 1997), pp. 184–94.

Cullen, P., Jones, R. and Parsons, D., *Thorps in a Changing Landscape* (University of Hertfordshire Press: Hatfield, 2011).

Cusack, C.M., The Rise of Christianity in Northern Europe, 300–1000 (Cassell: London, 1999).

Dumville, D. and Keynes, S., *Annals of St Neot's with Vita Prima Sancti Neoti* (D.S. Brewer: Cambridge, 1985).

Dumville, D.M., 'Kings of England 927–1066', in E.B. Fryde *et al* (eds) *Handbook of British Chronology* (Royal Historical Society: London, 3rd ed., 1986), pp. 25–9.

Finberg, H.P.R., *The Formation of England 550–1042* (Paladin: St Albans, 1976).

Fleming, R., *Domesday Book and the Law: Society and Legal Custom in Early Medieval England* (Cambridge University Press: Cambridge, 2003).

Fletcher, R., *Bloodfeud: Murder and Revenge in Anglo-Saxon England* (Oxford University Press: Oxford, 2003).

Foot, S., 'The Danish conquest of England', *BBC History Magazine*, vol. 7, number 4 (April 2006) pp. 48–51.

Foot, S., *Æthelstan: The First King of England* (Yale University Press: New Haven and London, 2011).

Foot, S., 'Canterbury's other martyr', *BBC History Magazine*, vol. 13, number 4 (April 2012), pp. 30–1.

Forte, A., Oram, R. and Pedersen, F., *Viking Empires* (Cambridge University Press: Cambridge, 2005).

Garmonsway, G. N. (ed. and transl.), *The Anglo-Saxon Chronicle* (J. M. Dent & Sons Ltd: London, 1972).

Gelling, M., *Place-names in the Landscape* (Phoenix: London, 1984).

Gillingham, J. (ed.), *Anglo-Norman Studies XXVI: Proceedings of the Battle Conference 2003* (Boydell Press: Woodbridge, 2004).

Graham-Campbell, J., *The Viking World* (Frances Lincoln Limited: London, 2001).

Hadley, D.M., *The Northern Danelaw: Its Social Structure, c. 800–1100* (Leicester University Press: London, 2000).

Hadley, D.M., *The Vikings in England, Settlement, Society and Culture* (Manchester University Press: Manchester, 2006).

Hadley, D.M. and Richards, J.D. (eds), *Cultures in Contact: Scandinavian Settlement in England in the Ninth and Tenth Centuries* (Brepols: Turnhout, 2000).

Haigh, C. (ed.), *The Cambridge Historical Encyclopedia of Great Britain and Ireland* (Cambridge University Press: Cambridge, 1990).

Haight Turk, M. (ed.), *The Legal Code of Ælfred the Great* (Lawbook Exchange: Clark, New Jersey, 2004).

Hall, R. A., *et al*, *Aspects of Anglo-Scandinavian York* (Council for British Archaeology: York, 2004).

Halsall, G., 'Playing by whose rules? A further look at Viking atrocity in the ninth century.' *Medieval History* vol.2, no.2 (1992), pp.3–12.

Haslam, J., 'King Alfred, Mercia and London, 874–86: A reassessment', in H. Hamerow (ed.), *Anglo-Saxon Studies in Archaeology and History*, 17 (Oxford University School of Archaeology: Oxford, 2011), pp.124–50.

Haywood, J., *The Penguin Historical Atlas of the Vikings* (Penguin: London, 1995).

Henson, D., *A Guide to Late Anglo-Saxon England, from Ælfred to Eadgar – 871 to 1074 AD* (Anglo-Saxon Books: Little Downham, Ely, 2006).

Higham, N.J., *The Death of Anglo-Saxon England* (Sutton: Stroud, 1997).

Higham, N.J. and Hill, D. (eds) *Edward the Elder, 899–924* (Routledge: London, 2001).

Hill, D., 'The origin of Alfred's urban policies', in T. Reuter (ed.), *Alfred the Great* (Ashgate Publishing: Aldershot, 2003), pp.219–234.

Hill, P., *The Age of Athelstan: Britain's Forgotten History* (Tempus: Stroud, 2004).

Hines, J., Lane, A. and Redknap, M. (eds), *Land, Sea and Home. Proceedings of a Conference on Viking-period Settlement, at Cardiff, July 2001* (Maney Publishing: Leeds, 2004).

Hinton, D.A., *Archaeology, Economy and Society: England from the Fifth to the Fifteenth Century* (Routledge: Oxford, 2002).

Holman, K., *The Northern Conquest: Vikings in Britain and Ireland* (Signal Books: Oxford, 2007).

Howard, I., *Swein Forkbeard's Invasions and the Danish Conquest of England, 991–1017* (Boydell Press: Woodbridge, 2003).

Howarth, D.A., *1066: The Year of the Conquest* (Penguin: London, 1981).

Hudson, B.T., *Viking Pirates and Christian Princes: Dynasty, Religion, and Empire in the North Atlantic* (Oxford University Press: Oxford, 2005).

Hunter Blair, P. and Keynes, S., *An Introduction to Anglo-Saxon England* (Cambridge University Press: Cambridge 3rd edn, 2003).

Johns, E., *Reassessing Anglo-Saxon England* (Manchester University Press: Manchester, 1996).

Karkov, C., *The Ruler Portraits of Anglo-Saxon England* (Boydell Press: Woodbridge, 2004).

Keynes, S. and Lapidge, M. (transl.), *Alfred the Great. Asser's Life of King Alfred and other contemporary Sources* (Penguin: Harmondsworth, 1983).

Keynes, S., 'The West Saxon charters of King Æthelwulf and his sons', *English Historical Review*, 109 (1994), pp.1109–49.

Keynes, S., 'The cult of King Alfred the Great', *Anglo-Saxon England*, 28 (1999), pp.225–356.

Keynes, S., 'Mercia and Wessex in the ninth century', in M.P. Brown and C.A. Farr (eds), *Mercia: An Anglo-Saxon Kingdom in Europe* (Continuum: London, 2001), pp.310–28.

Keynes, S., 'An abbot, an archbishop, and the Viking raids of 1006–7 and 1009–12', *Anglo-Saxon England*, 36 (2007), 151–220, pp.178–80.

Laing, L. and Laing, J., *Early English Art and Architecture* (Sutton Publishing: Stroud, 1996).

Lapidge, M., Blair, J., Keynes, S. and Scragg, D. (eds), *The Blackwell Encyclopaedia of Anglo-Saxon England* (Blackwell: Oxford, 2001).

Lavelle, R., *Alfred's Wars: Sources and Interpretations of Anglo-Saxon Warfare in the Viking Age* (Boydell Press: Woodbridge, 2010).

Lavelle, R., 'Fighting the Vikings', *BBC History Magazine*, vol. 12, number 1 (January 2011), pp.22–8.

Lawson, M., *Cnut: England's Viking King* (History Press: Stroud, 2011).

Livingston, M. (ed.), *The Battle of Brunanburgh: A Casebook* (Exeter University Press: Exeter 2011).

Mason, E., *The House of Godwin: The History of a Dynasty* (Hambledon Press: London, 2003).

McDonald, R.A., *The Viking Age: A Reader* (University of Toronto Press: Toronto, 2010).

McLynn, F., *1066: The Year of the Three Battles* (Pimlico: London, new edn, 1999).

Naismith, R., *Money and Power in Anglo-Saxon England, The Southern English Kingdoms, 757–865* (Cambridge University Press: Cambridge, 2012).

Nelson, J. L., '"A king across the sea": Alfred in continental perspective', *Transactions of the Royal Historical Society*, 36 (1986), pp. 45–68.

North, J.J., *English Hammered Coinage, Volume 1, Early Anglo-Saxon to Henry III, c.600–1272* (Spink and Son: London, 1994).

O'Brien, H., *Queen Emma and the Vikings: The Woman Who Shaped the Events of 1066* (Bloomsbury: London, 2005).

Page, R.I., *'A Most Vile People': Early English Historians on the Vikings* (Viking Society for Northern Research: London, 1986).

Page, R.I., *Reading the Past: Runes* (British Museum Publications: London, 1987).

Parker, J. *'England's Darling': The Victorian Cult of Alfred the Great* (Manchester University Press: Manchester, 2007).

Peirce, I.G. and Oakeshott, E., *Swords of the Viking Age* (Boydell Press: Woodbridge, 2002).

Pratt, D., *The Political Thought of King Alfred the Great, Cambridge Studies in Medieval Life and Thought: Fourth Series No. 67* (Cambridge University Press: Cambridge, 2007).

Redmond, A., *Viking Burial in the North of England, BAR British Series, 429* (Archaeopress: Oxford, 2007).

Reuter, T. (ed.), *Alfred the Great: Papers from the Eleventh-Century Conferences* (Ashgate Publishing: Aldershot, 2003).

Rex, P., *Hereward: The Last Englishman* (Tempus: Stroud, 2007).

Richards, J., *Blood of the Vikings* (Hodder and Stoughton: London, 2001).

Richards, J.D., *Viking Age England* (English Heritage/Batsford: London, 1991).

Roesdahl, E., Williams, K. and Margeson, S. (transl.), *The Vikings* (Penguin: London, 2nd edn, 1998).

Roffe, D., *Decoding Domesday* (Boydell Press: Woodbridge, 2007).

Sawyer, P.H., *The Age of the Vikings* (Edward Arnold: London, 1962, 2nd edn, 1971).

Sawyer, P.H., *The Oxford Illustrated History of the Vikings* (Oxford University Press: Oxford, 2001).

Stafford, P., *Unification and Conquest: Political and Social History of England in the Tenth and Eleventh Centuries* (Hodder Arnold: London, 1989).

Stephenson, I.P., *Viking Warfare* (Amberley: Stroud, 2012).

Swanton, M.J., 'King Alfred's Ships: Text and Context', *Anglo-Saxon England*, 28 (1999), pp. 1–22.

Whitelock, D. (ed.), *Sermo Lupi ad Anglos* (Methuen: London, 1939).

Whitelock, D., Douglas, D.C. and Tucker, S.I. (transl. and eds), *The Anglo-Saxon Chronicle* (Eyre and Spottiswoode: London, 1961).

Whitelock, D. (ed.), *English Historical Documents*, vol. I, c.500–1042 (Eyre Methuen: London, 1979).

Whittock, H, 'The Avon Valley as a Frontier Region, From the Fourth to the Eleventh Century' (unpublished BA dissertation in the department of Anglo-Saxon, Norse and Celtic, Cambridge University, 2010).

Whittock, H., 'Why does the north-western boundary of Wiltshire ignore the river Avon?', *The Wiltshire Archaeological and Natural History Magazine*, vol. 105 (2012), pp. 96–104.

Whittock, H., 'The Cult of Edward, King and Martyr and Bradford on Avon' (unpublished MPhil. dissertation in the department of Anglo-Saxon, Norse and Celtic, Cambridge University, 2012).

Whittock, H., 'The annexation of Bath by Wessex: The evidence of two rare coins of Edward the Elder', *British Numismatic Journal*, 82 (December 2012), pp.46–53.

Whittock, M., *A Brief History of Life in the Middle Ages* (Constable and Robinson: London, 2009).

Williams, A., Smyth, A.P. and Kirby, D.P., *A Biographical Dictionary of Dark Age Britain* (B.A. Seaby: London, 1991).

Williams, A., *Aethelred the Unready: The Ill-Counselled King* (Hambledon Continuum: London, 2003).

Williams, G. and Graham-Campbell, J. (eds), *Silver Economy in the Viking Age* (Left Coast Press Inc: Walnut Creek, California, 2007).

Wilson, D.M., *Anglo-Saxon Art: From the Seventh Century to the Norman Conquest* (Thames and Hudson: London, 1984).

Wood, M., *Domesday: A Search for the Roots of England* (BBC Publications: London, 1986).

Yorke, B., *Wessex in the Early Middle Ages* (Leicester University Press: London, 1995).

Yorke, B., 'Alfred the Great: the most perfect man in history?' *History Today*, vol. 49, issue 10 (October 1999), pp.8–14.

Yorke, B., 'Edward as Ætheling', in N. J. Higham, D. Hill (eds) *Edward the Elder, 899–924* (Routledge: London, 2001), pp. 25–39.

NOTES

Introduction

1 For example in: Haslam, J., 'King Alfred, Mercia and London, 874–86: A reassessment', in Hamerow, H. (ed.), *Anglo-Saxon Studies in Archaeology and History*, 17 (Oxford University School of Archaeology: Oxford, 2011), pp.124–50; Ferguson R., *The Hammer and the Cross: A New History of the Vikings* (Viking Penguin: London, 2009); Brink, S. and Price, N. (eds), *The Viking World* (Routledge: Abingdon, 2008); Forte, A., Oram, R. and Pedersen, F. (eds), *Viking Empires* (Cambridge University Press: Cambridge, 2005); and the BBC2 series 'Vikings', broadcast in autumn 2012.

2 Found in Whitelock, D. (ed.), *English Historical Documents*, vol. I, c.500–1042 (Eyre Methuen: London, 1979).

3 Whitelock, D., Douglas, D.C. and Tucker, S.I. (transl. and eds), *The Anglo-Saxon Chronicle* (Eyre and Spottiswoode: London, 1961).

4 Garmonsway, G.N. (ed. and transl.), *The Anglo-Saxon Chronicle* (J.M. Dent & Sons Ltd: London, 1972).

5 A detailed examination of issues relating to the *Anglo-Saxon Chronicle* can be found in: Jorgensen, A. (ed.), *Reading the Anglo-Saxon Chronicle: Language, Literature, History* (Brepols: Turnhout, 2010). Regarding how to understand and approach the different manuscripts, especially helpful is the chapter: Jorgensen, A., 'Introduction: Reading the *Anglo-Saxon Chronicle*'; pp.1–28 and especially Table 1, pp.6–7.

6 The problematic nature of Norse sagas as evidence for the actual events of the Viking Wars is well made by: Stephenson, I.P., 'Lies, Damn Lies and Sagas', *Viking Warfare* (Amberley: Stroud, 2012), pp.19–24.

7 www.jorvik-viking-centre.co.uk.

Chapter 1

1 Whitelock, D. (ed.), *English Historical Documents*, vol. I, c.500–1042 (Eyre Methuen: London, 1979), p.842.
2 Jeremiah, chapter 1, verse 14, New International Version of the Bible (Hodder and Stoughton: London, 1979).
3 Whitelock, D., *English Historical Documents*, p.843.
4 Whitelock, D., *ibid.*, p.896.
5 Whitelock, D., *ibid.*, p.845.
6 Whitelock, D., *ibid.*, p.845.
7 Whitelock, D., *ibid.*, p.181.
8 Aird, W.M., *St Cuthbert and the Normans: The Church of Durham, 1071–1153* (Boydell Press: Woodbridge, 1998), pp.24–5.
9 Owen-Crocker, G.R., *Dress in Anglo-Saxon England* (Boydell Press: Woodbridge, revised edn, 2004), p.170.
10 Catling, C., 'Raiders and traders', *Current Archaeology*, 245 (August 2010), p.14.
11 Whittock, H., 'The Avon valley as a frontier region from the fourth to the eleventh centuries,' unpublished BA dissertation (University of Cambridge, Department of Anglo-Saxon, Norse and Celtic, 2010). For further examination of the location of Malmesbury within a disputed frontier zone see: Whittock, H., 'Why does the north-western boundary of Wiltshire ignore the river Avon?', *The Wiltshire Archaeological and Natural History Magazine*, 105 (2012), pp.96–104.
12 Whitelock, D., *English Historical Documents*, p.180.
13 Whitelock, D., *ibid.*, p.413.
14 Quoted in Brimberg, S., 'In search of Vikings', *National Geographic* (May 2000), pp.8–27.
15 Balbirnie, C., 'The Vikings at home', *BBC History Magazine*, vol. 13, no. 9 (September 2012), p.25.
16 For an overview of the use of the term 'Viking' and the names used by others to describe them, see: Arnold, M., *The Vikings: Culture and Conquest* (Hambledon Continuum: London, 2006), pp.7–8. See also: Somerville, A. and McDonald, R.A., *The Viking Age: A Reader* (University of Toronto Press: Toronto, 2010), p.xiii
17 Ekwall, E., *The Concise Oxford Dictionary of English Place-Names* (Oxford University Press: Oxford, 1960).
18 For an accessible overview of Viking Age Scandinavia see: Haywood, J., *The Penguin Historical Atlas of the Vikings* (Penguin: London, 1995), pp.28–33; Forte, A., Oram, R. and Pedersen, F., *Viking Empires* (Cambridge University Press: Cambridge, 2005), pp.7–53.
19 Forte, A., Oram, R. and Pedersen, F., *Viking Empires* (Cambridge University Press: Cambridge, 2005), pp.51–3.
20 Hoggett, R., *The Archaeology of the East Anglian Conversion* (Boydell Press: Woodbridge, 2010), pp.22–3.
21 For an expansion of this argument see: Randsborg, K., *The Viking Age in Denmark: The Formation of a State* (St Martin's Press: London, 1980).

Chapter 2

1 Whitelock, D. (ed.), *English Historical Documents*, vol. I, c.500–1042 (Eyre Methuen: London, 1979), p.182.
2 Whitelock, D., *ibid.*, p.182, note 2 and p.830, note 3.
3 Whitelock, D., *ibid.*, p.182.
4 Whitelock, D., *ibid.*.
5 Whitelock, D., *ibid.*, p.184.
6 Naismith, R., *Money and Power in Anglo-Saxon England: The Southern English Kingdoms, 757–865* (Cambridge University Press: Cambridge, 2012), p.32.
7 Whitelock, D., *English Historical Documents*, p.186.
8 Smyth, A., 'The effect of Scandinavian raiders on the English and Irish churches: a preliminary reassessment', in Smith, B. (ed.), *Britain and Ireland, 900–1300: Insular Responses to Medieval European Change* (Cambridge University Press: Cambridge, 1999), p.7.
9 Ekwall, E., *The Concise Oxford Dictionary of English Place-Names* (Oxford University Press: Oxford, 1960), p.441, p.181, p.307.
10 Costen, M., *Anglo-Saxon Somerset* (Oxbow Books: Oxford, 2011), pp.150–1.
11 Sawyer, P.H., *Age of the Vikings* (Edward Arnold: London, 1962, 2nd edition, 1971), p.125.
12 Crumlin-Pedersen, O., 'The Vikings and the Hanseatic merchants, 900–1450', in Bass, G.W. (ed.), *A History of Seafaring* (Thames and Hudson: London, 1972), pp.182–207.
13 Smyth, A., 'The effect of Scandinavian raiders on the English and Irish churches', p.9.
14 Costen, M., *Anglo-Saxon Somerset*, p.39.
15 Vinner, M., *Viking Ship Museum Boats* (Roskilde Amtsmuseumsråd: Roskilde, 2002), pp.36–7. See also: Swanton, M.J., 'King Alfred's ships: text and context', *Anglo-Saxon England*, 28 (1999), p.12.
16 Crumlin-Pedersen, O., 'Large and small warships of the North', in Nørgård Jørgenson, A. and Clausen, B.L. (eds), *Military Aspects of Scandinavian Society in a European Perspective, AD1–1300* (PNM: Copenhagen, 1997), pp.184–94.
17 Nelson, J. (ed.), *Annales of St Bertin* (Manchester University Press: Manchester, 1991), p.59.
18 Whitelock, D., *English Historical Documents*, p.187.
19 Whitelock, D., *ibid.*
20 Bede, *A History of the English Church and People*, II.3, L. Sherley-Price (transl.) (Penguin: Harmondsworth, 1968) p.104.
21 Cowie, R., 'Mercian London', in Brown, M.P. and Farr, C.A., *Mercia: An Anglo-Saxon Kingdom in Europe* (Continuum: London, 2001), p.199, p.202.
22 Cowie, R., *ibid.*, pp.207–8.
23 Whitelock, D., *English Historical Documents*, p.188.
24 Sawyer, P.H., *Age of the Vikings*, p.17. See also p.126 for his rejection of numbers of '200' or '250' given in the *Chronicle's* account of an invasion fleet attacking Kent in 892.
25 Smyth, A., 'The effect of Scandinavian raiders on the English and Irish churches', pp.7–8.
26 Stefánsson, J., 'The Vikings in Spain. from Arabic (Moorish) and Spanish sources', *Saga Book of the Viking Society* 6 (1909–10), pp.31–46.
27 Whitelock, D., *English Historical Documents*, p.188.

28 Whitelock, D., *ibid.*, p.190.

29 Whitelock, D., *ibid.*, p.889, p.883.

30 Brown, M.P., *Manuscripts from the Anglo-Saxon Age* (The British Library: London, 2007), p.55 and Plate 41.

31 Sawyer, P.H., *Age of the Vikings*.

32 Sawyer, P.H., *ibid.*, p.205.

33 Page, R.I., *'A Most Vile People': Early English Historians on the Vikings* (Viking Society for Northern Research: London, 1986), p.3.

34 Foot, S., 'Violence against Christians? The Vikings and the Church in ninth century England', *Medieval History*, vol. 1 (1991), pp.3–16.

35 Halsall, G., 'Playing by whose rules? A further look at Viking atrocity in the ninth century', *Medieval History*, vol.2, no.2 (1992), pp.67. An excellent overview of the whole issue is provided by: Lavelle, R., *Alfred's Wars: Sources and Interpretations of Anglo-Saxon Warfare in the Viking Age* (Boydell Press: Woodbridge, 2010), pp.41–3.

36 Naismith, R., *Money and Power in Anglo-Saxon England*, pp.234–5, p.239.

37 Hadley, D.M., *The Vikings in England, Settlement, Society and Culture* (Manchester University Press: Manchester, 2006), p.208.

38 Abels, R., *Alfred the Great, War, Kingship and Culture in Anglo-Saxon England* (Longman: London, 1998), p.106.

39 Whitelock, D., *English Historical Documents*, p.843.

Chapter 3

1 An accessible overview of warfare in the Viking Age, from the perspective of both Anglo-Saxons and Scandinavians, can be found in: Lavelle, R., 'Fighting the Vikings', *BBC History Magazine*, vol. 12, no 1 (January 2011), pp.22–8.

2 Jones, G., *A History of the Vikings* (Oxford University Press: Oxford, 1984) p.218, note 1.

3 Mitchell, B. and Robinson, F. C., *A Guide to Old English* (Blackwell: Oxford, 7th edn, 2007), p.377.

4 Ekwall, E., *The Concise Oxford Dictionary of English Place-Names* (Oxford University Press: Oxford, 1960), p.236.

5 Whitelock, D. (ed.), *English Historical Documents*, vol. I, c.500–1042 (Eyre Methuen: London, 1979), p.195.

6 Whitelock, D., *ibid.*, p.183.

7 Whitelock, D., *ibid.*, p.187.

8 Whitelock, D., *ibid.*, p.190.

9 Most notably Hollister, C. Warren, *Anglo-Saxon Military Institutions on the Eve of the Norman Conquest* (Oxford University Press: Oxford, 1962), pp.38–102.

10 Abels, R.P., *Lordship and Military Obligation in Anglo-Saxon England* (University of California Press: Berkeley/Los Angeles, 1988).

11 See Bachrach, B.S., 'William Rufus' plan for the invasion of Aquitaine' in Abels, R.P. and Bachrach, B.S., *The Normans and their Adversaries at War* (Boydell Press: Woodbridge, 2001), pp.31–64, especially p.55, note 111.

12 Morillo, S., *Warfare Under the Anglo-Norman Kings, 1066–1135* (Boydell Press: Woodbridge, 1994), p.66.

13 See Hollister, C. Warren, 'The Personnel of the Select Fyrd' in R. Lavelle, *Alfred's Wars: Sources and Interpretations of Anglo-Saxon Warfare in the Viking Age* (Boydell Press: Woodbridge, 2010), especially pp.71–2.

14 Asser, *Life of King Alfred*, 56, in Keynes, S. and Lapidge, M. (transl.), *Alfred the Great, Asser's Life of King Alfred and Other Contemporary Sources* (Penguin: Harmondsworth, 1983), p.84.

15 For a study which suggests that the interlocking shield-wall was more a poetic device than a battlefield tactic, see: Stephenson, I.P., *Viking Warfare* (Amberley: Stroud, 2012), pp.77–8.

16 See: *Eyrbyggja Saga*, Pálsson, H. and Edwards, P.G. (transl.) (Penguin Books: London, 1989).

17 Peirce, I.G. and Oakeshott, E., *Swords of the Viking Age* (Boydell Press: Woodbridge, 2002), pp.7–8.

18 For the similarity between the two sides, in terms of both equipment and tactics, see: Stephenson, I.P., *Viking Warfare.*

19 Whitelock, D., *English Historical Documents*, p.201.

20 See: Snorri Sturluson, *King Harald's Saga*, Magnusson, M. and Pálsson, H. (transl.) (Penguin: London, 1976).

21 Haigh, C., *The Cambridge Historical Encyclopaedia of Great Britain and Ireland* (Cambridge University Press: Cambridge, 1990), p.73.

22 Darkes, G., http://www.cartography.org.uk/default.asp?contentID=749, 2008 and based on Ordnance Survey data recording the length of the mean high water mark.

23 Forte, A., Oram, R. and Pedersen, F., *Viking Empires* (Cambridge University Press: Cambridge, 2005), p.62.

Chapter 4

1 Naismith, R., *Money and Power in Anglo-Saxon England, The Southern English Kingdoms, 757–865* (Cambridge University Press: Cambridge, 2012), p.233, Fig. 8.10.

2 Forte, A., Oram, R. and Pedersen, F., *Viking Empires* (Cambridge University Press: Cambridge, 2005), pp.68–9.

3 Asser, *Life of King Alfred*, 20, in Keynes, S. and Lapidge, M. (transl.), *Alfred the Great, Asser's Life of King Alfred and Other Contemporary Sources* (Penguin: Harmondsworth, 1983), p.74.

4 Asser, *ibid.*, 21, p.74.

5 Forte, A., Oram, R. and Pedersen, F., *Viking Empires*, p.69.

6 Whitelock, D. (ed.), *English Historical Documents*, vol. I, c.500–1042 (Eyre Methuen: London, 1979), p.195.

7 Abels, R., *Alfred the Great, War, Kingship and Culture in Anglo-Saxon England* (Longman: London, 1998), p.113.

8 Whitelock, D., *English Historical Documents*, p.191.

9 Asser, *Life of King Alfred*, 21, p.74.

10 Whitelock, D., *English Historical Documents*, p.191.

11 Asser, *Life of King Alfred*, 27, p.76.

12 Whitelock, D., *English Historical Documents*, p.282.

13 Whitelock, D., *ibid.*, p.277.

14 Frank, R., 'Viking atrocity and Skaldic verse: the rite of the blood-eagle', *ASE Review*, 99 (1984), pp.340–1.

15 Grierson, P. and Blackburn, M., *Medieval European Coinage: The Early Middle Ages (5th–10th centuries)* (Cambridge University Press: Cambridge, 1986), p.308.

16 Ridyard, S., *The Royal Saints of Anglo-Saxon England* (Cambridge University Press: Cambridge, 1988), pp.61–9.

17 Asser, *Life of King Alfred*, 38, p.79.

18 Whittock, H., 'The Avon Valley as a frontier region, from the fourth to the eleventh century' (unpublished dissertation in the department of Anglo-Saxon, Norse and Celtic, Cambridge University, 2010), p.22.

19 For an archaeological insight into the Viking impact on Repton, see: Biddle, M. and Kjølbye-Biddle, B., 'Repton and the vikings', *Antiquity*, 250 (March 1992), pp.36–51. Also: Graham-Campbell, J. (ed.), *Cultural Atlas of the Viking World* (Facts On File Inc: New York, 1994), p.128.

20 Whitelock, D., *English Historical Documents*, p.194.

21 Whitelock, D., *ibid.*, p.195. Also see: Keynes, S., 'Mercia and Wessex in the ninth century', in Brown, M.P. and Farr, C.A. (eds), *Mercia: An Anglo-Saxon Kingdom in Europe* (Continuum: London, 2001), p.327.

22 Grierson, P. and Blackburn, M., *Medieval European Coinage*, p.308.

23 Blackburn, M., and Keynes, S., 'A corpus of the *Cross-and-Lozenge* and related coinages of Alfred, Ceolwulf II and Archbishop Æthelred', in Blackburn, M.A.S. and Dumville, D.N. (eds), *Kings, Currency, and Alliances: History and Coinage of Southern England in the Ninth Century* (Boydell Press: Woodbridge, 1998) pp.131–2.

24 Blackburn, M., 'The London mint in the reign of Alfred', in Blackburn, M.A.S. and Dumville, D.N. (eds), *Kings, Currency, and Alliances: History and Coinage of Southern England in the Ninth Century* (Boydell Press: Woodbridge, 1998), p.113.

25 Hadley, D.M., *The Northern Danelaw: Its Social Structure, c. 800–1100* (Leicester University Press: London, 2000), p.223.

26 Whitelock, D., *English Historical Documents*, p.194.

27 Whitelock, D., *ibid.*, p.195.

28 Asser, *Life of King Alfred*, 49, p.83.

Chapter 5

1 Whitelock, D. (ed.), *English Historical Documents*, vol. I, c.500–1042 (Eyre Methuen: London, 1979), p.195.

2 Whitelock, D., *ibid.*, p.195.

3 S362, http://www.trin.cam.ac.uk/chartwww/eSawyer.99/S%20358-85.htm.

4 Nelson, J.L., '"A king across the sea": Alfred in continental perspective', *Transactions of the Royal Historical Society*, 36 (1986), p.55.

5 Yorke, B., 'Edward as Ætheling', in Higham, N. J. and Hill, D. (eds), *Edward the Elder, 899–924* (Routledge: London, 2001), pp.35–6.

6 Whitelock, D., *English Historical Documents*, p.196.

7 Ekwall, E., *The Concise Oxford Dictionary of English Place-Names* (Oxford University Press: Oxford, 1960), p.18.

8 Whitelock, D., *English Historical Documents*, p.195.

9 Asser, *Life of King Alfred*, 53, in Keynes, S. and Lapidge, M. (transl.), *Alfred the Great, Asser's Life of King Alfred and Other Contemporary Sources* (Penguin: Harmondsworth, 1983), p.83.

10 Whittock, M., *Walking Somerset History* (Dovecote Press: Stanbridge, Wimborne, 1995), p.54.

11 For an overview of the growth of Alfred's reputation, including the legendary aspects see: Yorke, B., 'Alfred the Great: The Most Perfect Man in History?', *History Today*, vol. 49, issue 10 (October 1999), pp.8–14; and Keynes, S., 'The cult of King Alfred the Great', *Anglo-Saxon England*, 28 (1999), pp.225–356, examines the reputation of Alfred from the twelfth to the twentieth century.

12 Whitelock, D., *English Historical Documents*, p.196.

13 See: Currie, C.R.J. and Dunning, R.W. (eds), Baggs, A.P., Siraut, M.C., *The Victoria History of the County of Somerset: Volume VII: Wincanton and Neighbouring Parishes* (Victoria County History, University of London Institute of Historical Research: Oxford, 1999), pp.3–5 refers to the relevant information regarding Bruton, Horethorne and Norton Ferris Hundreds.

14 Gover, J.B.E., Stenton, F.M. and Mawer, A., *Place-Names of Wiltshire*, English Place-name Society 16 (English Place-name Society: Cambridge, 1939), pp.154–5.

15 To see how Alfred's achievements need to be set in the context of the developing sophistication of government administration in Wessex before him, see: Brooks, N., 'Alfredian government: the West Saxon inheritance' in T. Reuter (ed.), *Alfred the Great* (Ashgate Publishing: Aldershot, 2003), pp.153–74.

16 Asser, *Life of King Alfred*, 56, p.84.

17 Baxter, S.D., *The Earls of Mercia: Lordship and Power in Late Anglo-Saxon England* (Oxford University Press: Oxford, 2007), p.83–4.

18 See: Woolf, A., *From Pictland to Alba 789–1070* (Edinburgh University Press: Edinburgh 2007), p.147.

19 S346, http://www.esawyer.org.uk/charter/346.html.

20 S1628, http://www.esawyer.org.uk/charter/1628.html.

21 Yorke, B., *Kings and Kingdoms of Early Anglo-Saxon England* (B.A.Seaby: London, 1990), pp.150–1.

22 S271, http://www.esawyer.org.uk/browse/kinga/E.html.

23 Abels, R., *Alfred the Great, War, Kingship and Culture in Anglo-Saxon England* (Longman: London, 1998), pp.145–6.

24 Asser, *Life of King Alfred*, 83, p.98.

25 North, J.J., *English Hammered Coinage, Volume 1: Early Anglo-Saxon to Henry III, c. 600–1272* (Spink and Son: London 1994), p.124. See also: Whittock, H., 'The annexation of Bath by Wessex: The evidence of two rare coins of Edward the Elder', *British Numismatic Journal*, 82 (December 2012) pp.46–53.

26 For justification of this 'time-window' for the treaty see: Keynes, S. and Lapidge, M. (transl.), *Alfred the Great, Asser's Life of King Alfred and Other Contemporary Sources* (Penguin: Harmondsworth, 1983), p.171. For an argument for an earlier date, closer to 880, see: Abels, R., *Alfred the Great, War, Kingship and Culture in Anglo-Saxon England* (Longman: London, 1998), p.163.

27 Keynes, S. and Lapidge, M., *Alfred the Great*, p.171.

28 Baxter, S.D., *The Earls of Mercia*, pp.83–4.

29 Whitelock, D., *English Historical Documents*, p.207.

Chapter 6

1   Abels, R., *Alfred the Great: War, Kingship and Culture in Anglo-Saxon England* (Longman, 2005), p.15.

2   Keynes, S. and Lapidge, M. (transl.), *Alfred the Great, Asser's Life of King Alfred and Other Contemporary Sources* (Penguin: Harmondsworth, 1983), p.41.

3   Stenton, F.M., 'The South-Western Element in the Old English Chronicle', in Little, A.G. and Powicke, F.M. (eds), *Essays in Medieval History Presented to T. F. Tout* (Manchester, 1925), pp. 15–24; reprinted in Stenton, F.M. (ed.), *Preparatory to Anglo-Saxon England* (Oxford, 1970), pp.106–15.

4   Davies, R.N.C., 'Alfred the Great: Truth and Propaganda', *History*, 56 (1971), p.175.

5   Keynes, S. and Lapidge, M., *Alfred the Great*, p.41.

6   The Anglo-Saxons certainly seem to have felt that it was an Alfredian production and when it appears with other texts these are almost always Alfredian texts, Bredehoft T.A., *Textual Histories: Readings in the Anglo-Saxon Chronicle* (University of Toronto Press: Toronto/London, 2001), p.6.

7   Whitelock, D., Douglas, D.C. and Tucker, S.I. (transl. and eds), *The Anglo-Saxon Chronicle: A Revised Translation* (Eyre and Spottiswoode; London, 1961), p. xxii.

8   Whitelock, D., Douglas, D.C. and Tucker, S.I. *ibid.*, p.22.

9   Whitelock, D., Douglas, D.C. and Tucker, S.I. *ibid.*, p.11.

10 Whitelock, D., Douglas, D.C. and Tucker, S.I. *ibid.*, p.23.

11 Whitelock, D., Douglas, D.C. and Tucker, S.I. *ibid.*, pp.30–1.

12 Whitelock, D., Douglas, D.C. and Tucker, S.I. *ibid.*, p.45.

13 Wormald, P., 'The Age of Offa and Alcuin', in Campbell, J. (ed.), *The Anglo-Saxons* (Penguin: London, 1982), p.110.

14 Whitelock, D., Douglas, D.C. and Tucker, S.I., *The Anglo-Saxon Chronicle*, p.48.

15 Campbell, J., 'Placing King Alfred', in Reuter, T. (ed.), *Alfred the Great: Papers from the Eleventh-Century Conferences* (Ashgate Publishing: Aldershot, 2003), pp.3–23.

16 Keynes, S. and Lapidge, M., *Alfred the Great*, p.51.

17 Keynes, S. and Lapidge, M., *ibid.*, p.56.

18 Campbell, J., 'Asser's Life of Alfred', in Holdsworth, C. and Wiseman, T. P. (eds), *The Inheritance of Historiography 350–900* (Exeter, 1986), pp.115–35, p.116.

19 Campbell, J., *ibid.*, p.125.

20 Davies, R.N.C., 'Alfred the Great: truth and propaganda', *History*, 56 (1971), p.170.

21 Yorke, B., *Wessex in the Early Middle Ages* (London: Leicester University Press, 1995), p.106.

22 Asser, *Life of Alfred*, 23, in Keynes, S. and Lapidge, M. (transl.), *Alfred the Great. Asser's Life of King Alfred and other contemporary Sources* (Penguin: Harmondsworth, 1983), pp.74–5.

23 Asser, *Life of Alfred*, 76, *ibid.*, p.91.

24 Brookes, N., 'English identity from Bede to the Millennium', *Haskins Society Journal* (2003), pp.31–55, especially p.47.

25 Nelson, J., 'The political ideas of Alfred of Wessex', in Duggan, A. (ed.), *Kings and Kingship in Medieval Europe* (Short Run Press Ltd: Exeter, 1993), pp.125–58, p.155.

26 Keynes, S., 'King Alfred and the Mercians', in Blackburn, M.A.S, and Dumville, D.N. (eds), *Kings, Currency and Alliances: History and Coinage in Southern England in the Ninth Century* (Boydell Press: Woodbridge, 1998), pp.1–46, pp.25–7; Nelson, J., 'The political ideas of Alfred of Wessex', p.154.

27   Waite, G., *Old English Prose Translations of King Alfred's reign, Annotated Bibliographies of Old English and Middle English Literature* VI (D.S. Brewer: Cambridge, 2000), p.283.

28   Wormald, P., *The Making of English Law: King Alfred to the Twelfth Century I; Legislation and its Limits* (Wiley-Blackwell: Oxford, 1999), p.283.

29   Wormald, P., *ibid.*, p.426.

30   Wormald, P., *ibid.*, p.427.

31   Brookes, N., 'English identity from Bede to the millennium', p.48.

32   Alfred, Preface to the Pastoral Care, in Keynes, S. and Lapidge, M. (transl.), *Alfred the Great, Asser's Life of King Alfred and Other Contemporary Sources* (Penguin: Harmondsworth, 1983), p.126.

33   Bately, J., 'The Alfredian canon re-visited', in Reuter, T. (ed.), *Alfred the Great: Papers from the Eleventh-Century Conferences* (Ashgate Publishing: Aldershot, 2003), pp.111–19; Wormald, P., 'King Alfred', in Matthew, H.C. and Harrison, B. (eds), *Oxford Dictionary of National Biography: From the Earliest Times to the Year 2000*, 60 vols (Oxford, 2004), I, pp.718–23.

Chapter 7

1   Asser refers to a lost document, in which Æthelwulf divided his kingdom between his sons Æthelbald (to rule historic Wessex) and Æthelbert (to rule the eastern provinces); Alfred's *Will* – though specifically commenting on the inheritance of Æthelwulf's private property – suggests that in historic Wessex the brothers Æthelbald, Æthelred and Alfred would succeed each other. However, Æthelbald died in 860 and Wessex was reunited under Æthelbert and the planned brotherly succession then applied to the entirety of the West Saxon lands. See: Keynes, S. and Lapidge, M. (transl.), *Alfred the Great: Asser's Life of King Alfred and Other Contemporary Sources* (Penguin: Harmondsworth, 1983), p.15–16.

2   Whitelock, D. (ed.), *English Historical Documents*, vol. I, c.500–1042 (Eyre Methuen: London, 1979), p.207.

3   For an impressive analysis of the Victorian myth-making about Alfred, see: Parker, J. *'England's Darling': The Victorian Cult of Alfred the Great* (Manchester University Press: Manchester, 2007).

4   http://www.reformationsa.org/articles/King%20Alfred%20the%20Great.htm. Dr Peter Hammond. The Reformation Society, Cape Town, South Africa.

5   See: Stenton, F.M., *Anglo-Saxon England* (Oxford University Press: Oxford, 3rd edn, 1971), pp.245–55; Wood, M., *In Search of the Dark Ages* (BBC Books: London, 1981), pp.104–25.

6   Abels, R., 'Alfred the Great, the *micel hæðen here* and the Viking threat', in Reuter, T. (ed.), *Alfred the Great: Papers from the Eleventh-Century Conferences* (Ashgate Publishing: Aldershot, 2003), pp.265–80, specifically pp.267–9. The translations of the ' great army' versus the 'great host' are based on the terms used to differentiate them in Whitelock, D. (ed.), *English Historical Documents*, vol. I, c.500–1042 (Eyre Methuen: London, 1979), pp.214–15.

7   Hill, D., 'The origin of Alfred's urban policies', in Reuter, T. (ed.), *Alfred the Great: Papers from the Eleventh-Century Conferences* (Ashgate Publishing: Aldershot, 2003), pp.219–34.

8   Abels, R., 'Alfred the Great, the *micel hæðen here* and the Viking threat', p.278.
9   Abels, R., *ibid.*, p279.
10 Whitelock, D., *English Historical Documents*, p.409.
11 Brooks, N., 'Alfredian government: the West Saxon inheritance', in Reuter, T. (ed.), *Alfred the Great* (Ashgate Publishing: Aldershot, 2003), p.153.
12 Brooks, N., *ibid.*, p.155.
13 Keynes, S., 'The West Saxon charters of King Æthelwulf and his sons', *English Historical Review*, 109 (1994), pp.112–14.
14 Asser, *Life of King Alfred*, 29, in Keynes, S. and Lapidge, M. (transl.), *Alfred the Great: Asser's Life of King Alfred and Other Contemporary Sources* (Penguin: Harmondsworth, 1983), p.77.
15 Asser, *ibid.*, 13, p.71 and note 28, p.235–6.
16 See: Stafford, P., 'Succession and inheritance: a gendered perspective on Alfred's family history', in Reuter, T. (ed.), *Alfred the Great* (Ashgate Publishing: Aldershot, 2003), pp.251–64.
17 Yorke, B., 'Edward as Ætheling', in Higham. N.J. and Hill, D. (eds), *Edward the Elder, 899–924* (Routledge: London, 2001), p.35–6. See the charter S362 of 901, when Edward the Elder granted away one of Wulfhere's forfeited estates.
18 Whitelock, D., *English Historical Documents*, p.188.
19 Whitelock, D., *ibid.*, p.206.
20 Whitelock, D., *ibid.*, p.202.
21 See Pratt, D., *The Political Thought of King Alfred the Great, Cambridge Studies in Medieval Life and Thought: Fourth Series No. 67* (Cambridge University Press: Cambridge, 2007).
22 Haight Turk, M. (ed.), *The Legal Code of Ælfred the Great* (Lawbook Exchange: Clark, New Jersey, 2004) pp.50–1.
23 Karkov, C., *The Ruler Portraits of Anglo-Saxon England* (Boydell Press: Woodbridge, 2004), p.102.

Chapter 8

1   Interestingly, the *Anglo-Saxon Chronicle* does not find the arrival of a Scandinavian ship in England surprising and it seems likely that there was a long history of trade and contact between England and Scandinavia before the Viking Age.
2   Corrain, D.O., 'Pre-historic and Early Christian Ireland', in Foster, R.F. (ed.), *The Oxford Illustrated History of Ireland* (Oxford University Press: Oxford), p.31.
3   Whitelock, D., Douglas, D.C. and Tucker, S.I. (transl. and eds), *The Anglo-Saxon Chronicle: A Revised Translation* (Eyre and Spottiswoode, London, 1961), p.36.
4   Whitelock, D., Douglas, D.C. and Tucker, S.I. *ibid.*, p.45.
5   Asser, *Life of Alfred*, in Keynes, S. and Lapidge, M. (transl.), *Alfred the Great: Asser's Life of King Alfred and Other Contemporary Sources* (Penguin: Harmondsworth, 1983), p74.
6   Whitelock, D., Douglas, D.C. and Tucker, S.I., *Anglo-Saxon Chronicle*, p.46.
7   Whitelock, D., Douglas, D.C. and Tucker, S.I., *ibid.*, p.46.
8   Alfred the Great, *Preface to the Pastoral Care*, in Keynes, S. and Lapidge, M., *Alfred the Great: Asser's Life of King Alfred and Other Contemporary Sources* (Penguin: Harmondsworth, 1983), p.125.

9 Hadley, D.M., *The Vikings in England, Settlement, Society and Culture* (Manchester University Press: Manchester, 2006), p.208.

10 Brooks, N., *The Early History of the Church of Canterbury: Christ Church from 597 to 1066* (Leicester University Press: London, 1984), p.71.

11 Lapidge, M., 'Latin Learning in ninth-century England', in Lapidge, M., *Anglo-Latin Literature 60–900* (Hambledon: London, 1996), pp.452–3.

12 http://www.trin.cam.ac.uk/chartwww/Bishops/councils.html.

13 Abram, C., *Myths of the Pagan North: The Gods of the Norsemen* (Hambledon Continuum: London, 2011), p.98.

14 Leahy, K., 'Detecting the Vikings in Lincolnshire', *Current Archaeology*, 190 (February, 2004), pp.462–8.

15 http://finds.org.uk/contacts/staff/profile/id/90.

16 Leahy, K., 'History from fields and gardens', *British Archaeology*, 46 (July, 1999), p.3.

17 Mays, S., 'Wharram Percy: the Skeletons', *Current Archaeology*, 193 (August/September 2004), pp.45–9.

18 Richards, J.D., *Viking Age England* (Tempus: Stroud, 2000), p.56.

19 Hart, C., *The Early Charters of Northern England and the North Midlands* (Leicester University Press: London, 1975), p.14. See also: Hart, C., *The Danelaw* (Hambledon: London, 1992).

20 Makaorov, A., 'English silver pennies in Russia', *Coin News* (January 2003), p.43, draws attention to the large number of Anglo-Saxon silver coins that have been discovered in Russia. Their presence there testifies to the far-flung trade networks established by Scandinavians.

21 Hodges, R., *The Anglo-Saxon Achievement: Archaeology and the Beginnings of English Society* (Duckworth: London, 1989), p.162.

22 Naismith, R., *Money and Power in Anglo-Saxon England: The Southern English Kingdoms, 757–865* (Cambridge University Press: Cambridge, 2012), pp.248–9.

23 Scull, C., 'Urban centres in pre-Viking England?', in Hines, J. (ed.), *The Anglo-Saxons from the Migration Period to the Eighth Century* (Boydell Press: Woodbridge, 1997), p.274.

24 Hodges, R., *The Anglo-Saxon Achievement*, p.156.

25 Richards, J., *Blood of the Vikings* (Hodder and Stoughton: London, 1992), p.199.

26 Richards, J.D., *Viking Age England*, p.161.

27 Finberg, H.P.R., *The Formation of England 550–1042* (Paladin: St Albans, 1976), p.159.

28 Keynes, S., 'The Power of the Written Word: Alfredian England 871–899', in Reuter, T. (ed.), *Alfred the Great: Papers from the Eleventh-Century Conferences* (Ashgate Publishing: Aldershot, 2003), p.196.

29 Brooks, N., *The Early History of the Church of Canterbury, Christ Church from 597 to 1066*, pp.172–3.

30 Hart, C., *The Danelaw*, p.46. See also: Grierson, P. and Blackburn, M., *Medieval European Coinage 1. The Early Middle Ages (5th–10th centuries)* (Cambridge University Press: Cambridge, 1986), pp.319–20.

31 A point examined in detail in: Redmond, A., *Viking Burial in the North of England: a Study of Contact, Interaction and Reaction between Scandinavian Migrants with Resident Groups, and the Effect of Immigration on Aspects of Cultural Continuity*, BAR, British Series 429 (John and Erica Hedges Ltd: Oxford, 2007).

32 Richards, J.D., *Viking Age England*, p.125.

33 Hadley, D.M., *The Vikings in England*, pp.92–5.

34 Megaw, B., 'Norsemen and Native in the Kingdom of the Isles: A Reassessment of the Manx Evidence', *Scottish Studies*, 20 (1976), p.5.

35 Gelling, P., 'Celtic continuity in the Isle of Man', in Laing, L. (ed.), *Studies in Celtic Survival*, BAR British Series, 37 (British Archaeological Reports: Oxford, 1977), pp.77–82, p.79.

36 Kinvig, R.H., *History of the Isle of Man* (Oxford University Press: Oxford, 1944), p.68.

37 Megaw, B., 'Norsemen and Native in the Kingdom of the Isles', p.6.

38 Megaw, B., *ibid.*, pp.18–19.

39 Mays, S., 'Wharram Percy: The Skeletons', pp.45–9.

40 Richards, J.D., *Viking Age England*, p.49.

41 Cameron, K (ed.), *Place-name Evidence for the Anglo-Saxon Invasion and Scandinavian Settlements* (University of Nottingham: Nottingham, 1975), pp.139–56. See also: Cameron, K., *Scandinavian Settlement in the Territory of the Five Boroughs* (University of Nottingham: Nottingham, 1966).

42 Gelling, M., *Place-Names in the Landscape* (Phoenix: London, 1984), pp.220–6, pp.228–34.

43 Cullen, P., Jones, R. and Parsons, D., *Thorps in a Changing Landscape* (University of Hertfordshire Press: Hatfield, 2011).

44 In Ireland these include the towns of Dublin, Limerick, Waterford and Wexford.

45 Naismith, R., *Money and Power in Anglo-Saxon England*, p.231.

46 Hodges, R., *The Anglo-Saxon Achievement.*, p.166.

47 Draper, S., 'The Significance of Old English *Burh* in Anglo-Saxon England', *Anglo-Saxon Studies in Archaeology and History*, vol. 15 (2008), p.247

48 Draper, S., *ibid.*

49 Scull, C., 'Urban centres in pre-Viking England?', p.274

50 Astill, G, 'General Survey', in Palliser, D.M. (ed.), *The Cambridge Urban History of Britain 1:600–1540* (Cambridge University Press: Cambridge, 2000), p.35.

Chapter 9

1   See the overview of evidence in: Higham, N., 'Edward the Elder's Reputation' in Higham, N.J. and Hill, D.H. (eds), *Edward the Elder 899–924* (Routledge: London, 2001), pp.1–5.

2   For example: Fisher, D.J.V., *The Anglo-Saxon Age c.400–1042* (Longman: London, 1973), p.237; Hoggett, R., *The Archaeology of the East Anglian Conversion* (Boydell Press: Woodbridge, 2010), p.23.

3   Campbell, J., 'What is not known about the reign of Edward the Elder', in Higham, N.J. and Hill, D.H. (eds), *Edward the Elder 899–924* (Routledge: London, 2001), p.22.

4   Whitelock, D. (ed.), *English Historical Documents, vol. I, c.500–1042* (Eyre Methuen: London, 1979), p.207.

5   Whitelock, D., *ibid.*

6   Whitelock, D., *ibid.*

7   Dumville, D. and Keynes, S., *Annals of St Neot's with Vita Prima Sancti Neoti* (D.S.Brewer: Cambridge, 1985), p.104.

8   Whitelock, D., *English Historical Documents*, p.208, note 6.

9   Whitelock, D., *ibid.*, p.208, note 5.

10 Lavelle, R., 'Geographies of Power in the Anglo-Saxon Chronicle: The Royal Estates of Anglo-Saxon Wessex', in Jorgensen, A. (ed.), *Reading the Anglo-Saxon Chronicle: Language, Literature, History* (Brepols: Turnhout, 2010), p.211. The whole chapter

(pp.87–211) provided a fascinating insight into the importance of royal centres in the fighting of the Viking Wars.

11 Whitelock, D., *English Historical Documents*, p.208.

12 Campbell, J., 'What is not known about the reign of Edward the Elder', p.22.

13 Whitelock, D., *English Historical Documents*, p.208, note 12.

14 Whitelock, D., *ibid.*, p.209.

15 Whitelock, D., *ibid.*

16 Richards, J.D., *Viking Age England* (English Heritage/Batsford: London, 1991), p.33.

17 Whitelock, D., *English Historical Documents*, p.210, note 5.

18 Hill, D., *An Atlas of Anglo-Saxon England* (Basil Blackwell: Oxford 1981), p.55, map 81.

19 Richards, J.D., *Viking Age England*, p.31.

20 Hadley, D.M., *The Northern Danelaw: Its Social Structure, c.800–1100* (Leicester University Press: London, 2000), p.160.

21 Whitelock, D., *English Historical Documents*, p.214.

22 Thompson Smith, S., 'Marking Boundaries: Charters and the Anglo-Saxon Chronicle', in Jorgensen, A. (ed.), *Reading the Anglo-Saxon Chronicle: Language, Literature, History* (Brepols: Turnhout, 2010), pp.167–85.

23 Edgeworth, M., 'The waters of Bedford', *British Archaeology* (November/December 2011), no. 121, pp.22–7.

24 Whittock, H., 'The annexation of Bath by Wessex: The evidence of two rare coins of Edward the Elder', *British Numismatic Journal*, 82 (December 2012), pp.46–53.

25 Keynes, S., 'Edward, king of the Anglo-Saxons', in Higham, N.J. and Hill, D.H. (eds), *Edward the Elder 899–924* (Routledge: London, 2001), pp.57–8.

26 Whitelock, D., *English Historical Documents*, p.198.

27 Keynes, S., 'Mercia and Wessex in the ninth century', in Brown, M.P. and Farr, C.A. (eds), *Mercia: An Anglo-Saxon Kingdom in Europe* (Continuum: London, 2001), p.328.

28 For an overview of the issues see: Davidson, M.R., 'The (non) submission of the northern kings in 920', in Higham, N.J. and Hill, D.H. (eds), *Edward the Elder 899–924* (Routledge: London, 2001), pp.200–11.

29 Lapidge, M., Blair, J., Keynes, S. and Scragg, D. (eds), *The Blackwell Encyclopaedia of Anglo-Saxon England* (Blackwell: Oxford, 2001), p.136.

30 Lapidge, M., Blair, J., Keynes, S. and Scragg, D., *ibid.*

31 Lapidge, M., Blair, J., Keynes, S. and Scragg, D., *ibid.*, p.137.

Chapter 10

1 Foot, S., *Æthelstan: The First King of England* (Yale University Press: New Haven and London, 2011).

2 Hence the title of one of the few modern books exploring the king and his significance: Hill, P., *The Age of Athelstan: Britain's Forgotten History* (Tempus: Stroud, 2004).

3 Foot, S., *Æthelstan*, p.17.

4 Whitelock, D. (ed.), *English Historical Documents*, vol. I, c.500–1042 (Eyre Methuen: London, 1979), p.218.

5 Foot, S., *Æthelstan*, p.19.

6 Foot, S., *ibid.*, p.19.

7 Stenton, F.M., *Anglo-Saxon England* (Oxford University Press: Oxford, 3rd edn, 1971), p.351.

8 Whitelock, D., *English Historical Documents*, p.218.

9 North, J.J., *English Hammered Coinage, Volume 1, Early Anglo-Saxon to Henry III, c.600–1272* (Spink and Son: London, 1994), p.134.

10 Charter S434, '937' (for 935), www.trin.cam.ac.uk/kemble/pelteret/Malm/ Malm%2026.ht.

11 North, J.J., *English Hammered Coinage*, p.135.

12 North, J.J., *ibid.*, pp.136–7.

13 Whitelock, D., *English Historical Documents*, p.219.

14 *The Annals of Ulster (to AD1131), Part I, Text and Translation*, in Mac Airt, S. and Mac Niocaill, G. (eds) (Dublin Institute for Advanced Studies: Dublin, 1983), 937, 6, pp.384–7.

15 See Livingston, M. (ed.), *The Battle of Brunanburgh: A Casebook* (Exeter University Press: Exeter 2011). The location at Bromborough is also found to be the most convincing of a number of candidates in Foot, S., *Æthelstan*, p.178.

16 Hill, P., *The Age of Athelstan: Britain's Forgotten History*, pp.136–53, offers a detailed examination of the accounts of the battle and possible locations, and rejects the Bromborough option, being more in favour of a location in Yorkshire, whilst admitting the difficulty in reaching any definitive answer.

17 Whitelock, D., *English Historical Documents*, p.219.

18 Whitelock, D., *ibid.*, p.219.

19 Whitelock, D., *ibid.*, p.220.

20 Whitelock, D., *ibid.*, p.220.

21 Whitelock, D., *ibid.*, p.220.

22 See: *Egil's Saga*, Fell, C. (trans.) (Everyman's Library: London, 1975).

23 Interestingly, Athelstan's cousins who were killed at the battle – Ælfwine and Æthelwine – were also buried at Malmesbury. This is also found in William of Malmesbury, is a credible claim given Athelstan's later burial there and does illustrate the close relationship between Athelstan and Malmesbury.

24 See: Whittock, H., 'Why does the north-western boundary of Wiltshire ignore the river Avon?', *The Wiltshire Archaeological and Natural History Magazine*, vol. 105 (2012) pp.96–104.

Chapter 11

1 Whitelock, D. (ed.), *English Historical Documents*, vol. I, c.500–1042 (Eyre Methuen: London, 1979), pp.286–7.

2 Aird, W.M., *St Cuthbert and the Normans: The Church of Durham, 1071–1153* (Boydell Press: Woodbridge, 1998), pp.30–1.

3 Logan, F. D., *A History of the Church in the Middle Ages* (Routledge: London, 2002), pp.83–4.

4 Whitelock, D., *English Historical Documents*, p.279.

5 Whitelock, D., *ibid.*, p.221.

6 A tradition recorded by Roger of Wendover in his early-thirteenth-century, *Flowers of the Histories*, which appears to preserve northern material.

7 That for 943 and 944.

8 Richard Kemp (Jorvik Viking Centre), quoted in Brimberg, S., 'In search of Vikings', *National Geographic* (May 2000), p.16. The whole article can be found on pp.8–27.

9 Whitelock, D., *English Historical Documents*, p.325.

10 Ekwall, E., *The Concise Oxford Dictionary of English Place-Names* (Oxford University Press: Oxford, 1960), p.545

11 For an overview of how the discoveries from the Coppergate 'Viking dig' fit within the wider context of Anglo-Scandinavian York, see: Hall, R.A., *et al.*, *Aspects of Anglo-Scandinavian York* (Council for British Archaeology: York, 2004).

12 Examinations of the evidence from the Viking Age city of York can be found in: Richards, J.D., *Viking Age England* (English Heritage/B.T. Batsford: London, 1991).

13 Richards, J.D., 'The Scandinavian Presence', in Hunter, J. and Ralston, I. (eds), *The Archaeology of Britain: An Introduction from the Upper Palaeolithic to the Industrial Revolution* (Routledge: London, 1999), pp.205–6.

14 North, J.J., *English Hammered Coinage, Volume 1, Early Anglo-Saxon to Henry III, c.600–1272* (Spink and Son: London, 1994), pp.113–16.

15 Westcott, L., 'The Huxley Hoard', *Current Archaeology*, 248 (November 2010), pp.24–30.

16 Cooper, A., 'The Harrogate Hoard', *Current Archaeology*, 212 (November 2007), pp.26–30.

17 Boughton, D, Williams, G. and Ager, B., 'Buried wealth of the Norse North West', *Current Archaeology*, 264 (March 2012), pp.26–31.

18 Whitelock, D., *English Historical Documents*, p.223.

19 Whitelock, D., *ibid.*, p.284.

20 Somerville, A.A. and McDonald, R.A., *The Viking Age: A Reader* (University of Toronto Press: Toronto, 2010), p.96.

21 Whitelock, D., *English Historical Documents*, p.280.

22 According to John of Worcester and William of Malmesbury.

Chapter 12

1 See: Rex, P., *Edgar: King of the English 959–75* (Tempus: Stroud, 2007).

2 For accessible overviews of his reign see: Williams, A., *Æthelred the Unready: the Ill-Counselled King* (Hambledon Continuum: London, 2003) and Lavelle, R., *Aethelred II, King of the English* (The History Press: Stroud, 2008).

3 For an overview of the life and time of Wulfstan, see: Townend, M. (ed.), *Wulfstan, Archbishop of York: the proceedings of the second Alcuin Conference* (Brepols Publishers: Turnhout, 2004).

4 Whitelock, D. (ed.), *English Historical Documents*, vol. I, c.500–1042 (Eyre Methuen: London, 1979), p.932, the whole sermon being found on pp.928–34.

5 Whitelock, D., *ibid.*, p.932.

6 Whitelock, D., *ibid.*, p.220.

7 Haywood, J., *The Penguin Historical Atlas of the Vikings* (Penguin Books: London, 1995), p.108.

8 For a detailed exploration of the use of silver in the Viking Age see: Williams, G. and Graham-Campbell, J. (eds) *Silver Economy in the Viking Age* (Left Coast Press Inc: Walnut Creek, California, 2007).

9   The date of the start of Harald Finehair's reign is uncertain. Various dates between 860 and
    880 have been suggested. Even his death (though usually dated as being in 930) has, by
    some historians, been placed as late as 940. The most detailed account of his life is found
    in the much later saga written by Snorri Sturluson, *Heimskringla*, although he also features
    in a number of other Icelandic sagas. See: Somerville, A. and McDonald, R.A., *The Viking
    Age: A Reader* (University of Toronto Press Incorporated: Toronto, 2010), pp.434–9.

10 See: Snorrason, O. and Andersson, T.M. (transl.), *The Saga of Olaf Tryggvason* (Cornell
    University Press: Ithaca, New York, 2003).

11 Whittock, H., unpublished M.Phil. 'Review of Scholarship', in a study of the
    implications of the murder for the reign of Æthelred II and contemporary
    perceptions and the promotion of the cult of Edward King and Martyr, department of
    Anglo-Saxon, Norse and Celtic, Cambridge University, 2012.

12 Downham, C., 'England and the Irish-Sea Zone in the eleventh century', in
    Gillingham, J. (ed.), *Anglo-Norman Studies XXVI: Proceedings of the Battle Conference
    2003* (Boydell Press: Woodbridge, 2004), pp.59–60.

13 For an overview of some of the issues relating to the poem see: Cooper, J. (ed.), *The
    Battle of Maldon: Fiction and Fact* (Hambledon Continuum: London, 1993).

14 Whitelock, D. (ed.), *English Historical Documents*, p.324.

15 Whitelock, D., *ibid.*, p.236.

16 Boyle, A., 'Death on the Ridgeway. The Excavation of a Viking Mass Burial', Danes
    in Wessex conference, Wessex Centre of History and Archaeology, University
    of Winchester, September 2011.

17 Whitelock, D., *English Historical Documents*, p.239.

18 Whitelock, D., *ibid.*, p.591.

19 Howard, I., *Swein Forkbeard's Invasions and the Danish Conquest of England, 991–1017*
    (Boydell Press: Woodbridge, 2003), p.70.

20 *British Archaeology*, no. 125 (July/August 2012), p.8.

21 Whitelock, D., *English Historical Documents*, p.239.

22 Howard, I., *Swein Forkbeard's Invasions and the Danish Conquest of England, 991–1017*,
    pp.69–70.

23 Whitelock, D., *English Historical Documents*, p.241.

24 Stafford, P., *Unification and Conquest: Political and Social History of England in the Tenth
    and Eleventh Centuries* (Hodder Arnold: London, 1989), pp.64–5.

25 Lapidge, M., Blair, J., Keynes, S. and Scragg, D. (eds), *The Blackwell Encyclopaedia of
    Anglo-Saxon England* (Blackwell Publishing: Oxford, 1999) pp.150–1.

26 Whitelock, D., *English Historical Documents*, p.243.

27 Bradbury, I., *The Battle of Hastings* (Sutton Publishing: Stroud, 1998), p.14.

28 An accessible overview of this event and the start of the cult of St Ælfheah can be
    found in: Foot, S., 'Canterbury's other martyr', *BBC History Magazine*, vol. 13, no. 4
    (April 2012), pp.30–1. She accepts that the traditional account of the manner of his
    death may have a basis in reality. This seems a reasonable conclusion, since the event
    clearly was considered highly significant in the near-contemporary accounts.

29 Whitelock, D., *English Historical Documents*, p.245.

30 Whitelock, D., *ibid.*, p.245, note 5.

31 Page, R.I., *Reading the Past: Runes* (British Museum Publications: London, 1987), p.46.

32 Graham-Campbell, J. *The Viking World* (Frances Lincoln Limited: London, 2001), p.164.

33 Hunter Blair, P. and Keynes, S., *An Introduction to Anglo-Saxon England* (Cambridge
    University Press: Cambridge 3rd edn, 2003), pp.96–7.

34 Page, R.I., *Reading the Past: Runes*, p.46.

35 For a detailed examination of this murder and its aftermath, see: Fletcher, R., *Bloodfeud: Murder and Revenge in Anglo-Saxon England* (Allen Lane: London, 2002).

Chapter 13

1 Keynes, S., 'Re-reading Æthelred the Unready', in Bates, D. (ed.), *Writing Medieval Biography, 750–1150, Essays in Honour of Professor Frank Barlow* (Boydell Press: Woodbridge, 2006), p.94.

2 Keynes, S., *The Diplomas of King Æthelred* (Cambridge University Press: Cambridge, 1986), p.230.

3 Keynes, S. 'A Tale of Two Kings: Alfred the Great and Æthelred the Unready', in Wood, I. and Lund, N. (eds), *People and Places in Northern Europe 500–1600: Studies Presented to Peter Sawyer* (Boydell Press: Woodbridge, 1991), p.205.

4 Keynes, S., *ibid.*, p.203.

5 Keynes, S., *ibid.*

6 Whitelock, D., Douglas, D.C. and Tucker, S.I. (transl. and eds), *The Anglo-Saxon Chronicle* (Eyre and Spottiswoode: London, 1961), pp.83 and 93.

7 Whitelock, D., Douglas, D.C. and Tucker, S.I., *ibid.*, p.91.

8 Keynes, S., 'A Tale of Two Kings', p.211.

9 Keynes, S., 'The Declining Reputation of Æthelred the Unready', in Pelteret, D. (ed.), *Anglo-Saxon History: A Basic Reading* (Garland Publishing: New York and London, 2000), p.168.

10 Keynes, S., 'A Tale of Two Kings', p. 211.

11 Lavelle, R., *Aethelred II: King of the English, 978–1016* (History Press: Stroud, 2002), p.100.

12 Higham, N., *The Death of Anglo-Saxon England* (Sutton: Stroud, 1997), p.69.

13 Williams, A., *Aethelred the Unready: The Ill-Counselled King* (Hambledon Continuum: London, 2003), p. 150.

14 Higham, N., *The Death of Anglo-Saxon England*, pp.68–9.

15 Higham, N., *ibid.*

16 Higham, N., *ibid.*, p.70.

17 Howard, I., *Swein Forkbeard's Invasions and the Danish Conquest of England, 991–1017* (Boydell Press: Woodbridge, 2003), p.106.

18 Higham, N., *The Death of Anglo-Saxon England*, p.69.

19 Keynes, S., 'A Tale of Two Kings', p.213.

20 Keynes, S., *ibid.*, p.215.

21 Higham, N., *The Death of Anglo-Saxon England*, p.69.

22 Keynes, S., *The Diplomas of King Æthelred*, p.230.

23 Keynes, 'The Declining Reputation of Æthelred', p.175.

24 Whitelock, D., Douglas, D.C. and Tucker, S.I., *The Anglo-Saxon Chronicle*, p.95.

25 Keynes, S., 'A Tale of Two Kings', p.206.

26 Hunter-Blair, P., *An Introduction to Anglo-Saxon England* (Cambridge University Press: Cambridge, 1956), p.93.

27 Keynes, 'Re-reading Æthelred', p.94.

28 *Skaldic* verse is a metrically complex verse form often composed by named *skalds* or poets, as tribute or homage to a particular earl or king.

29 Lavelle, R., *Aethelred II*, p.11.
30 Whitelock, D., Douglas, D.C. and Tucker, S.I., *The Anglo-Saxon Chronicle*, p.85.
31 Whitelock, D. (ed.), *Sermo Lupi ad Anglos* (Methuen: London, 1939), p.56.
32 Yorke, B., 'St Edward, King and Martyr: an Anglo-Saxon Murder Mystery', in Keen, L. (ed.), *Studies in the Early History of Shaftesbury Abbey* (Dorset County Council: Dorchester, 1999), pp.99–116, p.112; Whittock, H., *The Cult of Edward, King and Martyr and Bradford on Avon* (unpublished MPhil. dissertation in the department of Anglo-Saxon, Norse and Celtic, Cambridge University, 2012).
33 Keynes, S., 'An Abbot, an Archbishop, and the Viking Raids of 1006–7 and 1009–12', *Anglo-Saxon England*, 36 (2007), pp.151–220, pp.178–80.
34 Keynes, S., *ibid.*, p.190. See also: Keynes, S. and Naismith, R., 'Four New Agneus Dei Pennies of Æthelred the Unready', *Anglo-Saxon England*, 41 (2012), forthcoming.
35 Keynes, S., 'An Abbot, an Archbishop, and the Viking Raids', p.184.
36 Keynes, S., 'A Tale of Two Kings', p.201.
37 Keynes, S., 'Re-reading Æthelred', p.85.
38 Keynes, S., 'A Tale of Two Kings', p.202.
39 Higham, N., *The Death of Anglo-Saxon England*, p.70.
40 Johns, E., *Reassessing Anglo-Saxon England* (Manchester University Press: Manchester, 1996), p.142.
41 Keynes, S., 'A Tale of Two Kings', pp.211–12.
42 Johns, E., *Reassessing Anglo-Saxon England*, p.143.
43 Lavelle, R., *Aethelred II*, p.102.
44 Williams, A., *Aethelred the Unready*, pp.148–9.
45 Keynes, S., *The Diplomas of King Æthelred*, p.229.
46 Finberg, H.P.R., *The Formation of England 550–1042* (Paladin: St Albans, 1976), pp.190–1.
47 Foot, S., 'The Danish Conquest of England', *BBC History Magazine*, vol. 7, no. 4 (April 2006), pp.48–51.
48 Lavelle, R., *Aethelred II*, p.80.
49 Keynes, S., 'The Declining reputation of Æthelred', p.159.
50 Keynes, S., *ibid.*
51 Keynes, S., *ibid.*, p.164.
52 Hunter-Blair, P., *An Introduction to Anglo-Saxon England*, p.92.
53 Keynes, S., 'The Declining Reputation of Æthelred', p.167.

Chapter 14

1 For an overview of the issues see: Whittock, M., *A Brief History of Life in the Middle Ages* (Constable and Robinson: London, 2009), pp.4–12.
2 Whitelock, D. (ed.), *English Historical Documents*, vol. I, c.500–1042 (Eyre Methuen: London, 1979), pp.439–42.
3 Whitelock, D., *ibid.*, p.439.
4 Wormald, P., *The Making of English Law: Legislation and its Limits volume 1: King Alfred to the Twelfth Century* (Blackwell: Oxford, 1999), p.328.
5 Richards, J., *Blood of the Vikings* (Hodder and Stoughton: London, 2001), p.203.

6   For an examination of this issue see: Hadley, D.M and Richards, J.D. (eds), *Cultures in Contact: Scandinavian Settlement in England in the Ninth and Tenth Centuries* (Brepols: Turnhout, 2000), Introduction, pp.3–13; Reynolds, S., 'What do we mean by "Anglo-Saxon" and "Anglo-Saxons"?', *Journal of British Studies*, xxiv (1985), pp.395–414.

7   Pohl, W. and Reimitz, H. (eds), *Strategies of Distinction: the Construction of Ethnic Communities, 300–800* (Brill: Leiden, 1998).

8   Whitelock, D., *English Historical Documents*, p.435.

9   Hadley, D.M., *The Northern Danelaw: its Social Structure, c.800–1100* (Leicester University Press: Leicester, 2000), p.300.

10 Holman, K., *The Northern Conquest: Vikings in Britain and Ireland* (Signal Books: Oxford, 2007), p.162.

11 Hadley, D.M., *The Northern Danelaw*, p.301.

12 See, Rex, P. *Edgar, King of the English, 959–75* (Tempus: Stroud, 2007), pp.69–73.

13 For a revealing parallel from near-contemporary Francia (France) see: Amory, P., 'The meaning and purpose of ethnic terminology in the Burgundian Laws', *Early Medieval Europe*, 2 (1993), p.23.

14 Hadley, D.M., *The Northern Danelaw*, p.302.

15 Holman, K., *The Northern Conquest: Vikings in Britain and Ireland*, p.162, explores how Cnut allowed regional variations in fines, but within a unified national system of justice, just as Æthelred II had done.

16 Hadley, D.M., *The Northern Danelaw*, p.303.

17 Stafford, P.A., *Unification and Conquest: a Political and Social History of England in the Tenth and Eleventh Centuries* (Hodder Arnold: London, 1989), p.66.

18 Reynolds, S., 'What do we mean by "Anglo-Saxon" and "Anglo-Saxons"?', p.409.

19 Whitelock, D., *English Historical Documents*, p.896. See also: Brooks, N., *Anglo-Saxon Myths: State and Church, 400–1066* (Hambledon Press: London, 2000), p.3.

20 Whitelock, D., *English Historical Documents*, p.843. See also: Fugelso, K., *Studies in Medievalism Volume XV, 2006: Memory and Medievalism* (D.S.Brewer: Cambridge, 2007), p.58.

21 Brooks, N., *Anglo-Saxon Myths*, p.3.

22 O'Brien, H., *Queen Emma and the Vikings: The Woman Who Shaped the Events of 1066* (Bloomsbury: London, 2005), p.50.

23 Whitelock, D., *English Historical Documents*, p.246.

24 Richards, J., *Viking Age England* (BT. Batsford/English Heritage: London, 1991), p12.

25 Fisher, D.J.V., *The Anglo-Saxon Age, c.400–1042* (Longman: Harlow, 1973), p.347.

26 Stafford, P., 'One English Nation', in Smith, L.M. (ed.), *The Making of England, Volume 1: The Dark Ages* (LWT4/Macmillan: Basingstoke, 1984), p.122.

27 Redmond, A., *Viking Burial in the North of England*, BAR British Series, 429 (Archaeopress: Oxford, 2007), p.28.

28 Wareham, A., *Lords and Communities in Early Medieval East Anglia* (Boydell Press: Woodbridge, 2005), pp.84–5.

29 Redmond, A., *Viking Burial in the North of England*, p.28.

30 Smyth, A.P., 'The Vikings in Britain', in Smith, L.M. (ed.), *The Making of England, Volume 1: The Dark Ages* (LWT4/Macmillan: Basingstoke, 1984), p116.

31 Laing, L. and Laing, J., *Early English Art and Architecture* (Sutton Publishing: Stroud, 1996), p.186.

32 Graham-Campbell, J. *The Viking World* (Frances Lincoln Limited: London, 2001), p.152.

33 Discovered in 1852, in the south-eastern part of the churchyard, it had probably originally been in a different area of the churchyard but had been reused as a slab in a

wall enclosing the church precinct in the thirteenth century. Schofield, J, 'Revealing the full story of St Paul's Cathedral', *British Archaeology*, no. 124 (May–June 2012), p.20.

34 Wilson, D.M., *Anglo-Saxon Art: From the Seventh Century to the Norman Conquest* (Thames and Hudson: London, 1984), pp.208–9.

35 Laing, L. and Laing, J., *Early English Art and Architecture*, p.186.

36 Backhouse, J., *et al* (eds), *The Golden Age of Anglo-Saxon Art, 966–1066* (British Museum Publications Ltd : London, 1984), no. 105.

37 Brown, M.P., *Manuscripts from the Anglo-Saxon Age* (The British Library: London, 2007), p.131, notes the limited nature of the Scandinavian impact on eleventh century English manuscripts, compared with sculpture and metalwork.

38 Backhouse, J., *et al*, *The Golden Age of Anglo-Saxon Art*, p.209.

39 Laing, L. and Laing, J., *Early English Art and Architecture*, p.186.

40 Laing, L. and Laing, J., *ibid.*, p.211.

41 Hadley, D.M., *The Vikings in England, Settlement, Society and Culture* (Manchester University Press: Manchester, 2006), p.130.

42 Hinton, D.A., *Archaeology, Economy and Society: England from the Fifth to the Fifteenth Century* (Routledge: Oxford, 2002), p.109.

43 Hinton, D.A., *ibid.*, pp.109–10.

44 Hudson, B.T., *Viking Pirates and Christian Princes: Dynasty, Religion, and Empire in the North Atlantic* (Oxford University Press: Oxford, 2005), p.67.

45 Giandrea, M.F., *Episcopal Culture in Late Anglo-Saxon England* (Boydell Press: Woodbridge, 2007), p.58.

46 This helps to explain the occurrence of Christian-inspired tomb markers.

47 Cusack, C.M., *The Rise of Christianity in Northern Europe, 300–1000* (Cassell: London, 1999), pp.147–8.

48 Lapidge, M., Blair, J., Keynes, S. and Scragg, D. (eds), *The Blackwell Encyclopaedia of Anglo-Saxon England* (Black Publishing: Oxford, 1999), p.449.

49 Allsopp, B. and Clark, U., *English Architecture: An Introduction to the Architectural History of England from the Bronze Age to the Present Day* (Oriel Press: London, 1979), p.55.

50 Translated by Elisabeth Okasha, in Watts *et al*, 'Kirkdale – The Inscriptions', *Medieval Archaeology*, 41 (1997), p.81.

51 See: Blair, J., 'The Kirkdale Dedication Inscription and its Latin Models: *Romanitas* in Late Anglo-Saxon Yorkshire', in Hall, A., Timofeeva, O. and Kiricsi, A. (eds), *Interfaces Between Language and Culture in Medieval England: A Festschrift for Matti Kilpio* (Brill: Leiden, 2010), pp.139–45.

52 Jesch, J., 'Scandinavians and cultural Paganism in Late Anglo-Saxon England', in Cavill, P. (ed.), *The Christian Tradition in Anglo-Saxon England* (D.S. Brewer: Cambridge, 2004), pp.58–60.

53 Bolton, T., *The Empire of Cnut the Great: Conquest and the Consolidation of Power in Northern Europe in the Early Eleventh Century* (Brill: Leiden, 2009), pp.209–11.

54 Jesch, J., 'Scandinavians and cultural Paganism', pp.61–3.

55 Godden, M. and Lapidge, M., *The Cambridge Companion to Old English Literature* (Cambridge University Press: Cambridge, 1991), p.127.

56 Brown, M.P., *Manuscripts from the Anglo-Saxon Age*, p.131.

57 Jesch, J., 'Scandinavians and cultural Paganism in Late Anglo-Saxon England', p.61.

58 Most notably the *Northumbrian Priests' Law*.

59 Jesch, J., 'Scandinavians and cultural Paganism in Late Anglo-Saxon England', p.67.

60 Whittock, M., *A Brief History of Life in the Middle Ages*, p.12.

Chapter 15

1 Campbell, A. (ed.), *Encomium Emmae Reginae* (Camden 3rd series 72 Royal Historical Society: London, 1949), pp.15–16.

2 Whitelock, D., Douglas, D.C. and Tucker, S.I. (transl. and eds), *The Anglo-Saxon Chronicle: A Revised Translation* (Eyre and Spottiswoode: London, 1961), p.97.

3 Lawson, M.K., *Cnut: England's First Viking King* (Tempus: Stroud, 1993), p.84.

4 Whitelock, D., Douglas, D.C. and Tucker, S.I., *Anglo-Saxon Chronicle*, p.97.

5 Whitelock, D., Douglas, D.C. and Tucker, S.I., *ibid.*, p.133.

6 Whitelock, D. (ed.), *English Historical Documents*, vol. I, c.500–1042 (Eyre Methuen: London, 1979), p.312.

7 Williams, A., Smyth, A.P. and Kirby, D.P., *A Biographical Dictionary of Dark Age Britain* (B.A. Seaby: London, 1991), p.115.

8 Emma is the Norman version, while in Old English her name is Ælgifu. In order to make it simpler to differentiate the two women, Queen Ælfgifu will be referred to as Emma, while Ælfgifu of Northampton will be given her Old English name.

9 Lawson, M.K., *Cnut: England's First Viking King*, p.86.

10 Lawson, M.K., *ibid.*, p. 90.

11 Trow, M. J., *Cnut: Emperor of the North* (Sutton Publishing: Stroud, 2005), p.191.

12 Lund, N., 'Cnut's Danish Kingdom', in Rumble, A.R., (ed.), *The Reign of Cnut: King of England, Denmark and Norway* (Leicester University Press: London, 1994), p.38.

13 Lund, N., *ibid.*, p. 35.

14 Lawson, M.K., *Cnut: The Danes in England in the Early Eleventh Century* (Tempus: Stroud, 1993), pp.93–4.

15 Lawson, M.K., *ibid.*, pp. 93–4.

16 Lawson, M.K., *ibid.*, p. 94.

17 Lawson, M.K., *ibid.*, p. 96.

18 Saxo Grammaticus, *Danorum Regum* X, 16, in Christensen, E. (ed. and transl.) (BAR International Series, 84), pp.31–4.

19 Lund, N., 'Cnut's Danish Empire', p.38.

20 Whitelock, D., *English Historical Documents*, pp.476–7.

21 Lund, N., 'Cnut's Danish Empire', p.97.

22 Sawyer, P.H., 'Cnut's Scandinavian Empire', in Rumble, A.R. (ed.), *The Reign of Cnut: King of England, Denmark and Norway* (Leicester University Press: London, 1994), p.19.

23 Sawyer, P.H., *ibid*, p.20.

24 Campbell, W.M., 'Queen Emma and Ælfgifu of Northampton: Canute the Great's women', *Mediaeval Scandinavia* 4 (1971), pp.3–4.

25 Campbell, W.M., *ibid.*, p.75.

26 Henry of Huntingdon, *The Chronicle of Henry of Huntingdon, comprising The History of England, From the Invasion of Julius Caesar to the accession of Henry II*, in Forester, T.A.M. (ed. and transl.) (Henry, G. Bohn: London, 1853), p.199.

27 See: http://www.bbc.co.uk/news/magazine-13524677, 'Is King Canute Misunderstood?', May 2011, for the way the tradition was misunderstood by some in the press and politics over injunctions and twitter.

28 Trow, M.J., *Cnut: Emperor of the North*, p.125.

29 Trow, M.J., *ibid.*

30 Campbell, A., *Encomium Emmae Reginae*, p. 33.

31 Whitelock, D., Douglas, D.C. and Tucker, S.I., *Anglo-Saxon Chronicle*, p. 103.
32 Whitelock, D., Douglas, D.C. and Tucker, S.I., *ibid.*, p.104.
33 Whitelock, D., Douglas, D.C. and Tucker, S.I., *ibid.*, p.105.
34 Whitelock, D., Douglas, D.C. and Tucker, S.I., *ibid.*, p.106.

Chapter 16

1 Barlow, F., *Edward the Confessor* (Yale University Press: New Haven and London, 2nd edn,1997), p.54.
2 Barlow, F., *ibid.*, p.55.
3 Higham, N., *The Death of Anglo-Saxon England* (Sutton: Stroud, 1997) p.122.
4 Barlow, F., *Edward the Confessor*, pp.287–8.
5 John, E., 'Edward the Confessor and the Norman Succession', *English Historical Review*, 94 (1979), p.243.
6 Garmonsway, G.N. (ed. and transl.), *Anglo-Saxon Chronicle* (J.M. Dent & Sons Ltd: London, 1972), p.152.
7 Whitelock, D. (ed.), *English Historical Documents*, vol. I , c.500–1042 (Eyre Methuen: London, 1979), p.242.
8 John, E., 'Edward the Confessor and the Norman Succession', p.244.
9 Barlow, F., *Edward the Confessor*, p.117.
10 Whitelock, D., Douglas, D.C. and Tucker, S.I. (transl. and eds), *The Anglo-Saxon Chronicle* (Eyre and Spottiswoode: London, 1961), p.124.
11 Whitelock, D., Douglas, D.C. and Tucker, S.I., *ibid.*, p.138.
12 Baxter, S., 'MS C of the Anglo-Saxon Chronicle and the Politics of Mid-Eleventh-Century England', *English Historical Review*, 122 (2007), p.1198.
13 Baxter, S., *ibid.*, p.1224.
14 Baxter, S., *ibid.*, p.1215.
15 Baxter, S., *ibid.*, p.1224.
16 The thirteenth-century Icelandic writer, Snorri Sturluson, gives an account of the collaboration between Tostig and Harald Hardrada in the months leading up to the Norwegian invasion in September 1066. This is found in *King Harald's Saga*, which forms part of the *Heimskringla*.
17 McLynn, F., *1066: The Year of the Three Battles* (Pimlico: London, new edn, 1999), pp.15–16.
18 Howarth, D. A., *1066: The Year of the Conquest* (Penguin: London, 1981), pp. 69–70.
19 McLynn, F., *1066: The Year of the Three Battles*, p.15.
20 Bates, D., 'In search of the Normans', *BBC History Magazine*, vol. 13, no. 8 (August 2012), p.33.
21 Lewis, P., 'The French in England before the Norman Conquest', *Anglo-Norman Studies* 17 (1995), p.123.
22 Lewis, P., *ibid.*
23 Lewis, P., *ibid.*, p.124.
24 Lewis, P., *ibid.*, p.126.
25 Lewis, P., *ibid.*, pp.126–7.
26 John, E., 'Edward the Confessor and the Norman Succession', p.242.
27 John, E., *ibid.*, p.247.

28 John, E., *ibid.*, p.248.

29 John, E., *ibid.*, p.251.

30 Barlow, F., *Edward the Confessor*, p.109.

31 William of Poitiers, *Histoire de Guillaume de Conquérant*, Foreville, R. (ed.) (CHF: Paris, 1952), p.154.

32 Beckerman, J.S., 'Succession in Normandy, 1087, and in England, 1066: the Role of Testamentary Custom', *Speculum*, 47 (1972), pp.259–60.

33 Beckerman, J.S., *ibid.*, p.246. See also: Bradbury, J., *The Battle of Hastings* (Sutton: Stroud, 1998), pp.121–2.

34 For a detailed examination of this invasion see: DeVries, K., *The Norwegian invasion of England in 1066* (Boydell Press: Woodbridge, 1999).

35 Wace, *Le Roman de Rou*, Holden, A.J. (ed.) (A. & J. Picard: Paris, 1970–73), ii, p.173.

36 John of Worcester, *The Chronicle of John of Worcester*, Darlington, R.R. and McGurk, P. (eds), Bray, J. and McGurk, P. (transl.) (Clarendon Press: Oxford, 1995), ii., p.604.

37 Only Anglo-Saxon warriors are shown using two-handed axes on the Bayeux Tapestry. See: Bradbury, J., *The Battle of Hastings*, pp.90–92. And at Stamford Bridge the battle-axe was described as a peculiarly Scandinavian weapon by Henry of Huntingdon (died c.1157). See: *Henry, Archdeacon of Huntingdon, Historia Anglorum (History of the English People)*, Greenway, D. (ed. and transl.) (Oxford Medieval Texts: Oxford, 1996). For a more recent examination of the Viking origins of the broad-axe see: Stephenson, I.P., *Viking Warfare* (Amberley: Stroud, 2012), pp.59–62 and for an examination of Cnut's role in the formation of the *huscarls* see: pp.80–1.

38 John, E., 'The End of Anglo-Saxon England', in Campbell, J. (ed.), *The Anglo-Saxons* (Phaidon: London, 1982), p. 214.

Chapter 17

1 See Haigh, C. (ed.), *The Cambridge Historical Encyclopedia of Great Britain and Ireland* (Cambridge University Press: Cambridge, 1990), p.76 for an overview of how the ambitions of Scandinavian rulers, post-1066, fitted into the pattern of competition for the English throne which stretched back to the 1030s.

2 Garmonsway, G.N. (ed. and transl.), *The Anglo-Saxon Chronicle* (J. M. Dent & Sons Ltd: London, 1972), p.203, note 3.

3 Whitelock, D., Douglas, D.C. and Tucker, S.I. (transl. and eds), *The Anglo-Saxon Chronicle* (Eyre and Spottiswoode: London, 1961), p.148.

4 Green, J.A., *The Aristocracy of Norman England* (Cambridge University Press: Cambridge, 1997), pp.63–4.

5 Barlow, F., *The Godwins* (Pearson: Harlow, 2002), p.169.

6 McLynn, F., *1066: The Year of the Three Battles* (Pimlico: London, new edn, 1999), pp.15–16; Strickland, M., 'Military Technology and Conquest: the Anomaly of Anglo-Saxon England', in Harper-Bill, C. (ed.), *Anglo-Norman studies XIX: proceedings of the Battle Conference, 1996* (Boydell Press: Woodbridge, 1997), p.377.

7 Arnold, M., *The Vikings: Culture and Conquest* (Hambledon Continuum: London, 2006), p.128.

8 Haywood, J., *The Penguin Historical Atlas of the Vikings* (Penguin Books: London, 1995), p.126–7.

9 Haywood, J., *ibid.*

10 For an overview of the revolt of Hereward, see: Rex, P., *Hereward: The Last Englishman* (Tempus: Stroud, 2007).

11 Rex, P., *ibid.*

12 Wareham, A., *Lords and Communities in Early Medieval East Anglia* (Boydell Press: Woodbridge, 2005), p.85.

13 Whitelock, D., Douglas, D.C. and Tucker, S.I., *The Anglo-Saxon Chronicle*, p.151.

14 See the mid-twelfth-century *De Gestis Herwardi Saxonis* (*The exploits of Hereward the Saxon*) of Hugh Candidus.

15 Whitelock, D., Douglas, D.C. and Tucker, S.I., *The Anglo-Saxon Chronicle*, p.157.

16 According to the Danish chronicles, *The Anglo-Saxon Chronicle, Manuscripts E* and *D* date his death to 1076. Whitelock, D., Douglas, D.C. and Tucker, S.I., *The Anglo-Saxon Chronicle*, p.158.

17 Graham-Campbell, J. (ed.), *The Viking World* (Frances Lincoln Limited: London, 3rd edn, 2001), p.35.

18 Fleming, R., *Domesday Book and the Law: Society and Legal Custom in Early Medieval England* (Cambridge University Press: Cambridge, 2003), p.3.

19 Wood, M., *Domesday: A Search for the Roots of England* (BBC Publications: London, 1986), pp.22–5.

20 *The Ecclesiastical History of Orderic Vitalis*, Chibnall, M. (ed), 6 vols (Oxford University Press: Oxford, 1969–80), ii, p.267.

21 Orderic Vitalis, *ibid.*, iv, pp.52–3.

22 The *Anglo-Saxon Chronicle* separates the account of the threat of Cnut's invasion from William's plan to investigate the land ownership of England. However, it could be read as implying that they were related events. See: Whitelock, D., Douglas, D.C. and Tucker, S.I., *The Anglo-Saxon Chronicle*, p.161.

23 Roffe, D., *Decoding Domesday* (Boydell Press: Woodbridge, 2007), pp.7–10.

24 Roffe, D., *Domesday: the Inquest and the Book* (Oxford University Press: Oxford, 2002).

25 See the detailed critique of Roffe's thesis by Stephen Baxter, Christ Church College, Oxford, which challenges the arguments that the production of Domesday Book itself was not one of the objectives envisaged from the outset and that it was not commissioned until the reign of William Rufus. Stephen Baxter, review of *Domesday: the Inquest and the Book* (review no. 216) URL: http://www.history.ac.uk/reviews/review/216 (October 2001).

26 Ealdgyth and Edith are actually the same female personal name. It helps, in this context, to reserve one form of the name for Edith Swan-neck and one for Ealdgyth daughter of Ælfgar. It avoids confusion a little and is quite a common convention in writing about these two women.

27 Darlington, R.R. and McGurk, P., (eds), Bray, J. and McGurk, P. (transl.), *The Chronicle of John of Worcester* (Oxford Medieval Texts: Oxford, 1995), ii, pp.604–5. See: Scott, T., Starkey, P. (eds), *The Middle Ages in the North-West: papers presented at an international conference sponsored jointly by the Centres of Medieval Studies of the Universities of Liverpool and Toronto* (Leopard's Head Press in conjunction with the Liverpool Centre for Medieval Studies: Liverpool, 1995), p.168.

28 Gerald of Wales, Thorpe, L. (ed. and transl.), *The Journey Through Wales and the Description of Wales* (Penguin Books: London, 1978), chapter 11.

29 Mynors, R.A.B., Thomson, R.M., Winterbottom, M. (eds and transl.), *William of Malmesbury De Gestis Regum Anglorum* (Oxford Medieval Texts: Oxford, 1998), ii, p.318.

30 William of Malmesbury, *ibid.*, note 329, p.285. The other recorders of this campaign of Magnus Barelegs were John of Worcester and Orderic Vitalis.

31 William of Malmesbury, *ibid.*, ii, p.318, p.376.

32 Forte, A., Oram, R. and Pedersen, F., *Viking Empires* (Cambridge University Press: Cambridge, 2005), p.288.

33 Palsson, H. and Edwards, P. (transl.), *Orkneyinga Saga: The History of the Earls of Orkney* (Penguin Classics: London, 2004).

34 Haywood, J., *The Penguin Historical Atlas of the Vikings*, p.130.

35 Ballin Smith, B., Taylor, S. and Williams, G. (eds), *West Over Sea: Studies in Scandinavian Sea-borne Expansion and Settlement Before 1300* (Brill: Leiden, 2007), p.327.

36 For a conclusion on the way in which the Viking Age ended, see: Forte, A., Oram, R. and Pedersen, F., *Viking Empires*, p.171.

Chapter 18

1 Lang, S., *British History for Dummies* (John Wiley & Sons: Chichester, 3rd edn, 2011), p.83.

2 Lang, S., *ibid*, p.85.

3 While the BBC website no longer lists the results in voting order (now only showing the alphabetical list) the ranked list can be seen on: http://alchemipedia.blogspot.co.uk/2009/12/100-greatest-britons-bbc-poll-2002.html

4 Sellar, W.C., and Yeatman, R.J., *1066 and All That* (Methuen and Co. Ltd: London, 1930), Chapter V.

INDEX